## About Island Press

Island Press is the only nonprofit organization in the United States whose principal purpose is the publication of books on environmental issues and natural resource management. We provide solutions-oriented information to professionals, public officials, business and community leaders, and concerned citizens who are shaping responses to environmental problems.

In 1994, Island Press celebrated its tenth anniversary as the leading provider of timely and practical books that take a multidisciplinary approach to critical environmental concerns. Our growing list of titles reflects our commitment to bringing the best of an expanding body of literature to the environmental community throughout North America and the world.

Support for Island Press is provided by Apple Computer, Inc., The Bullitt Foundation, The Geraldine R. Dodge Foundation, The Energy Foundation, The Ford Foundation, The W. Alton Jones Foundation, The Lyndhurst Foundation, The John D. and Catherine T. MacArthur Foundation, The Andrew W. Mellon Foundation, The Joyce Mertz-Gilmore Foundation, The National Fish and Wildlife Foundation, The Pew Charitable Trusts, The Pew Global Stewardship Initiative, The Rockefeller Philanthropic Collaborative, Inc., and individual donors.

## About Regional Plan Association

The nation's oldest independent planning organization, Regional Plan Association promotes sustainable economic development, sound environmental stewardship, and broad social equity for the New York–New Jersey–Connecticut Metropolitan Region. Supported by a wide array of corporations, foundations, and individuals from all over the region, RPA prepares long-range comprehensive plans for the region and advocates for their implementation across the 2,000 political jurisdictions that fragment the metropolitan area. Over the years RPA's recommendations have shaped the network of highways, railways, parks, communities, and urban centers that define the region as we know it today, enabling the region to remain at the forefront of the global economy.

# A Region at Risk

# A Region at Risk

THE THIRD REGIONAL PLAN FOR
THE NEW YORK–NEW JERSEY–CONNECTICUT
METROPOLITAN AREA

*Robert D. Yaro and Tony Hiss*

REGIONAL PLAN ASSOCIATION

**ISLAND PRESS**

Washington D.C. ■ Covelo, California

ISLAND PRESS is a trademark of The Center for Resource Economics.

Credit lines for photographs and illustrations reproduced in this book appear on page 265.

Library of Congress Cataloging-in-Publication Data
Yaro, Robert D.
    A region at risk: the third regional plan for the New York–New Jersey–Connecticut metropolitan area/Robert D. Yaro and Tony Hiss (Regional Plan Association).
        p.    cm
    Includes bibliographical references and index.
    ISBN 1-55963-492-8 (paper)
    1. Regional planning—New York Metropolitan Area. 2. Regional planning—Environmental aspects—New York Metropolitan Area. 3. Municipal powers and services beyond corporate limits—New York Metropolitan Area. 4. Municipal services—New York Metropolitan Area. I. Hiss, Tony. II. Regional Plan Association (New York, N.Y.) III. Title.
    HT392.5.T7Y37    1996
    338.9747'1—dc20                                    96-16612
                                                                              CIP

Printed on recycled, acid-free paper ✪

Manufactured in the United States of America

10 9 8 7 6 5 4 3 2 1

THIS PLAN IS DEDICATED to the spirit of three people whose vision, confidence, and gentle good humor inspired everyone involved in the preparation of this plan to aim high in addressing the tough issues facing the region, but who did not live to see its completion.

*Robert F. Wagner, Jr.*

Bobby helped organize and then chaired the Committee on the Third Regional Plan just before his untimely death in 1993. In this capacity and his many other civic and government roles he touched the lives of so many people in his beloved home-town, New York City. Bobby's insights, enthusiasm, and optimism confirmed the out-look among all of us that the region's serious problems can be overcome and its potential realized.

*Charles McKim Norton*

Kim inspired three generations of civic and business leaders in the region and provided a bridge back to RPA's origins. Kim served as RPA's president from 1940 to 1968; his father, Charles Dyer Norton, founded the Association in the 1920s, and Kim was a presence in RPA's work from its inception in 1921 until his death in 1991. Kim helped shape the plan in its early stages, advised the staff on some of the region's most vexing and persistent problems, and inspired the plan's Greensward concept.

*Bill Simmer*

A playwright by training and avocation, as RPA's communications director until his death in 1990, Bill understood the importance of appealing to people's hearts as well as their minds. He set a high standard for RPA's communications, and we hope the plan lives up to his expectations by inspiring his largest audience: the concerned citizens and leaders of the region.

# Contents

# PART III. FIVE MAJOR CAMPAIGNS

# Figures

# Plates

# Foreword

***From the Chairman***

Historically, the reason people have come to this region has been to pursue economic opportunity and prosperity. During the first half of this century, Regional Plan Association helped to manage the region's enormous growth—proposing and planning the transportation, housing, and parks that the burgeoning population needed. Using RPA's plans, public authorities and government agencies built the infrastructure that allowed the region to develop and expand.

But the past few decades have brought us a new reality: we have seen our economy and quality of life decline steadily. We now realize that our success is no longer guaranteed and that a new plan for the future of the region should not be about managing growth that is inevitable, but about finding new ways to stimulate growth that is uncertain. If we do not act boldly to create new opportunities to grow and prosper, the quality of life will surely continue to deteriorate, for our region, our communities, and our families.

The recession that hit in the late 1980s struck us earlier, harder, and deeper than any other region in the country, as we lost over three-quarters of a million jobs. This recession and our slow recovery from it was an alarm, telling us that we had basic problems in the structure of the region and its economy. It led us to conclude that RPA would have to prepare a third plan, fundamentally different from the first two, that would address these concerns and rededicate efforts at building the region's economy in the new landscape of global competition.

I would like to thank all the contributors who understood the urgency of these issues and supported us in this endeavor. But for this region to succeed, business and civic leaders must continue to support these efforts—not only financially but intellectually and personally. I urge all concerned citizens to join together and act on the critical issues discussed in this plan, before it is too late, to recapture our historic promise of opportunity and prosperity.

*Gary C. Wendt*
*Chairman, RPA*

### From the President

Having studied the Second Regional Plan in graduate school and having spent much of my career in state and local government in New York, I have long been aware of the special importance of Regional Plan Association. To serve as president of RPA during the creation of the Third Regional Plan has therefore been a unique privilege. My goal in assuming this honored position was to provide an atmosphere in which bold thinking and a commitment to excellence would flourish. I knew that the peerless staff at RPA would do the rest.

Preparing the plan was a collaborative effort of all of RPA's staff and consultants: Robert Yaro directed the plan development process, developed key plan concepts, and authored or co-authored a number of sections of the plan; Tony Hiss also co-authored and edited several sections of the plan; Thomas Wright co-authored other sections, edited the entire document, and directed the Quality of Life Poll; Jack Dean coordinated production of plan sections and graphics, conducted research on transportation and demographic issues, and co-authored the housing section; Christopher Jones was the primary author of the Economy and Workforce chapters; William Shore co-authored the Equity chapter and served as RPA's conscience throughout the process; Regina Armstrong developed forecasts and authored sections on immigration, the economy, the capital budget, and sustainable economics; Robert Pirani wrote the Environment and Greensward chapters; Jeffrey Zupan wrote the Mobility chapter; Raymond Gastil co-authored the Centers chapter; John Feingold wrote the Governance chapter; Graham Trelstad co-authored the section on housing issues; Elizabeth McLaughlin contributed to sections on state planning and governance; Linda Morgan contributed sections on brownfields development and centers; Albert Appleton contributed to sections on smart infrastructure and the regional capital budget; Winifred Armstrong wrote sections on changing work structures, business practices, and regional indicators; and Nicole Crane contributed to several sections.

But above all, this project could not have been completed without the vision, leadership, and persistence of RPA's chairman, Gary C. Wendt, Chief Executive Officer of GE Capital. From the beginning of the process of developing the plan, Gary saw both the importance of quality of life to the region's future well-being and the need to rebuild the region's competitiveness. These themes were later confirmed in public forums and RPA's 1995 Quality of Life Poll, and they suffuse the plan. The success of his tireless efforts to communicate the importance of the plan to business leaders was critical to RPA's ability to secure the means to complete this project.

All of us were dedicated to developing a plan that would live up to the dauntingly high standards set by the plans of 1929 and 1968. I believe we have succeeded, but ultimately that is up to the region's citizens to decide.

*H. Claude Shostal*
*President, RPA*

# A Region at Risk

# Introduction

NOT THAT MANY years ago, a visionary group of civic and business leaders came together to consider new ways to deal with the daunting problems facing their city and its surrounding countryside. This place, which had once been a collection of frontier outposts at the edge of a vast, undeveloped continent, was fast becoming the economic, political, cultural, and communications capital of the world. At the same time it was being transformed into a new kind of place, a *metropolitan region.*

Rapid growth was expanding the region beyond long-established political boundaries and the capabilities of existing government institutions. Millions of new residents, many of them poor immigrants from strange and distant places, threatened to overwhelm urban schools and neighborhoods, and, some thought, the social fabric as well. New communications technology and industrial institutions were revolutionizing the structure of the economy and the nature of work. And urban sprawl, promoted by widespread automobile ownership and use, was creating uncontrollable traffic congestion and transforming traditional communities and familiar rural landscapes—almost always, it seemed, for the worse.

This group of concerned citizens determined that to take charge of these trends this place needed a *regional plan*—a comprehensive, long-range, region-wide blueprint for the future.

The group was the Committee on the Regional Plan for New York and its Environs, established 75 years ago and incorporated in 1929 as Regional Plan Association. The plan that they completed that year—the world's first long-range metropolitan plan—provided a compelling new vision for the New York–New Jersey–Connecticut Metropolitan Region, which they projected would double in population to nearly 20 million by 1965.

Lewis Mumford criticized the plan's assumptions that the region would inevitably grow and that Manhattan could accommodate a larger share of the projected growth in white collar employment. He suggested instead that stronger efforts should be made to restrain development and deconcentrate the urban core. RPA's first planning director, Thomas Adams, replied that it would be folly even to attempt to prevent in-migration or control economic expansion, and that the challenge was to accommodate growth in the best way possible. The failure of more recent efforts to control migration and economic growth in Moscow, Beijing, and other cities, even in authoritarian societies, has vin-

1

dicated Adams' conclusion. And much of the plan's concrete agenda of highways and bridges, parkways and parks, and proposals to create new kinds of urban and suburban communities was achieved (in large part through the efforts of master builders Robert Moses, Austin Tobin, and John D. Rockefeller, Jr.), enabling the region to improve its efficiency and quality of life even as its population and economy grew and decentralized. The plan provided a foundation for these efforts by enabling the region to attract an inordinate share of federal funds in the New Deal and postwar eras.

A second regional plan, completed in 1968, dealt with a new set of concerns, in particular the emerging trends of suburban sprawl and urban decline that were the results of the region's excesses in planning and building exclusively for automobiles. It proposed a bold program of concentration of employment in satellite centers and the rebirth of the regional rail system as alternatives to isolated suburban office parks accessible only by automobile. Among its many accomplishments, this second plan helped to protect hundreds of thousands of acres of open land and guided the rebuilding of regional commuter rail systems.

Implementation of the plans has not always come easily or without controversy and second guessing. As a not-for-profit civic group with no official standing, RPA's "power" has rested on the credibility of its research, the influence of its board, and ultimately the wisdom of its recommendations. In many cases—such as the first plan's proposals to expand the regional rail system and the second plan's warnings against continued sprawl—RPA's advice has gone largely unheeded.

In the late 1980s, it became clear to RPA's leadership and staff that the region faced a new and very different set of challenges, leading to the decision in 1989 to produce a third regional plan. Our economy faces new pressures from technology and global competition. Communities are threatened by sweeping economic and demographic changes as concerns once associated with inner-city communities spread to a wider range of established suburbs. Our last remaining intact ecological systems are finally caught in the shadow of development as we expand to new areas instead of addressing these issues where they occur.

And the rapid transfer of federal powers and

funds to states and regions, now gathering momentum in Washington, requires more than ever that this region identify and assert its own priorities. The current approach presents the very real danger that the national government will abrogate responsibility for urban centers and the needs of the poor and elderly. However, this process also presents us with an opportunity, in that this region may once again be able to chart its own course and finance its own needs, less encumbered by federal dictates and priorities.

In an era in which narrowly focused, one-issue-at-a-time strategic planning predominates, the decision to proceed with a long-range, comprehensive plan once again represents a radical departure. By proceeding in this way, RPA reaffirmed a long-standing conviction that the region's concerns are indeed regional and interrelated—recognizing the concept that if you "pull on a thread, you move the stars." This perspective is apparent in the third plan's "Three E" formulation, in which the relationships between economy, equity, and environment are seen as driving the region's concerns.

While suburbanization has irrevocably changed the face of North America, on all the other continents of the globe large central cities are undergoing explosive growth. What remains unrecognized is that both American suburbanization and global urbanization are part of an even more profound shift in human geography that is rapidly redefining circumstances of people's lives. The fundamental economic truth of our times is that, on their own, the suburbs are just as vulnerable as the shrinking cities of North America and the expanding mega-cities elsewhere in the world. That is because a far larger form of settlement has, almost imperceptibly, been taking root all around us. Far more suddenly than people realize, super-sized metropolitan regions—areas hundreds of miles wide crowded with a dense mixture of aging cities, expanding suburbs, newer edge cities, and older farmlands and wildernesses—are emerging not just as a recognizable place but as humanity's new home base.

Only a handful of other regions—notably Portland, Oregon, with its new *2040 Plan*, and Toronto, with its new *Greater Toronto Area Task Force* report—are recognizing these trends and the comprehensive approach they demand. The 1991 Intermodal Surface Transportation Efficiency Act

(ISTEA) requires that metropolitan planning organizations prepare long-range transportation plans that address land use and air quality concerns, but in only a few places are these plans truly integrating these issues. And none of them addresses the broader set of environmental, economic, social, urban design, and governance concerns facing these regions. Continued devolution of authority from Washington will require that metropolitan regions develop their own plans and investment strategies.

The most urgent of the new concerns facing the New York–New Jersey–Connecticut Metropolitan Region is the region's changing role in national and world markets as a result of new telecommunications technologies and economics. Our share of the national economy has declined for decades as the market share of even our leading industries in national and world markets has eroded. Companies, and even whole industries, that had been the mainstay of the regional economy are no longer "bolted down" here. Virtually every economic sector is undergoing restructuring that will, in the short term, continue to limit employment opportunities. The burden of these changes is greatest for low-skill workers, at the same time that millions of immigrants, many lacking advanced skills, have come to the region from developing countries. Declining income and employment opportunities for both native and foreign low-skill workers are likely to persist as these trends continue.

The result is that the region's century-old unwritten social contract—that we owe all our citizens the opportunity to gain the education and technical skills to attain a job and a decent standard of living in an expanding economy—is threatened. This contract has long been the cornerstone of our economic and social well-being, and its loss represents a significant threat to the region's future success. Consequently, for the first time the challenge facing RPA and the region is not managing growth, but preventing decline.

Related to these deteriorating economic prospects is the widespread notion that the region's quality of life is in decline, as measured by perceptions of incivility, crime, homelessness, failing schools, gridlocked and crumbling highways and bridges, and impaired air and water quality. Cherished landscapes, encompassing much of the region's public water supplies, agricultural lands, and scenic beauty, are succumbing to an unprecedented wave of suburban sprawl. And rapidly escalating housing prices and congested suburban highways mean that fewer residents of the region can afford to escape to the remaining places perceived to be safe and attractive. We seem to have lost the will to create the public institutions, adopt the policies, and make the investments that this place and its people need.

We are not alone in these concerns. To a significant degree these same challenges face most North American metropolitan regions and many of their counterparts in other developed countries.

To many people, more than ever, metropolitan regions—and in particular, large regions like those surrounding New York, Los Angeles, Tokyo, and London—seem out of control, even as they play a larger role in world commerce, culture, and communications. But these challenges are not restricted to these world centers. Virtually every North American metropolitan region, both large and small, faces many of the same concerns: shifting employment prospects created by global competition, industry restructuring, and immigration; growing disparities between poor central cities and inner suburbs and rich outer suburbs; environmental and transportation impacts of decentered, automobile-based growth; and other issues. In this sense, the approach taken by RPA to develop a comprehensive, long-range, region-wide plan could become a model for other regions.

RPA's plan concludes that these concerns can and must be addressed, and that the "pay back" to this region from doing so—in terms of expanded economic opportunity for all its citizens, improved quality of life, and enhanced environment—could be enormous. RPA believes that by implementing the plan and strengthening our connections to world markets we can reverse decades of relative economic decline. By sustaining our current share of the national economy rather than continuing the trend of declining share, we could add up to $200 billion per year to the gross regional economy by 2020.

This region, as the first to begin growing out of its 20th century infrastructure systems, is facing these problems a little bit sooner than anyone else. The size of the Tri-State Metropolitan Region, and its role as a world center of business, finance, culture, and communications, ensures that trends happen here first, or they happen in such a way that they cannot be ignored. RPA's third regional plan attempts to deal with issues that face most North American metropolitan regions to a greater or lesser degree. While it can suggest solutions in other places, it should not be seen as a cookbook to be employed by these places. Rather, it can be seen as an "early warning system" for other regions and as a testing ground for the initiatives needed to bring metropolitan areas successfully into the 21st century.

# *Part I*

# Overview: A Region at Risk

TODAY, IN THE TWILIGHT of the 20th century, the Tri-State Metropolitan Region of New York, New Jersey, and Connecticut should be the undisputed capital of the new global economy. This region is a magnet for the world's best minds and the destination of choice for the hopes of millions of people. Tokyo, London, and Paris also exert economic leadership, but it is our metropolitan region that offers the world's most diverse and talented population. And no place else on earth can demonstrate such extraordinary leadership in global finance, media, information management, the arts, and culture. For nearly four centuries, the region's prosperity and inventiveness have sprung from the diversity and talent of our people and the richness afforded by an exceedingly bountiful environment.

As the dawn of the millennium approaches, however, it is evident from an assessment of our economic, social, and environmental landscape that the formula of our success has been disturbed. Despite the region's strength in the global economy, we are facing decades of slow growth and uncertainty following our worst recession in 50 years. Despite the billions of dollars spent every year by the public and private sector on infrastructure, office space, and housing, the uncomfortable truth is that we have been living off the legacy of investments of previous generations. Despite a history of strength from diversity, a shadow of social division has fallen across the region. Despite strict laws and renewed public concern, we continue to pollute our air and water and consume our last portions of open land.

The region faces a future in which it must compete in a global economy that offers new challenges and opportunities. The question posed is whether the next 25 years will represent the final chapter in a story of prosperity and momentum that dates to the purchase of Manhattan in the 17th century. The warning is that modest growth in the next few years could mask the beginning of a long, slow, and potentially irreversible and tragic decline.

A regional perspective is the proper scale and context for analyzing and addressing these issues. Regions will be the dominant economic, social, and environmental components of the next century, because cities and suburbs in the nation's metropolitan regions now rise and fall together. During the 1980s, the 25 metropolitan regions in the United

States that had the most rapid growth in income in the suburbs all had central cities that also grew rapidly. In the 18 areas where suburban incomes declined, all but four central cities also experienced income decline.[1] Nearly one-third of income earned in New York City ends up in the pockets of commuters, around $44 billion annually. More than ever, the economies, societies, and environments of all the communities in the Tri-State Metropolitan Region are intertwined, transcending arbitrary political divisions. Our cities and suburbs share a common destiny.

To recapture the promise of the region, RPA has produced a plan to reconnect the region to its basic foundations. RPA calls these interlocking foundations the "Three E's"—economy, environment, and equity, the components of our quality of life. The fundamental goal of the plan is to rebuild the "Three E's" through investments and policies that integrate and build on our advantages, rather than focusing on just one of the "E's" to the detriment of the others. Currently, economic development is too often border warfare, as states within the region try to steal businesses from each other in what amounts to a zero-sum game. Social issues are either ignored or placated by a vast welfare system that fails to bring people into the economic mainstream. And environmental efforts focus on short-term solutions that attack the symptoms rather than the causes of problems.

With all our diversity, sometimes it is hard to see how each of the "E's" unites us:

- We all inhabit the same landscape, breathe the same air, and drink the same water.

- However and wherever we earn our living, the economies of our cities and suburbs are interdependent, and they succeed or fail as one.

- Our lives are embedded in far-reaching networks of neighbors, family, friends, and colleagues that stretch across all social, racial, economic, physical, and political boundaries.

The region's steep recession from 1989 to 1992 and its slow recovery are part of a wrenching transformation to an economy in which some of our leading industries are no longer as dominant in global and national markets as they used to be. Something else has changed, too: when these businesses improve their performance and competitive-

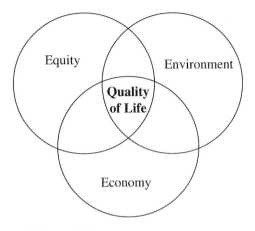

*Figure 1*: *Three E Diagram.*

ness, they do so with fewer people, so the region is no longer guaranteed widespread growth in jobs and income. A more open and fiercely competitive global economy, accompanied by new technologies that are radically changing how goods and services are produced, adds to the uncertainties of the situation, because now the fortunes of any firm or industry can turn around almost overnight. In spite of our region's impressive strengths, we face unprecedented challenges to our shared economic prosperity—challenges that are not unique to this region, but ones for which we must devise our own solutions.

Some planners speak of a jobless future or an end to growth. However, the greater likelihood is that new technological capabilities and expansion in the world economy are not inevitably imposing any one future on the region, but instead are setting in motion forces that could lead to either of two very distinct futures—sustainable growth through new patterns of cooperation, competitiveness, and investment, or declining growth and diminished prosperity. Our opportunity to shape the future has to do with choosing between these two alternatives.

To preview a declining future, we need only look at the extent to which we are currently losing ground in the global economy.

- From 1989 to 1992, the region lost 770,000 jobs— *the largest job loss of any U.S. metropolitan region since World War II*— eliminating virtually all of the region's growth during the prosperous 1980s. While national employment grew by 5% from the end of the 1990 to 1991 recession through 1994, jobs in the region grew by only 1% since the bottom of the recession in 1992.

• Unlike in previous recessions, *all areas of the region suffered downturns of similar magnitude*—from a loss of nearly 10% in southwestern Connecticut to a decline of 7% in northern New Jersey and the Hudson Valley.

• From 1982 to 1992, which included both the strong growth of the mid-1980s and the 1989 to 1992 recession, *the region had the slowest job growth of any major metropolitan area in the nation*—slower than Detroit, Chicago, Cleveland, or Boston.

• Over that same period *the region lost nearly one-quarter of its share of national output in key industry sectors*, including business services, media and communications, and advanced manufacturing.

Just as troubling as this recent economic stagnation are the stubbornly rooted inequities between rich and poor and between racial and ethnic groups. This region has long been identified with great extremes of wealth and poverty. In the last 15 years, however, the income gap has become wider, driven partly by global economic forces but also by neglect of our human resources. Two million residents of the region are officially poor, including 30% of children under the age of 18. In spite of impressive gains, African-Americans, Hispanics, and Asians are still far more likely than whites to be excluded from opportunities to achieve economic prosperity. And although the poor remain concentrated in urban communities, many suburban areas are no longer free from poverty and related social costs. In both human and economic terms, the burdens of widespread poverty and inequities are staggering. We can no longer afford either the price or the shame of this loss to humanity. Economic growth that comes without success in moving the region's poor into the economic mainstream, that doesn't return steady economic gains to the middle class, and that can't budge racial and ethnic divisions is neither desirable nor sustainable.

Our current dilemma is the result of global changes coinciding with our own failure to change—of 25 years of economic transformation unfolding worldwide during a generation of under-investment in our own human and physical assets. Had we made our communities more attractive and reduced our business costs with smarter investment in schools, rail systems, community design, and natural resources, our transition to the post–Cold War era would have been less painful and might even have begun to run its course. As it is, we are facing an extended period of continued adjustment and slow recovery.

In addition to a lack of investment, our transition to the demands of the new global economy is also being undercut by the land-hungry, sprawl-and-congestion growth pattern that pervades the area—the same pattern that now pervades every large American metropolitan area. Land-consuming growth does not just foul the region's air, or merely cost the regional economy billions of dollars a year in lost sales and extra wages because of time spent tied up in traffic. It now directly threatens the integrity of our life-support system, the region's environment. In the last 30 years the region's population grew by 13%. But from 1962 to 1990 the amount of land devoted to businesses and residences shot up by 60%.

A generation ago, only 19% of the region's 12,000-plus square miles were covered by roads, offices, and houses. The current total is 30%. If we do not start growing smarter, it will be 45% by 2020. Among the 2,000-plus square miles now at risk are the vast northern watershed lands that have always provided this area with the purest, best-tasting drinking water of any urbanized region on earth. Also at stake are the beautiful wildlands, shorefronts, farming communities, and recreational areas that are such an essential part of the region's quality of life.

It is odd how few metropolitan areas have yet seen what is happening. Many of the largest American metropolitan areas are now designing "outer beltways" for their peripheries—talking about third rings, fourth rings, and even fifth rings of suburban sprawl that can lead them to the promised land.

Very few regions—among them Portland, Oregon, the San Francisco Bay area, and, hopefully, our own—are now beginning to leap free from this kind of thinking. *Beyond Sprawl*, a 1995 report by a coalition of California groups that includes the Bank of America, California's largest bank, starkly concludes that sprawl now hurts all: "Unfettered sprawl will make the state less competitive, burden taxpayers with higher costs, degrade the environment, and lower the quality of life for every Californian." The report concentrates on the costs of sprawl, which are staggering. A Rutgers University study concluded that by 2010 local taxpayers in

New Jersey alone will spend $9.3 billion that could be saved by more compact development.[2]

Because we are a world-leadership region, we have other compelling reasons to grow smart. Economists recognize that metropolitan regions—not cities, not suburbs, not even countries—are the building blocks of the 21st century, and that regions that will thrive are regions that have strong centers as well as healthy suburbs. These are the areas in which global businesses feel secure. And that is because a region, economically, is a single job and housing market, which means that suburban wages rise and fall in tandem with the ups and downs of central cities. One reality envelopes all: when the inner cities stumble, the suburbs stagger. And when inner cities prosper, suburbs can boom.

An alternative future is possible—not inevitable, but *possible*—because of new opportunities inherent in the transformed world economy. But this is not destiny. It is choice. It needs thought, caring, and commitment, and it *requires* investments to make the region smarter, more efficient, and more attractive. This future is not illusory—indeed, it is already well within our grasp, if we take advantage of some very real reasons for optimism:

1. The world economy is poised for a period of robust growth in the early part of the 21st century, a period during which the productive capacities of new technologies may be fully realized while the economies of developing nations expand global markets. New products and media will emerge, as we are already seeing with CD-ROMs, the internet, and other products that were little more than ideas a decade ago. Greater efficiencies could also free up more resources—and create jobs in the process—to devote to a host of unmet human needs, from child care to environmental enhancement.

2. The region continues to be a leader in information-based industries and technologies, in the arts, and in numerous fields of creative talent, forces that will furnish much of the coming growth in the global economy. Over half of all the securities transactions in the world take place in Manhattan's stock exchanges, and we have the largest concentration of corporate management services in the nation, if not the world. Our preeminent arts and cultural institutions, universities, and research institutes provide a foundation for continuing leadership in creativity-based industries, including advertising, broadcasting, and publishing.

3. Despite sprawl, we are still a strongly centered, compactly developed region. Nearly half of the region's jobs are in its cities, and these include far more than just downtown and midtown Manhattan. The region's Central Business District has been spreading across two rivers and beyond the New York City limits, and it now takes in Downtown Brooklyn, Long Island City, and the Jersey City waterfront. Supplementing the expanded center is a tri-state constellation of regional downtowns in cities such as Newark, White Plains, and Stamford. The traditional centers and all of our newer suburban edge cities are found within the region's core, a semi-circle of lower-lying land along the coast still largely bounded by intact forests and farmlands. Two generations of development in suburban corridors have altered the form of the region from uniform concentric rings of development to a pattern in which each subregion connects with the region's core. To describe this new regional form, Robert Geddes has suggested the analogy of the subregions being the petals of a rose, each with its own life-supporting connection to the center. The recommendations in this plan are designed to reinforce these connections both between the petals and the core and among the petals themselves.

4. The region has the basic infrastructure, human resources, and natural assets—everything we need, in fact—to play catch up with the world's economy. With 40% of all the commuter rail, subway, and light-rail stations in the country, our existing rail infrastructure is not only unique but in a state of reasonable health thanks to 15 years of steady public reinvestment. An hour's drive north of Manhattan's Central Park is the core's natural northern edge (the roof of the region), a million-acre ecosystem, a tri-state band of lightly settled, densely wooded highlands that preserve the quality of air and water and provide an oasis from the stresses of urbanized areas. Perhaps most importantly, in an era when distances between nations and cultures continue to shrink, we have one of the most diverse, talented, and innovative populations on the planet.

This period of recovery is the time to build on our successes, pull back from past mistakes, and for the first time create a permanent framework for regional growth that can sustain our competitiveness, prosperity, and well-being far into the future. Our choice will be largely determined in the few remaining years of the 20th century. It will, of course, take a decade or more to build new rail connections, revitalize downtowns and suburban centers, and reform outdated institutions and regulatory systems. It will take even longer before today's school children enter the workforce. But to be ready for a growing and highly competitive economy in the next century, we must begin the reinvestment process now.

There is more good news: These investments will also bring *immediate* benefits. Infrastructure spending translates into jobs for construction workers and others who have been particularly hard hit in the transition. Improved schools will make the region more attractive to families of skilled workers. Along with strategic actions to support the region's key industries, this renewed investment can provide added income and jobs during a decade of otherwise sluggish growth.

The Third Regional Plan calls for an immediate campaign to recapture the promise of the New York–New Jersey–Connecticut Metropolitan Region—and it must be citizen-led to invigorate fragmented and often short-sighted political leadership. We need to start now, and we need to sustain our energy through the inevitable cycles of the economy and changes in political leadership.

This broad-based action program marks a sharp departure from prior approaches to regional planning, both in its organization and its basic assumptions:

- Automatic success is no longer part of our destiny, and it can no longer be defined in simple terms of overall economic growth without accounting for social and environmental costs and benefits.

- The ideas presented here are not being handed down by an elite group of professional planners and soothsayers, but instead they represent a distillation of the best thinking of the region itself because citizens and civic groups have participated over the past five years in developing this plan.

- The plan requires creation of a new force in the region, a grand coalition of city residents and suburbanites, as represented by hundreds of civic, business, labor and environmental organizations who are now realizing that they need each other because the region's continuing prosperity has become their joint responsibility.

To address the dilemma of regional competitiveness in the global economy, RPA turned to the region's business leadership in eight key industry sectors. Their insights have been critical to formulating a regional strategy that integrates economic strength, an improved quality of life, and a more inclusive prosperity. Working together, these business leaders were able to identify four prerequisites for the successful regions of the future:

1. The talents, creativity, and initiative of the region's people are its primary advantages as a global center of finance, communication, and culture.

2. An exceptional quality of life, efficient infrastructure systems, good schools, and competitive tax rates and housing prices are needed to educate, attract, and retain the creative people who drive the economy.

3. Collaboration between business and government in specific industries is required to capitalize on new technologies and emerging markets.

4. A diverse economy that includes healthy industrial sectors as well as advanced service industries is needed to provide sufficient employment opportunities and adequate income levels.

The Third Regional Plan also makes a critical distinction between real growth and "pseudo-growth." If we add people or jobs but do so at the expense of the other "E's," that is not true growth—it is a form of decline, postponed for the moment perhaps, but all the more inevitable when it comes. Because anything that further undermines the region's environment or equity will eventually drive away the global businesses that now—in a post–Cold War, deregulated, Internet and inter-linked world—can pack up shop any time and head for some place that has not already been fouled up.

## Notes

1. Larry C. Ledebur and William R. Barnes, *All In It Together*, National League of Cities, February 1993.

2. *Beyond Sprawl: New Patterns of Growth to Fit the New California*, Executive Summary, 1995; and *Impact Assessment of the New Jersey Interim State Development and Redevelopment Plan*, Executive Summary, prepared by Rutgers University Center for Urban Policy Research for the New Jersey Office of State Planning, February 1992.

# Chapter 1

# The Three E's

EACH OF THE "THREE E'S" also has broad applicability to metropolitan regions throughout the industrialized world. Virtually every North American metropolitan region, both large and small, faces similar concerns—among them are shifting employment prospects created by global competition, industry restructuring, and immigration; growing disparities between poor central cities and inner suburbs and rich outer suburbs; and sprawl and gridlock as a result of decentered, automobile-based growth. It has become clear that the "Three E's" now provide a universal context for discussing regional issues.

## Economy

With national governments less able to regulate economic activity, regions have a growing need to develop their own strategies. They must focus on their particular advantages in the global marketplace—the clusters of related industries that anchor their economy, the talents of their population, and the character of their communities and environment—to move beyond policies that rely solely on tax cuts, business incentives, and promotional campaigns. The right mix of investments in advanced infrastructure, workforce skills, and quality of life improvements are crucial to long-term success, and this will require collaborative relationships between business, government, and labor to succeed.

The strategies outlined in this plan—maintaining a diverse, high-skill workforce, investing in an extensive but aging transit system, and energizing people's entrepreneurial talents with more efficient, flexible systems of governance—emerge from the particular strengths and industry profile of the Tri-State region.

## Equity

Every world center faces daunting challenges to reverse the divisive trends resulting from economic transformation and global resettlement patterns. Global competition, technological change, and corporate restructuring have resulted in widening income disparities between the affluent and the poor, exacerbating long-standing racial and class divisions. Simultaneously, a handful of regions—including New York, Chicago, Miami, and Toronto—are attracting most of the vast number of immigrants flocking to North America, creating a truly multicultural society. Declining numbers of low-skill jobs, stagnant incomes for the middle-class, and increasing numbers of newcomers are creating larger concentrations of poor residents in metropolitan areas at a time when economic conditions are particularly fluid.

New residents bring with them enormous talent and cultural diversity—New York City, for one, could never have come into being without them. However, accommodating new residents requires new investments in schools, in workforce training, and in housing and public services. Federal funding has not been provided for these purposes. Localities have been left to deal with these new demands while conditions for many native-born residents are worsening, particularly for those in low-skill jobs. The benefits of immigration are certainly worth the effort to address its short-term costs, but it is equally important to ensure that people already here have the same kind of amenities and opportunities that we extend to newcomers.

In the metropolitan context, these forces have also had an impact on the gap between cities and suburbs. The movement of middle-class residents of all racial and ethnic groups from cities to the outer suburbs has left central cities for the poorest residents. And in many regions, inner suburbs now have more in common with center cities than they do with outer suburbs. Most regions continue to develop new rings of suburban growth, threatening to further isolate downtowns and center-city neighborhoods and diminish their tax base at the same time that urban welfare, police, education, and other costs continue to escalate. At the same time, middle-income whites continue to migrate out of this region—and from metropolitan Chicago, Los Angeles, Boston, and similar places—to smaller communities. Continuation of this trend could lead to even deeper racial and social polarization for the entire country.

## Environment

The extreme deconcentration of North America's metropolitan regions has played havoc with the green infrastructure of watersheds, farmland, estuaries, woodlands, and other resources that make life in these places possible and desirable. While open "greenfields" are increasingly prone to development, vast areas of our cities have become desolate "brownfields"—contaminated urban lands abandoned by both business and government. Conventional solid waste management and pollution control facilities seem to have only limited success in protecting the environment. And they are expensive because they rely on "end of the pipe" treatment and focus on cleaning up toxic materials after they have already been made rather than redesigning industries so that they process only benign materials. Many taxes and regulations designed to protect the environment have the perverse effect of discouraging both traditional and neo-traditional compact development, which generates far less pollution than sprawl.

# Chapter 2

# Toward Solutions: Five Campaigns

IN MANY AREAS of post-modern and post-industrial life, changes are accelerating beyond anyone's ability to see more than a few years ahead. Places, on the other hand, have qualities that can endure and gather strength, age after age. And this region, by simply anchoring itself firmly to its own superb natural abundance and extraordinary human achievements and talents, can create a permanent quality of life and structure for living that can both accommodate and weather all the changes that may come its way.

RPA has identified five crosscutting campaigns designed to respond in a comprehensive way to the issues defined by the "Three E's." Most of these initiatives could be adapted to the needs of other large and small North American metropolitan regions. In the Tri-State Metropolitan Region, the continuing "Three E" strengths of the place—our ecosystems, our centers, our transportation systems, our people, and our history of working together—can form a secure basis for future prosperity. Treasure them now and, whatever happens, we will have all the ingredients for success: our watersheds, mountains, rivers, and beaches; the cities and towns that embody 400 years of know-how, aspirations, and satisfactions; the infrastructure that keeps us all hooked together; new skills and an expanded ability to participate in each new economy that arises; and inclusive and flexible systems of governance, taxation, and regulations.

These inheritances are the bedrock on which the Third Regional Plan builds. Five initiatives anchor the plan—*Greensward, Centers, Mobility, Workforce,* and *Governance.* Together, they have been designed to re-energize the region by re-greening, re-connecting, and re-centering it. The *Greensward* safeguards the region's green infrastructure of forests, watersheds, estuaries, and farms, and it establishes green limits for future growth. *Centers* makes the region's existing major employment and residential areas the focus for the next generation of growth. *Mobility* transforms our transportation network to knit together the re-strengthened centers. *Workforce* provides groups and individuals living in these centers with the skills and connections needed to bring them into the region's economic mainstream. Achieving these ends will require new ways of organizing and energizing our political and civic institutions, as outlined in *Governance.* Collectively, all of these strategies underpin the region's quality of life and competitiveness, and they can guide us to sustainable growth as we enter the 21st century.

## Greensward

An astounding 40% of the region's landmass—more than 3 million acres—is covered by intact ecosystems, watersheds, rivers, estuaries, forests, and farmlands of national or regional significance that naturally organize themselves into five kinds of treasured landscapes: pineland reserves, mountain reserves, river valley reserves, maritime reserves, and farmland reserves. RPA's position about these great reserve areas is clear: they are special places that define the region, and they must always remain such. Because they have always supported vital human communities, they have never been off limits to development, but it has always been development that respects the natural systems in place.

These natural systems are not suitable for large-scale sprawl. Instead, these reserves should form a permanent "green edge to rapid growth," encircling the core of the region. To encourage the reserves to support appropriate smaller scale growth, RPA is working, where feasible, to encourage locally controlled, subregional commissions that could take on the joint task of managing the conservation of these vital places. A prototype of these regional reserve commissions already exists: the new Long Island Pine Barrens Commission, which is protecting 50,000 acres of land on top of eastern Long Island's only aquifer, while also supervising suitable development on an adjacent 50,000 acres. Building on this precedent, in 1995 a coalition of watershed towns and New York City agreed to create a balance between conservation and development in the city's upstate watersheds. By promoting the right kind of necessary growth, the 11 reserves proposed in this plan can protect 2.5 million acres that would otherwise succumb to unsustainable sprawl.

The Greensward is not a brand-new idea—rather it is a case of this region playing catch up with much of the rest of the industrialized world. To control suburban sprawl, a growing number of world centers have created permanent green belts, protecting large natural resource systems at the periphery of their urbanized areas and creating regional growth management systems to contain sprawl. London's Green Belt, established half a century ago, has become a model for other regions, even as development has moved to concentrated cities, towns, and villages beyond the Green Belt. Paris' new *Plan Vert*, or Green Plan, calls for creation of a similar network of protected landscapes and natural resource systems in that region. Planners in Tokyo are investigating ways to create a similar system in the mountains surrounding the capital region. In 1994 an RPA-sponsored team of American and Japanese planners prepared a green belt plan for the Miura area south of Tokyo as part of the U.S.–Japan Metropolitan Planning Exchange.

In North America, San Francisco, Chicago, and Philadelphia have initiatives led by civic groups to create metropolitan green belts. Portland, Oregon's Metropolitan Greenspaces plan represents a collaboration between environmental and community groups and Portland Metro, the regional service district. And in Greater Toronto, a mosaic of private initiatives to save the Oak Ridge Moraine and Niagara Escarpment, ridge lines that define the region's northern and western edges, complement public efforts to reclaim and preserve the region's lakefront.

At the same time that green belts are established to limit outward sprawl, new initiatives are needed to green and revitalize urban spaces. Attractive parks, playgrounds, and streetscapes help make cities livable and attractive for residents and businesses. Better management of the urban forest of street trees and woodlots has proven benefits for environmental quality, energy use, and property value. There is also an opportunity to transform abandoned and underutilized urban waterfronts of the New York–New Jersey Harbor and the Long Island Sound into new public spaces and development projects. Improving the environmental quality of the region's cities will make it easier for people to choose to live and work in urban areas.

## Centers

The region's cities and other centers have retained much of their economic vitality, although the loss of entry-level and middle-income jobs has had a devastating effect on many urban communities. The region's urban core still retains almost half of the jobs and people—an impressive achievement considering the decline of centers in many other American metropolitan areas. At the same time the region's highway-oriented suburbs gained 2 million payroll jobs during the last 25 years and have now essentially run out of room to grow. It is time to set up a three-way split of the next 2.5 million jobs that could come our way between 1995 and 2020.

Because of the way work is changing, 500,000 of those new jobs are likely to be arranged as "homework" or "telecommuting" situations. What RPA is proposing is a 50-50 split of the remaining 2 million jobs, with 1 million going to "re-centering" suburbs. ("Re-centering" suburbs are edge cities working to overcome their rawness by becoming more town-like, where offices, shops, and parks are for the first time grouped within walking distance of each other.)

The centers certainly have the land to support another million jobs. RPA estimates that the region has more than 50,000 "brownfield" acres—abandoned industrial sites, landfills, and waterfronts. RPA has already helped a Danish developer find one such site for a 200-store factory outlet mall in Elizabeth, New Jersey. Thanks to RPA's help in cutting through red tape (the permitting process required the consent of 25 different agencies), the developer's costs are now comparable to what they might be on a less-accessible "greenfield" site, meaning one never before developed, out on the edge of the region. As a result, he can afford to create a 10-acre marsh on the edge of his land that will serve as habitat for the endangered least tern.

Of course, centers need to be re-magnetized in two other ways before jobs can flow freely to them: they need to be places where people feel safe and welcomed. And they need to be reconnected to the millions of people that have been excluded from their benefits, by linking urban schools and community groups with downtown employers.

The plan also builds on the "pro-centering" approaches already successfully adopted in other first-world regions. Proposals here to recycle thousands of acres of abandoned brownfields are refinements of highly acclaimed initiatives in metropolitan London, Paris, Tokyo, Berlin, and Toronto. These include:

- London's efforts to reclaim the East Thames industrial corridor and the success of Groundwork trusts throughout the United Kingdom in reclaiming thousands of acres of derelict industrial land.

- Berlin's plans to reclaim its docks and the derelict areas adjoining the former Berlin Wall.

- Paris' efforts to recycle former industrial land along the Seine.

- Toronto's successful efforts to recycle former lakefront industrial and port facilities.

The plan's transit-friendly communities initiative emulates policies in Western Europe and Japan that promote lucrative, livable compact patterns of growth around rail systems. It builds on the historic transit-oriented patterns of growth that still characterize most of the mature northeastern and midwestern metropolitan regions in North America.

At the heart of the Tri-State Metropolitan Region, the plan's proposals to couple *Rx* rail improvements with civic design improvements in Manhattan's midtown and downtown districts builds on Paris' *RER* regional express rail and *Grands Projets* urban redevelopment initiatives; this strategy could also be replicated in every North American region that retains or plans to strengthen its regional rail system and core downtown district.

## Mobility

In our region—in any region—the kind of transportation available shapes the growth that occurs, both where it goes and the form it takes. In addition, a region's transportation system has as much to do with the pace of growth as it does with the speed of traffic, which means that an improved transportation network can accelerate growth rates, sometimes quite dramatically. In the 19th century, for instance, completion of the Erie Canal and a new breed of ocean-going clipper ships and, later, iron-hulled steamboats brought this region to early prominence.

In the 20th century, the region's unique transportation system—which in its current configuration includes 2,000 miles of major highways and 1,250 miles of rail lines—has already made possible two sustained waves of region building. First came the rail-supported growth—the centered growth, a massive program of (for the most part) highly concentrated development during the latter half of the 19th century and the first half of this century. This was the Tri-State Metropolitan Region's coming-of-age, the great age of skyscrapers and "canyons of steel," the boom time that solidified dozens of downtowns and made the Manhattan skyline one of the wonders of the modern world.

Then came the highways, mostly during the 1950s, '60s, and '70s, setting up the now-familiar postwar growth pattern, when the big centers went on hold and some of the smaller centers spiraled into decline, while highway-focused, de-centered development spread out across most of the region. The inner half of the region—the land south of the Appalachian highlands—now holds both its older, railroad-grown centers and a much larger number of highway-served newcomers, including 20 "edge city" suburban office clusters, almost 40 mega-malls (probably the world's greatest concentration of giant shopping malls), and hundreds of smaller strip malls.

Despite enormous regional spending to maintain and rebuild them, our highways and our railroads, as every driver and passenger knows, each still have problems that must be addressed immediately: they are both far more crowded and less dependable than they need to be. But, in addition to such problems, we now face two brand-new problems:

1. Our transportation system was not set up to serve a generation in which both cities and suburbs will be undergoing growth.

2. Our roads and railroads are not yet configured to support a more concentrated form of suburban growth that stays largely within the core, instead of over-spilling into the critical, hilltop watershed lands on which we depend for pure drinking water.

*Rx* is RPA's name for a reconfigured regional rail system only 25 miles longer than the present system—but suddenly endowed with far greater capacity to support the far stronger centers at the heart of the region and equipped to offer high-speed rail access to the region's three major airports. What is *Rx*'s secret? "Seamlessness," as it is called, meaning interconnectivity, something the region's highways have had from the start: after all, when you get off I-287 you don't have to park your car and then find another one before you can get onto I-78.

But the region's railroads and subway lines, originally built by separate operators, still function as seven discrete systems. This was the situation Tokyo and Paris found themselves in 35 years ago—one they now consider foolish. Paris' *RER*

*Figure 2: The region's commuter rail system provides a strong foundation for the future.*

network, built over the past quarter-century, has integrated *Metro* and commuter rail services, providing faster and more direct commutes for hundreds of thousands of commuters. And as a result of Tokyo's rebuilding, a commuter train from one end of that region can slide onto subway tracks near the center of Tokyo and then drift back onto a second commuter line over on the far side of the city. It is a one-ticket, one-seat ride for through-passengers. Just 25 miles of new track can perform the same trick of railroad togetherness for this region, giving birth to an entirely new kind of Regional Express Service.

Nearly every North American metropolitan region faces a mobility crisis because almost all new buildings are accessed only by automobile. Over the past decade, most suburban highways have necessarily become increasingly congested: highway mileage has hardly grown at all. But with every new building that goes up along these highways, more people have to drive; and drivers have to make more trips than they used to; and each trip gets longer. RPA's Regional Express Rail, or *Rx*, proposal would create new mobility for the region by transforming the existing transit infrastructure, mostly through creative reuse of existing abandoned or under-utilized routes. This approach could be replicated in every other large North American region with a well-developed transit system. The plan's proposal to make better use of the region's existing highway system, by instituting market pricing and eliminating bottlenecks, among other measures, would also have broad application in any North American region.

## Workforce

In a time of rapid economic change, the postwar guarantee of lifetime employment in large companies began to unravel in North America more than a decade ago, and the same phenomenon is now emerging in Western Europe and even in Japan. The only acceptable substitute for lifetime employment is a new system of lifelong learning that will guarantee that every worker is always ready to do well at a succession of jobs. This is an issue that every advanced economy must tackle, not just the Tri-State Metropolitan Region. And, like us, all U.S. regions face the additional challenge of troubled urban school systems and the frustrating lack of connections between urban workers looking for jobs and suburban employers looking for workers.

RPA's workforce campaign outlines a comprehensive strategy to deal with these concerns. For over a decade, workforce preparedness and education reform have risen to the top of national, state, and local agendas. Not only has the speed of technological change outpaced the ability of education and training systems to upgrade workforce skills, but comparisons with systems in other industrialized societies have revealed the weaknesses in our own. While this issue clearly has both national and local elements, its regional dimensions cannot be ignored. Substantial differences between urban and suburban education systems are central to the nation's workforce dilemmas, as are development patterns that separate urban workers from suburban employment opportunities.

Several states and regions, often with impetus from the business community, have accepted the daunting challenge of transforming their systems of learning and worker training. However, the complexity of the issues, resistance from many constituencies with an interest in maintaining the status quo, and the large-scale costs and efforts involved have made these transformations difficult to sustain. RPA's workforce campaign calls for a mobilization of business, labor, civic, local, and state leadership to scale up, coordinate, and sustain existing reform efforts. The objectives of reconnecting work and education with a system of lifelong learning, connecting the region's new workforce to a changing labor market, and improving the physical connections between communities and employers are applicable throughout metropolitan areas of the United States.

## Governance

Everywhere in the world, expanding metropolitan regions have extended beyond political boundaries that were often set in place centuries ago. Metropolitan New York now encompasses parts of three states; metropolitan Tokyo includes three suburban prefectures beyond the jurisdiction of the official Tokyo Metropolitan Government; and Greater London stretches out far beyond the boundaries of the former Greater London Council to cover much of southeastern England. Even in North America, metropolitan or county-wide governments in Indianapolis, Miami, Memphis, and Toronto no longer fully encompass all their growing suburban employment, retail, and residential districts. Only the "elastic" cities of America's southwest, with their broad powers to annex their urbanizing fringe, seem able to stay ahead of the metropolitan growth curve.

The universal disdain for big, distant government led to RPA's conclusion that a general purpose metropolitan government should not be proposed for the Tri-State Metropolitan Region. And recent taxpayer revolts in all three states also lent an urgency to RPA's search for ways to make government more efficient and accountable, and to control the fiscal impacts of sprawl. For these reasons, the plan's governance initiatives focus on ways to rationalize the activities of existing authorities, "right size" spending programs and encourage service sharing among municipal governments, and lend support to more effective state and regional land use planning programs.

## Conclusion

The size of the Tri-State Metropolitan Region and its role as a world center of business, finance, culture, and communications often means that many global trends appear here first—or, if not first, they erupt here in a way in which they cannot be ignored. RPA's Third Regional Plan comes to terms with issues that to a greater or lesser degree face most North American metropolitan regions. While it is the responsibility of our citizens to heal our own communities, and to recapture the promise and finally fulfill the potential of a region that has always had so much to offer, we hope that our solutions will also be useful to other places. Bringing the world's metropolitan areas safely and successfully into the 21st century is a job that will require much cooperation, both among the regions and within each of them.

# Part II

# Where We Are,
# Where We Are Headed

WHAT IS THE "Tri-State Metropolitan Region?" Throughout this book, the phrase is brought up again and again. This section of the plan reviews how our economy, society, and environment function as a modern, unified region—though our political structures reflect our colonial past. The Tri-State Metropolitan Region today consists of nearly 20 million people, more than most countries in the world. Its more than half-trillion dollar regional economy rivals many leading nations—if we were a country, we would have one of the ten largest economies in the world, about the same as that of Canada. We live in nearly 1,600 cities, towns, and villages that encompass nearly 13,000 square miles and comprise 31 counties at the heart of the Boston-to-Washington "megalopolis."

Referring to Figure 3, the Tri-State Metropolitan Region includes:

- *Connecticut:* Fairfield, Litchfield, and New Haven counties.
- *New Jersey:* Bergen, Essex, Hudson, Hunterdon, Mercer, Middlesex, Monmouth, Morris, Ocean, Passaic, Somerset, Sussex, Union, and Warren counties.

- *New York:* The five boroughs of New York City; Nassau and Suffolk counties on Long Island; and Westchester, Rockland, Orange, Putnam, Dutchess, Sullivan, and Ulster counties in the Hudson Valley.

The basic projections of the Third Regional Plan are discussed in the following section: who we are as a region and where we are headed if current trends continue. Two threads weave through this section: by and large, we are victims of our own desires; and second, our old "security blanket" of comfortable notions that helped us out of jams in the past is now threadbare and offers little comfort.

Anthony Downs, in his recent book *New Visions for Metropolitan America,*[1] succinctly captures the idea that metropolitan America's problems are not the work of some diabolical plot hatched by dark conspirators—it is us. Downs notes that for the last 50 years we got precisely what we asked for: good highways to travel fast and frequently; spread out homes with equally big lots for those who could afford them; well-stocked, bright, air conditioned "one-stop" shopping malls, close to home; and office buildings nearby that resembled home, set back

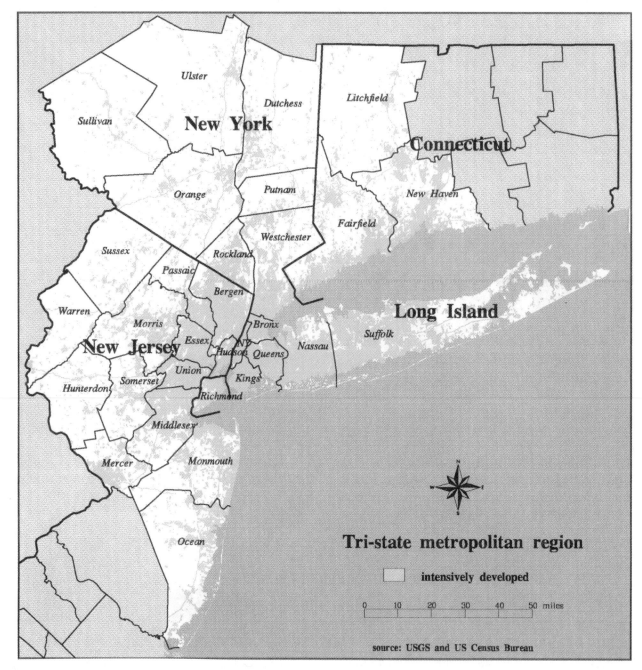

**Figure 3:** *The Tri-State Metropolitan Region.*
Source: USGS and U.S. Census Bureau.

on large lawns and nestled under the tree line. The country—people, government, and industry—that could put a man on the Moon could and did deliver on these wishes.

These dreams were grounded in the notion that we, as individuals, have complete independence to come and go as we see fit and can associate or dis-

associate with whomever we choose. But the way these dreams play out on the landscape is causing serious problems today: for example, our insistence to drive anywhere at any time, with no apparent cost. Now that more people insist on exercising this right simultaneously, it is causing true gridlock on our highways. Another example is our wish to live wherever we choose, coupled with our rejection of the notion that we are interconnected and depend on one another, which has led us to threaten our life-support systems: our watersheds in the Hudson and Delaware basins, the north Jersey highlands, or the Long Island Pine Barrens. Maximizing our individual independence is diminishing our collective independence. And those who have few choices and options, who are outside of this dream as a result of poverty, race or ethnicity, often live instead in a world of crime, despair, abuse, and addiction. The tension between independence and interdependence in the region is chronicled in this plan.

The second theme in this section is that the old notions of how to fix things when they break are no longer viable solutions. Indeed, they are becoming dangerous because they probably never were particularly effective, and continuing to count on them can lead us into even worse problems. A good example is seen in considering how we might solve the highway congestion problems we have created. Our traditional response is simply to widen the existing roads and build new ones. That path is very expensive politically, financially, and environmentally. Yet we cannot just walk away from the problem. Another example is evident in our manner of providing housing for new families. The traditional response is to pave over farms and forests and build homes. But that path continues to destroy valuable farmland, sensitive habitats, and critical watershed lands, while regulations that force new homes to be bigger and costlier than necessary are now keeping our children from living in the towns in which they grew up.

This section of the plan is meant both to help us take stock of who we are and where we are headed and to help hold up a mirror to ourselves so we can forge a new, more secure path to the future.

## Note

1. Anthony Downs, *New Visions for Metropolitan America*, The Brookings Institute, Washington, DC, and Lincoln Institute of Land Policy, Cambridge, MA, 1994.

# Chapter 3

# Economy: Transformation to a Competitive Global Economy

THE TRI-STATE Metropolitan Region is one of the world's leading centers of trade, finance, communications, and corporate management. It produces more goods and services than all but a handful of nations. However, the region is only slowly emerging from its worst recession since the Great Depression. Incomes for low-skill workers are barely affected by good times and decline substantially when the economy turns sluggish. And the relentless pace of technological change and corporate restructuring adds great uncertainty to the amount and type of economic growth that we can expect for years to come.

While the nation as a whole is struggling with similar issues concerning its role in the global economy, these issues are particularly acute for this region. After growing at a pace only moderately lower than the nation's from the late 1970s through the mid-1980s, the region suffered much greater employment losses during the last recession and has had a much more uneven and sluggish recovery. As a result, while the nation's employment has grown by 11% since 1987, jobs in the region have declined by 5%.

Although other mature metropolitan economies have also struggled, the Tri-State Metropolitan Region has grown more slowly than any other large metropolitan area in the United States over the decade ending in 1992, including other mature, densely developed regions such as Boston, Cleveland, Philadelphia, Chicago, and Detroit. By contrast, employment in rapidly growing areas such as Seattle and Atlanta increased by over 40%, while jobs in this region grew by less than 10%.

This section presents RPA's projections and analysis of the region's economy for the next quarter century. Considered in the context of an historical transformation in economic activities, short- and long-term economic projections are presented. Following these projections, this section identifies the challenges and advantages of competing in a global economy.

A central assumption of this analysis is that no village, town, city, state, or neighborhood in the region can think realistically about its own future until it realizes what an enormous stake it has in the prosperity of the areas that surround it. The flow of trade, capital, and jobs is determined by the performance of economic regions, not political jurisdictions. The future prosperity of this region's separate parts and places depends far more on their combined ability to compete effectively with other

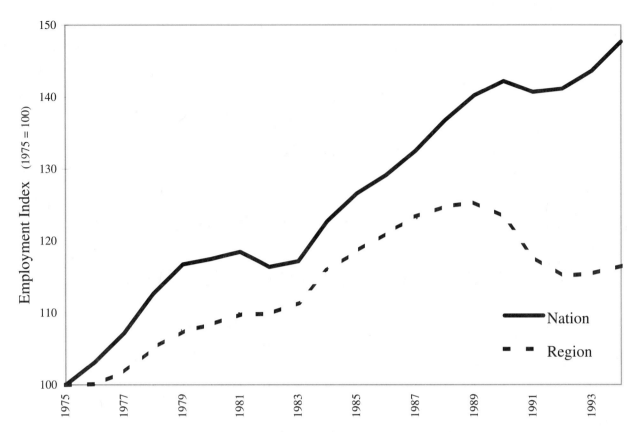

**Figure 4**: *Employment Growth, 1975 to 1994, United States vs. Tri-State Metropolitan Region.*
Sources: United States, Connecticut, New Jersey, and New York Departments of Labor.

| Region | 1982 | 1992 | Change |
|---|---|---|---|
| 1. Seattle–Tacoma | 1,310,000 | 1,919,000 | 46% |
| 2. Atlanta | 1,319,000 | 1,924,000 | 46% |
| 3. Dallas–Ft. Worth | 1,930,000 | 2,605,000 | 35% |
| 4. Washington–Baltimore | 3,355,000 | 4,373,000 | 30% |
| 5. Los Angeles–Long Beach | 6,247,000 | 7,876,000 | 26% |
| 6. San Francisco–San Jose | 3,172,000 | 3,915,000 | 23% |
| 7. Miami–Ft. Lauderdale | 1,384,000 | 1,706,000 | 23% |
| **United States** | **114,152,000** | **139,289,000** | **22%** |
| 8. Denver | 1,131,000 | 1,377,000 | 22% |
| 9. Detroit–Ann Arbor | 2,208,000 | 2,690,000 | 22% |
| 10. Chicago | 4,046,000 | 4,733,000 | 17% |
| 11. Philadelphia | 2,751,976 | 3,192,000 | 16% |
| 12. Cleveland–Akron | 1,400,000 | 1,579,000 | 13% |
| 13. Houston–Galveston | 2,006,000 | 2,247,000 | 12% |
| 14. Boston | 2,978,000 | 3,322,000 | 12% |
| **15. New York–NJ–Conn Region** | **9,675,000** | **10,465,000** | **8%** |

**Figure 5**: *Employment Growth, 1982 to 1992, Largest U.S. Metropolitan Areas.*
Source: U.S. Bureau of Economic Analysis; areas are BEA-defined Consolidated Metropolitan Statistical Areas.

regions, such as greater Los Angeles or London, than on their ability to compete individually with each other.

In all parts of the world, metropolitan areas have grown past the boundaries of their central cities and now constitute the integrated economy formerly represented by cities alone. In the United States, the suburban portion of metropolitan areas grew from 30% in 1950 to over 60% in 1990.[1] And while regions have been changing internally, conditions around them have been going through equally dramatic changes. Advances in telecommunications, global deregulation, and the decline of military alliances have weakened the control that nations can exert over global economic developments. This has allowed goods, services, and people to flow more freely between economic regions.

This continuing interdependence of cities and suburbs and the growing primacy of metropolitan regions has been documented in a number of compelling analyses. Anthony Downs, Neil Pierce, David Rusk, William Barnes, and Larry Ledebur, to name a few, have documented how the economic fortunes of suburbs are linked to the fates of their central cities.[2]

In the Tri-State Metropolitan Region, evidence from a number of sources demonstrates that the region is part of a worldwide trend, a place where every locality must be concerned with the welfare of its neighbors.

• *Rather than growing at each other's expense, employment growth in the region's cities and suburbs complement one another.* A report for RPA by Rutgers University's Center for Urban Policy Research found that growth in the suburbs of the region is strengthened by growth in New York City. The only exception to this is in manufacturing, where the effect of the city on the suburbs appears instead to be substitutional: when manufacturing employment in the city drops, it rises in the suburbs. Suburban manufacturing employment has not suffered as much in recent years as the city's manufacturing sector has, in part because the suburbs have grown at the expense of the city. But in both financial and other service employment, the city and suburbs have either grown or declined together. Of the region's four subregions, Long Island is the most strongly tied to the fortunes of the city's economy, followed by New Jersey, Connecticut, and the Mid-Hudson.[3]

• *The region's cities depend on suburban areas for much of their labor force, while suburbs rely on cities for employment opportunities and income growth.* New York City depends on its suburbs for over one-fifth of its workforce, and a much higher share of its managerial and professional workforce. Consequently, 31% of the income earned in New York City goes to suburban commuters. This $44 billion represents approximately one-fifth of the earned income of suburban residents, and it benefits many people in addition to the suburban wage earners who work in the city. Local suburban businesses and their employees benefit from the purchases made by these commuters, and all suburban residents benefit from a larger tax base. In addition to commuters to New York City, other intra-regional commuters are essential to local economies throughout the region, such as the 50,000 residents from the Hudson Valley working in Bergen and Fairfield counties, or the 220,000 New York City residents working in New Jersey, Long Island, or Westchester.[4]

• *All parts of the region suffered declines of similar magnitude in the 1989 to 1992 recession.* The steep toll of falling financial markets reverberated throughout the region's economy as growth in Wall Street–generated commuter incomes ground to a halt. Defense cutbacks hit hardest in Connecticut and Long Island, with their large defense contractors, but soon affected the network of suppliers that extends into New York City, New Jersey, and the Hudson Valley. Corporate downsizing affected all parts of the region, with decisions by individual firms often leading to workforce reductions in several locations throughout the region. Since 1992, all areas have emerged slowly from the recession, although the range of employment change has been somewhat larger than from 1989 to 1992.

Similar patterns of growth occur in part because every local industry is an interlocking part of a regional network, or "cluster," of suppliers, clients, partners, institutions, and infrastructure. A good example of this is the region's cluster of publishing, broadcasting, and communications firms. Although centered in Manhattan, media companies have research, sales, production, and back office operations throughout the Tri-State area. They rely on, and provide business to, printing firms in New Jersey, film studios in Queens, and technology research institutes on Long Island. Educational institutions throughout the region train and give homes to the scientific and creative talent that drive the media services industry, and the region's telecommunications network is critical for linking media service operations throughout the area.

To address the sources of our economic stagnation, we must acknowledge that both a healthy core and attractive and vibrant suburban and exurban

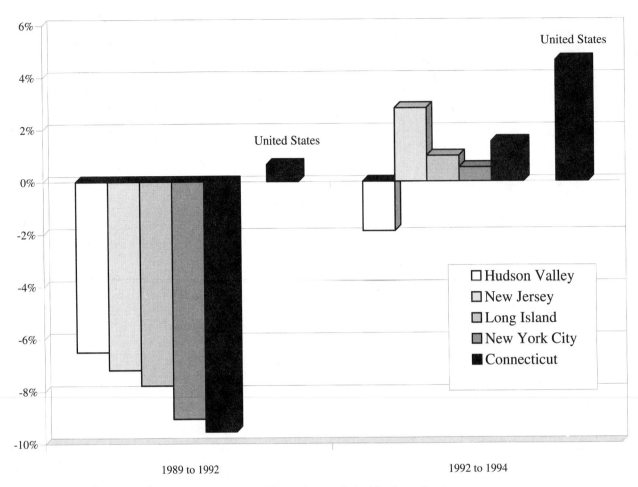

***Figure 6:*** *Employment Change, 1989 to 1994, Major Areas of the Tri-State Region.*
Sources: United States, Connecticut, New Jersey, and New York Departments of Labor.

areas are needed to attract national and international business. The concentration of globally oriented firms at the region's core stands as the primary reason for new international firms to come to the region, whether or not they end up in the core. Many of the successful activities in other parts of the region, whether it is financial services in Stamford or business service centers in New Jersey, depend on the region remaining a center for global economic activities. At the same time, centers outside the core provide cost-effective space for critical support services and for activities that need to be close to, but not a part of, the Central Business District. More importantly, the enormous variety of life-styles and recreational opportunities offered by the region's many communities are an essential part of this equation. They are why the region can attract and hold onto the kind of sophisticated

workforce that global firms rely on. The irony of the global economy is that we must cooperate in order to compete. Business, state and local governments, and citizens have a shared interest in ensuring that economic prosperity extends throughout the region, and that collaborative actions proceed from a shared understanding of our interdependence.

## Projections: From Recession to Growth

Over the past two decades, the diffusion of computer technology and telecommunications in American business and the widespread automation of manufacturing have brought about a major structural transformation in the region's economy. Long

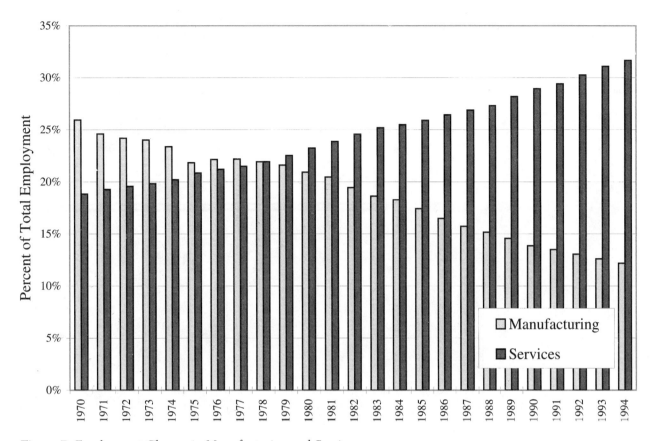

**Figure 7**: *Employment Change in Manufacturing and Services.*
Sources: Connecticut, New Jersey, and New York Departments of Labor.

the center of corporate and financial activity, the region has become the nation's most advanced knowledge-based service economy, linked directly to global markets as a result of fundamental changes in consumption, products, and processes. Services eclipsed goods production in the region as long ago as 1977.[5] Since then, service production has evolved in nature and market orientation to become the driving force in the region's economy.

As markets have transformed in scope from a national to an international focus—tied together by global networks of information transmission, production, and distribution, and given new range by liberalized agreements on trade in goods and services—knowledge-based world cities have emerged as global capitals in design, management, and financial services for high value-added products. New York, London, and Tokyo are the premier centers of a constellation of world cities that also includes Paris, Frankfurt, and Hong Kong. Each city–region has some representation of all essential world city functions, but the Tri-State Metropolitan Region, with New York City at its center, is the most diverse.

In capital market functions, this region accounts for half of all securities traded on a global basis, leading London and Tokyo by a wide margin. In 1994, turnover exceeded $3 trillion in equities traded on our stock exchanges, compared to under $1 trillion in Tokyo, the second most active market. Today, more foreign companies are listed on New York's exchanges than in London or in Frankfurt, Paris, and Tokyo combined. In international law and accountancy, where Anglo-American structures are the acknowledged standard, London is our only competition, and this region dominates the market with 12 of the 20 largest international law firms. We are also headquarters to five out of the six largest accounting firms in the world.

As world cities compete, and major trading blocs form to strengthen linkages within world regions, national borders have given way to a free flow of money and information across global networks that, at times, override national economic policies

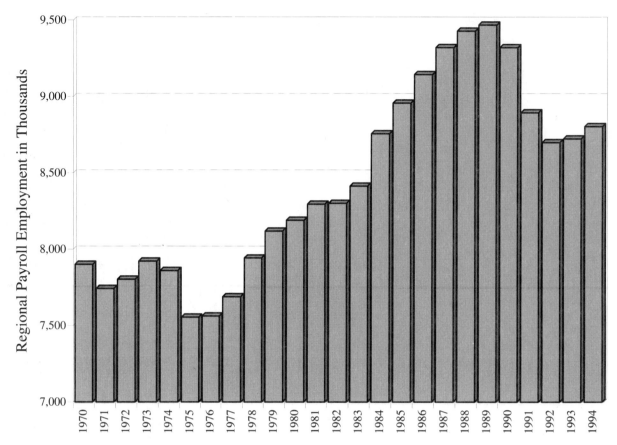

***Figure* 8:** *Employment Change, 1970 to 1994.*
Sources: Connecticut, New Jersey, and New York Departments of Labor.

and cultural differences. As a center of global financial transactions and international business decision-making—and as a major trading partner with the European Community, Western Hemisphere, and Pacific Rim blocs—the region's economic performance is far less dependent on domestic markets. Between 1970 and 1989, payroll employment in the region's economy rose from 7.9 to 9.5 million jobs, with all of that growth coming after 1977, a period of rapid acceleration in international trade and the integration of global markets.

Between 1989 and 1992, preceding and following a national recession but coinciding with the worldwide collapse of property and equity markets, the region lost 770,000 jobs, or 8% of its payroll employment. In the midst of the national recession of 1990 to 1991, the region lost three of every eight jobs lost in the United States. Since 1993, as Europe and Japan began to emerge from deep recessions, the region began its own recovery, generat-

ing 200,000 jobs by mid-1995. The new jobs differ markedly from those lost during the turbulent 1989 to 1992 period and from many of the jobs created in the expansion of 1971 to 1989.

Since early 1993, the region has restored all sector job losses outside of manufacturing, government, and construction. More new opportunities have been added in business, nonprofit, and personal services than were lost between 1989 and 1992, and not quite so many have been replaced in trade and financial services. Today, nonagricultural payroll employment stands at 8.9 million jobs in the region, up from 8.7 million in 1992 but down from 9.5 million in 1989. Jobs continue to disappear from goods-producing industries, though at one-quarter the volume of losses experienced for 1989 to 1992, and public sector activities are also continuing to decline. Compared to the 1977 to 1989 period, the current pace of job generation in selected services is comparable, but new growth is

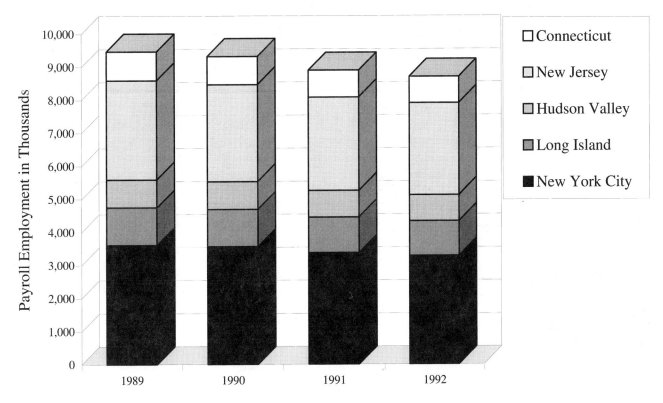

*Figure 9: Employment Change in the Region, 1989 to 1992.*
Sources: Connecticut, New Jersey, and New York Departments of Labor.

significantly behind in retail trade and financial service activity.

The distribution of new employment growth is unlike that of recovery periods in the recent past. Over the entire 25-year period, New York City failed to restore the peak level of employment achieved in 1969 of 3.8 million jobs, and all net new job formation in the region occurred outside the city. To be sure, the 1977 to 1989 period of increasing globalization generated a gain of 420,000 payroll jobs in New York City, or nearly one in every four jobs created in the region. But fully 42% of all jobs lost between 1989 and 1992 were jobs in the city. New York City itself has lost three of every four jobs created between 1977 and 1989. Since early 1993, roughly 46,000 jobs have been added in New York—a weak but not inconsistent share of the region's job recovery.

In 1995 total employment stood at 10.5 million jobs in the region, up from 10.2 million in 1992 but down from 10.8 million in 1989. Total employment outnumbers payroll employment by the inclusion of "proprietors," or self-employment. Over the en-

tire 1989 to 1995 period, self-employment increased from a level of 1.3 million to 1.6 million workers. Growth occurred more rapidly in the 1989 to 1992 contraction period than in recent years, as displaced payroll workers turned to independent contracting on a full- or part-time basis. Because of the involuntary and provisional nature of many proprietary jobs, and the uncertainty as to their location, greater reliance is placed on payroll jobs as the more reliable measure of economic growth and development in the region.[6]

As new jobs are gradually generated, the structural transformation of the economy can be seen not only in changes in products, industrial composition, and final markets, but also in the application of advanced technologies and enhanced factors of production. By 1993 more than 51 million people—43% of the U.S. employed workforce—were using computers at work.[7] On average, twice as many computers are now in use per person in the United States than in Germany, and three times as many as in Japan. While complex global transactions demand extensive computer systems, along

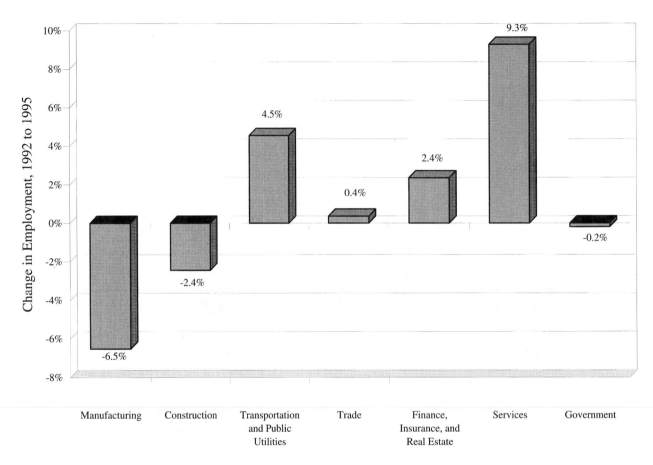

*Figure 10: Employment Change by Industry, 1992 to 1995.*
Sources: Connecticut, New Jersey, and New York Departments of Labor. (Estimate for 1995 by Urbanomics.)

with well-defined legal, financial, and accounting structures, they also require reliable and ample telecommunications infrastructures. Over the past decade, increases in trans-oceanic cable and satellite telecommunications systems that link the region with competing world cities have grown tenfold in total capacity.

Even more than technology, however, quality knowledge and workforce skills are major determinants of the economy's competitiveness. Highly skilled workers critical to global competitiveness are attracted to a world city–region not solely by its economic opportunity, but also by its quality of life. Against the declining importance of other factors of production, and even the advantages of location, the knowledge-based economy stresses elevation of cognitive skills and interpersonal communication, with educational attainment the best predictor of successes. Between 1980 and 1990 more than two

in every three new jobs created in the region were filled by college graduates. Advanced white collar skills—in executive, managerial, professional, and technical occupations—were part of nearly three in every four net new jobs.

The question of how human skills mesh with mechanical substitutes for them, and the broader issue of whether technology—especially information technology—destroys more employment opportunities than it creates, cannot be answered with certainty. It is clear, however, that technology elevates the level of skill required of the workforce and creates new demand for goods and services—by increasing productivity and therefore real incomes, and by generating new products for consumption. The new products can include those created directly by new technology, such as interactive video, as well as those made affordable by increased incomes, such as home help. Thus, rather than expe-

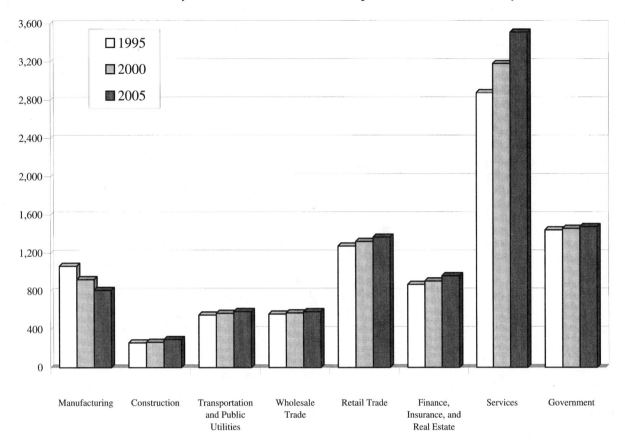

*Figure 11: Short-Term Employment Outlook for the Region, 1995 to 2005.*
Source: New York Metropolitan Transportation Council.

riencing a net loss of employment from the infusion of technology, it is more probable and historically more consistent that compensating effects will hold—that the region's economy will generate jobs that are both more and less skilled, and that the distribution of income in the region will reflect the growing disparity in productivity.

### The Short-Term Outlook: Slow Recovery from a Steep Downturn

*From 1995 to 2005 the outlook for the region is characterized by a slow recovery of the 1989 to 1992 job losses. This short-term outlook assumes modest growth in national and international demand and continued decline in the region's share of national employment.*

The short- and long-term projections in the sections that follow are demand-driven forecasts. They represent the region's expected capture of projected national and international growth based

on evolving trends in different industries. They assume that the region will make sufficient investments in infrastructure, workforce, and facilities to achieve the capacity necessary to grow at demand-driven levels. As such, they are neither "best" nor "worst" case scenarios. If the region fails to raise skill levels or infrastructure capacity sufficiently, it will not achieve the growth levels forecast. Conversely, the right level and mix of investments and policies could give the region an even larger share of international growth.[8]

Nonagricultural payroll employment, which stood at 8.9 million jobs in 1995, will grow to 9.6 million jobs by 2005, or 120,000 above the peak level of employment in 1989. Over the next ten years, payroll employment in the region will grow at the compound annual rate of 0.75% per year, or roughly half of the nationally projected rate of job growth of 1.4% per annum. While the region is expected to generate 690,000 new jobs between 1995 and 2005, it would be creating 1.4 million new jobs if it were to expand at industry-wide national average rates of growth. The shortfall of 730,000 jobs will be particularly noticeable in services, government, retail trade, and manufacturing.

By 2005 the region should finally have achieved recovery from the 1989 to 1992 recession. In New York City, however, the recovery will not be complete until sometime between 2005 and 2010, when the 1989 employment level of 3.6 million jobs will have been regained as a result of growth in private services industries. Manufacturing jobs are expected to decline further throughout the region, with one in every three in New York City facing elimination. Other goods handling activities, such as those in contract construction, wholesale trade, and warehousing, will show very modest growth. Despite manufacturing job losses, factory output and manufactured goods shipments, both into and out of the region, will continue to grow in response to domestic markets and foreign trade activity. But further automation of production facilities, both nationally and regionally, will curb any net job formation.

The service industries in business and advanced corporate services, communication and information, financial and real estate services, nonprofit institutions, personal care and health, travel and tourism, entertainment, and retail trade activity will account for more than the total of the region's net new growth, generating 820,000 jobs over the next ten years. This may sound robust, but, were these industries to grow as rapidly here as they are expected to in the nation as a whole, over 400,000 additional service producing jobs would be created. Public sector jobs in the region, meanwhile, will barely hold their own, as deep cuts in government budgets virtually eliminate job growth. Between 1995 and 2005, public employment at all levels of government will remain essentially unchanged in the region. This also contrasts sharply with national projections. If the region's public sector were to expand at expected national average rates of government employment growth, the region would gain 190,000 new government jobs over the next decade. By continuing to lag behind national economic performance, the region is likely to forfeit 590,000 jobs it might otherwise have created by 2005.

The general outlook for the short-term period is one of modest recovery with the opportunity to address our fundamental deficits. During this period, physical capacity is adequate to accommodate the jobs; capital is sufficient for private sector investment; and existing circulation, power, and communication systems have the needed capacity to move workers and information. But the region will lack the capacity—initially in its transportation systems and later in its environment, labor force, and other systems—to accommodate significant new business and employment activity beyond 1989 levels. Therefore, this is the time to invest in what has been ignored and what must be restored to a state of good repair or sufficiency: adult education and training for labor market needs, elementary and secondary education for long-term preparedness, affordable housing, and transportation and environmental infrastructure systems.

### The Long-Term Outlook: Opportunity for Sustainable Economic Growth

*The long-term outlook for the region (2005 to 2020) is characterized by a promise of sustainable economic growth driven by a robust world economy. It assumes that the region will make sufficient investments in its infrastructure, workforce, and communities to capture a share of international growth that is consistent with its current industrial and population trends.*

The region will fail to capture this promise if it does not invest in the skills, advanced infrastructure, and quality of life required in an even more competitive and technologically sophisticated global economy. But if in the next decade the region does make investments that expand capacity sufficiently, its long-term growth will, for the first time in decades, equal or even outpace growth in the nation as a whole. The global economy, upon which the region is increasingly dependent, will significantly outperform the national economy in the long term.

After 2005 demographic constraints will be exerted on the United States economy by passage of the "baby boom" generation into retirement age and the consequent steep slowdown in labor force formation. While the rate of job creation in the national economy is constrained by its rate of labor force growth, job growth in a regional economy—which can add to its labor force from both domestic and foreign sources—is a primary determinant

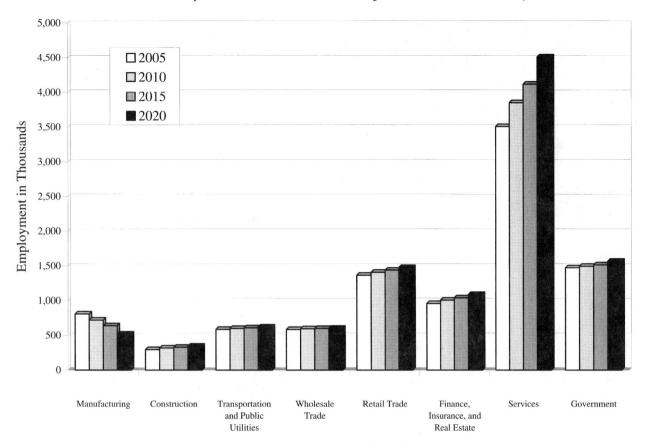

***Figure 12:*** *Long-Term Employment Growth, 2005 to 2020.*
Source: New York Metropolitan Transportation Council.

of population growth. Between 2005 and 2020 the national economy will grow at an average annual rate of 0.7%, approximately half of its rate of growth in the 1995 to 2005 period. The region will—if we invest in our workforce, infrastructure, and quality of life—first converge, then advance beyond national growth rates, driven by faster growth in the global economy. While the region's projected rate of employment growth, 0.75%, is no larger than the rate projected for 1995 to 2005, its relative performance is considerably stronger in the context of slowing national growth.

Global market forces are expected to generate regional job growth in advanced information-based services: financial services, multinational business management, telecommunications and multimedia computer services, design and engineering, high technology research and development, and arts and tourism. Robust demand in the world economy is expected from two sources. Some developing coun-

tries are expected to see accelerated growth as their economies mature, and the revolution in information technology can be expected to significantly increase productivity and economic activity in the long run, even as its tendency to widen income disparities continues.

To be sure, these sectors are not expected to support labor-intensive growth, but rather knowledge-intensive jobs characterized by high productivity and commensurably high earnings. While highly skilled global market jobs will be limited in number, local consumption by high-income workers will produce demand for in-person services that are not easily displaced by technology. Personal care, health care, education, environmental services, hospitality, and entertainment are but a few such activities.

Collectively, by industry, services are expected to grow over the long term from 3.5 to 4.5 million jobs, finance from 1.0 to 1.1 million jobs, retail

*Figure 13: New services, such as Bloomberg Business News, exemplify the wired economy's emphasis on delivery of specialized information.*

trade from 1.4 to 1.5 million jobs, and government from 1.5 to 1.6 million jobs. Manufacturing will continue to decline from 800,000 to 500,000 jobs, while construction and transportation will add fewer than 100,000 jobs each between 2005 and 2020.

The demand for skills in the region will likely diverge along two paths: at the high end, with emphasis on cognitive skills, communications, and the ability to manage complex systems, and with compensation based on the amount of valued knowledge provided; and at the low end, stressing personal service, manual skills, a pleasant demeanor, and technical training, with compensation based on the number of hours worked.

This dynamic will push the region toward an even wider gap between the "haves" and the "have nots," propelled in part by new forms of work. Knowledge-based compensation, technology-driven productivity increases, and the competitive advantages of agglomeration will benefit and hold the high-end service producers—the global business managers; financial, legal, design, or other business services; professionals and research scientists; consultants; and the media, arts, and cultural community. Many of the self-employed will function alone or in teams as "virtual corporations," forming and reforming different competitive configurations.

By contrast, routine goods and service–producing skills, including many blue collar and standardized white collar occupations, will devolve offshore, be displaced by technology, or be used by employ-ers on an as-needed basis. Workers in these occupations will be under continual pressure to lower wage rates to remain cost-competitive in global markets. Those that provide in-person services to the regional market—in retail, health care, social services, government, and consumer services—will be in demand locally but will require relatively less training and capital investment, a factor that will be reflected in their productivity and earnings.

## Economic Trends and Issues

To become competitive in the emerging global economy, the region must recognize the new challenges that it faces. But there are also comparative advantages to build on   advantages that could become stronger as international linkages become more vital to economic success.

### Challenges to Competitiveness and Equitable Growth

The global transformation, and its impact on the region, is best captured in two phrases—the "wired economy" and the "hourglass economy."

The "wired economy" is changing the geography, labor market needs, and marketing strategies of American and international business. The emergence of footloose businesses tied together only via telework on "information superhighways" reduces the need for many workers to be close to customers, or bosses, or even each other. Existing networks for the distribution of goods and services must adapt to new, often home-based modes of electronic purchase and delivery, and long-established patterns of journey-to-work are being reconfigured by 24-hour production processes and increased telecommuting. A workforce already weighed down with too many people who lack even basic skills must now cope with new needs for computer literacy.

The "hourglass economy" is increasing the number of both high- and low-income jobs, while the ranks in the middle are dwindling. The shift from a middle class growing in income and proportion during the immediate post–World War II decades began to level off in the 1970s. Mean national family income increased by 21% between 1969 and 1979, and by only 5% between 1979 and 1992. But

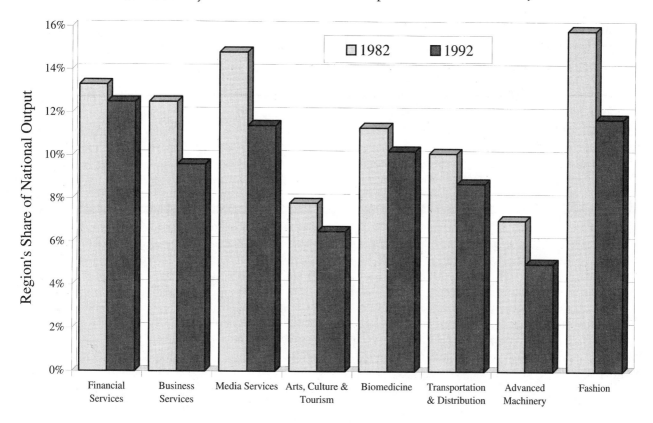

*Figure 14: Share of U.S. Output in Major Industry Clusters, 1982 and 1992.*
Source: DRI/McGraw-Hill, Inc., *The Tri-State Competitive Region Initiative, Diagnostic Assessment,*
April 1994.

the share of aggregate U.S. income earned by the middle 60% of American families fell between 1979 and 1992: only the top 20% gained substantially in absolute amount and relative share, to 44.6%, while the incomes of the bottom 20% of families fell by 14%, to a share of 4.4% of the aggregate.[9]

Furthermore, the drive for cost competitiveness in global markets and shareholder value in stock markets has led corporations to restructure labor relations toward more short-term employment contracts and performance-related pay. Corporate re-engineering has contributed to the growth of a part-time, or contingent, labor force lacking job security, benefits, and adaptive retraining, while, simultaneously, rapid expansion occurs among a highly skilled cadre of independent professionals who trade on knowledge, contacts, and virtual office technology. Compounding these forces in the region are the effects of heavy foreign immigration, continued job and housing discrimination, unequal access to capital and educational resources, and im-

pending cutbacks that may open holes in the social safety net.

### The Competitive Region Initiative

To determine the region's competitive strengths and challenges, RPA and the economic consulting firm of DRI/McGraw-Hill conducted an assessment of the region's leading industries and engaged industry leaders in a collaborative process to determine industry priorities and to develop strategies to address competitive challenges. Eight clusters of export industries, along with their networks of local suppliers, were examined. These clusters represent the industries driving the region as a global center of capital markets, corporate management, information production, trade and goods production, and the arts and popular culture.[10]

- *Financial Services*—banking, securities, insurance, and real estate—define the region as the world's leading financial center and account for almost 20% of the region's economic output.

- *Business Services*—accounting, law, advertising, consulting, and other professional and office services—provide the support network for the region's complex of corporate headquarters and international financial services; the region is a leading exporter of these services to the rest of the world.

- *Media Services*—publishing, broadcasting, printing, and telecommunications—anchor the region as a leading center of global communications and provide an immeasurable competitive advantage in an information-driven economy.

- *Arts, Culture, and Tourism*—theater, museums, art galleries, performing arts centers, hotels, restaurants, and travel services—are not only a major source of jobs and income in their own right, they are a shining star in the region's quality of life, and a wellspring of creativity that infuses the entire economy.

- *Biomedicine*—health services, drugs and biotechnology, and medical equipment—accounts for 10% of the region's jobs and provide an important research and technology base for the region.

- *Transportation and Distribution*—airlines and ocean carriers, truckers and rail lines, warehouses, and freight services—maintain the region as a center for commerce and are the region's physical link to the global economy.

- *Advanced Machinery and Systems*—electronic components, communications equipment, aircraft, instruments, and industrial machinery—employ nearly 300,000 workers and are central parts of the economic base of many local communities.

- *Fashion Cluster*—apparel, cosmetics, and jewelry—maintains the region as a leading international fashion capital in both design and high-value production and remains a major source of manufacturing jobs.

The priority challenges identified by leaders in each industry cluster reflect the workforce composition, production inputs, and market changes specific to the cluster. Together, they provide a basis for both strategic investments and collaborative actions by the private and public sectors.

In *financial services*, the highest priorities reflect the critical importance of human resources and the concern that changes in telecommunications and regulatory environment could erode the region's concentration of financial expertise and global services:

- Respond proactively to decentralization with actions to promote the region's strengths as a financial center, retain exchanges and other key institutions, and attract foreign financial firms.

- Enhance the region's quality of life, including improving public safety, lowering relative costs of housing for young professionals, reducing work travel times, and preserving arts and culture.

- Upgrade workforce skills for entry- and mid-level occupations.

The priority challenges for *business services* were similar to those of financial services in their emphasis of quality of life and workforce issues, but also reflect a decline in the cluster's traditional client base of large corporate headquarters:

- Improve quality of life to retain and attract professional talent, which represents 55% of the workforce in the cluster.

- Diversify the cluster's client base by expanding in international markets and supporting the development of emerging local industries.

- Upgrade the ability of the region's schools and universities to provide skills required.

The central importance of creative talent to *media services* is shown in its priorities, while concern for technology utilization and regulatory environment reflect a dynamic industry where the pace of new product development is overwhelming industry and regulatory structures:

- Retain and attract creative talent, not only by addressing negative quality of life factors but also by maintaining a vibrant cultural life in the region.

- Nurture the growth of new entrepreneurs by lowering regulatory barriers and assisting firms in emerging industries.

- Develop a coordinated investment strategy for telecommunications infrastructure that transcends industry and political boundaries.

- Develop an industry-ready workforce that is computer-literate and possesses both basic communication and media-related technical skills.

Challenges to *arts, culture, and tourism* center on maintaining the cultural assets that generate activity for tourism and the economy as a whole, and on growing recognition of the role of the arts in cre-

*Figure 15: Congestion on the region's roads and highways is a competitive disadvantage.*

ativity-based industries from fashion design to multimedia products:

- Maintain the region as a destination for creative individuals, with particular focus on the housing, work space, and professional needs of artists.

- Integrate the arts more closely with the agendas of business, government, and civic communities.

- Meet the financial needs of the arts with both adequate government support and encouragement of private support.

- Maintain leadership in arts training and education, particularly with a recommitment to arts education as core curriculum in schools.

- Improve access to the region's diverse cultural assets and tourist attractions with both transportation and information improvements.

In *biomedicine*, a growing concern for the ability to attract intellectual resources is combined with a need to develop new alliances to respond to extensive industry restructuring and the urgent necessity of strengthening our individual institutions of biomedicine and health to compete with other major centers of biomedical research:

- Retain and improve the supply of talent with quality of life improvements and increased research funding.

- Build mechanisms for collaboration between industry and health care providers, such as partnerships for clinical trials and product development.

- Enhance opportunities for commercial research and entrepreneurial development, addressing issues of in-

tellectual property and information links between researchers and biomedical firms.

- Create a regional identity for the biomedical cluster to promote the region's assets and develop coordinated regulatory policy.

Physical infrastructure needs supersede all other issues for *transportation and distribution*, where limited rail freight capacity, highway congestion, land costs, and other factors contribute to a high cost structure for commercial freight:

- Reduce congestion throughout the highway system, but particularly at intermodal access points for commercial traffic.

- Reform land use policies that restrict the development of new facilities, particularly environmental constraints that limit the reuse of industrial property.

- Coordinate tax and regulatory policies of different states, such as their truck size and weight restrictions, to create a seamless flow of goods in the northeastern United States.

For *advanced machinery and systems*, the priority challenges respond to the combined issues of shrinking defense budgets, more competitive commercial markets, and high production costs:

- Create a "manufacturing matters" mindset among public officials to develop land use, tax, and regulatory policies that support industrial activities that can still thrive in the region.

- Invest in public infrastructure, particularly transportation, that will reduce production costs and insure access to a large workforce.

- Strengthen skills in key occupations with industry-supported training and improved coordination between industry and educators.

- Increase financial, technical, and managerial support for small firms that are particularly vulnerable to the costs and complexities of operating in the region.

The priorities for the *fashion cluster* reflect its transformation to an industry built around the region's advantages in design, high-value production, sample and reorder production, and merchandising:

- Improve the image of the region's fashion cluster with both improved service and coordinated promotion to attract international buyers.

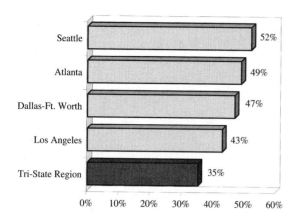

**Figure 16:** *Percentage of Residents Very Satisfied with Their Local Community.*

• Develop flexible production capacities with coordinated investments in technology upgrades, workforce training, and marketing.

• Maintain the region's creative energies and abilities by making urban centers more attractive as places to live and work.

In identifying the competitive challenges to their own industries, these leaders helped establish the priorities for shaping a regional economy that is in sync with needs of the global marketplace. Across these industries, three priority themes emerged:

1. With the ability to attract and retain creative talent repeatedly cited as the major competitive issue for most of our leading industries, improvement in the region's quality of life is clearly a leading competitive priority.

2. With rapidly increasing requirements for communication skills, reasoning abilities, and technical skills, continual development of skills in our existing workforce is becoming an ever-greater concern.

3. Efficient infrastructure and regulatory systems are required, both to keep costs of doing business competitive and to provide businesses with the flexibility to respond to rapid changes in both global and domestic markets.

In each of these three competitive priorities, there is mounting evidence that current trends have us headed in the wrong direction.

### Quality of Life Comparisons to Other Regions

Quality of life is a common expression used to describe the concerns of residents of the region. Re-

gional Plan Association, in conjunction with Quinnipiac College Polling Institute, surveyed residents of the Tri-State Metropolitan Region and four other regions in the United States to determine just what issues people felt were most important to determining their quality of life, and how satisfied they were with it.[11] The four other regions polled were the major regions outside the northeast that experienced the highest rates of growth during the 1980s—Atlanta, Dallas–Fort Worth, Los Angeles, and Seattle.

The poll found that people in the Tri-State Metropolitan Region are generally less satisfied with their quality of life than people in the other metropolitan regions. Only 35% of the people in this region were very satisfied with their quality of life, and 17% were somewhat or very dissatisfied. This compared to 49% of Atlanta residents who were very satisfied, 52% in Seattle, 47% in Dallas, and 43% in Los Angeles. The poll also found significant differences among income and age groups. Only 28% of the Tri-State Metropolitan Region's residents who earn less than $25,000 a year were very satisfied, and only 26% of those earning between $25,000 and $50,000 a year were very satisfied—giving strength to the idea that the middle class is the most dissatisfied in this region. Furthermore, only 27% of the people in this region between the ages of 18 and 29 were very satisfied.

The poll also determined what issues people consider most important to a good quality of life. Safe streets was the most important issue, followed by a strong community or neighborhood, good public schools, and good financial institutions. But when the poll asked people what they liked most about their local communities, the most frequent responses were convenience and access to work, entertainment and schools, and being part of a good neighborhood or community.

### Skill Deficiencies

In spite of the region's high level of professional and entrepreneurial talent, 75% of the region's labor force are not college graduates and 16% have not completed high school.[12] Drop-out rates and academic achievement in many urban schools, while showing improvements in some areas, remain alarmingly high. For example, only two-thirds of Newark high school students graduate within four years of entering high school.[13]

*Figure 17: The region's aging and crumbling infrastructure requires billions of dollars of reinvestment each year simply to maintain current conditions.*

In several areas of critical importance to employers, there is evidence that the region's workforce is not keeping pace with employer demands. Basic literacy is clearly of paramount importance to employers, yet a 1989 study for the Tri-State United Way estimated that 22% of the region's population, and 18.5% of its adults, were functionally illiterate. That study estimated that, if trends continued, 70,000 more illiterate persons would be added to the region's population each year, bringing the total to over 4.5 million by 1995.[14]

A recent study by the New York City Department of Employment has also documented a high level of skill deficiencies. Although computer skills were felt to be of growing importance among surveyed employers, 49% of employees in service occupations and 33% in professional occupations were found to be deficient in computer skills. Among all occupation groups, 10% of employees and 31% of applicants were found to be lacking in basic skills. Technological skills were deficient in 28% of employees and 51% of applicants, while 11% of employees and 45% of applicants were deficient in linguistic skills.[15]

In addition to the clear implications for productivity on the firm level, the region's ability to respond rapidly to changes in the economic climate depends on a workforce adept with the tools of the information age. Increasingly, this is not just a concern for office workers or professionals, but encompasses everyone from machinists working with computer-automated design to sales workers assisting customers with a larger variety of products and service options.

## Crumbling Infrastructure

The region spends approximately $12 billion annually on infrastructure—$5.5 billion alone for transportation in the New York State portion of the region.[16] Yet "crumbling infrastructure" is now one of the standard clichés about the area. For example, literally thousands of local bridges are either functionally deficient, which means they were not built to handle the weight or size of modern vehicles, or structurally deficient, which means they might actually collapse. There is an economic and an equity issue buried in the middle of all this—the so-called hidden subsidies that lead drivers to think it costs less to drive than it really does. Because driving seems cheaper people drive more, and bridges and roads therefore wear out faster. At the same time, because drivers are not covering their own costs, the system is starved for dollars that could and should be put back into repair and maintenance. One conservative calculation of the net direct and indirect costs of automobile use not borne by users is about $330 billion per year nationally, or about 15 cents per vehicle mile. These costs are in the form of highway capital, maintenance, and administration; the cost of vehicle parking, ownership, and operation; accident losses; and pollution, including air, noise, and water.[17] Locally, direct subsidies to New Jersey drivers exceed $700 million, according to one estimate, and more than $1 billion of local road costs are paid for out of property taxes rather than through charges imposed on drivers.[18]

One element of the hidden subsidy problem is that state and local departments of transportation (DOTs) seem to get as badly fooled as drivers about the true costs of construction and repair. This sets DOTs apart from all other utilities, both private and public, because they appear to have unlimited capacity to provide any and all services that are demanded of them—or that they think are being demanded. Within this faulty logic, building and operating roads seems to be free. By comparison, public water or sewer utilities, transit providers, toll roads, and private telecommunications and energy utilities have very strict, transparent accounting processes in which costs, prices, cost-recovery, and cost-benefits are immediately known, and so prices, rates, and subsidy requirements can be discussed and debated rationally. This transparency, now mandated by stockholders, investors, and other creditors and required by the federal government

*Figure 18: Manhattan anchors the region as a premiere global capital marketplace.*

for transit investments, encourages market-based supply and demand solutions to capacity questions. For example, if an electric utility finds that increasing supply by constructing new generating capacity will be too expensive, it will damp down demand instead, by promoting and offering customers incentives to weatherize their homes, or giving them rebates if they buy energy-efficient appliances. In the case of public water and sewer utilities, moratoria on new connections to the system are frequently used if they currently cannot afford new capacity to accommodate that demand. While many of the region's DOTs have begun to reinvent themselves as operators and managers of transportation systems, rather than thinking of themselves as road-builders, they have yet to calculate cost-recovery ratios or identify necessary subsidy levels to maintain a given level of performance.

A huge and perverse irony emerges from this tangled pricing problem. The country's richest region is now in a state of hand-to-mouth public financing as local and federal sources of additional funds for both infrastructure and environmental investment dry up. And critical components, such as mass transit, educational facilities and open space preservation, are now being specifically defunded. While there are many causes for this fiscal austerity, the regional impact is clear: the five-year MTA Capital Programs, which helped pull the subway and commuter rail systems back from the brink of extinction 15 years ago, now already seem a thing of the past. And the newest federalism currently in vogue in Washington—shifting program and funding responsibility down to states and municipalities—brings with it considerable cuts to transit aid and other infrastructure maintenance. In addition, future revisions to the federal Clean Water Act are likely to cut the federal funding available for pollution control.

### Advantages of a Global Center

Both immediate actions and long-term investments must build on our existing strengths: networks of high-value industries, talented human resources, and sophisticated infrastructure. As a constantly evolving center of commerce, core industries in the region develop clusters of suppliers and spin-off industries that spread throughout the region. "Wall Street" now encompasses a diverse set of financial service firms with operations in Brooklyn, Jersey City, and Stamford, and it relies on a labor force, transportation system, and telecommunications network that is regional in scope. Similarly, the pharmaceutical industry in New Jersey was an important contributor to the growth of medical research, biotechnology, and support services that have spread across the region.

The human talent and support services that have developed around these concentrations of high-

*Figure 19: The region's leadership in the arts is central to its role as a global center. The Stamford Arts Center is part of the region's unparalleled collection of museums, performing arts centers, theaters, galleries, film studios, and artists. The arts generate more than $9 billion in economic activity in the region and are essential to its tourist- and creative-based industries.*

value industries have given the region a number of interrelated leadership roles in the global and national economies:

- *Global Capital Marketplace:* An increasing share (now 45%) of national earnings in securities and commodities trading are generated in Manhattan, where the world's largest equity, futures, and options markets and leading financial service firms conduct the essential transactions, deal-making, and product development that keep capital in circulation on a global scale.[19] And it is not just in Manhattan. Insurance and banking centers in Newark and Stamford extend the reach of this marketplace, which represents by far the largest concentration of financial services in the Western Hemisphere. Although London has more international representation of foreign banks, and Tokyo has a larger asset base, New York is the most active and innovative center of global capital management.

- *Command Post of Management:* Over 10,000 international businesses with both American and foreign parent firms direct a worldwide network of production and distribution in goods and services from locations in the region, and they return to gross regional product fully 43% of national profits in rest-of-world earnings.[20] Many U.S. multinationals have now re-engineered their corporations to streamline headquarters employment, re-scale operations, and relocate production facilities on a global basis. These productivity advances have yielded greater cost competitiveness in worldwide markets and a decided edge over European and Japanese firms that have yet to undergo such corporate restructuring.

- *Producer of Information:* The nation's three major television broadcasting networks, several specialized cable viewing networks, six out of ten large book publishers, leading newspapers, magazines, and print services, major on-line information providers, and the giants of communications and interactive multimedia are concentrated in the region, where they underpin the knowledge-based sectors of its economy. They are all here because face-to-face communication still confers a critical advantage, even in a business environment imbued with telecommunications technology. The region's manufacturing industries and educational institutions produce a vast amount of the research and development in biomedicine, telecommunications, and other fields that set global and national standards.

- *Designer of the Arts and Popular Culture:* Through its diversity of creative talent, its world-class arts institutions, and its concentration of both traditional and new media, the region is a premier center for the design and export of both art and popular culture. Along with Los Angeles, it largely determines new trends in American consumption in the arts, film, music, and fashion. These resources, coupled with an increasingly diverse and multicultural population, equip the region to provide consumers and audiences around the world with American arts and entertainment in their own languages.

- *Center for Intergovernmental Relations:* The United Nations, its affiliated agencies and intergovernmental organizations (IGOs), the permanent missions of nearly 200 nations, and several thousand nongovernmental organizations (NGOs) conduct the deliberative and executive functions of intergovernmental relations from a central location in the region, drawing an unparalleled diversity of people, interests, new ideas, and approaches. With the decline of the nation-state and increasing fractionalization in global relations, agencies with continental and global administrative functions have increased in importance.

- *Center of Trade and Production:* As a producer, consumer, and transporter of goods, the region remains a national center of commerce. Twelve percent of the nation's imports and exports arrive and depart through the region's ports and airports. In spite of the region's decline in manufacturing, it still produces one-quarter of the nation's drugs and pharmaceutical products, over one-fifth of its cosmetics and jewelry, one-tenth of its apparel, and significant shares of its communications equipment, aircraft, electronics, and instruments.

## Toward a Competitive Region: Investing in Economic Development

Both the outlook for slow recovery over the next decade and the potential for sustainable growth in the years beyond justify a decade of region-shaping investments. In the near term, the region's challenge is not one of expanding capacity but rather of stimulating job growth while improving the competitive position of key industries. Over the long term, our goal is to attract and develop a highly skilled workforce, build systems of advanced infrastructure, and create community environments that meet the requirements of a knowledge-based economy.

Stimulating growth in the near term will be difficult in part because of modest growth in the world economy and because current quality of life, workforce, and infrastructure deficiencies will take years to address. However, reductions in business costs through intelligent regulatory reform and reduced public sector inefficiencies can have some impact on immediate growth prospects. For the specified needs of industrial clusters, private–public partnerships could also have short-term impacts. For example, the emergence of the multimedia industry has spawned efforts, such as the New York Information Technology Center and RPA's Silicon Alley Initiative, to enhance the region's position as a center of this fast-growing industry.

For the long term, the five major campaigns of RPA's Third Regional Plan provide an action agenda that addresses competitive priorities while laying the foundation for a period of sustainable and more equitable growth in the 21st century. RPA's proposals for a *Greensward, Centers,* and *Mobility* are three integrated strategies that would greatly enhance the region's quality of life by preserving open space, reducing congestion and commuting times, improving air and water quality, enhancing community design and housing opportunities, and insuring sustainable land use development. *Workforce* outlines a system of lifelong learning and skill development that would reconnect our education and training institutions with the needs of employers in a knowledge-based economy. And *Governance* describes the restructuring necessary for these other initiatives to succeed.

Clearly, the investments recommended in these initiatives will require an increase in both public and private expenditures in infrastructure and human capital development. We must certainly be smart about our investments to achieve the largest return, but even in our difficult fiscal climate we cannot allow our economic foundations to continually decline. Investments during the next decade will also address some of our short-term challenge. Expenditures for new construction and education and training services will ripple through the economy, sustaining job growth in a period when there is likely to be less stimulus from the national and international economies.

Collectively, these initiatives recognize that social equity and environmental quality are not at odds with a competitive economy, but are integral parts of one. They are designed to address the economy, equity, and the environment simultaneously, instead of considering economic development as a separate objective from meeting human and natural resource needs.

## Notes

1. 1950-1990 U.S. Census of Population, calculated in David Rusk, *Cities Without Suburbs,* The Woodrow Wilson Center Press, 1993, p. 5.

2. Larry C. Ledebur and William R. Barnes, *All In It Together,* National League of Cities, February 1993, pp. 3–7. See also Anthony Downs, *New Visions for Metropolitan America,* The Brookings Institute, 1994; Neil R. Pierce, *Citistates: How Urban America Can Prosper in a Competitive World,* Seven Locks Press, 1993; and Rusk (see note 4).

3. Rutgers University Center for Urban Policy Research, *Is New York City Still Propelling Growth in the Tri-State Region?* Prepared for Regional Plan Association, August 1995.

4. 1990 U.S. Census of Population.

5. Unless otherwise stated, employment in this section refers to nonagricultural payroll employment as provided by the United States, Connecticut, New York, and New Jersey Departments of Labor.

6. Data from the U.S. Bureau of Economic Analysis.

7. U.S. Census Bureau, "Computer Use in the U.S.," PPL 22, Education and Social Stratification Branch, 1995.

8. Employment, population, and labor force projections in the plan were developed by Regina B. Armstrong of Urbanomics, who is also a senior fellow for economics at Regional Plan Association. The projections were developed as interagency consensus forecasts for the New York Metropolitan Transportation Council (NYMTC) to create a basis for accordant approaches to transportation planning in the Tri-State Metropolitan Region. They therefore provide a consistent basis for comparing infrastructure proposals in this plan with those of the region's transportation agencies.

9. Bureau of the Census, Current Population Reports: Consumer Income, Series P60-184, 1992, "Money Income of Households, Families and Persons in the United States."

10. *The Tri-State Competitive Region Initiative, Diagnostic Assessment,* prepared for Regional Plan Association by DRI/McGraw-Hill, April 1994.

11. Regional Plan Association and Quinnipiac College Polling Institute, *The 1995 Quality of Life Polls,* April 1995.

12. 1990 U.S. Census of Population.

13. New Jersey School Report Card, *The Statewide Summary of 1993,* New Jersey Department of Education.

14. Urbanomics, "Illiteracy in the Tri-State Region," a report prepared for the United Way of Tri-State, 1989.

15. New York City Department of Employment, "What Employers Require for Employment," New York City Employer Survey, Research Report #1, June 1995.

16. NYMTC 1994/95-1998/99 Transportation Improvement Program, page 46. The 10 counties used for this analysis include the five New York City boroughs and Nassau, Suffolk, Westchester, Putnam, and Rockland.

17. Douglas Lee, *The Full Cost of Highways*, paper delivered at Transportation Research Board, January 1995. Lee included the highway capital, maintenance, and administration; the cost of parking, vehicle ownership, and operations; accident losses; and pollution (air, noise, and water).

18. Charles Komanoff and Margaret Sikowitz, *Crossroads: Highway-Finance Subsidies in New Jersey*, Tri-State Transportation Campaign, 1995.

19. Information provided by Morgan Stanley Group, Inc.

20. Estimate based on unpublished data from the U.S. Bureau of Economic Analysis.

# Chapter 4

# Equity: The Region's Society in the Past, Present, and Future

THIS REGION is one of the largest and most diverse in human history. Comprising 8% of the total U.S. population, residents of this region speak more languages, offer a wider array of skills, reside in more extreme densities, and live under the broadest range of incomes in the nation.

The region has always been home to a large and diverse population, and RPA forecasts that it will remain so long into the future. Yet this diversity, perhaps our greatest strength, is also seen by some as a threat. And even as we become a more diverse and vigorous society, disturbing trends show us becoming a more isolated, segregated, and fragmented society. This section of the plan consists of two parts: a discussion of regional population characteristics and projections, and a discussion of the social issues that, if ignored, truly threaten our survival as a prosperous and sustainable region.

## Projections: Increasing Diversity

The region's population has historically grown in tandem with its economic fortunes. Recently, however, a global resettlement of people has brought a steadily increasing foreign population, even as periods of economic boom and bust have resulted in

changing rates of out-migration by the domestic population. The result is a population with more racial and ethnic diversity than the region has had since the early years of this century.

As the population has changed in age, race, and nativity, new demands have been placed on the region's educational system, housing, job market, and social cohesiveness. This global resettlement has coincided with economic changes that are limiting job opportunities at a living wage, exacerbating long-standing racial and class divisions. Too many people now see diversity not as the enormous advantage it provides in the world economy, but as a hindrance. But immigrants have always provided, and will continue to provide, the growth and vitality this region is based on. They provide a multicultural and multilingual base for global economic expansion that is unparalleled.

A brief survey of past and projected demographic trends in the region illustrates the changes underway.

### Major Demographic Trends, 1970 to 1995

Over the entire quarter century since 1970, the region's population grew a scant 2%, from 19.7 to 20.2 million, or by fewer than one in every one hundred new U.S. residents. As most of the nation's settlement moved southward and westward, a steep economic contraction occurred in the region during the 1970s, and population correspondingly declined by 3%. In the robust 1980s, an offsetting expansion occurred and population rose by 3.4%. Since then, growth has been continuous, amounting to a population gain of 1.6% from 1990 to 1995, despite an even greater loss in employment and weaker economic recovery.

The dramatic growth in the region's population from 1980 to 1995 can be traced largely to the expansion of foreign immigration since the late 1970s and the concentration of new immigrants in a handful of major metropolitan areas in the nation. Of somewhat lesser importance has been the impact of favorable economic conditions, stemming the net outflow of native born white and black non-Hispanics from the region.[1]

- During the turbulent 1970s net out-migration of whites from the region amounted to 2.1 million persons, drawn from every subregion, although New York City's losses accounted for two in every three.

- During the 1980s white net out-migration retreated to 1 million persons leaving the region, with two in every five departing from New York City. But during this period some 60,000 African-Americans joined the outflow. African-American net out-migration from New York City and urban portions of New Jersey was even greater, as some inner-city households moved to suburbs of the region.

- Since 1990 there has been an increase in both white and black net out-migration from the region, the effect of sharp reductions in corporate, defense, and production line employment. Altogether, nearly 700,000 whites and 100,000 blacks have left the region on balance between 1990 and 1995.

By contrast, over the entire quarter century, 1970–1995, Asians and Hispanics have resettled here in ever-growing numbers. In terms of net in-migration, some 800,000 Asians and 700,000 Hispanics have taken up residence in the region since 1970, with Asians increasing in importance as the total influx rose from 375,000 in the 1970s, to 780,000 in the 1980s, to over 350,000 thus far in the 1990s. As a result, the region's racial and ethnic composition has shifted dramatically in relatively few years.

Today, 12.4 million whites reside in the region, composing 61% of the total population, down from 15.7 million in 1970 when they comprised 79% of the total population. Hispanics, the second largest group, are now growing more rapidly from natural increase than net in-migration and currently account for 3.3 million persons or nearly 17% of the region's population, up from 1.6 million persons in 1970, or 8% of the total. African-Americans, the third largest group, are now growing only from natural increase and number 3.2 million persons, or 16% of the 1995 population, compared to 2.3 million persons or 12% of the population in 1970. Lastly, Asians, the smallest but most rapidly expanding group, top 1.2 million persons or 6% of the existing population, up from 200,000 in 1970 when they comprised just 1% of the total.

A growing diversity in the population characterizes not only New York City but also the suburban portions of the region, though only New York and New Jersey are more diverse than the nation as a whole. Five in every eight residents of New York City are now minority Hispanic, African-American, or Asian. In northern New Jersey, minorities comprise nearly one in every three people. In the Mid-Hudson, about one in every four residents belongs to a minority group, and in Connecticut and Long Island, roughly one in every five, or less than the average percentage for the nation as a whole.

Throughout the region, extreme conditions of segregation persist, with minorities heavily concentrated in older central places and relatively few, despite their rapid growth, integrated even on an income-adjusted basis across all residential settlement.

### Who Are the New Immigrants?

Since 1970 nearly 3 million immigrants have been admitted to the region, or more than one in every five legal alien admissions to the United States.[2] Coming in ever-larger waves of resettlement, immigrants with announced intentions to reside in the Tri-State Metropolitan Region averaged roughly 85,000 persons per year in the 1970s, about 125,000 per year in the 1980s, and nearly 170,000 per year in the 1990s. Compared to the 1970s and 1980s, new immigrants display an increasing propensity to settle outside New York City when they first arrive, primarily in older cities in the suburban

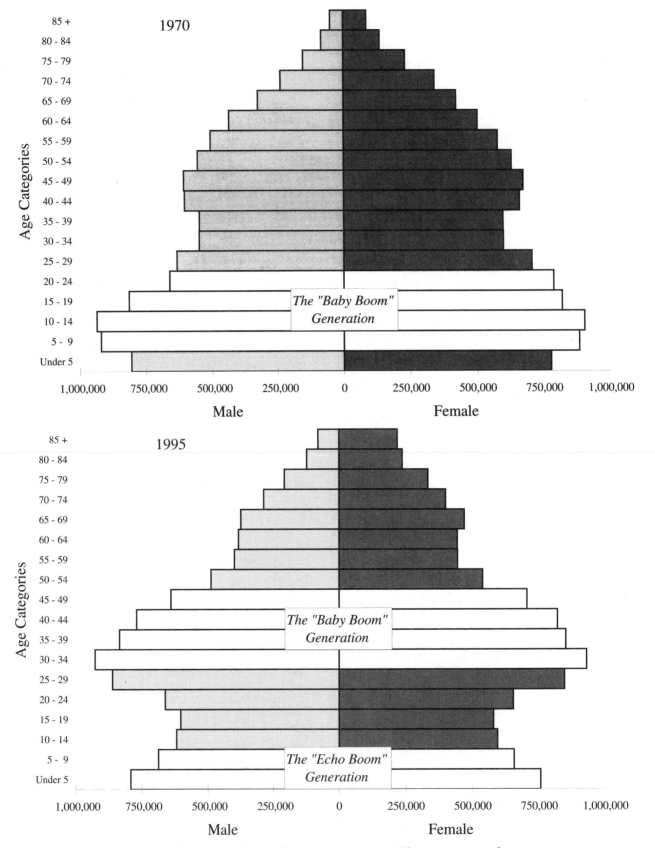

**Figure 20:** Age Composition of the Region's Population, 1970 to 1995. The progression of the "baby boom" generation from adolescence (1970) to middle age (1995) has had significant effects on the region's workforce, housing, and transportation.

portion of the region. However, two of every three immigrants to the region still locate in New York City, and the city's existing immigrant population shows little proclivity to relocate to the rest of the region.

Over half of the region's immigrant population has been admitted under family reunification provisions of immigration law, while less than 10% have arrived with employment-related visas. New provisions of the Immigration Act of 1990 have increased immigrant admissions to the region largely under refugee, diversity, and other preference tracks. Although the region remains ahead of the nation on family-related visas, it is substantially behind on employment-related visas. The strong family reunification character to the region's immigration contributes to the tight concentration of newcomers in ethnic enclaves.

A disproportionate share of the nation's immigrants from the Caribbean and South America are drawn to the region, which attracted 60% and 40%, respectively, of these admissions over the past few decades. Although only one in every eight Asian immigrants to the United States settles in the region, Asians still comprise the second largest group of newcomers, having dominated all immigrant admissions to the nation in the past quarter century. Rank ordered, the region's largest source countries have been: the Dominican Republic, Jamaica, China, Guyana, India, Haiti, and newly independent states (NIS) of the former Soviet Union. While immigration from West Indian countries has abated in recent years, immigration from the Dominican Republic, China, and the NIS has accelerated.

*The Changing Age Structure of the Population*

Aside from the effects of net migration, including foreign immigration and racial or ethnic composition, the region's population has undergone change from natural causes. In the past quarter century, major demographic transformations related to aging, fertility, and mortality have altered the growth and structure of the region's population. Average lifetime expectancy has increased markedly with advances in health care, more than offsetting the effects of new causes of death such as AIDS. The bulge in the region's population created by the

"baby boom" generation has passed through youthful ages to reproductive stages, causing a "baby bust" and then "echo boom" effect on birth rates. While deaths have declined in relative terms, in recent years births have increased both absolutely and relatively.

Over the past quarter century, births have risen from an average of 264,000 per year in the 1970s, to 280,000 per year in the 1980s, to 327,000 per year in the 1990s. By contrast, deaths have remained relatively constant at 185,000 per year, despite growth in the population. Thus growth in the region's population is now under greater pressure from natural increase. Today, Hispanic, African-American, and Asian minorities account for 49% of all births, while a white majority accounts for 76% of all deaths. Fertility rates are especially high among African-American and Hispanic residents, whose births per thousand women in reproductive ages average 81 and 71, respectively, compared to 62 births for Asian women and the sub-replacement rate of 52 births per thousand for white women.

Coupled with a more youthful age profile among new foreign residents, the forces of natural increase and aging have altered the basic structure of the region's population. Today, 10.8 million residents are in the working ages of 25 through 64, some 2.7 million are of retirement ages at 65 years and over, 1.5 million are preschoolers under 5 years of age, another 2.6 million are of elementary school ages 5 through 14, some 1.2 million are of secondary school ages 15 through 19, and 1.3 million are of college and postgraduate ages 20 through 24.

Compared to prior population profiles of the past quarter century, never before have so many residents of the region been of prime (35 to 44 years) and young (25 to 34 years) working ages, and of retirement (over 65) and house-buying (typically 30 to 34) ages. There were more preschoolers and elementary school aged children in the region in the early 1970s—though recent growth is fast approaching the "under 5" peak—and more secondary school and college aged youth in the early 1980s. The region continues to have a smaller mature (45 to 54 years) and older (55 to 64 years) working age population than in 1970, or even 1980, though maturation of the "baby boom" generation will soon alter this relationship. Still today, there exists the largest working age population in the re-

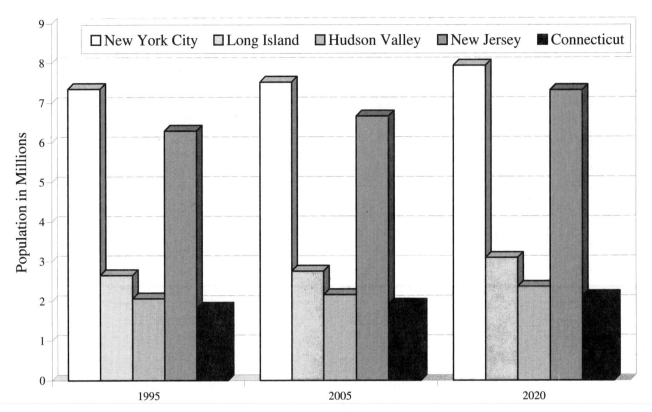

**Figure 21**: *Forecasted Growth by Subregion.*
Source: New York Metropolitan Transportation Council.

gion's history and a more favorable ratio of dependent ages to working ages, despite a growing elderly generation.

### Effect on the Region's Labor Force

The strong concentration of working age population and high rates of labor force participation, particularly among women and immigrants, support a large and diverse labor force in the region. In 1995 the labor force numbered 10.4 million persons aged 16 years and over who were working or actively seeking work in the formal economy. Officially, just over 7% are now unemployed. As a share of the nation, the region's labor force comprises nearly 8%, having declined steadily from 10% in 1970. Regional rates of unemployment were below national averages throughout the 1980s, but joblessness has had a far more severe effect on the region's labor force in the 1990s.

A growing diversity on a racial and gender basis has transformed the region's labor force over the past quarter century. Today, nearly half of all those working or seeking work are women (47% of the labor force) and over one in three (36%) are Hispanic, African-American, or Asian. In New York City diversity is even greater, with 59% of the resident labor force drawn from racial or ethnic minorities. Over the past decade more than all of the net growth in the regional labor force resulted from gains in minority and female participation, with white male workers actually declining in absolute terms. In the past quarter century nearly all of the net growth occurred outside New York City, with the City accounting for one in every three labor force participants in the region by 1995.

### The Near-Term Outlook: More New and Old Faces

In the near term between 1995 and 2005, the region's population is expected to grow by 830,000 as foreign immigration remains unabated throughout the 1990s and natural increase plays a more promi-

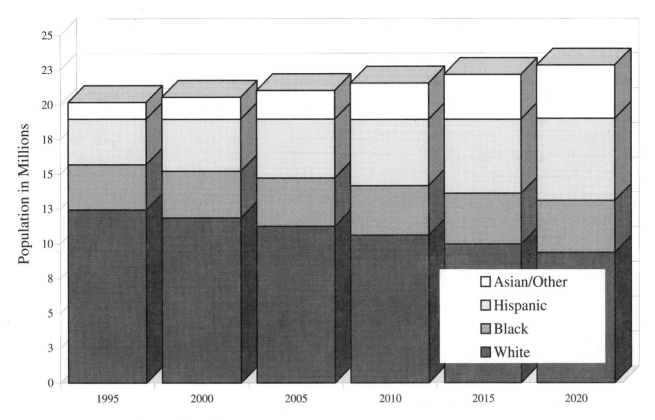

***Figure 22****: Forecasted Growth by Ethnicity.*
Source: New York Metropolitan Transportation Council.

nent role. Net out-migration is projected to continue among white and even black non-Hispanics. By 2005 the region's population is projected to reach 21 million persons from the combined effects of more natural increase at 1.1 million (births of 300,000 per year less deaths of 190,000 per year) and foreign immigration at 1.25 million, offset by more white and African-American out-migration at 1.5 million persons over the decade. Because immigration is expected to continue to play a strong role in the region's near-term growth, population in New York City will rise to 7.5 million, or account for one in every four new persons. By 2005 the region will likely be about half white non-Hispanic (54%) and half minority (20% Hispanic, 16% African-American, and 10% Asian).

About half of new growth projected over the next decade will be persons of working ages 25 through 64. Together with younger and older labor force participants, as well as new entrants, the region can expect a substantial increase of some 700,000 persons working or seeking employment. In the near

term, labor force growth will be strongest among workers aged 35 through 54, supporting greater productivity in the economy. Working age persons 25 to 34 are expected to decline absolutely, despite immigration, as the "baby bust" generation hits young working ages. It is likely that many minorities and less-skilled older workers will be held back in lower paying entry-level positions.

Pressure will also mount on elementary and secondary school facilities if the number of residents aged 5 through 19 increases by more than 1% per year, as projected. Coupled with increasing immigrant-related demands, educational systems will need new resources to cope with this growth. The typical house-buying age group (30 to 34 years) will show the first signs of decreasing in more than a quarter century, but because there are strong pent-up demands for affordable housing, the decline in this age group will not relieve strains in the demand for housing. Lastly, the elderly are projected to continue to increase, as much from increased longevity as from aging of the population. Elderly growth in the coming decade, however, pales in contrast to a virtual explosion of the older generation that will emerge past 2005, despite out-migration, as the "baby boom" reaches retirement ages.

### The Long-Term Outlook: A Nonwhite Majority

By 2020 the region's population is projected to reach 23 million, or grow by 2.1 million persons over the 2005 to 2020 period. Assuming moderate level fertility, births are expected to number 4.3 million or roughly 350,000 per year, and deaths 2.8 million or 190,000 per year. Thus natural increase will account for 1.5 million more persons, or seven in every ten new residents. If, as projected, the region's economy expands beyond the national rate of growth, from 2005 to 2020 net migration will turn positive, drawing in some 650,000 residents on balance from foreign and domestic sources. By 2010 African-Americans, Asians, and Hispanics are projected to become a majority of the region's population. And by 2020 whites will likely comprise only 42% of the region's population. Rapid growth among Asians and Hispanics would eclipse African-American population increases as Hispanics comprise one-quarter of the population and Asians become as numerous as African-Americans by 2020.

According to long-term population projections, 2005 to 2020, growth in the working age population will characterize the major gain in the region's age profile. In addition, more than 400,000 persons will be added to retirement ages of 65 and over, another 400,000 to college and postgraduate ages of 20 through 24, and some 250,000 to early home-buying ages of 30 through 34 years. Whereas school ages declined in the 1980s, secondary school and the preschool ages will expand between 2005 and 2020. Some 1.3 million additional persons will be of working ages, but the net gain will be unbalanced. The prime labor force years of 35 through 44 will contract, while growth will split between young workers aged 25 through 34, and mature and older workers aged 45 through 64. At projected rates of racial/ethnic participation in the labor force, Asians and Hispanics will comprise more than all of the net gain in persons working or seeking work, with new Asian entrants likely exceeding Hispanics because of higher rates of labor force participation.

From a demographic perspective over the long term, projections indicate that the region will become a much more dynamic and diverse place than the nation as a whole. With 7% of the total U.S. population in 2020, it will contain nearly 8% of the nation's working age persons. Whereas the median age will rise sharply in the rest of the nation—with today's one in every six people of retirement ages becoming one in every five by 2030—the region will provide a much more active population. In 2020 on average there will be only 58 dependents per 100 persons aged 18 to 64 in the region, compared to 67 per 100 in the nation. Productively engaged, the vitality that derives from a larger working age population that is both younger and more ethnically diverse can only reinforce the creative, innovative attributes that have long been competitive advantages of this region. The challenge is to realize the potential of diversity through greater equality of opportunity.

## Social Trends and Issues

Americans have always striven for equal opportunity, not only from a sense of fairness but also from an understanding that if we do not defend others' rights, we, too, could someday be pulled under. Freedom of expression and religion are more than federal laws—they are fundamental values that protect all our rights. And the economic arguments for equality are just as compelling: limiting anyone's opportunities in a free enterprise system reduces the output of the entire economy. Finally, the good communities that people are seeking cannot come into being in an atmosphere of resentment.

The huge challenge we face is the fact that this region is becoming more inequitable as it becomes more diverse. From 1979 to 1989, a period of strong economic growth for the region, household incomes grew by 40% for the wealthiest one-fifth of the 17-county region monitored by the Port Authority of New York and New Jersey. But the poorest one-fifth saw its income increase by only 7%.[3] This increasing inequality is due to a number of factors, such as foreign competition for relatively well-paying manufacturing jobs, unions losing their bargaining power, and corporate restructuring. However, the greatest impact appears to be technological change that displaces routine labor and increases the productivity and bargaining power of workers with higher cognitive and technical skills.

| | 1979 | 1993 | Change | Share of U.S. Aggregate Income, 1993 |
|---|---|---|---|---|
| Top 5% | $137,482 | $191,612 | 39.4% | — |
| Highest 20% | $90,805 | $111,017 | 22.3% | 48.6% |
| Fourth 20% | $52,405 | $54,946 | 4.8% | 23.7% |
| Third 20% | $38,056 | $37,066 | -2.6% | 15.1% |
| Second 20% | $25,198 | $23,390 | -7.2% | 9.1% |
| Lowest 20% | $11,421 | $9,739 | -14.7% | 3.5% |

**Figure 23**: *Changes in U.S. Mean Family Income (in 1993 dollars before taxes), by Quintile, 1979 to 1993.*
Source: U.S. Bureau of the Census, Current Population Reports, Series P60-184 and P60-188.

The trends analyzed in the region are mirrored nationally. In the United States as a whole, the share of aggregate income earned by 60% of the population fell between 1979 and 1993, with the lowest quintile of families dropping nearly 15% in income. Only the share of the top 20% got substantially larger. The percentage of families below the poverty line increased from 9.2% in 1979 to 12.3% in 1993.[4]

This section of the plan identifies inequities in the region's society today and projects how current trends and policies are likely both to exacerbate existing problems and to create new ones. Major inequities are identified in the region's education system, in the geographic isolation of impoverished communities, and in continuing racial segregation. Two other major areas of concern, access to housing and the neglect of urban communities, are also examined in detail.

### Limitations on Opportunity

Obstacles to full participation in the economy are the most important causes of our social problems, both to individuals and to the health of the region as a whole. Over 2 million residents of the region currently live in poverty. The greatest obstacles to their prosperity have been identified as poor education, geographical isolation, and persistent segregation.

### Education

With the sharp shift in the economy toward knowledge-based jobs, education and training are the primary keys that open the way to economic opportunity. Part of the growing demand for cognitive

skills is illustrated by the changing employment structure of the region's workforce. The region added over 1 million managers, professionals, and technicians to the workforce in the 1980s, while jobs that required primarily manual skills, such as production, craft, and repairs, declined by 140,000. By 1990 managers and professionals accounted for 35% of the employed workforce, compared to 21% for manual workers. In 1980 these two groups had been much closer, at 30% and 26% of the total workforce, respectively.[5]

As a result of both changing occupation demand and rising skill requirements, the education profile of the workforce changed dramatically from 1980 to 1990. Jobs held by college graduates grew by 53%, while jobs available to those who had not completed high school went down by 18%. By 1990 some 63% of the native-born African-American males in the region between the ages of 25 and 34 who did not have a high school diploma also did not have a job.[6] In the future, jobs that do not require a college degree will remain a majority of the region's jobs, but will still require higher levels of communication and technical skills.

These trends reinforce and exacerbate existing inequities, primarily because of unequal access to education and job skills. Schools in which low-income students predominate have much lower performance levels and far fewer resources, relative to need, than schools with affluent or middle-income students. With education being the most important single determinant of success in the labor market, equitable access to quality education is of paramount importance.

Although very high percentages of immigrants manage to find jobs, it is often through ethnic enclaves, limiting their opportunity to branch beyond

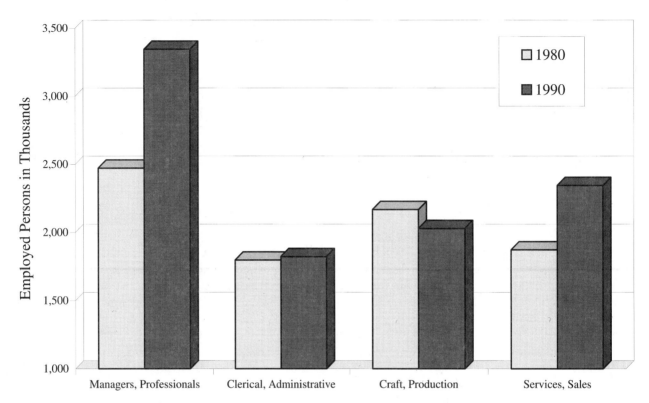

**Figure 24**: *Occupation Change.*
Source: U.S. Census of Population.

certain fields. Their principal obstacle to wide job opportunities is lack of competence in English, but there are long waiting lists for English literacy classes. A decade ago, studies estimated that less than 5% of the 2.5 million people who needed English-language or adult literacy education were enrolled in publicly funded programs. The need has undoubtedly increased as immigration has expanded.

As prosperity returns to the region, higher personal incomes among skilled employees are likely to result in somewhat more low-skill jobs to serve them. However, there will be nowhere near enough of these jobs to employ all the region's unskilled residents or to reduce the competition for them so that wages can rise to a level that can support a family. Cuts now proposed at all levels of government in education and college tuition assistance do not match the growing need for education, nor do current immigration formulas that allow in far more unskilled than skilled people.

*Isolation*

New employment opportunities and housing have increasingly been inaccessible to inner-city and minority communities. In the past 30 years, a new pattern of land use has swept the region, a pattern that involves the construction of massive campus-style commercial and industrial facilities in residential suburbs that are inaccessible by public transportation. From 1970 to 1995, the core urban counties in the region lost more than 300,000 jobs, while the outer suburban ring gained 2 million jobs.[7] Although the urban counties have only 46% of the region's population, they are home to 74% of the region's poor.[8]

Four of five of the 1.7 million housing units built since 1970 were also constructed in the region's outer ring, as residents sought affordable housing and taxes. This spread out pattern of homes and jobs has led people to drive more than ever.

Meanwhile, half the households in New York City and 40% in Newark do not have cars, which

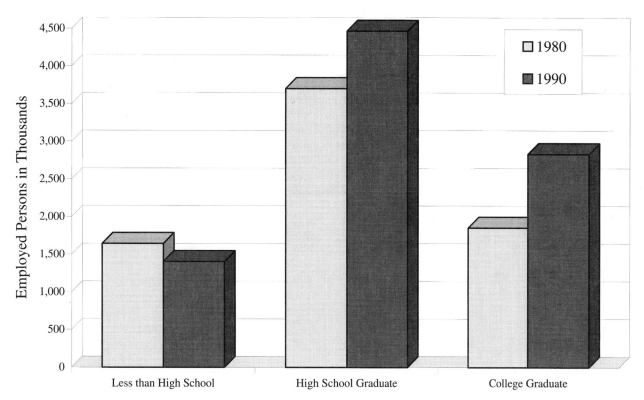

**Figure 25**: *Education Change.*
Source: U.S. Census of Population.

consume an estimated $3,000 annually from a household budget.[9] And information about new jobs often does not reach inner-city neighborhoods. A few suburban employers venture into inner-city neighborhoods to recruit and transport workers to suburban jobs, but those workers find themselves tied to the employer who recruited them, often unable to explore other opportunities outside the city.

Federal policies have contributed to this geographic isolation by favoring new development in less dense suburban areas over established urban communities. Government policies enacted after World War II—from construction of an interstate highway network to disinvestment in mass transit—have favored suburban over urban residents. For example, policies to encourage and increase home ownership in the country, such as low interest and low down payment loans—making new homes affordable to two-thirds of the nation's households for the first time—promoted new suburban development, even as many urban neighborhoods were

red-lined or denied access to similar financial packages. Finally, a higher percentage of suburban residents tend to own, rather than rent, their houses, so federal tax deductions for mortgage payments have become a *de facto* subsidy for suburban living. While many of these policies have justifiable goals, such as home ownership, they have also had the effect of sapping investment and opportunity from urban areas.

### Segregation

*Brown v. Board of Education* established that separate education could never be equal, and it effectively banned institutional and governmental practices that had created widespread racial segregation. However, segregation persists in our society, and young African-Americans "who grow up in areas of concentrated poverty are much less likely to learn how to get and keep a job or to advance in school; rather they come to expect a life of joblessness, single parenthood, and welfare dependency."[10] Not surprisingly, poor education and isolation beget further segregation, as these problems reinforce each other in a vicious cycle.

This segregation cannot be explained solely by income disparities or other economic factors.[11] Studies have shown that African-Americans in this region are more segregated than in all but five of the nation's metropolitan areas with the largest African-American populations. Worse, the region has become more segregated between 1970 and 1990, while most other metropolitan areas in the nation are becoming less so.[12]

High crime rates have added to fear and mistrust among racial and ethnic groups, further increasing tendencies to maintain segregated communities. If this trend toward greater segregation continues, minorities will be deprived of progress in the mainstream economy and the region could be faced with untenable social relations.

Education and access have been identified as primary components to ending this cycle. But other social issues, the results of segregation, continue to compound the problem. Communication skills have become extremely important in the economy, but students in segregated schools often do not learn the communication skills they will need to get a job. An example: many graduates who have mastered the demanding course work at Polytechnic University of New York still need special training in communication before meeting with prospective employers.[13] Successful job preparation includes not just schooling but acquaintance with the world of work and role models.

|  | Employment Change 1970–1995 | Below Poverty 1990 |
|---|---|---|
| Bronx | -700 | 29% |
| Kings | -72,700 | 22% |
| New York | -273,400 | 20% |
| Queens | 12,800 | 11% |
| Richmond | 54,000 | 8% |
| Essex | -39,200 | 14% |
| Hudson | -5,400 | 15% |
| Union | -7,400 | 7% |
| **Urban Counties** | **-307,000** | **18%** |
| Dutchess | 31,800 | 5% |
| Nassau | 149,400 | 4% |
| Orange | 55,600 | 9% |
| Putnam | 15,400 | 4% |
| Rockland | 50,100 | 6% |
| Suffolk | 298,700 | 5% |
| Sullivan | 7,800 | 13% |
| Ulster | 23,800 | 8% |
| Westchester | 89,300 | 7% |
| Bergen | 152,500 | 4% |
| Hunterdon | 36,600 | 3% |
| Mercer | 78,400 | 7% |
| Middlesex | 183,600 | 5% |
| Monmouth | 133,900 | 5% |
| Morris | 173,200 | 3% |
| Ocean | 101,600 | 6% |
| Passaic | 11,200 | 10% |
| Somerset | 118,200 | 3% |
| Sussex | 22,000 | 3% |
| Warren | 12,500 | 5% |
| Fairfield | 160,500 | 6% |
| Litchfield | 33,200 | 4% |
| New Haven | 79,100 | 8% |
| **Suburban Ring** | **2,018,400** | **5%** |

*Figure 26: Employment Change and Poverty in Urban and Suburban Counties.*
Source: U.S. Bureau of Economic Analysis, U.S. Census of Population.

### Access to Housing

Geographic isolation of poor communities and continued racial segregation are perpetuated by trends in the region's housing markets. These conditions are not only a source of social inequity but also constitute a competitive disadvantage for the entire region. The American dream of single-family home ownership has driven national and regional development patterns and financial policy for nearly half a century. But now, as the housing stock of the region becomes increasingly unaffordable, the dream has become little more than a myth. The enormous disparity between regional and national housing prices makes it increasingly difficult to attract new residents and businesses to the region, or even to get employed people from other parts of the nation to accept a transfer into the area. Businesses, in large part, look for cheap labor and low taxes when they move—but housing costs for current and prospective employees also play a significant role in their decision-making. Key indicators of the region's housing problem include:

• Rising costs of housing are increasingly unbearable. These costs include mortgage or rent payments, property taxes, association fees, and operating costs (water, sewer, and energy bills)—all of which are high in the region. Nearly two-thirds of all households with incomes less than $20,000 that rent their homes are spending more than 35 percent of their income on rent.[14] Households unable to pay the increasing prices are compelled to double-up in apartments, accept unsatisfactory housing, try to find affordable housing at the periphery of the region, or move away altogether.

• The perception and reality that the region has no acceptable and affordable housing options seriously undermines the competitiveness of the region's economy. Business leaders participating in RPA's Competitive Region Initiative stressed that poor housing opportunities have seriously affected their ability to attract national and international talent to the region. And many large companies have abandoned the region for just this reason.

• Nontraditional households are becoming a larger portion of the housing market, and their dreams cannot be accommodated by the standard suburban American dream ideal. Two-income and single-parent families and other nontraditional households need different types of housing and services than seemed adequate 50 years ago. These new needs might mean sharing some responsibilities with others, such as supervising children's play areas, or reducing other responsibilities such as outside maintenance. And it is not just a matter of the site and shape of rooms, because people are also looking for access to daycare facilities, for instance, and closeness to transportation and shopping centers, which means rethinking not just the "what" of housing, but where and how new homes can be located within the urban and suburban landscape.

• The region is burdened by continuing racial and economic residential segregation, as well as homelessness. While the number and degree may vary by subregion and community, leaving others out of the economy

and society is unsustainable and weakens the economic and social foundations of the region.

Figure 27 summarizes the changes in the number of people, households, and housing units in the region. Households grew much more rapidly than the overall population, primarily the result of the population becoming relatively older, with significant increases in the "baby boomer" age groups (as detailed elsewhere in the Equity chapter). This group entered the prime "settling down" age, roughly between ages 25 and 40, where finding a home is not only desirable, but more financially attainable. In response, more housing units were created, but the affordability and desirability of the overall housing stock remains a key question.

Since the 1980s we have seen a dramatic bidding up of housing prices. As employment increased during the economic boom of the 1980s and large numbers of baby boomer households sought housing for the first time, housing demand far exceeded supply, particularly for choice homes in choice neighborhoods. It seemed for a while as if prices would never stop rising. Simultaneously, our ability to build enough affordable homes has been constrained by increasingly scarce developable land in the near suburbs, low-density residential zoning which reduces the number of homes possible and further consumes scarce land, and regulatory delays that could add as much as one-quarter to the cost of a new home.

In 1981 the ratio of regional housing prices to national housing prices was approximately 1.1 to 1. This ratio increased steadily in the first two years of the 1980s and then shot up dramatically in 1983. By the end of 1987 the ratio of regional to U.S. housing prices peaked at 2.2 to 1, meaning that housing

| Subregion | Population | | | Households | | | Housing Units | | |
|---|---|---|---|---|---|---|---|---|---|
| | 1980 | 1990 | Change | 1980 | 1990 | Change | 1980 | 1990 | Change |
| Connecticut | 1,725,237 | 1,805,956 | 4.7% | 599,656 | 676,112 | 12.8% | 633,130 | 725,708 | 14.8% |
| New Jersey | 5,856,975 | 6,079,453 | 3.8% | 1,992,819 | 2,206,663 | 10.7% | 2,127,117 | 2,391,413 | 12.4% |
| Long Island | 2,605,813 | 2,609,212 | 0.1% | 805,139 | 856,234 | 6.3% | 859,761 | 927,609 | 7.9% |
| Mid-Hudson | 1,773,135 | 1,860,668 | 4.9% | 593,985 | 651,647 | 9.7% | 643,136 | 707,149 | 10.0% |
| New York City | 7,071,639 | 7,322,564 | 3.5% | 2,785,527 | 2,819,401 | 1.2% | 2,941,661 | 2,992,169 | 1.7% |
| **Region Total** | **19,032,799** | **19,677,853** | **3.4%** | **6,777,126** | **7,210,057** | **6.4%** | **7,204,805** | **7,744,048** | **7.5%** |

*Figure 27:* *Regional Population, Households, and Housing Units, 1980 to 1990.*
Source: U.S. Census Bureau, *County and City Data Book,* 1992.

| Area or County | 1980 Income | 1990 Income | Change in Income, 1980–1990 | 1980 Median House Value | 1990 Median House Value | Change in House Value, 1980–1990 | Change in House Value in Relation to Income |
|---|---|---|---|---|---|---|---|
| New York | 16.3 | 36.8 | 125.6% | 92.4 | 487.3 | 427.4% | 340.29% |
| Queens | 20.5 | 40.4 | 97.1% | 51.4 | 191 | 271.6% | 279.71% |
| Bronx | 13.2 | 25.5 | 93.6% | 48.2 | 173.9 | 260.8% | 278.63% |
| Kings | 14.7 | 30 | 104.8% | 50.5 | 196.1 | 288.3% | 275.10% |
| Hudson | 17.7 | 35.3 | 99.6% | 43.5 | 168.5 | 260.9% | 261.95% |
| Nassau | 28.4 | 60.6 | 113.1% | 56.6 | 209.5 | 270.1% | 238.82% |
| Suffolk | 24.2 | 53.2 | 120.1% | 45 | 165.9 | 268.7% | 223.73% |
| Orange | 20.6 | 44 | 114% | 42.2 | 141.7 | 235.8% | 206.84% |
| Westchester | 27.3 | 58.9 | 115.8% | 83.5 | 283.5 | 239.5% | 206.82% |
| Richmond | 23.8 | 50.7 | 112.5% | 60 | 186.3 | 210.5% | 187.11% |
| Union | 25.3 | 48.8 | 93.4% | 65.8 | 180.5 | 174.3% | 186.62% |
| Rockland | 28.2 | 60.5 | 114.1% | 69.6 | 217.1 | 211.9% | 185.71% |
| Ulster | 18.8 | 40.1 | 113.7% | 37.5 | 114.3 | 204.8% | 180.12% |
| Bergen | 27.5 | 57.6 | 109.5% | 76.7 | 227.7 | 196.9% | 179.82% |
| Dutchess | 23.1 | 49.3 | 113.2% | 49.3 | 149.2 | 202.6% | 178.98% |
| Putnam | 26.3 | 58.9 | 123.9% | 61.5 | 195 | 217.1% | 175.22% |
| Essex | 19.9 | 42.2 | 111.5% | 67.1 | 163.8 | 192.3% | 172.47% |
| Passaic | 21 | 43.1 | 105% | 66.3 | 185.5 | 179.8% | 171.24% |
| Middlesex | 25.6 | 51.8 | 102.5% | 60.7 | 164.7 | 171.3% | 167.12% |
| Mercer | 23 | 48.5 | 111.1% | 49.7 | 137.9 | 177.5% | 159.77% |
| Litchfield | 22.3 | 49.1 | 119.6% | 57.8 | 166.3 | 187.7% | 156.94% |
| New Haven | 21.7 | 46.1 | 112.6% | 59.7 | 165.2 | 176.7% | 156.93% |
| Warren | 21.4 | 45.8 | 113.8% | 51.9 | 143.9 | 177.3% | 155.80% |
| Monmouth | 24.5 | 53.6 | 118.5% | 64.7 | 180.4 | 178.8% | 150.89% |
| Morris | 29.3 | 62.7 | 114.3% | 81.4 | 217.3 | 167% | 146.11% |
| Fairfield | 26.6 | 58 | 118% | 91.7 | 249.8 | 172.4% | 146.10% |
| Ocean | 18.8 | 39.8 | 111.7% | 48.2 | 126 | 161.4% | 144.49% |
| Somerset | 29.2 | 62.3 | 113.4% | 77.8 | 196.3 | 152.3% | 134.30% |
| Sullivan | 15.9 | 33.9 | 112.8% | 37.2 | 93.4 | 151.1% | 133.95% |
| Hunterdon | 26.6 | 61.1 | 129.7% | 78.7 | 209 | 165.6% | 127.68% |
| Sussex | 23.5 | 53 | 125.4% | 61.2 | 156.3 | 155.4% | 123.92% |
| **U.S. Average** | **7.3** | **14.4** | **97.6%** | **47.2** | **79.1** | **67.6%** | **69.26%** |

*Figure 28*: *Ratio of Home Price Change to Income Price Change (in thousands).*

in this region cost over twice what comparable housing cost in other parts of the country. Since the stockmarket crash of 1987, prices have deflated slightly, thereby decreasing the ratio somewhat—although not because the regional housing prices are falling significantly, but because prices are just not rising as rapidly as prices across the country.[15] Median home values in New Jersey and Connecticut are still twice as high as the national average.[16]Another way of looking at the issue is to compare the ratios of home price change to median family incomes during the decade, as shown in Fig-

ure 28. Incomes in the region rose by roughly 100 percent in the decade, while home prices rose more than 200 percent. Sussex County had the least differential between home price and income increases, but still home prices rose 124% faster than incomes and over twice the national average.

While regional incomes grew at a somewhat faster pace than the national rate, house values in the region literally exploded, growing at nearly three times the country's pace. One rough gauge of affordability is that when a person is buying a home, banks will provide a mortgage worth approximately 2.5 times a person's annual household income. Back in 1980 the approximate ratio of regional house values to household income stood at roughly three-to-one, which meant that, at closing, families would have to come up with about one-sixth of the purchase price. By 1990, however, the same ratio had jumped to four-to-one or higher. The new ratio obligates families to make a down payment of three-eighths of the purchase price, and potentially puts home ownership beyond the reach of many people—particularly young families or minorities, who tend to have lower incomes.[17,18]

One further housing trend involves changes in the composition of households. Between 1980 and 1985 alone, the expansion of "nonfamily households" accounted for 71% of the region's increase in occupied housing, while families comprised only 29% of the growth. In addition, five of every six new families were formed by female heads of household. This pattern is expected to continue beyond the 1990s and into the early years of the 21st century.[19] And RPA projects decreasing household incomes for many new households. Between 1990 and 2005, households with annual incomes below $17,500 (in 1982 dollars) may increase by 1 million, to comprise 45% of new growth.[20] Using the household income to mortgage ratio of 2.5, such households could not afford housing valued on the open market at more than $50,000, or less than one-third the price of an average home in the region today.

Figure 29 highlights additional county-level indicators of the condition and quality of the regional housing stock. The first two indicators, housing affordability index and percentage of renters paying more than 35% of their income in rent, are measures of the affordability of both rental and owned units. The second pair, percentage of units built prior to 1939 and percentage of units with more than 1.01 persons per room, attempt to gauge the possible condition of the unit and its degree of crowding. While crowding does not appear on the surface to be a major problem, "doubling-up" of households in the same home is a quiet but pressing issue. RPA's 1990 "New Directions for the Bronx" report estimated that over 43,000 families in that borough were doubled-up.[21] While some families may see an advantage to doubling-up, it reflects an unmet demand for new housing and creates an equity and quality of life issue, as greater

numbers of the region's citizens are forced to endure reduced family privacy and comfort. The index omits homeless families altogether.

The housing affordability index in Figure 29 reinforces the idea introduced above of the overall lack of affordable housing, especially in the wealthiest parts of the region. This index reveals that the median household has only 70% of the income needed to afford the median-priced home.[22] Additional burdens, if not outright barriers, include the operating cost of the home: taxes, energy, water, and sewer fees. Geographically, the index shows that housing is least affordable in the urban core, where incomes are lowest, with larger supplies of more affordable housing out on the periphery. Nearly one-third of all households that rent are paying more than 35% of their income in rent, a threshold beyond which the householder will likely have difficulty paying. The highest rent-to-income ratio is in Ocean County, perhaps a function of the many senior communities there, while the ratio is lower in the suburbs. Over 30% of the region's housing stock was built before 1939, which may not seem particularly surprising, considering the region's maturity. The historic preservation movement has taught us all to be proud of our historic homesteads, yet, at the same time, the youngest pre-war homes are now 56 years old, and are more apt to have inferior, inefficient, or less reliable heating, plumbing, or electrical systems, perhaps decayed due to deferred maintenance. A further concern in older units is the likely presence of lead and asbestos materials. As would be expected, the counties with the biggest share of older housing are in New York City and adjacent areas—the areas that predate sprawl. In addition, the crowding indicator shows considerable crowding conditions in urban areas, particularly in New York City and in Essex, Hudson, and Passaic counties in New Jersey. Such crowding does not just cramp lives; it also brings with it more rapid decay of housing units and premature dilapidation if increased maintenance needs go unmet.

Although much of the preceding discussion has focused on suburban needs, Figure 29 suggests that a higher percentage of housing resources be devoted to urban locations—New York City, Hudson County, and the urban parts of Essex County—so as to address problems of crowding, affordability, and a large stock of older homes that may need sig-

| County or Area | Housing Affordability Index | Paying Over 35% of Income in Rent | Housing Stock Built Before 1939 | Units with More Than 1.01 Persons per Room |
|---|---|---|---|---|
| Fairfield | 62.3 | 31.1% | 24.4% | 2.9% |
| Litchfield | 80 | 23.5% | 30.6% | 1.1% |
| New Haven | 72.8 | 31.4% | 27.6% | 2.2% |
| Connecticut | 70.4 | 30.7% | 26.5% | 2.4% |
| Bergen | 67.6 | 29.5% | 26.0% | 2.5% |
| Essex | 55 | 32.3% | 36.7% | 7.4% |
| Hudson | 61.5 | 29.2% | 48.7% | 9.5% |
| Hunterdon | 81.3 | 29.8% | 25.5% | 8.0% |
| Mercer | 93.4 | 27.9% | 28.4% | 3.2% |
| Middlesex | 86.6 | 26.7% | 14.7% | 3.3% |
| Monmouth | 79.5 | 31.6% | 20.2% | 2.1% |
| Morris | 80.9 | 24.4% | 17.9% | 1.6% |
| Ocean | 82.1 | 40.6% | 6.6% | 1.7% |
| Passaic | 63.3 | 32.8% | 30.7% | 7.0% |
| Somerset | 88.4 | 24.6% | 15.9% | 1.8% |
| Sussex | 97.6 | 34.0% | 17.8% | 1.2% |
| Union | 72.4 | 29.9% | 30.3% | 4.6% |
| Warren | 86.7 | 30.5% | 33.2% | 1.1% |
| New Jersey | 77.5 | 30.2% | 25.8% | 4.1% |
| Nassau | 81 | 32.5% | 21.3% | 2.8% |
| Suffolk | 92.5 | 38.6% | 11.7% | 2.5% |
| Long Island | 86.1 | 35.6% | 16.3% | 2.7% |
| Dutchess | 88.5 | 28.5% | 23.8% | 2.1% |
| Orange | 86.4 | 35.1% | 28.7% | 3.3% |
| Putnam | 86 | 31.6% | 20.5% | 1.6% |
| Rockland | 75.9 | 33.6% | 15.2% | 4.5% |
| Sullivan | 92.3 | 37.9% | 26.2% | 4.0% |
| Ulster | 93 | 31.8% | 32.9% | 2.2% |
| Westchester | 53.4 | 30.5% | 35.3% | 4.4% |
| Mid-Hudson | 77.9 | 31.5% | 29.3% | 3.7% |
| Bronx | 39.4 | 34.5% | 31.3% | 16.6% |
| Kings | 40.9 | 34.0% | 48.0% | 13.8% |
| New York | 20.7 | 28.9% | 47.2% | 10.1% |
| Queens | 55.9 | 30.8% | 34.7% | 11.8% |
| Richmond | 73.6 | 30.3% | 24.1% | 3.7% |
| New York City | 40 | 31.9% | 40.9% | 12.3% |
| **Region Total** | **70** | **31.6%** | **30.9%** | **6.9%** |

*Figure 29*: *Selected Regional Housing Indices, 1990.*
Source: U.S. Census of Population, STF 3A, 1990.

nificant amounts of rehabilitation before they can once again be listed as a regional asset.

### Urban Neglect

Despite a generation of effort, the region has been unable to stop the continued hollowing out of its cities. Numerous federal, state, and local initiatives have been launched to try to ease urban poverty, improve housing conditions, control crime, and rebuild infrastructure. RPA's own efforts in Downtown Brooklyn, Jamaica Center, Newark, and New Brunswick have had positive impacts in many ways. On balance, sadly, the problem is every bit as ur-

| City | Population Change, 1982 to 1992 | Infant Deaths per 1,000 Births, 1988 | Crimes Reported per 100,000 Persons, 1991 | Children Living Below Poverty Level, 1989 |
|------|------|------|------|------|
| Bridgeport, CT | -3.9% | 10 | 12,253 | 2.9% |
| New Haven, CT | -1.7% | 16.2 | 14,922 | 33.8% |
| Jersey City, NJ | 2.3% | 13.9 | 9,201 | 29.7% |
| Newark, NJ | -18.6% | 19.8 | 14,806 | 37.2% |
| Paterson, NJ | 1.0% | 13.2 | 7,643 | 26.7% |
| Trenton, NJ | -4.7% | 17.7 | 10,863 | 26.8% |
| Bronx, NY | 2.2% | 15.5 | na* | 28.7% |
| Brooklyn, NY | 2.5% | 14.7 | na* | 22.7% |
| Manhattan, NY | 4.3% | 13.6 | na* | 20.5% |
| Queens, NY | 3.2% | 9.8 | na* | 10.9% |
| Staten Island, NY | 11.1% | 8.3 | na* | 7.8% |
| Danbury, CT | 8.0% | 6.4 | 5,588 | 8.2% |
| Fair Lawn, NJ | -4.2% | 11 | 2,231 | 2.3% |
| Valley Stream, NY | -3.6% | 7.1 | na | 3.4% |

*Data not broken out for each borough. For all of New York City the number was 9,236 per 100,000.

**Figure 30**: *Selected Indicators of Urban Quality of Life.*
Source: U.S. Bureau of the Census, *County and City Databook*, 1994, Washington, D.C., 1994.

gent as it was a generation ago. And regionally the problem has intensified, now that crime and poverty are no longer strangers in the suburbs. There are many causes for continuing urban decay, as have been noted in previous sections, including poor schools, economic restructuring that eliminates many living wage jobs, and residential housing segregation. Figure 30 highlights some of the grim indicators. The three communities below the dotted line represent contemporary conditions in nearby suburbs.

## Toward an Equitable Region: Creating Opportunity for All

Each of the five campaigns detailed later in the plan addresses ways to make the region more equitable while also strengthening our economy and environment. *Workforce* seeks to address the deficiencies in our educational system and institutions and link technological change to opportunities, particularly in inner city communities. *Governance* is critical in enabling communities to link resources, breaking down discriminatory barriers and effecting changes called for in the other campaigns. *Mobility* finds transportation alternatives to diminish infrastruc-

ture barriers which limit employment and housing opportunities for communities. *Centers* refocuses investment, employment, and housing in existing urban centers across the region, also making a higher quality of life more accessible to a greater portion of the region. *Greensward* would protect our environment and preserve clean air and drinking water and access to open space for all the region's residents.

## Notes

1. The region's population has been divided into four mutually exclusive racial/ethnic groups: white non-Hispanic, black non-Hispanic, Asian and other non-Hispanics, and Hispanics. Henceforth, references to white, African-American, or Asian populations should be understood to exclude Hispanic members of these groups.

2. Legal alien admissions will not match net migration estimates by race/ethnicity because relocations occur within the United States, some immigrants return to their native countries, and net migration can contain native born second generation population.

3. Port Authority of New York and New Jersey.

4. Bureau of the Census, Current Population Reports: Consumer Income, Series P60-184, 1992, "Money In-

come of Households, Families and Person in the U.S.," updated; and P60-188, 1993, "Income, Poverty and Valuation of Non-Cash Benefits."

5. U.S. Census of Population.

6. Ibid.

7. RPA defines the *urban core* of the region as New York City's five boroughs and Essex, Hudson, and Union counties in New Jersey.

8. U.S. Census of Population.

9. Patrick Hare, *Clunker Mortgages and Transportation Redlining: How the Mortgage Banking Industry Unknowingly Drains Cities and Spreads Sprawl*, Washington, DC, 1995.

10. Massey and Denton, *American Apartheid*, Harvard University Press, 1993.

11. Regional Plan News, No. 104, July 1979, *Segregation and Opportunity in the Region's Housing.*

12. Massey and Denton, *American Apartheid*, Harvard University Press, 1993.

13. Interview with Jeanette Grill, Director, Career Services Office, Polytechnic University, 4/26/95.

14. U.S. Census Bureau, Summary Tape File 3a, 1990.

15. Port Authority of New York/New Jersey.

16. Hughes and Seneca, *Ranking the Municipalities: Incomes and House Values*, A Rutgers Regional Report, 1994.

17. An examination of selected areas and municipalities finds that all households with heads aged 25 to 34—the core of the "nesting period" where first-home buying aspirations are quite likely—and black households of all ages tend to have incomes roughly 10% below the median for all ages and races.

18. It should be noted that mortgage lenders have introduced new products during the decade to help serve this end of the market, including variable rate mortgages, and lower down payment requirements.

19. Regional Plan Association. "Household Formation in the Tri-State Region & the Demand for New Housing, 1980–2015. Working Paper No. 3." Prepared by Regina B. Armstrong for the Metropolitan Transportation Authority, September 1990.

20. Ibid.

21. Regional Plan Association, "New Directions for the Bronx," 1990.

22. This index is created by multiplying each county's median household income by the 2.5 mortgage factor and dividing by 80% to reflect a down payment of 20%. This number is then divided into the median house value for the respective county.

# Chapter 5

# Environment:
# Green Infrastructure Under Siege

THE EARTH CHARTER—The 1992 Rio Declaration on Environment and Development that has now become the world's official 21st century growth policy—states that environmental protection must be an "integral part of the development process and cannot be considered in isolation."[1]

This simple phrase reflects a new global understanding of the relationship between the planet's economy and ecology. As we enjoy the benefits of recent advancements in environmental protection, such as cleaner water and air, and as we grapple with emerging issues, such as new manufacturing methods that minimize or eliminate the production of wastes, we can now understand that the old paradigm of economic progress and environmental quality as opposing forces was never quite true.

In the past 30 years, the region has made tremendous investments in improved environmental quality and has been well rewarded for this effort:

- We all breathe a little easier now as aggressive measures to reduce emissions and technological advances to tame them, such as the catalytic converter, have improved air quality. New York City did not record a single violation of federal carbon monoxide standards in both 1992 and 1993. As recently as 1987, the city had 90 violations.[2]

- Fish, as well as boaters and waterfront developers, have returned to the Harbor and Long Island Sound as investments in sewage treatment plants have cleaned the water. The New York–New Jersey Harbor is the cleanest it has been in the 84 years since systematic harbor surveys began. As a result, South Beach and Midland Beach on Staten Island were re-opened in 1992 for the first time in 20 years. Seagate Beach on Coney Island was opened in 1988 for the first time in 40 years.[3]

- The region has added about 350,000 acres of public parkland since 1964, creating a public trust that safeguards the jewels of the region's natural areas and invests in urban public spaces, such as Gateway National Recreation Area, one of the country's very first big-city national parks.[4]

The formula for this success has been relatively straightforward: New York, New Jersey, and Connecticut are national leaders in environmental protection because they have set up comprehensive and far-reaching environmental standards and regulations. Once such laws went on the books, the states spent both money and political capital to make them work.[5]

It is important to emphasize these remarkable achievements, because they are often overshadowed

61

**Figure 31:** *Thanks to environmental laws and investments in water pollution control, the New York–New Jersey Harbor is the cleanest it has been since surveys began 84 years ago.*

by the very serious problems that have yet to be solved. Most of the region's residents still breathe air that fails to meet federal health standards.[6] Drinking water that once arrived at the tap with a minimum of treatment must now be filtered in many areas.[7] Far too many urban neighborhoods do not meet minimum standards for park acreage, and most of the parks that already exist are increasingly unkempt and unsafe. And suburban development continues to sprawl across the mountains and farmlands.

The continuing impact of this ongoing mismanagement is a slow but steady decline in the region's quality of life. One week we may taste a little more chlorine in the water from the tap, and start buying drinking water from the store. The next week a favorite fishing hole or hiking trail will be replaced by a new subdivision, and we have to travel farther for vacations and weekend outings. We suffer in traffic jams almost daily, whether on the way to work or off to the beach, stuck behind trucks in a haze of

smoke and partially burned diesel fuel. Inevitably, as environmental quality costs more and becomes more elusive, businesses and families pick up stakes and resettle elsewhere.

Many of the biological and land resources now at risk in the region are simply irreplaceable. The eastern timber rattlesnake, to take one example of the region's extensive and often surprising biodiversity, nests in ancestral den sites that have been continuously occupied for 5,000 to 8,000 years. When these den sites are destroyed, as they are with some regularity throughout the Appalachian Highlands in New York and New Jersey, the snakes simply cannot find a new home, and they are destroyed as well.[8] While all of us may not mourn the loss of this threatened species, it represents an important fact: As long as there are still rattlesnakes less than 40 miles from Manhattan, biodiversity and untamable wilderness can continue to coexist with civilization.

How the region manages its interactions with the

environment is at once an example and a major component of a worldwide pattern of resource depletion, bringing with it effects such as global warming, decreased biodiversity, and declining fisheries. Climate change is perhaps the most far-reaching consequence: 1994 was the fifth warmest year on record since 1880, and the ten warmest years on record have all occurred since 1980.[9] Direct and indirect consequences of a predicted sea level rise and other changes could be substantial: increased storms and flooding could affect coastal homes, roads, and bridges, while a rise in sea level will affect water supply intakes and sewage treatment plant outflows. As we better understand the relationship of this warming trend to the production of greenhouse gases such as carbon dioxide, it is clear that this region, like others, must do a better job of meeting global accords on reducing carbon releases into the atmosphere.

All these issues, and their potential solutions, are in many ways very different from those that confronted the region a generation ago. Often enough the pollution that remains to be addressed cannot be pinpointed to a smokestack but is diffused throughout the environment or involves the actions of multiple players:

- Water quality experts are now concerned with pollutants that reach streams and estuaries from stormwater carrying fertilizers, oils, and sediment washing away from homes and roadways. In New York State over 80% of the remaining water pollution problem is believed to be caused by such "nonpoint" pollution.[10]

- The key contributor to air quality problems is no longer tall factory smokestacks but short, mobile, horizontal smokestacks—tailpipe emissions from the growing number of automobiles.[11]

- Habitat needs of many of the region's species, from river otter to warblers, cannot be met by setting aside small individual tracts of land, but often require linking together these islands of habitat through landscape-scale conservation efforts.

Such issues do not lend themselves to traditional, after-the-fact or "end-of-the-pipe" treatment technology. Complex problems demand systemic solutions, and are inexorably leading to strategies that prevent pollution from being generated in the first place or address entire systems of land and water.

The political context for this work has also become more delicate. While environmental protection continues to be of the utmost importance to

*Figure 32: Many of the region's environmental challenges cannot be traced to a single smokestack but are diffused throughout the region or involve the actions of multiple players.*

the public, there is widespread dissatisfaction on the part of businesses and public officials with the way environmental management is practiced.[12] The growing complexity of regulations and environmental science in general is viewed as a burden by landowners, businesses, and governments. Smaller companies, municipalities, and developers lack the resources and technical expertise to address land and resource management issues. So developers try to avoid the problems altogether by seeking out opportunities in smaller, less-affluent communities with simple or no land use controls.

Federal and state governments are increasingly unwilling or unable to provide capital funds necessary to address environmental issues, leading local officials to criticize the proliferation of unfunded mandates as regulatory objectives are shifted to

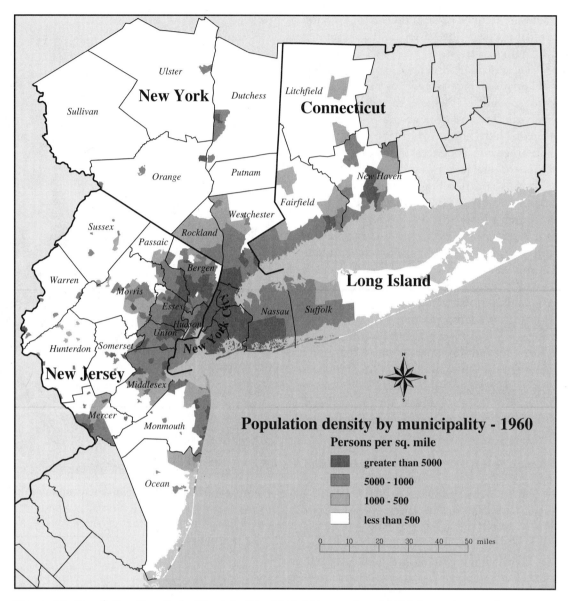

**Figure 33:** *Population Density by Municipality, 1960 (this page) and 1990 (opposite page).*

lower levels of government. Federal appropriations to New York and New Jersey to help communities meet federal Clean Water Act goals have dropped from around $600 million annually between 1972 and 1987 to around $235 million annually today. Moreover, funding is now being used to grant low-interest loans to communities, rather than direct grants in aid.[13] Federal appropriations from the Land and Water Conservation Funds, which buy parkland or make capital improvements to existing parks, have dropped by more than 50% since 1978.

New York State's share of this funding dropped by over 90%, to only $1.3 million in 1994.[14] As a result, local governments have to shoulder an increasing share of environmental costs.[15]

And people and their elected representatives are increasingly reluctant to host environmental improvement facilities in their communities. Some communities in the region feel—often justifiably—that they already have more than their fair share of such facilities. The concerns of lower income and minority communities on this issue have created a

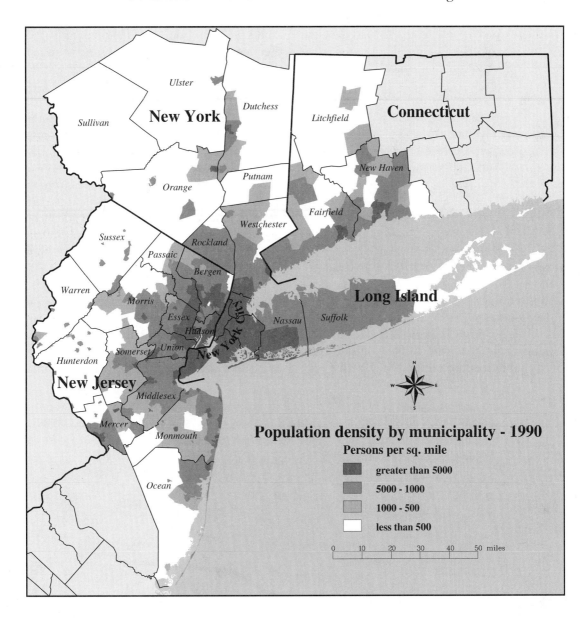

new social movement—the quest for environmental justice. And since almost every neighborhood is eager to see unwanted land uses constructed elsewhere, the result often is that environmental improvement facilities cannot be built at all.

## Projections: Land Consumption at the Region's Edge

Nowhere is the complexity or urgency of these concerns so evident as in the issue of the region's dwindling supply of open land. For more than 350

years, the New York–New Jersey–Connecticut region has experienced successive waves of development and outward growth. Expanding the region has conferred benefits on each successive generation, building new homes and setting aside space for new businesses. There has always been a price for this success—each generation has had to watch as farms, forests, waterways, and cherished countryside disappeared.

We used to grow fast and spread out slowly. Now our growth is much slower—but we spread out very quickly, consuming vast areas of open land and shattering traditional patterns of community. Population in the region has grown only 13% in the last 30 years, but the amount of developed land has grown 60%.[16] That means that, since 1962, development in the region has raced across 1 million acres. It used to be that forests and farms surrounded us. Thirty years ago 81% of the region was open space; now only 70% of the region's land base is still green. We have sacrificed our landscapes for high-cost sprawl and endless miles of traffic congestion.

### Suburban Growth

While large-scale suburban expansion has been a force in this region since the 1920s, a generation ago it underwent a significant change. Massive campus-style commercial and industrial development jumped out from central areas into previously residential suburbs. From 1975 to 1992, some 90% of the region's new jobs were located outside the core urban counties of the region (New York City

and Essex, Hudson, and Union counties).[17] In Connecticut alone, three out of four new jobs have been located in the suburbs since 1950.[18] As a result, the leading edge of housing development has moved even farther away from Manhattan, Newark, White Plains, Stamford, and other urban centers. This places suburban development in rural communities, where construction costs are cheaper and regulations are looser. Of the 1.7 million housing units built since 1970, some 40% were built in the outer ring of counties. Towns like Brookfield and Sherman in Connecticut, and Monroe and Brookhaven in New York tripled in size between 1960 and 1990. Places like Vernon and Plainsboro in New Jersey grew tenfold.[19]

Once such a pattern takes hold, it builds its own momentum. Federal and state policies to build highways and sewers far from existing towns get such a pattern started, but thereafter it is nurtured by individual decisions. People are drawn ever outward by their need for affordable housing. But as

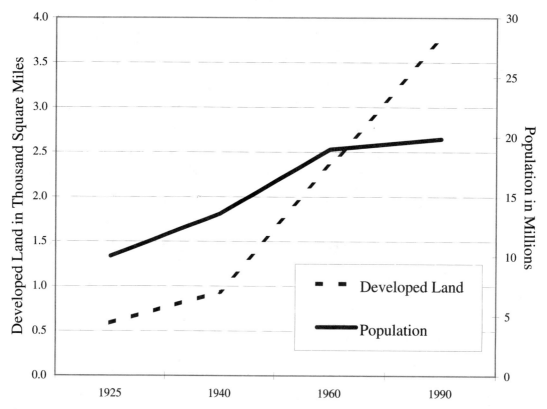

**Figure 34:** *Developed Land and Population Changes in the Region: 1925, 1940, 1960, and 1990.*

Sources: RPA and U.S. Census Bureau.

new communities fill with new families who want quality schools and infrastructure, property taxes rise. The response of local elected officials is rational under the circumstances—they revise their land use codes to bring in commercial uses that pay taxes without requiring schools or other services. They discourage smaller lot, higher density housing, whose property taxes are unlikely to pay for the services they require. And housing gets pushed even farther out into the fields.

The region has, in effect, wrapped new suburbs around old suburbs in ever expanding rings. We

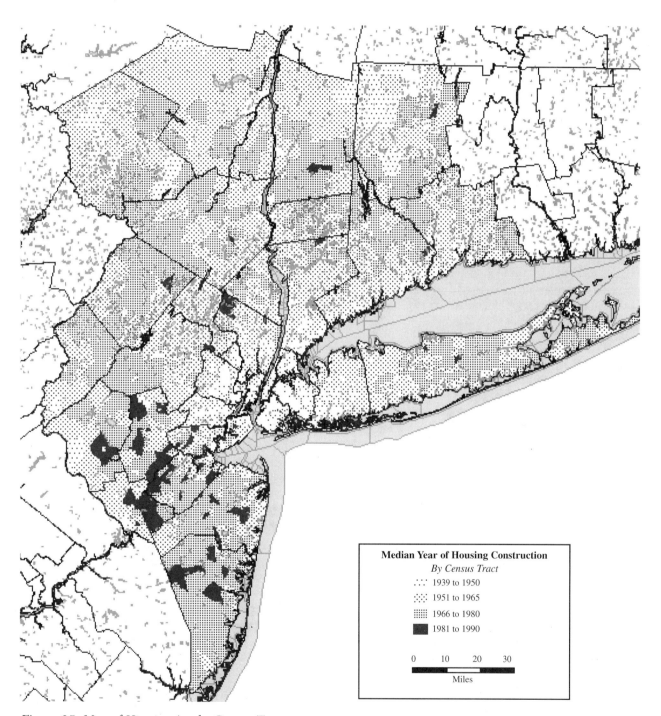

*Figure 35: Map of Housing Age by Census Tract.*
Source: U.S. Census Bureau.

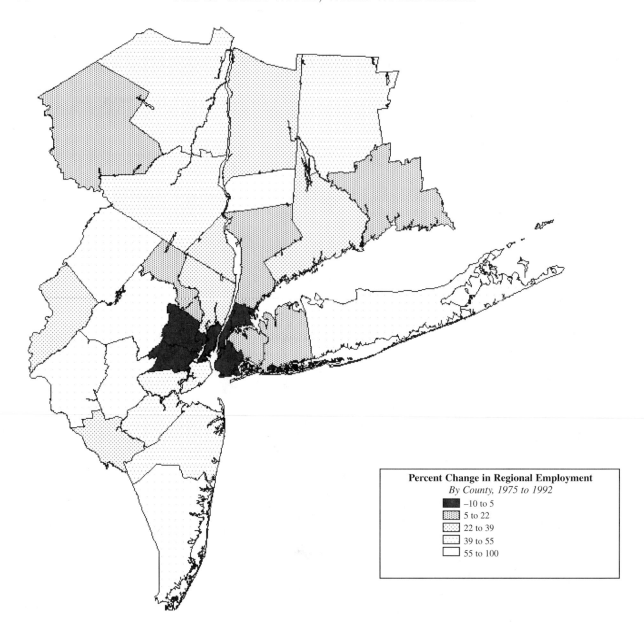

**Percent Change in Regional Employment**
*By County, 1975 to 1992*
■ −10 to 5
▨ 5 to 22
▧ 22 to 39
░ 39 to 55
□ 55 to 100

**Figure 36:** *Map of Employment Change by County.*
Source: U.S. Department of Commerce, Bureau of Economic Analysis.

have succeeded in creating 75 miles of formless suburban sprawl.

### Urban Decline

At the same time that the region has been devouring land at its periphery, we have been abandoning our urban areas, hollowing out the cities that historically have been the locus for jobs and people. Cities such as Hicksville, Trenton, and Poughkeep-

sie lost 10% or more of their populations between 1970 and 1990. Newark lost almost 30%.[20] And while some of the region's downtowns were able to attract business investment, since 1975 these centers on the whole lost 30,000 private sector jobs as businesses were creating 1 million jobs elsewhere. Cities such as Newark, Trenton, New Haven, and Bridgeport were particularly hard hit.[21]

By 1980 the majority of the region's residents did not live in urban areas. By 1990 the decline of the

| Center | Population | Employment | Population | Employment | Population | Employment |
|---|---|---|---|---|---|---|
| New York City | 7,894,862 | 2,712,800 | 7,071,639 | 2,931,400 | 7,322,564 | 2,698,500 |
| Manhattan CBD | | 1,510,385 | | 1,671,600 | | 1,411,912 |
| Downtown Brooklyn | | 37,289 | | 23,282 | | 40,882 |
| Jamaica | | 16,488 | | 13,931 | | 17,616 |
| Long Island City | | 75,054 | | 68,791 | | 64,819 |
| Jersey City, NJ | 260,545 | 59,506 | 223,532 | 59,559 | 228,537 | 61,441 |
| New Haven, CT | 137,707 | 74,630 | 126,019 | 74,610 | 130,474 | 65,400 |
| Bridgeport, CT | 156,542 | 60,390 | 142,546 | 61,240 | 141,686 | 42,980 |
| Stamford, CT | 108,798 | 49,290 | 102,453 | 72,920 | 108,056 | 68,400 |
| White Plains, NY | 50,125 | 34,334 | 46,999 | 55,031 | 48,718 | 51,350 |
| Poughkeepsie, NY | 32,029 | 22,419 | 29,757 | 41,016 | 28,844 | 34,144 |
| Hicksville, NY | 48,075 | 17,351 | 43,245 | 25,398 | 40,174 | 20,711 |
| Mineola, NY | 21,845 | 12,338 | 20,757 | 13,654 | 18,994 | 14,346 |
| Trenton, NJ | 104,638 | 30,123 | 92,124 | 23,199 | 88,675 | 21,601 |
| New Brunswick, NJ | 41,885 | 24,641 | 41,442 | 22,256 | 41,711 | 23,357 |
| Newark, NJ | 382,417 | 145,659 | 329,248 | 123,651 | 275,221 | 110,766 |
| **Centers Total** | **9,239,468** | **3,243,481** | **8,269,761** | **3,503,934** | **8,473,654** | **3,212,996** |
| **31-County Region** | **19,747,964** | **6,214,900** | **19,190,960** | **7,568,800** | **19,843,157** | **7,292,100** |

*Notes:*
New York and New Jersey employment data is for 1975, 1985, and 1993.
Connecticut employment data is for 1975, 1985, and 1994.
The 31-County Region data is for 1975, 1985, and 1993.

*Figure 37: Populations and Private Employment in the Region's Centers.*
Sources: State Departments of Labor.

cities combined with suburban growth in formerly rural towns and villages meant that a plurality of the population lived in suburban counties. In 1960 urban counties had a 53% share of the region's population. By 1990 that figure was down to 43%. In contrast, the suburbs' share of the population went from 36% to 44%.[22]

There are many complex reasons for this dramatic shift. Some are related to our tax structure and where we have chosen to invest public infrastructure dollars. Historically, this has meant building a highway system that enabled people to live in distant suburbs. Other reasons have to do with cultural biases and persistent issues of segregation by race, class, and ethnic background. Still another explanation relates to personal cost–benefit analyses conducted by each household in the region, as individuals and families weight factors such as housing, schools, environmental quality, and job availability in deciding whether and where to move.

As compared to the region's suburbanites, urban residents are twice as likely to think that the lack of open space, the quality of their schools, or the level of crime are big problems in their communities. On the other hand, there is little distinction between urban and suburban residents' views on employment opportunities, traffic congestion, racial tension, or lack of community.[23]

## Environmental Trends and Issues

There are a number of important fiscal and social costs associated with scattering people and jobs over the landscape. Rural communities transformed almost overnight into suburban centers lack schools, transportation, and other public service infrastructure, while tax-starved urban areas fall into final crisis and decay. Unrelieved automobile congestion adds costly delays to the movement of goods and people. Mounting residential property taxes burden rural and suburban communities, as residential development is separated from commercial ratables. There are environmental costs as well, and it is difficult to separate the causes of sprawl from these effects.

### Parks and Open Space

The immediate and most visible effect of continued suburban sprawl is the conversion of forests, farms, and wetlands to urban uses and the paving of wildlife habitat, recreational and scenic resources, and productive agricultural lands. For example, the region lost 42% of its agricultural land between 1964 and 1992.[24]

Harder to see is the breakdown of the biological and physical processes within this green infrastructure. Green open space keeps us healthier by trapping and breaking down pollutants in the air and water. It moderates air temperature so that we use less energy to stay cool in summer and warm in winter. And it buffers our homes and businesses from flooding. These services are provided at a fraction of the cost needed for the hard engineering solutions, such as storm sewers that are built when natural systems have been mismanaged, disrupted, or paved over.

The condition of New York City's drinking water supply is perhaps the clearest example. The quality of water in the complex of upstate reservoirs and aqueducts that provide drinking water for New York City and Westchester County is threatened as homes, businesses, and other urban facilities have been built in the hills, wetlands, and stream valleys that drain into the reservoirs. Recent development in the Croton Basin in Westchester and Putnam counties, which supplies 10% of the overall 1.4 billion gallon supply, has degraded water quality to the degree that, for the first time, water drawn from these reservoirs will have to be filtered before it is safe to drink. The threat of future development in the Catskill and Delaware basins west of the Hudson, coupled with federal surface water treatment rules, may require New York City to spend an estimated $6 billion on what would be the world's

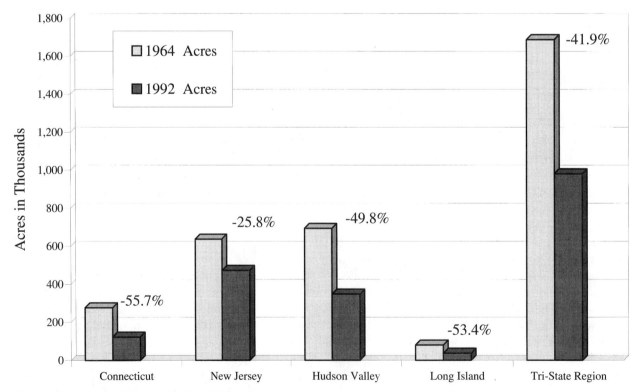

**Figure 38:** *Farmland Loss, 1964 to 1992.*
Source: USDA Census of Agriculture.

largest filtration plant to treat the remaining 90% of the water.

Driven by these public health concerns and by the oversight of federal regulators at the Environmental Protection Agency, in 1990 the New York City Department of Environmental Protection launched a watershed protection program designed to find alternatives to expensive filtration requirements. Rather than filtration of water once it reaches New York City reservoirs, the program's goal is to create a "multiple barrier" approach that seeks to minimize the introduction of pathogens and pollutants in the water by protecting hydrologically sensitive lands and by creating green buffers around streams and reservoirs.

In response to this initiative, communities in the watershed created the Coalition of Watershed Towns, a group that opposed further land acquisition and the city's proposed regulations, setting the stage for nearly five years of contentious debate over the issue. In 1995 Governor George Pataki initiated a series of negotiations between New York City, the coalition, and the U.S. Environmental Protection Agency. The agreement reached by these groups balances water quality and local economic goals and creates a new commitment by the city to finance pollution control and economic development activities in the watershed area.

In the short term, the success of this program will be based primarily on New York City's ability to acquire hydrologically sensitive lands and the towns' acceptance of a comprehensive set of watershed rules and regulations. Such rules will control, for example, how close homes and businesses are to watercourses and whether vegetation clearing, chemical use or storage, and paved surfaces are allowed near them. The agreement represents a new understanding between 234,000 people living in the 2,000-square-mile watershed and more than 9 million downstate water drinkers. To succeed in the long run, the partnership must recognize that the city cannot forsake the stewardship of its water supply, that watershed residents and businesses have a right to pursue their lives with a minimum of intrusive oversight, and that both parties will benefit from clean water and good conservation practices.

While additional New York City–directed regulations and land acquisition programs will be needed to safeguard the water supply of half of the state's citizens, the fate of the 2,000-square-mile watershed will also depend on the governing boards

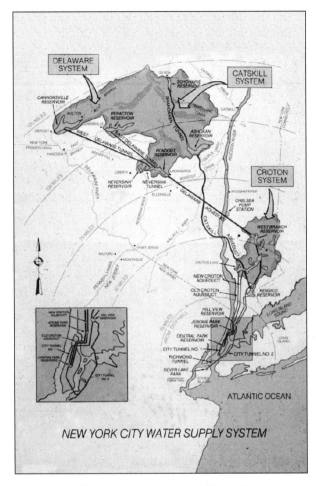

*Figure 39: The New York City Drinking Water Supply System.*

of the 79 towns and villages and thousands of private landowners in the watershed area. It is important to recognize that far more is at stake than an unending supply of pure drinking water. The mountains, wetlands, and stream valleys of the Croton, Catskill, and Delaware basins are also special places that help make the region an attractive place in which to live and work. They offer world-class recreational opportunities, spectacular scenery, and cultural traditions and experiences to visitors and residents. They are the only homes for threatened and endangered species of plants and animals found nowhere else in the world. Furthermore, tourism, which depends on the maintenance of a healthy and attractive environment, is a vital element of the economy in both the watershed area and the downstate metropolitan area.

The issues and debate over the future of the New York City water supply system are not unique.

They are mirrored by similar situations in the Appalachian Highland watersheds that supply surface water for more than 3 million New Jersey residents[25] and the vast groundwater aquifers that underlie the Long Island Pine Barrens.[26]

While we are losing the race for open space at the edge of the region, urban public spaces suffer as chronic budget problems have so starved city park budgets that many urban parks do not have the maintenance they need and have little hope for capital improvements or expanded recreational programming. While all the cities in the region suffer from this problem, the situation is most acute in New York City. Over the past 20 years, New York City park spending has dropped by more than one-third. As a result, the city now ranks next to last among 19 major U.S. cities in the amount of money it spends per person on park operations.[27] This disinvestment is felt in many ways. The number of street trees is declining at a rate of 2,000 a year.[28] And only 35% of the city's parks are deemed to be in acceptable condition.[29] As a result, city residents flee to the countryside seeking environmental quality, fueling the demand for new homes and businesses.

### Derelict Urban Land

More than parks and playgrounds are being neglected. The lack of reinvestment and redevelopment in urban centers has left behind tens of thousands of acres of empty urban land.[30] These former industrial areas, brownfields as opposed to greenfields, are frequently located in close proximity to major transportation lanes and centers of commercial and industrial activity. Many are even owned by the government, including *in rem* properties seized for back taxes, former solid waste facilities, military bases, and ports and terminals. Of particular note are those tracts located on the region's urban waterfronts, where cleaner water could offer potential developers and the public remarkable views and recreational opportunities.

As a result of their former use, some of these sites have been contaminated to some degree by toxic chemicals. There are more than 100,000 leaking underground fuel tanks, spill sites, or former industrial sites included in the government's register of known or potential toxic sites in the region.[31] In certain cases, these sites may pose a threat to peo-

**Figure 40:** *Derelict tracts of land exist throughout the region. RPA's Union County Land Recycling Project is helping transform this site in Elizabeth, New Jersey, into an urban retail center.*

ple who live nearby. But many of these sites have limited, if any, contamination problems. These sites are simply eyesores that undercut the viability of urban communities, limiting their quality of life and property values.

But regardless of the actual degree of cleanup required, the prospect of liability plagues any developer bold enough to take an interest in a brownfield site.[32] In order for such sites to be reused, new owners must clean them to meet public health standards set by state and federal governments. The people who actually created the contamination in the first place are often no longer around to correct the situation, and additional uncertainty may loom over the known costs: health standards may change as medical and technical science advance. And since many of the sites have been only cursorily examined, there is always the possibility that further contamination will turn up once remediation is underway. Such worst case scenarios are driving potential developers away, adding further momentum to the forces of sprawl.

### Cars and Pollution

The deconcentration of homes and jobs has meant that people are driving more than ever. The number of vehicle miles traveled in the region grew by 60% from 1970 to 1990. And while this is partly due to the convenience, comfort, and utility that cars offer, the impetus toward an automobile-centered economy and life-style has also been driven by changes in land use.

By trading in our cities for suburban subdivisions and office parks, the region's residents have far fewer choices when it comes to how they get to work, school, or leisure time pursuits. The automobile becomes the preferred and in many cases the only way for people to get around.

Increased use of automobiles and trucks is the key reason why the Tri-State Metropolitan Region is second only to Los Angeles in the number of days each year that our air fails to meet federal health standards. New standards for the discharges of air pollutants, technological advances like catalytic converters, and aggressive measures to inspect and maintain our auto fleet have improved air quality in the region, but these benefits have been considerably offset by the increase in vehicle miles traveled. Each tailpipe may be cleaner, but every day there are more vehicles driving longer distances.

The region is, to use the official federal language, a "severe" nonattainment area for ozone and a "moderate" nonattainment area for carbon monoxide.[33] Manhattan fails to meet federal health standards for fine particulate matter, or soot.[34] Cars, trucks, and buses account for approximately 90% of the carbon monoxide and 50% of the region's ozone pollution. They are also significant contributors to soot and atmospheric carbon dioxide levels.[35]

This poor air quality is a serious threat to health. The young, the old, people who suffer from allergies and severe respiratory ailments, and those who exercise outdoors are most severely at risk.[36] Asthma has been increasing in incidence and is now the leading cause of days lost from school among children.[37]

Recognizing this, the Clean Air Act Amendments of 1991 require a two-pronged attack on mobile source emissions. One approach requires the introduction of cleaner vehicles over the next decade. Early steps involve cleaner-running gasoline and even more intensive motor vehicle inspections.[38] The second approach requires a change in travel behavior. It includes a far-reaching and much-disliked requirement that employers with 100 or more workers who reach their jobs between 6:00 A.M. and 10:00 A.M. must promote carpooling vigorously enough so that the ratio of employees-to-automobiles increases by 25% over the existing average in

**Figure 41:** *Even though tailpipes have been getting cleaner, more cars driving longer distances clog the region's roads and contribute greatly to air pollution.*

their area. Known as the Employee Trip Reduction Programs, or ETRP, employers must submit plans in each state where air quality is poor, which includes all parts of New York, New Jersey, and Connecticut in the Tri-State Metropolitan Region. ETRP goals will be exceedingly difficult to achieve. Urban areas that already have high public transit ridership have to boost transit use substantially. For example, people working in Queens will have to increase their transit use by 44%. In typical suburban locations where public transit is altogether unavailable, ridesharing in cars will need to increase threefold. Most measures to increase ridesharing are likely to fall far short of the mark. Evidence suggests that in the short term, only strong pricing measures, and in the long term, only land use measures that change the locations of where we live and work, will reduce single-occupant driving enough to meet such stringent goals.

### Managing Waste Materials

The region spends a great deal of money on infrastructure, natural resource management, and pollution control. In 1994 over $4.6 billion in state, federal, and local funds were allocated for water pollution control projects in the coastal waters of the region.[39] That same year, $2.8 billion was spent disposing of our garbage.[40]

And we will be spending even higher amounts in the future. Meeting the water quality goals outlined in the recently completed Long Island Sound

Study, for instance, will require over $17 billion in capital costs alone over the next 20 years.[41] The region will spend almost $9 billion to build the transfer stations, landfills, and recycling facilities to manage its solid waste over the same time period.[42]

Given the increased complexity of need and the scarcity of funds, public and private officials throughout the region are developing new ways of protecting the environment: increasing production efficiencies so as to produce less waste in the first place; recycling what waste we do produce, both to control environmental costs as well as to create downstream economic benefit streams; using biological systems rather than hard engineering solutions for natural resource management and pollution control to both save costs and to broaden the environmental benefits; and thinking comprehensively about solutions, so that the limited capital dollars that are spent perform as many tasks as possible.

Two sets of issues, solid waste and sewage treatment plant capacity, show how this new thinking can be implemented.

### Solid Waste

The region produces 20 million tons of solid waste a year.[43] Approximately 50% of that waste will be disposed of in landfills within the region. The remainder is managed through recycling programs, incineration, or export to disposal facilities outside of the region.

As long as sufficient landfill space was available far enough away from residents, localities found this approach to solid waste acceptable—both politically and financially. Today, however, a combination of factors has created a solid waste management crisis. All of the region's existing and planned landfills are scheduled to reach capacity by the year 2000; rates of per capita waste generation continue to rise; and the political problems of exporting garbage are becoming so intractable that this option may soon be legislatively closed. Unless other actions are taken, within only a few years the region will be unable to find space for approximately two-thirds of the waste it currently generates.

The capacity crisis is becoming all too familiar to state and local officials. A new wave of planning has brought new and more sophisticated approaches to waste management. What leaves the house is no longer just "garbage." Instead, it is an amalgam of "nutrients" for the next generation of production processes. Guided by a state-mandated hierarchy, today's solid waste managers separate the total solid waste stream into its individual components—glass, paper, plastic, metal, and so forth—and then select the most appropriate management option for each. Different materials are targeted for reduction, recycling, composting, energy production, or burial.

Shifting from garbage collection and disposal to integrated materials management—while keeping up with increased needs—will require a substantial retooling of our solid waste management system. In the next 25 years:

- The region's public and private sectors will have to invest more than $9 billion in capital projects to build recycling, composting, incineration, and landfill facilities.

- Producers and consumers will have to learn how to reduce the overall volume of materials that actually enters this reconfigured waste management system.

- Industry will have to expand its use of recycled material, replacing fiber from trees with fiber from old newspapers and office paper, and substituting steel found in scrap metal and empty steel cans for virgin steel produced from coal and iron ore.

These substantial commitments come at a time when government and business face a number of other environmental and economic pressures.

The most important step toward containing waste management costs is to reduce the amount of waste generated. If projected increases in waste generation rates are not reversed in the next ten years, the region will have to spend an extra $267 million a year in collection and management costs.[44] The current trend in waste generation does not bode well for the region. If the trend continues, the amount of waste produced here is expected to increase 29% over the next 25 years. This anticipated growth is based on projected increases in population and employment and the rate of waste generation per person and per job. Much of the expected growth is attributed to industry forecasts of increases in the production and disposal of materials per employee.

All three states in the region realize the critical importance of waste prevention and have set aggressive goals. Connecticut and New Jersey are seeking "no net increase" of waste production, a

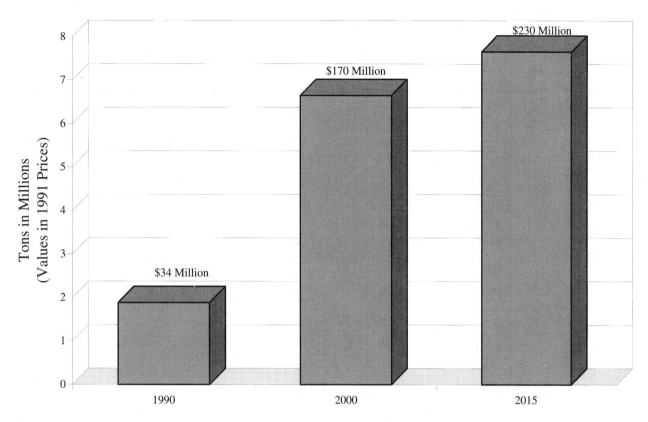

**Figure 42:** *Projected Growth in Recycled Materials in the Tri-State Metropolitan Region, 1990 to 2015.*

Source: Regional Plan Association/Tellus Institute.

standard which translates to a 26% waste prevention target for New Jersey and a 22% target for Connecticut. New York State is calling for a 10% reduction. Region-wide these goals reflect a 2 million ton per year decrease in the production of waste by the year 2000. By 2015 this total would rise to a 3.7 million ton decrease. From 2000 to 2015, success in waste reduction would be worth $4.2 billion in avoided solid waste management costs.[45]

Producing less waste has many environmental benefits as well. It will improve the region's air and water and lower the costs of maintaining environmental quality. Moreover, tremendous political and social benefits would be derived by avoiding future struggles to site unneeded (and locally unwanted) processing facilities, incinerators, and landfills. Under current plans, three more incinerators would have to be built and 15 more acres of landfill set aside for goals to be met.

The three states in the region have also set goals for recycling. Recycling over 40% of the region's waste stream is a fiscally responsible, cost-effective, and environmentally beneficial strategy for managing solid waste. The long-term cost of creating large-scale recycling and composting programs in the region—capable of achieving the 25% to 60% rates called for by the three state legislatures—is no higher than that of our current system or of alternative systems based on export or incineration. The cost increases associated with restructuring the collection system to facilitate material separation is matched dollar-for-dollar by the savings created by replacing more expensive landfills and incinerators with recycling and composting facilities.[46]

The solid waste management costs of conventional alternatives are roughly equal, but the environmental costs of a recycling-based system are much lower. It is important to understand that this environmental benefit is derived primarily from substituting recycled materials for virgin resources in production facilities. Not burning or burying our waste is only the first step. The subsequent substitution of those collected materials for virgin resources is where the environmental benefits will be largely realized.

In order for these recovered materials to actually be recycled, however, manufacturers will have to expand significantly their capacities to absorb non-virgin feedstocks. The volume of materials recovered through recycling programs is expected to increase 430% by 2015. But there are important benefits as well. Expanding secondary manufacturing capacity would produce economic benefits to the region on the order of an estimated $230 million per year in revenue from the sale of the material, with the potential expansion of local manufacturing contributing another $100 million per year in sales, taxes, and wages.

### Sewage Treatment

In the late 1980s increasing per capita demand for drinking water prompted New York City to plan on regularly using its Chelsea Pump Station on the Hudson River. This proposal produced a bitter controversy among the city, Hudson River advocates, and state officials.

At the same time, the Newtown Creek treatment plant, New York City's largest, was receiving waste flows of 30 million gallons a day over capacity. As a result, New York State threatened to impose a moratorium on sewer hookups for buildings, a situation that would have shut down construction in Lower Manhattan and Downtown Brooklyn. This created concern among people involved in real estate who were pressing for additional treatment capacity. It raised alarms in Brooklyn's Williamsburg community that hosts the Newton Creek facility, where citizens were bitterly opposed to expanding the existing plant. And it caused panic among city officials who did not want to try to find a site for a new treatment plant elsewhere.

The city's solution to both issues was to look at the water system as an integrated whole. From that perspective, it became clear that traditional policies would mean billions of dollars in facility construction after years of controversy, lawsuits, and uncertainty. The better solution was to promote water conservation as an alternative to both capital projects.

By investing $750 million in a water conservation program that included leak detection, meters, low flow plumbing fixtures, and public education, the city was able to save $3 billion and reap enormous environmental benefits. In 1992 New York City formally abandoned any plans to utilize the Hudson River for water supply and ameliorated capacity problems not just at Newtown Creek but at six other sewage treatment plants as well.

### Business Practices

Companies worldwide and in the region are also changing their approach to environmental management. Businesses are creating innovative ways to recycle and to change or redesign materials so they can be recycled. Pollution prevention and waste reduction are replacing the earlier emphasis on cleanup. Businesses are producing and promoting goods and services that require fewer resources to produce and have less environmental impact. Environmental accounting methods are being integrated into company practices, from day-to-day site management to capital investment decisions—with professional accounting organizations teaching, and selling, environmental accounting services. Some banking and insurance groups are seeking out environmental enterprises and requiring, and sometimes assisting, prospective borrowers to develop environmental plans as a condition of their loans. And the concepts of source reduction, product life cycle, and balanced materials flow are increasingly recognized as business goals, embodying the acceptance that we all operate in an ecosystem where resource use must balance with resource regeneration.

Some businesspeople are picking up these challenges with alacrity and imagination; others are moving ahead more slowly. The International Chamber of Commerce acknowledged the direction business must take in opening its 1992 report: "We are all in the process of learning that the environment is not a free good or externality but . . . an indispensable asset . . . that needs to be invested in, maintained and developed like any other asset." But no one thinks it is easy. "The task of switching from consuming environmental assets to treating them as an investment on whose income everyone depends is daunting," continued the ICC report.[47]

Business leaders acknowledge that these changes would not have been undertaken without environmental mandates and public pressure. They urge that a combination of regulation and goal-based incentives be used to achieve the intended integration of economic and environmental policy.[48] EPA and state environmental agencies acknowledge the need to move beyond their early emphasis on waste cleanup to both mandatory and incentive programs that support pollution prevention, energy efficiency, source reduction, and other practices that provide a greater return to both the environment and the investor.[49]

Some brief examples of businesses in the region that are implementing environmental strategies include:

• *Revising Production Processes.* The owner of a 24-year-old New York City–based firm that prints company business forms has gone to great lengths to reduce the operation's impact on health and safety in the workplace. They have installed a closed-loop system for rinsing pre-processed film and they recycle all film scraps, making money from the silver recovered. A current issue is ink: solvent-based tinting solutions are unhealthy for workers and ultimately damaging to the ozone layer; but traditional water-based solutions take too long to dry and shrink the paper. By experimenting with different formulas for the inks and applications and drying techniques, the company is now able to use only water-based inks and, as an unexpected benefit, has found them to be less expensive.

• *Tracking Packaging and Purchasing.* For Home Box Office (HBO), making internal operations environmentally sound is a continuous quest. Are their packaging materials nontoxic, made from recycled materials, recyclable? Can the waste handlers hired by HBO find a market for the materials they take away, and if not, can HBO alter their waste or help find a suitable market? Can HBO leverage its annual $2 million purchasing budget to assure that the companies from which they buy are using environmentally sound processes? Does HBO's building use paint, fabric, and building materials that are durable, repairable, and recyclable? Can office machines, furniture, and supplies no longer in use have an afterlife with nonprofit organizations? Answering one question leads to another, to improve both company performance and the wider environment.

• *Pursuing Product Life Cycle.* "Every product we make and every service we perform has the potential to . . . impact the environment," states Bristol-Myers Squibb's Chair and CEO. Every division and every employee is responsible for what goes into and what comes out of every pharmaceutical, personal, and medical prod-

uct the company makes and sells. The company's "Pollution Prevention Throughout the Product Life Cycle" manual provides directives to every division[50]:

• Materials used in making products are designed to be re-utilized or recycled.

• Preventing pollution is both an aim and a condition for all R & D activity.

• Packaging, which in this country accounts for one-third of the waste stream, takes as its in-order priority scale: (a) none; (b) minimum; (c) returnable, reusable, or refillable; (d) recyclable.

• The Purchasing Department sets as a criterion for suppliers whether their products use fewer and renewable resources, contain recycled content or are recyclable, and are energy efficient.

What does Bristol-Myers Squibb think it gains from this "cradle to grave" approach? "Thousands of pounds of pollution prevented and millions of dollars saved." These practices also build market share, create competitive advantage, reduce liability, enhance the corporate image, and enable the company, in the words of the Brundtland Commission, to better meet its present needs without compromising the ability of future generations to meet theirs.

These examples suggest what can be done when business takes a lead. How to produce more with less resources and less waste is becoming a practice in both the public and private domains. Yet neither business nor public organizations have yet elevated it to "business as usual." Businesses asking the government to lighten its cleanup regulations say they want a "floor" of government standards and goals with freedom to work out their own processes for pollution prevention and other practices. Yet the business community's request for regulatory reform will attain greater credibility only as more companies take initiative to advance their own environmental practices.

## Integrating Economic and Environmental Accounts

The shift from "regulate the process" to "set the standard for the outcome" is slowly being reflected in public policy. Collaborative pilot projects, incentive (but not subsidy) programs, and transmission of information through communication networks are approaches both public agencies and private groups have begun to implement. But too often current public policies intended to encourage growth in fact support and even subsidize resource-consumptive, waste-producing investments with low employment—the opposite of what the public should be asked to support.

Both public and private decision-makers still fail to count environmental costs and benefits in management and investment decisions. There are both public and private costs when pollution dirties the air; there are both public and private benefits when waste is prevented from fouling a water supply. Such full-cost accounting is rarely applied by business or government—and hence prices, costs, and benefits are skewed.

There is need to further develop methods for the full-cost accounting of environmental costs and benefits—factors now often treated as imponderable externalities in traditional economics and accounting. Recent initiatives to develop and apply integrated economic and environmental corporate accounting methods, a first step toward full cost accounting, include the EPA's Corporate Environmental Accounting and Capital Budget Project, with an academic/business contacts group of nearly 700 associates; publications and programs of the Institute of Management Accountants; and the 28 corporations that lead the Global Environmental Management Initiative (GEMI), which has recently published a Cost Effective Pollution Primer.[51]

The methods for integrating economic and environmental accounts are in use as supplementary or "satellite" accounts in several European and other countries. They can be used to show "Green GDP," an environmentally adjusted domestic product that reflects the use of natural and environmental resources in the production of goods and services and that accounts for the depletion and degradation of natural resources. RPA, which pioneered the development of regional income and product accounts, is urging the further development and application of environmentally adjusted accounting for state and city bodies in the region.[52]

The use of "green fees" as a way to restructure fiscal systems so as to raise the tax burden on activities damaging to productivity (such as congestion, resource waste, and pollution) and lower the tax burden on essential activities (i.e., employment, investment) has been little explored to date and merits serious investigation. At the regional level, green fee policies could translate into competitive advan-

tages in the costs of doing business and the quality of life.[53]

## Toward a Sustainable Region: Protecting Our Natural Infrastructure

RPA recognizes that there are many ways of thinking and of doing business that we now take for granted—from the way we make things to where we build houses to how much trash each household throws away every night—that will have to change before this region can operate on a sustainable basis. Meeting current needs without depriving current or future generations of a quality environment is a long-term process.

Taken as a whole, RPA's five initiatives launch a program for beginning the process of building a sustainable region by conserving open space, redirecting growth, and improving the management of our natural resources.

Of key concern to RPA is the need to bend the trends of the past 30 years and locate the next generation of growth in urban and suburban centers. The region also needs to ensure that key natural resource systems, especially water supply landscapes and estuaries, are protected. *Greensward* creates a region-wide open space system that helps shape growth and protect environmental infrastructure through conservation of 11 designated reserves and by investing in urban open space and greenways. *Centers* describes how the region can make urban areas more viable, through brownfield restoration and transit friendly development, to ease development pressures on our critical open spaces. *Mobility* describes strategic investments to improve a transit system oriented around these centers, and *Workforce* ensures that residents of those centers have employable skills, making them more viable alternatives for investment and growth. *Governance* shows how state growth management policies that direct development to the right places and revise an antiquated property tax system can encourage local communities to develop in an appropriate manner.

## Notes

1. United Nations, *Agenda 21: The United Nations Programme of Action from Rio*, United Nations Publication # E.93.1.11, June 1992.

2. Based on the number of days exceeding federal standards for an eight-hour running average, Department of City Planning, *Annual Report on Social Indicators,* 1994, Figure 8-1.

3. In 1993 estimated compliance with New York State total and fecal coliform standards was the best ever recorded by the New York Harbor Water Quality Survey. Measures of dissolved oxygen, nitrogen, and phosphorous also show improvements, although many sites continue to violate standards. Thomas Brosnan and Marie L. O'Shea, *New York Harbor Water Quality Survey: 1993 Executive Summary,* New York City Department of Environmental Protection.

4. Regional Plan Association, *Where the Pavement Ends, The Open Space Imperative #2,* 1987, p. 5.

5. New York, New Jersey, and Connecticut environmental policies rank 6th, 2nd, and 5th, respectively, in the nation according to the *1991–1992 Green Index,* August 1991, Island Press, Washington, D.C.

6. The EPA considers only Ulster and Sullivan counties and the northern part of Orange County as attainment zones for ozone. Putnam, Dutchess, and Warren counties are "marginal" nonattainment areas. Litchfield and New Haven counties are "serious" nonattainment zones. The remaining 23 1/2 counties are considered "severe."

7. New York City is now building a filtration plant for the Croton River reservoirs, which for the past 150 years have delivered safe drinking water using only chlorination and holding time as treatment.

8. Dr. William S. Brown, *Impact on the Timber Rattlesnake of Proposed Development Project of Sterling Forest,* report to Palisades Interstate Park Commission, June 25, 1995.

9. Vinikov et al., 1994, Trends 93, Oak Ridge National Laboratory in EDF Letter Vol. XXVI, No. 3. May 1995. see also *The Baked Apple: Metropolitan New York in the Greenhouse,* preprints of a conference sponsored by the American Society of Civil Engineers, Metropolitan Section et al., November 3, 1994.

10. New York State Department of Environmental Conservation, *Non-Point Source Assessment Report,* 1989.

11. Motor vehicles contribute nearly 50% of the region's ozone pollution and 90% of its carbon monoxide. U.S. EPA 1992 Transportation and Air Quality Planning Guidelines, EPA 420/R-92-001, July 1992, p. 4; Center for Resource Economics, Annual Review of the U.S. EPA, Island Press, May 1993, p. 92 (from TSTC report).

12. In RPA's 1995 *Quality of Life Poll,* having clean air and water was considered to be of primary importance to virtually all of the region's residents, ranking only behind safe streets in the list of issues polled. Greenery and open space ranked fourth. Perhaps more significantly, 56% of the region's residents said they would personally spend more money to preserve open space and parks and 66% would spend more money to ensure clean air and water. In contrast, only 24% of the residents in the region would be willing to spend money to eliminate traffic congestion.

13. Environmental Protection Agency, Region II Clean Water Act Title II and Title VI outlays.

14. The Wilderness Society et al., *Land and Water Conservation Fund: The Conservation Alternative for Fiscal Year 1994,* 1993;

and Environmental Advocates, *Shortchanged: New York State and the Land and Water Conservation Fund,* 1995.

15. Policy Planning and Evaluation, *Municipal Sector Study: Impacts of Environmental Regulations on New Jersey Municipalities* (Draft), prepared for the New Jersey Department of Environmental Protection, 1990.

16. Population estimates based on U.S. Census Population data for 1960 and 1990. Land use data from 1962 is "The Tri-State Region and Environs," Regional Plan Association, 1965, and "Urban Land Use in the Tri-State Metropolitan Region," Regional Plan Association and the Center for Remote Sensing and Spatial Analysis, Cook College, Rutgers University, 1995.

17. U.S. Department of Commerce.

18. Council on Environmental Quality, *Connecticut Environmental Review,* 1990, p. 14.

19. U.S. Census of Population.

20. Ibid.

21. New Jersey and Connecticut State Departments of Labor.

22. U.S. Census of Population.

23. Regional Plan Association, *The Quality of Life Poll,* 1995.

24. USDA Census of Agriculture.

25. See *Drinking Waters at Risk: A Strategy to Protect New Jersey's Drinking Water Watersheds,* Environmental Defense Fund and New Jersey Public Interest Research Group, 1994.

26. See Central Pine Barrens Joint Planning and Policy Commission, *Central Pine Barrens Comprehensive Land Use Plan Vol. 2: Existing Conditions,* January 13, 1994.

27. The Parks Council, *Public Space for Public Life,* pp.13–16.

28. Office of the Public Advocate, *The Services Scorecard: Quality of Life Indicators,* 1995.

29. City of New York, *Mayor's Management Report,* 1994.

30. Estimate based on extrapolating RPA's survey of brownfield sites: Linda P. Morgan et al., *Union County Model Site Redevelopment Project: Final Report,* Regional Plan Association/New Jersey, June 1994.

31. The U.S. EPA and NYS DEC have identified 80,000 sites in New York City, Long Island, and Westchester and Rockland counties alone.

32. See, for example, "Staff Report to the New York State Joint Legislative Commission on Toxic Substance and Hazardous Wastes," *The Voluntary Cleanup of New York's Contaminated Property: Barriers and Incentives,* October 1994.

33. See note 51.

34. PM-10 (particulate matter) levels in Manhattan have exceeded national air pollution standards for every measuring period since 1988 (from TSTC Report).

35. U.S. EPA 1992 Transportation and Air Quality Planning Guidelines, EPA 420/R-92-001, July 1992, p. 4; Center for Resource Economics, Annual Review of the U.S. EPA, Island Press, May 1993, p. 92.

36. RPA, The Health Affects of Ozone, Project Clean Air No. 3, April 1990.

37. William Taylor and Paul Newacheck, "Impact of Childhood Asthma on Health," *Pediatrics,* Nov. 1992, Vol. 90, No. 5 pp. 657–662 (from TSTC).

38. Many people are working on alternative fuels and car types (e.g., Inform and NRDC are looking at natural gas and hydrogen powered cars, and Amory Lovin has proposed a "super car" of composite plastics).

39. Interstate Sanitation Commission, *1994 Annual Report,* 1995.

40. Regional Plan Association, *Existing and Future Solid Waste Management Systems in the Regional Plan Association Region,* RPA Working Paper #16, 1992.

41. EPA, *The Long Island Sound Study,* July 1994, p. 19. EPA 842-S-94-001.

42. Regional Plan Association, *Existing and Future Solid Waste Management Systems in the Regional Plan Association Region,* RPA Working Paper #16, 1992.

43. All data in this section derived from Working Paper #16, *Existing and Future Solid Waste Management Systems in the Regional Plan Association Region;* Working Paper #17, *Environmental Impacts of Alternative Waste Management Options in the Regional Plan Association Region;* and The Region's Agenda, #1, *Putting a Price Tag on Solid Waste Management.*

44. Regional Plan Association, *Existing and Future Solid Waste Management Systems in the Regional Plan Association Region,* RPA Working Paper #16, 1992.

45. Ibid.

46. Ibid.

47. Jan-Olaf Willums and Ulrich Goluke, *From Ideas to Action: Business and Sustainable Development,* The ICC Report on the Greening of Enterprise, The International Environmental Bureau of the International Chamber of Commerce, 1992.

48. Richard Barth, Chair and CEO of CIBA Geigy; David Buzzelli, Vice President of Dow Chemical; and Stephan Schmidheiny, a leading Swiss industrialist and founder of the International Business Council for Sustainable Development each emphasized these points in presentations at Columbia University's Business School in 1995. Mr. Buzzelli also co-chairs the U.S. President's Council on Sustainable Development. Mr. Barth is a Council member and co-chairs its Natural Resources Task Force.

49. EPA and other agencies have set up voluntary collaborative pilot programs with businesses in the region to provide technical assistance and share information to enable participants to make environmental improvements and achieve cost savings. Among them are EPA's "Green Lights" (energy-efficient lighting), "Energy Star" (for computers), and "Waste Wise"; ITAC-the Industrial Technology Assistance Corporation, which works with New York City's small and medium-sized manufacturers; and a new program of the New Jersey Department of Environmental Protection whereby a standing group of knowledgeable business representatives and environmentalists work with the department to improve its regulatory and management efficiency.

50. *Environment 2000: Pollution Prevention Throughout the Product Life Cycle.* Bristol-Myers Squibb Company, 1992.

51. New publications in a growing literature include *Green Ledgers: Case Studies in Corporate Environmental Accounting,* published in 1995 by the World Resources Institute and EPA; and EPA's *An Introduction to Environmental Accounting as a Business Management Tool: Key Concepts and Terms.*

52. Regina B. Armstrong et al., *Regional Accounts: Structure and Performance of the New York Region's Economy in the 1970's.* Bloomington: Indiana University Press, 1980.

53. In *Green Fees: How a Tax Shift Can Work for the Environment and Economy,* Robert Repetto and others argue that such a corrective change could generate an annual savings of more than $50 billion nationally. (Washington: World Resources Institute, 1992.)

# *Part III*

# Five Major Campaigns

THE "THREE E'S" define the goals of the Third Regional Plan. Strategies for improving the region's quality of life must reinforce all three areas and demonstrate how the region's economy, equity, and environment are vitally linked to each other. Each campaign addresses aspects of each "E" and strengthens the synergy between them. While the "E's" represent RPA's goals, the campaigns are the means to achieve them.

- The Greensward makes economic sense, protecting the environmental infrastructure that would otherwise require costly cleanup facilities and pollution controls. It is good for our society, safeguarding access to recreation and natural landscapes for everyone. And it is good for the environment, providing a long-term and comprehensive plan to reconcile local land use and development with broader regional objectives.

- Centers provide a more efficient use of resources and reduce costs for the entire regional economy. Centers also reduce land consumption and conserve a greater portion of our remaining open space. And centers are more accessible to less-advantaged communities, so investing in and bringing new employment to centers brings new opportunities to the residents who need them most.

- Mobility would strengthen the region's economy by facilitating travel to employment centers, improving freight connections, and using the road system more efficiently to produce less congestion. It would improve our society, as less-advantaged communities would become better connected to employment and housing opportunities and downtowns would become more accessible. And regional mobility would improve our environment, allowing people and goods to travel more quickly with less pollution.

- Workforce development will support economic growth by supplying the trained workers and entrepreneurs necessary for new technology-based activities and increasing productivity. It addresses equity by closing the skill gap that creates larger disparities in income. And it improves our environment by focusing growth into urban centers rather than allowing it to sprawl across open spaces.

- Reforming governance will encourage local governments and current single-purpose agencies to plan their best resource use in relation to regional needs. Limited resources can thus spread further and be directed to filling multiple purposes, getting more "bang for the buck." Governance is critical to providing equity for the region's society, particularly public education. And governance is crucial to protecting our environment as we reform land use regulations that currently encourage sprawl and work to integrate environmental and economic accounts.

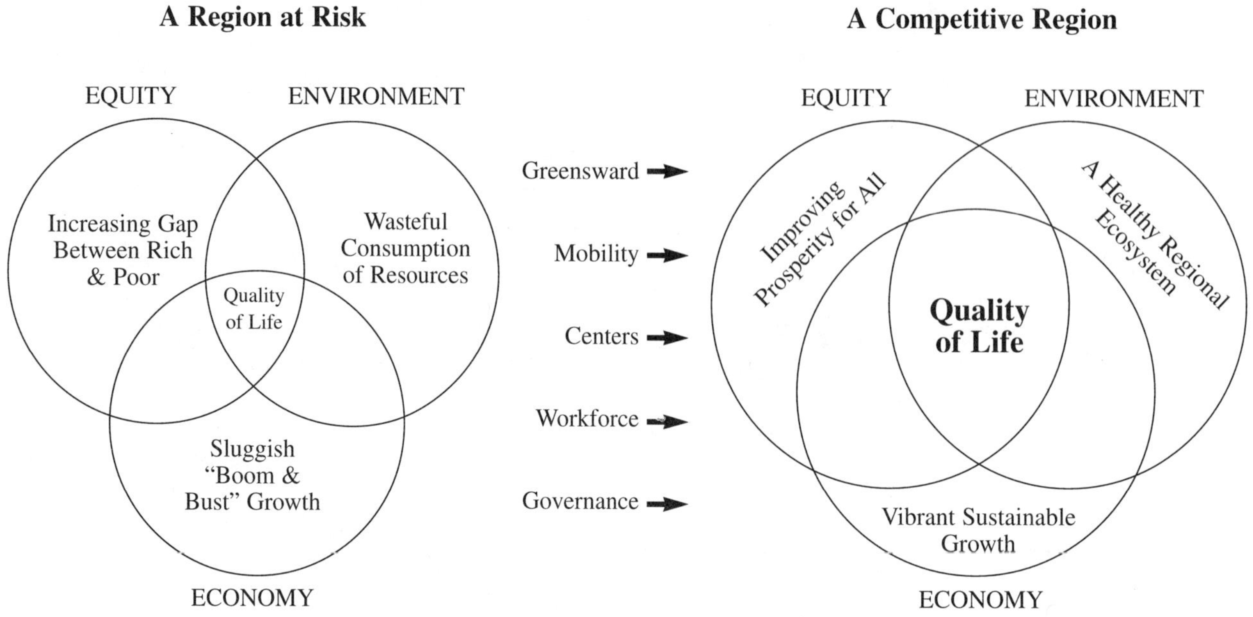

**A Region at Risk**

**A Competitive Region**

*Figure 43: The Three E's Transformed by the Five Campaigns.*

So RPA's campaigns all integrate the "Three E's" into policies and investments that can improve quality of life and lead to a better future for the entire region.

Old habits make it easier to look at the region's problems in a parochial, single-disciplinary, "vertical" way. The public agencies of this region (or of any region), such as departments of transportation, social services, economic development, or environmental protection, have been organized primarily to deal with one aspect of a problem. It is much like the old adage, "if you have a hammer, all your problems look like nails." This way of viewing the region's problems leads to solutions that are less effective than if both the problem and solution were approached in a broader manner. For example, the conventional "vertical" approach to solving water

pollution in Jamaica Bay in Queens is to build water treatment plants, at enormous political and economic cost. But seeing the problem in a holistic, systemic way led New York City to help the natural biological systems of the bay heal themselves, cleaning the water, acquiring key open space, and saving precious public funds while avoiding expensive treatment facilities.

RPA's proposals are grouped into five campaigns that each attack the region's problems with this new type of thinking. The alternative to this type of broad and decisive action is a continuing decline in our region's economy, social equity, environment, and quality of life. If we do not change our traditional ways of doing business, we will become a region that is neither competitive, fair, nor sustainable.

# Chapter 6

# The Greensward Campaign

THE METROPOLITAN GREENSWARD has been conceived of as a 21st century counterpart to Frederick Law Olmsted's visionary mid-19th century concept for Central Park, the green heart of New York City. Although New York grew explosively in the century that followed the construction of Central Park, it was this one extraordinary, pre-skyscraper, pre-highway public development project, since imitated around the world, that established New York as a great modern city and gave its citizens a sense that they lived in a place that had now become a permanent part of the world. Olmsted's design, which he himself called the Greensward, had, as we would now say, a "Three E" impact on New York: it dramatically increased the economic value of then-northern Manhattan; it rebalanced the city's society by creating what Olmsted called a "democratic space," in which all groups were treated as equals; and, in the face of early industrialism, it reestablished the green environment as the most important setting for human activities.

RPA's vision of a Metropolitan Greensward also seeks to shape a cherished place—the entire Tri-State Metropolitan Region. This regional open space system will re-anchor urban centers while at the same time protecting and restoring the natural systems and open spaces that serve as an environmental life support system for our cities, suburbs, and rural hamlets. By thinking of urban greenspaces, large-scale regional landscapes, and an emerging network of greenways between cities and landscapes as the leaves, roots, and trunk of a single green system, the Greensward addresses both aspects of one interlinked regional problem: suburban sprawl and urban disinvestment.

## Issues

RPA's 1929 and 1968 Regional Plans called for protection of dozens of stunning natural areas. RPA, along with the inspired advocacy of hundreds of groups, has helped protect close to 1 million acres of regional parkland. Many of the jewels of the region recognized in these plans—from the Delaware River Water Gap to Minnewaska to Fire Island—are now safeguarded for future generations to treasure and enjoy.

Despite this glorious success, the traditional focus of park creation did not always account for how the conservation of individual greenspaces relates to the region as a whole. The many functions

*Figure 44*: *Thanks to years of advocacy and regional investments, the region has close to one million acres of protected open space.*

provided by the region's open spaces and related ecological systems—from protecting water quality to cooling the air to enhancing property values—are rarely incorporated into land use planning and decision-making. Little thought has been given to setting up a metropolitan green belt, or how those great green spaces relate to the needs of the region's urban residents.

As a result, the potential of parks to shape the overall form and functioning of our built and natural environments has never been realized. Expanding our vision from individual parks to larger systems of open space is now required. Two generations of decentralized growth have dramatically expanded the urban portion of the Tri-State Metropolitan Region. In the last 30 years the amount of urban land has increased by more than 60% despite only a 13% increase in population. Continuing exurban development—at a rate of more than 30,000 acres a year—threatens large areas of open land and

environmental resources at the region's outer edge, more than 50 miles from Manhattan.[1] At the same time the outward flow of money resulting from this sprawl has helped contribute to the deterioration of the region's urban public spaces and natural resources.

What is at stake? A great deal:

- Accessible public space for the region's 7 million households and the swelling number of school-age children. There is growing demand for space for hiking, picnicking, swimming, and other outdoor recreation.[2] This is an important measure of our quality of life and, as the benefits of regular exercise and access to nature become more documented, is increasingly recognized as a public health concern.

- The viability of the metropolitan area's remaining large-scale ecosystems—many containing species found nowhere else in the world—and last vestiges of wilderness. These resources are threatened as habitat is fragmented into smaller and more isolated patches.

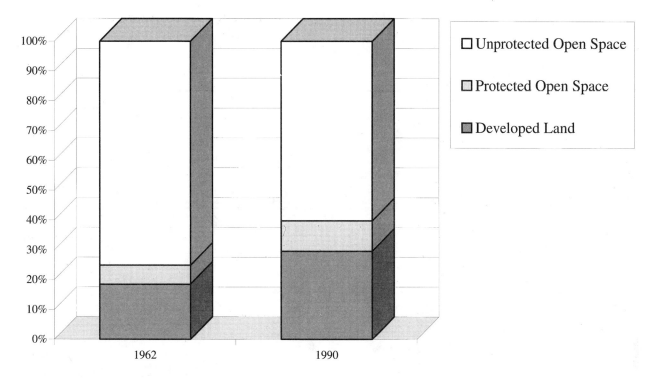

**Figure 45:** *Land Use in the Region, 1962 and 1990.*
Sources: RPA and U.S. Census.

- The quality of our region's unmatched water resources, as suburban development spreads across previously pristine watersheds. Of particularly vital concern are threats to the water supply landscapes of the Catskills, Appalachian Highlands, and Pine Barrens.

- The last local farming communities and agricultural landscapes. While still important to the economy in some counties, the amount of land in agricultural production has declined by 42% in the Tri-State Metropolitan Region between 1964 and 1992.[3]

- The financial and social health of rural communities straining to meet sudden new demands for services, urban areas starved for redevelopment and taxes, and everyone who must cope with mounting traffic congestion.

The new form of the region—sprawling suburbs ringing declining center cities—demands a new form of response. To propose strategies that seek only to run up the total number of public parks would miss the fundamental regional threats we face. Whole systems of land and the permanence and health of the region's cities are at risk 100 years after Olmsted. The goal of *Greensward* is to create a system of protected open spaces that will safeguard the region's environmental infrastructure while encouraging and celebrating resource-efficient patterns of growth.

### A Lesson from the Past

This is not the first time that the region has faced massive problems associated with urbanization and change. In the mid-19th century, New York and other emerging U.S. cities confronted a seemingly insurmountable set of challenges: rapid population growth threatened to outstrip water supplies; growing water pollution contributed to repeated and widespread epidemics; waves of immigration threatened to tear apart the social fabric; and revolutionary improvements in the technology of industry and transportation allowed for rapid decentralization of formerly compact, pedestrian-scale cities.

One of the concerned public citizens to whom this frightening array of challenges cried out was America's first landscape architect, the pioneer city planner and park designer, Frederick Law Olmsted. In 1858 Olmsted advanced his visionary Greensward plan for Central Park, a concept that was later

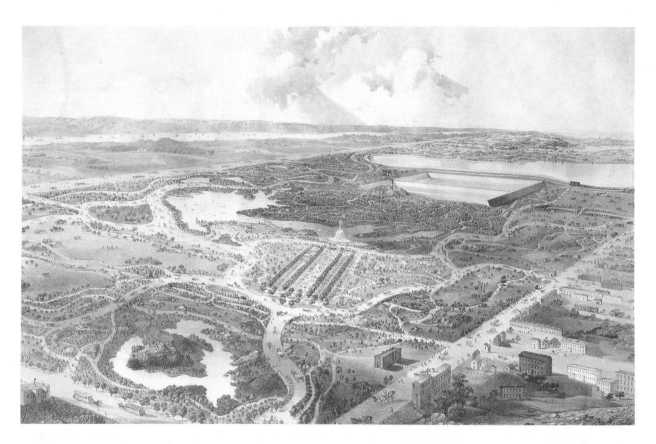

**Figure 46:** *Central Park provided form and function to a growing Manhattan Island.*

expanded to include parkways and networks of parks, and then adopted in Brooklyn, Newark, Elizabeth, Bridgeport, and dozens of other growing cities both within and beyond the region.

Olmsted correctly saw these new park systems as places that could heal most of the ills then facing urban America. Olmsted designed parks to serve as democratic spaces, institutions that would integrate waves of immigrants into the mainstream of metropolitan life. His parks provided the fresh air and light that had been banished from crowded city streets, a healthy oasis at the center of the dirt, disease, and congestion of 19th century urban life. Olmsted also made a place in his parks for the then-novel environmental infrastructure of cities, thus integrating water supply, sewer, and flood control systems into the recreational open space system. In addition, he deliberately made use of derelict, abused, and bypassed places within the city limits—the brownfields of his day—thereby giving them new value and helping set in place a framework for subsequent urban growth.

### A New Vision

Olmsted and his equally audacious successor, Robert Moses, were able to bring their great green visions into reality almost single-handedly, as it sometimes seemed. But even they required the support of public officials and community groups to realize their visions. Carrying their work forward today, in a larger, far more decentralized and even more diverse region, will take an effort that draws together communities scattered across thousands of square miles of land. This new vision must address itself to even more issues than Olmsted or Moses had to face: the need for reinvestment in our cities and mature suburbs; the need to devise land conservation and ecological management strategies that will protect and restore the region's air, water, and biological quality; the need for distinct, perceptible, stable, and dependable green boundaries to an increasingly outsized and unvarying built environment; and the need to maintain publicly important natural areas and working landscapes that are largely in the hands of private owners who serve, unpaid, as their guardians and stewards.

The Greensward Plan is a grand concept of what our open spaces collectively can and should be. It is a framework that reflects the ongoing work of hundreds of local and regional conservation organizations and agencies. And although it makes some recommendations for action, it does not contain the final prescriptions. These must be created by the actions of individuals, community groups, and local and state governments throughout the region.

Neither an Olmsted nor a Moses is here to lead us, but that is not what is needed in today's more complex and diverse region. If thousands of regional citizens can learn how to work together on region-scale greening, we can as a community accomplish projects that would have been beyond their dreams.

There are three components to the Greensward Plan:

1. The creation of 11 Regional Reserves to conserve the waterways and broad working landscapes that provide the region with fresh drinking water, harbor the area's most significant ecosystems, constitute our best recreational destinations, and delimit the outward expansion of the region's urbanized core.

   - In each of the reserve landscapes, conservation efforts should be coupled with efforts to reconcile local land use planning with the management of regionally significant natural resources. With local initiative, new plans and regulations could emerge through a state planning framework, through regional commissions, or through inter-community compacts.

   - Funds for planning, pollution prevention, and land acquisition could be provided by state-level initiatives that would target consumption of natural resources. These could include small surcharges on downstream drinking water consumers, a dedicated property tax surcharge or real estate transfer tax in reserve areas, a tax on extractive industries, or a tax on hotel/motel rooms or other tourism-related activities.

2. A full-scale reinvestment in urban parks, public spaces, and natural resources to improve the environmental quality of our cities, provide a fair share of parkland to urban residents, and help cities attract businesses and residents. Of special significance is this generation's opportunity to create dramatic new public spaces along the region's redeveloping urban waterfronts.

   - These goals should be pursued through a combination of citizen initiative, public action, and creative funding strategies. These strategies include targeted user fees, the creation of park improvement districts, community management strategies, an Olmsted Park restoration initiative, dedication of public waterfront property for public access, and smart infrastructure strategies that pay for the restoration of wetlands and urban forests as part of the region's water quality and air quality improvement programs.

3. The founding of a network of greenways to connect and nurture our cities, suburbs, and protected landscapes. These linked open space corridors will safeguard and restore trails, scenic roads, rivers, and wildlife habitat, bringing open space and recreational opportunities close to everyone's home.

   • Greenways could be created through a combination of local initiatives and public technical assistance grants and programs, such as that recently created in the state of Connecticut. These locally directed efforts should be guided by ongoing state-level coordinating councils and planning efforts.

Together, this framework of regional reserves, urban public spaces, and greenways will provide a "green blueprint" for the region, setting a form for further and more sustainable growth while guaranteeing the health of the region's environmental life support systems for generations to come. Regional Plan Association's goal is to have the Greensward substantially in place by the year 2008, some 150 years after completion of the landmark Central Park "Greensward" plan.

Achieving this vision will require new alliances between regional objectives and local concerns. It will require new tools to accommodate the concerns of private landowners. Creative models for doing this already exist right here in the region; many of these ongoing efforts are recognized in the pages that follow. They must now be expanded and adapted to fit each distinct community and landscape.

Of course, funding and political resolve will also be required to turn this collective vision into reality. But in an era where mistrust of government and government spending is widespread, Greensward offers both public officials and taxpayers a positive framework for the future.

## Summary of Recommendations

The time has come to strike a new balance with nature—and not just because healthy ecosystems, mighty rivers, and lofty mountains give us clean air and pure water. The region should develop, and redevelop, around its natural systems, instead of at their expense. Where we have not yet sprawled, we still have big natural systems of breathtaking majesty—3 million acres of pinelands, mountains, river valleys, seashores, and farms. People live in these landscapes, and always will, but for all of our sakes these areas must be allowed to grow in ways that respect and honor their innate integrity. RPA is proposing a system of 11 Regional Reserves as a no-sprawl zone that encompasses all of the major natural areas that are still intact.

But the Greensward is more than just the reserves. Striking a new balance with nature means renewing the open spaces in our cities to provide the environmental quality and recreational opportunities desired by current and prospective residents and businesses. While a generation ago we might have been satisfied to create new parks, now we must be in the business of restoring and improving the great urban ecosystems—our urban forests and estuaries—so that this green infrastructure can help provide us with clean air and water.

The Greensward is also a new kind of regional transportation system: an extensive network of greenways—hiking paths, bicycle routes, and natural corridors—that directly reconnects the cities to the big natural systems at the water's edge or just beyond the urban core. The following is a summary of the Greensward Campaign recommendations.

1. Establish 11 Regional Reserves
   • The Long Island Pine Barrens and Peconic Estuary
   • The New Jersey Pinelands
   • The Catskill Mountains
   • The Shawangunk and Kittatinny Mountains
   • The New York–New Jersey–Connecticut Appalachian Highlands
   • The Delaware River
   • The Hudson River
   • Long Island Sound
   • The New York–New Jersey Harbor
   • The Atlantic seashore
   • Active farmland throughout the region

2. Reinvest in urban parks, public spaces, and natural resources
   • Create new public spaces along the region's redeveloping urban waterfronts

- Create and restore parks in underserved urban neighborhoods
- Improve the quality of the region's urban forest resources
3. Create a regional network of greenways
   - Establish state-level coordination and support for local initiatives

## Eleven Regional Reserves

At the heart of the Greensward vision is the protection of 11 region-shaping landscapes and coastal waterways. Together, these areas provide the region's cities, suburbs, and rural towns with fresh drinking water and local produce. They offer recreation and spectacular scenery—a chance to enjoy the outdoors—to visitors and residents, from children to the elderly. They safeguard threatened and endangered species of plants and animals found nowhere else in the world. Tourism, which relies on a healthy and attractive environment, is a vital and growing element of each reserve area's economy.

And together, these 11 reserves encompass the largest estuarine systems, the longest rivers, the most extensive pine barrens, and the highest mountain chains in the region. They incorporate the major water supply watersheds, aquifers, and surface water resources of the region. They are clearly marked by still-intact natural boundaries that, in several cases, look from the air almost like a knife-edge between wilderness and intense urbanization. They are regional in scale, ranging in size from at least 100,000 acres to as large as 3 million acres. All of them have also been recognized in a number of official planning documents, past and current, including "Conserving Open Space in New York State," the New Jersey "State Development and Redevelopment Plan," and Connecticut's "Plan for Conservation and Development."

The 11 reserves are the truly special places, the quintessential landscapes that have helped attract residents and investments in the past and can make the region a desirable place to live and work far into the future.

Historically, these reserve landscapes have always played a critical role in shaping the region's urban form. If conservation of these areas moves forward hand in hand with two other Third Regional Plan initiatives, *Rx* and *Centers*, and in conjunction with state planning and local policies to encourage development in existing city and town centers, the reserves can be a principal instrument for containing urban sprawl and adopting more compact, energy-efficient, and less land-consuming patterns of growth.

Each of these landscapes has been an important locus for past conservation efforts. Indeed, they now collectively contain the majority of the region's existing public lands. But maintaining the environmental quality of both the private and the public lands in the reserve landscapes is an increasingly difficult challenge. The number of people living and working in these areas has increased dramatically over the past several decades. Suffolk County, for instance, encompassing the Long Island Pine Barrens and Peconic Estuary, doubled its population between 1960 and 1990. Towns in the Appalachian Highlands of Connecticut, New York, and New Jersey grew by 85% during the same period. Even once-remote rural towns in the Catskill Mountains drew in 40% more residents. These rates of growth far exceeded the overall regional increase of 13% in the same 30-year period.[4]

Too often, meeting the residential and commercial needs of these new reserve area residents has resulted in over-eager and insensitive development in the wrong places: filling in the wetlands, fragmenting the forests, cutting steep slopes, and obscuring the scenic views that define these places and provide important ecological functions. To maintain the integrity of these regional open space treasures we need to make conservation investments in each one of the reserve areas, acquiring land where appropriate and, more importantly, ensuring that the long-term environmental quality of the region is not dismembered parcel by parcel.

This is not an easy challenge. Time is running short if we hope to protect these landscapes. Development has already begun to fragment intact landscapes and ecological systems into open spaces too small to provide recreational value or to support species—such as warblers or other songbirds—that are dependent on interior forest habitat. In the New York–New Jersey Highlands researchers found that only 1% of the land area consists of forest patches larger than 5,000 acres. Only 5% consists of patches larger than 500 acres. Seventy-one percent of the land area on the Highlands—one of the most undeveloped areas in the region—was in forest patches of less than 50 acres.[5] Smaller tracts of land also mean addressing the needs of more landowners who must be part of any conservation solution. In the Central Long Island Pine Barrens a regional commission is working to conserve a 100,000-acre area with 36,000 separate parcels.[6]

Moreover, the towns and villages within the reserve areas are the homes and workplaces for more than 1 million residents. For that reason, the reserve process cannot simply rely on land acquisition or even development regulations alone. These are places where economic development and land use must move forward together, but where such activity should be built around natural resources and other landscape values.

Finding the right answers will not be easy. But it is clear that many people do not have faith in our current system. As noted in the report of the New York–New Jersey Highlands Work Group, a recently convened, working committee of conservationists, developers, private landowners, and state and local officials, "The current system of regulations to manage land use and protect natural resources is ineffective and costly due to duplication, inconsistencies, a lack of integration and a lack of political will to make difficult administrative decisions about development and conservation."[7]

The Highlands Work Group uncovered five areas of concern in which land use progress is routinely blocked. While these findings were specifically drawn from experiences in the Highlands, they reflect the state of land use and natural resource management in the region in general:

- Lack of regional coordination or consistency among existing legal authorities.
- Inadequate funding for land use and natural resource programs.
- Lack of adequate incentives to lead municipalities to exercise authority they already have over land use and natural resources.
- Disincentives for landowners who wish to keep their land open.
- Development projects plagued by lengthy permitting reviews and the overlapping jurisdictions of concerned government agencies.[8]

The good news is that in each of the proposed reserves, residents, conservation groups, and all levels of government are beginning to tackle these issues and see the need to work toward the linked goals of a healthy local economy and a healthy local environment. The region's collective experience in creating regional land use institutions—from the New Jersey Pinelands and Long Island Pine Barrens to the Upper Delaware River to the Whole Farm Program in the Catskills—demonstrate that various stakeholders can join together to address common land use and natural resource management issues.

Here are some of the highlights of what is in place in the reserve landscapes and what needs to be accomplished if the Greensward vision is to be achieved.

### New Jersey Pinelands

Of the five great land areas in the proposed reserve system—the Pine Barrens in New Jersey and in Long Island, the Catskills, Shawangunk and Kittatinny mountains, and the Appalachian Highlands—only one is managed on a landscape basis. Since 1979 the federal Pinelands Reserve and the state-level Pinelands Commission have guided development decisions in the New Jersey Pinelands—a 1.1 million acre area covering land in seven counties and 56 municipalities. Recognized as a Biosphere Reserve by the United Nations, the Pinelands covers a vast groundwater aquifer estimated at over 17 trillion gallons—three times the size of the New York City water supply system—and is home to 54 species classified as rare or endangered by state or federal officials. With almost all of its production located in the damp and sandy soils of the Pinelands, New Jersey ranks as one of the top three states in the country in cranberry and blueberry farming.[9]

The 15-member Pinelands Commission regulates land use in a 337,000-acre Preservation Area, where essentially no development is allowed, and a much larger Protection Area, where development is encouraged in specific growth areas. An innovative and equitable system to transfer development rights from conservation areas to suitable development sites has been a remarkable success. Since the program's inception the value of credits transferred and the volume of transactions recorded have increased markedly.[10] The result is that, in comparison to surrounding southern New Jersey, residential land values in the Pinelands have increased by 10%.[11] The success of this integrated conservation and development program has resulted in broad public support

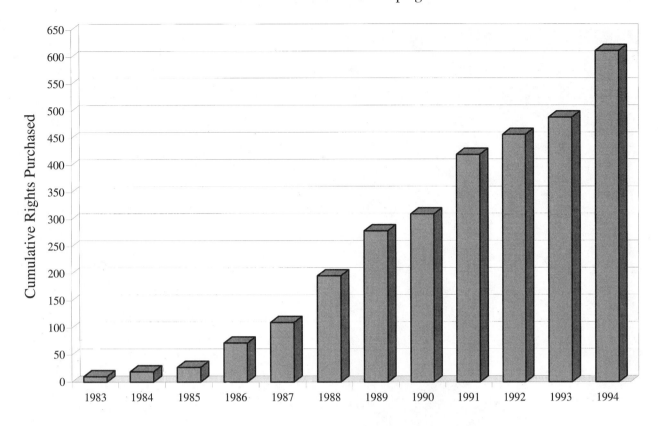

**Figure 47**: *Pinelands Development Credit Program—Rights Purchased by Private Parties.*
Source: Pinelands Development Credit Bank.

for the Pinelands Commission. In a 1994 poll, 79% of New Jersey residents favored continued protection for the Pinelands landscape.[12]

### Long Island Pine Barrens and Peconic Bay Estuary

A mid-1990s version of the New Jersey model has been established in the Pine Barrens on Long Island's East End. The Pine Barrens ecosystem is one of the state's biological treasures, harboring the greatest concentration and diversity of rare and endangered species in New York State. And like their geologic cousins in New Jersey, the sandy, scrubby Long Island Pine Barrens sit on top of an enormous aquifer—water that is critical to the economic future of Long Island. But East Enders also see protection of the Pine Barrens as equally critical to Long Island's future. The island's enormous second home and tourist economy is threatened by sprawl patterns of growth that are consuming open spaces and filling roadways. The town of Brookhaven, 250 square miles at the center of the island, which less

than a generation ago defined the start of the rural East End, added more than 1,000 people per square mile in the past 30 years—the greatest increase of any town in the region.[13]

As a means of permanently protecting this important resource and as a way of settling bitter and long-standing courtroom battles between conservationists, developers, and local officials, New York State in 1993 created the state's third forest preserve: the 100,000-acre Central Pine Barrens area in the towns of Brookhaven, Riverhead, and Southampton. The Long Island Pine Barrens Act also established a Central Pine Barrens Commission and charged this body with preparing a comprehensive land use plan for the forest preserve area. A key aspect of the legislation is that the commission is locally controlled and staffed. Of the five members of the Pine Barrens Commission, only one is a state official. The other four are the supervisors of the three member towns along with the Suffolk County Executive. The Pine Barrens plan, which was adopted on June 28, 1995, divides the forest preserve into two zones.[14] A 52,500-acre

*Figure 48*: *The sandy soil and unique vegetation of the Pine Barrens landscape overlie important groundwater aquifers.*

The next challenge for the East End of Long Island is to extend the cooperative spirit that established the Pine Barrens Commission eastward to take on equally serious resource issues in the Peconic Bay Estuary, a complex of over 100 distinct bays and tributaries extending along the Island's North and South Forks that was recently designated by The Nature Conservancy as one of the 75 "Last Great Places" in the Western Hemisphere. The estuary has historically supported several major fisheries. As recently as 1982 bay scallop catches in the estuary accounted for almost 30% of the national harvest. But brown tide and declines in water quality have sharply reduced the viability of this industry and now threaten the area's tourism economy, which generates more than $200 million a year from boaters alone.[15]

Research conducted under the Peconic Bay Estuary Program—a partnership between federal agencies, New York State, local government, and the private sector—suggests that the future of the estuary will hinge largely on the fate of 30,000 acres of land that still remain open and undeveloped in the estuary watershed. Comprehensive approaches like the Pine Barrens Commission may be one answer to ensure that land uses in the estuary watershed are compatible with the biological health of this important ecosystem. Indeed, one option, already authorized in the original Pine Barrens Act, will be to simply extend the Pine Barrens management planning process eastward to encompass the Peconic ecosystem.

### Appalachian Highlands

The largest reserve area is the 2 million acres of Appalachian Highlands of New Jersey, New York, and Connecticut. In 1921 the pioneering regionalist Benton MacKaye first described his vision of a protected, wild Appalachian Highlands landscape stretching from Maine to Georgia, a green vastness to serve as the open space backbone of the industrializing northeastern United States.[16] MacKaye's best-known legacy, the 2,100-mile-long Appalachian Trail, was intended to be only the central thread of a much more extensive system of wilderness areas and backcountry farms.

Remarkably, almost 70 years later, this long-ignored vision still could be brought to life—and not just in Maine, but right here, in a broad band of

Core Preservation Area encompasses the largest intact areas of still undeveloped Pine Barrens. About half of this core area is already public parkland, and development in the remainder will be strictly limited. The other zone is a 47,500-acre Compatible Growth Area where development will continue, although with special concern for uncompromised Pine Barrens resources.

The heart of the plan is a land strategy to protect property owners. Within the core area privately held land that must remain open for ecological reasons will either be bought by the public, or landowners may transfer out their preexisting development rights. The plan will set standards for managing the Pine Barrens' recreational and biological resources and also create a mechanism for reimbursing towns and school systems for revenues that may be lost by leaving land undeveloped.

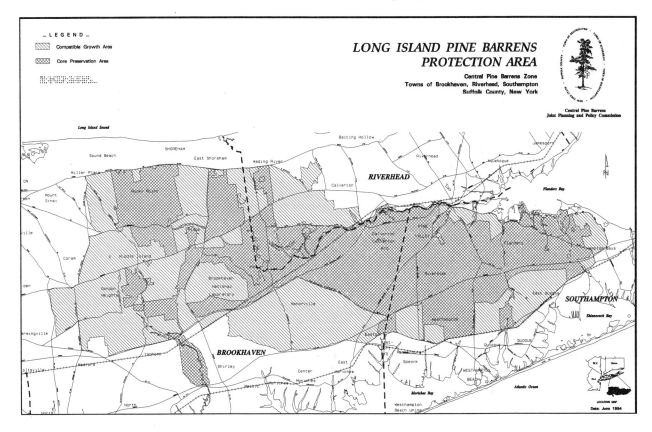

*Figure 49*: *Central Long Island Pine Barrens Commission Area.*

stunning lands that cuts across the heart of the most urbanized region in the United States. It is a landscape rich in wildness, charm, serenity, natural resources, and recreational opportunities, including:

- More than 200,000 acres of public open space hosting at least 9 million recreation visits yearly.[17] Most notable are the famous parks in the Hudson Highlands: Bear Mountain, Fahnestock, and Harriman State Park.

- Clean drinking water for 2.8 million metropolitan northern New Jersey residents who depend on publicly owned reservoirs and surface water systems west of the Hudson River and for 9 million people in New York City and Westchester County who drink water that flows through the Croton River basin east of the Hudson.

- Much of the region's biological heritage. Almost 30% of the regional sites that host threatened, rare, and endangered plants and animals are found in the Appalachian Highlands.[18] The highlands also hold the largest patches of unfragmented forest in the region south of the Catskills, forests that are critical to the

survival of migratory songbirds whose numbers are in alarming decline.

- An extraordinary historic resource with Native American rock shelters and early European settlements, roads, and forts. The iron mines and furnaces that still dot the Highlands were used to produce the great chain across the Hudson that kept the British from dividing the colonies and the cannon and shot used by Washington's army to win the nation's freedom.[19]

The highlands have long served as an unannounced and unofficial boundary to the urban core of the New York–New Jersey–Connecticut Metropolitan area, effectively partitioning the region into the dense suburbs and urban centers to the south and east and the more rural landscape of western New Jersey and the Hudson Valley. The vast open spaces of the highlands still function as an effective, if undesignated, green belt. The highlands' ability to provide such shape and form to the region is now in jeopardy.

The towns that encompass the highlands have already become home to 1.3 million people in 132

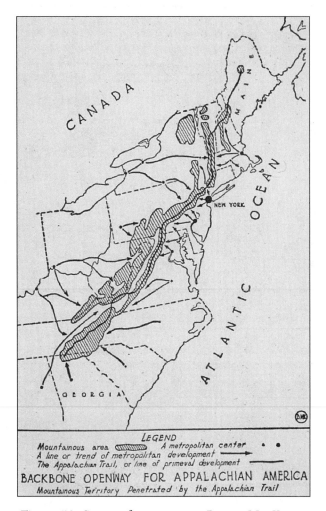

LEGEND
Mountainous area [symbol]   A metropolitan center • •
A line or trend of metropolitan development ——→
The Appalachian Trail, or line of primeval development ——

BACKBONE OPENWAY FOR APPALACHIAN AMERICA
Mountainous Territory Penetrated by the Appalachian Trail

*Figure 50:* *Seventy-five years ago, Benton MacKaye described a protected Appalachian Highlands from Maine to Georgia.*

gional cooperation and coordination, including the proposal by the Highlands Work Group for a Highlands Regional Council.[21] In addition several individual planning and conservation projects are moving ahead, including a local planning demonstration project developed by RPA and the town of West Milford that will help protect hydrologically sensitive land by transferring development rights from more sensitive land within the Newark drinking water watershed; conservation of the key "Treasures of the Highlands" identified by the Highlands Coalition and RPA; and the development of a Highlands Trail extending from the Hudson River to the Delaware, which will thread together most of the dozen jewels of this landscape.[22]

In New York the most important ongoing initiative is the conservation of the 17,500-acre Sterling Forest tract, where the Palisades Interstate Park Commission, Regional Plan Association, and others have assembled an historic combination of New York, New Jersey, and federal money to buy the property and put a stop to region-busting development plans for a new city of 35,000 people and 8 million square feet of commercial and office space. On the east side of the Hudson River, the Northern Putnam Greenway Plan has set out a long-term vision for protecting the integrity of the Hudson Highlands in Putnam County, an area that includes important sections of the New York City drinking water watershed.

In Connecticut, RPA and the Housatonic Valley Association have teamed to create the Litchfield County Open Space Forum. The forum is a first-ever county-wide assembly of local conservation organizations. Its long-term goal is to encourage open space protection at the grassroots level by providing local conservation organizations with technical assistance and support. An initial demonstration project in Norfolk is creating a local inventory of open space resources, one step toward the forum's goal of creating a bottom-up, county-wide inventory. The forum will then help local organizations protect key open space resources within their local settings.

### Shawangunk and Kittatinny Mountains

The Shawangunk (NY) and Kittatinny Mountains (NJ) are a 90-mile-long range of continuous ridgelines extending from the town of Rosendale in Ul-

towns and 11 counties—and these areas are likely to grow by about 20%, meaning more than 250,000 people in the next 20 years if current policies and trends continue.[20] Accommodating these expected new residents (and businesses, roads, and public services) in typical development patterns could result in the highlands disappearing as a landscape and simply becoming a more mountainous part of the suburban sprawl that already extends north and west from New York City. Addressing this issue appropriately will mean crafting different strategies in each of the component parts of the Appalachian Highlands.

The success of the New Jersey Pinelands Commission has led the way for several proposals for re-

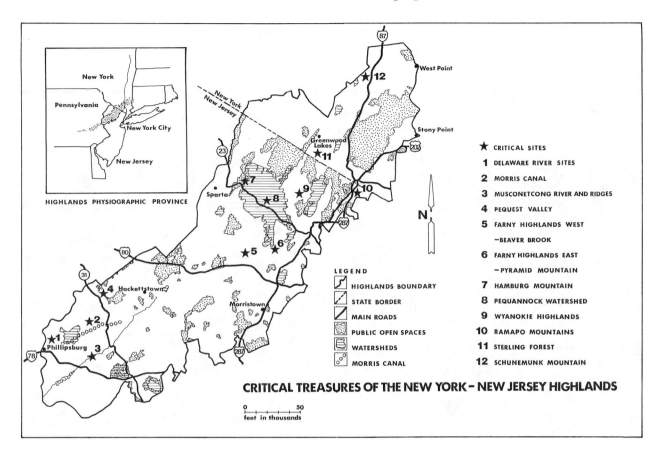

**Figure 51:** *The Treasures of the Highlands.*

ster County in New York to the Delaware Water Gap in New Jersey.[23] These mountains contain unusual and visually striking quartz conglomerate and limestone cliffs, "sky lakes," rare ecological communities including the globally unique mountain-top dwarf pine community, and exceptional recreational resources, including 75 miles of 19th century carriage trails and some of the best rock climbing east of the Rockies. Like the Peconic Bay Estuary, the Shawangunks are another of The Nature Conservancy's "Last Great Places."[24]

As with many of the areas in the region offering high environmental quality and affordable housing, the 17 towns surrounding the Shawangunks and Kittatinny have almost doubled in size in the past 30 years, growing by about 80%.[25] Together with this growth has come some notable conservation efforts. Kittatinny Mountain in New Jersey and the Shawangunks in New York north of Route 52 have been largely protected. Kittatinny Mountain is largely owned by park agencies, notably in places

like High Point State Park and the Delaware River Water Gap National Recreation Area. The 18,000-acre core of the northern Shawangunks is included in Minnewaska State Park and the nonprofit Mohonk Preserve—a National Historic Landmark. There are still, however, a number of unprotected northern tracts where active conservation initiatives, if successful, would either complete or help buffer these publicly accessible lands.

Conservation of the southern Shawangunks has not received as much attention. While much of the area is still forested and undeveloped, most of the ownership is divided into smaller lots that will be difficult to preserve solely through land purchases. Two important initiatives are currently underway that could help protect this area for the future. One is the swift recent creation of the 36-mile Shawangunk Ridge Trail by the National Park Service and the New York–New Jersey Trail Conference, which runs between the Appalachian Trail at High Point and the Long Path at Minnewaska State Park. An-

**Figure 52:** *The Shawangunks contain important biological, recreational, and scenic resources.*

other is the growing realization on the part of local municipalities that conventional zoning will need to be bolstered if the ridgeline is to survive as a resource. Several area towns are examining ways and means by which they could cooperatively protect the area. This could include the adoption of Ridge Overlay Districts, which make environmental treasures and scenic vistas into resources that local zoning can recognize and protect.[26]

### Catskill Mountains

The Catskill Mountains encompass two overlapping landscapes of concern: The Catskill Park and the New York City water supply watershed. Catskill Park gives official New York State recognition to a world-famous landscape region by drawing a line on a map—the celebrated "Blueline"—around the heart of an extensive wilderness area. The Park includes about 288,000 acres of publicly owned land, the 100-year-old "Forever Wild" State Forest Preserve. Mountain peaks of 4,000-plus feet, world-

renowned trout streams, and extensive public and private recreation facilities, including several major ski areas, make the park one of the region's most important recreational and natural open spaces.

Unlike Adirondack Park, which was also set up by New York State a century ago, there is no regional management or coordination of land use activities in the 705,500 acres included within the Catskill Park "Blueline." The state has undertaken a long-term process of improving the use of its Forest Preserve holdings by developing Unit Management Plans for individual sections of the preserve. Of particular importance is the completion of the Catskill Interpretive Center, the development of which on Route 28 would give the park an increased visibility and presence to the estimated 530,000 visitors who travel there each year.

The Catskill region is also the headwaters for about 90% of the New York City drinking water supply system. The Esopus, Schoharie, Rondout, and Delaware basins drain into an extensive system of reservoirs and aqueducts that help deliver over a

**Figure 53:** *The Catskill region is also the headwaters for about 90% of the New York City drinking water supply system.*

billion gallons of pure drinking water every day to downstate communities. While this water supply has always been of excellent quality, clean, and sweet-tasting, concerns over future growth and development and newly promulgated federal surface water treatment rules have led a health-conscious and cost-conscious New York City to comprehensively overhaul its watershed protection program. Under a watershed partnership agreement recently signed by the Environmental Protection Agency, New York State, and the coalition of watershed towns, New York will be investing $1.5 billion over the next 15 years to safeguard the quality of this water. The program will triple the acreage of city-owned land in the watershed (New York City currently owns 60,000 acres in the Catskills). The program also includes funds for improving local water quality infrastructure and for creating economic development programs compatible with the area's role as a water supply landscape.[27] The stakes are high: If water quality is compromised, the city, under federal mandate, will have to filter the

water—at an estimated capital cost of over $5 billion and annual operating costs of approximately $200 million.

While efforts by the state and the city, the area's two largest public land owners, are important, the future of the Catskills, both as wild forest and as watershed, is still largely in the hands of the 50 towns and villages that have local jurisdiction. Only two-thirds of these towns and villages have any zoning or other local land use management programs at all. Less than half have local comprehensive plans. In much of the watershed, as a result, development and land use decisions pay little attention to the effects of growth on water quality and to how growth will affect town character, traffic, open space, and long-term economic viability.

What is needed is a "Three E" approach to help localities safeguard the future of natural resources in a way that does not detract from the health of the local economy or the interests of local citizens and property owners. Some models for this kind of conservation development have already started, ranging from the New York City–sponsored Whole Farm Program, which gives grants to individual farmers to prevent pollution through best management practices; to the land conservation efforts of the Catskill Center and the Woodstock Land Trust to protect the Little Beaverkill watershed; to RPA-assisted municipal projects to revitalize the traditional, compact villages of Hunter and Fleishmans as an alternative to the suburban-style subdivision and highway commercial development patterns found in developing rural areas. Ultimately, a grand alliance of equal partners—the local communities, the state, and the city—is needed to defend and care for the Catskills through the century ahead.

### Hudson and Delaware Rivers

The two great rivers of the region, the Delaware and Hudson, have been the ongoing focus of efforts to create multi-town greenways intended to help

riverfront communities protect, enhance, and celebrate these rich ecological and recreational resources.

Outstanding water quality and an abundance of wildlife, splendid vistas, and recreational opportunities have galvanized conservation efforts along the Delaware River. Revenues from fishing, hunting, and boating alone bring in more than $17 million a year to the local economy in the upper Delaware.[28] Downstream the river provides drinking water for some 13 million people in New Jersey and Pennsylvania before feeding important bird and fish habitat along the Delaware Bay estuary. Thanks to years of effort from local towns, private landowners, civic organizations, and the National Park Service, a continuous 206-mile river greenway could be created from Hancock, New York, to the Delaware Water Gap and down through Trenton, New Jersey.

As a result of the designation of the upper Dela-

*Figure 54: The upper Delaware River—the 73 miles between Hancock and the Delaware Water Gap National Recreation Area—is one of a handful of rivers in the Northeast that have been included in the National Wild and Scenic River System.*

ware River as part of the National Wild and Scenic River System, the National Park Service (NPS) works with the Upper Delaware Council to help local governments meet certain minimum land use guidelines. In addition, the council offers technical assistance grants to help member towns address river management issues.[29] While only 11 out of the 15 towns in the basin are members of the council and not all of its members have met NPS standards, the relationship between the council and the NPS offers a valuable means for encouraging local cooperation.

In the lower Delaware, a cooperative partnership of over 120 public and private organizations hosted by the Heritage Conservancy in Pennsylvania has been formed with the intended purpose of establishing a greenway along the river from the National Recreation Area south to Trenton. Through the greenway program, local landowners and municipalities are being encouraged to identify and protect significant public and private lands in the corridor.

A similar greenway program legislated by New York State is helping to create a greenway along the Hudson River. Since 1991 the Hudson River Valley Greenway Communities Council has been encouraging communities along the Hudson River to protect and provide access to the river by providing technical assistance and funding for local planning projects. The ultimate goal is to create a river-long compact of communities actively working together to protect and enhance the Hudson. A partner agency, the Greenway Heritage Conservancy, is working on the long-term goal of building a Hudson River Trail that can be walked and biked along both banks, from the mouth of the Hudson north beyond Albany.

This biologically rich and tidally influenced river supports major fisheries, including shad and striped bass populations that are among the healthiest on the east coast. The river is an important stop-over point on the Atlantic Flyway for migrating birds: bald eagles, an endangered species, soar over the Hudson every winter.[30] Yet most people know the Hudson only for its spectacular scenery. The birthplace of American landscape paintings, its natural elegance is still remarkably intact. The Hudson River was the first area in New York State to be designated as a Scenic Area of Statewide Significance.

Voluntary greenway programs have raised the

*Figure 55: The Hudson River Valley is one of the region's most famous open spaces.*

visibility and standing of the Hudson and Delaware rivers both within the communities that share their banks as well as throughout the region. Ultimate success in protecting the river resources will depend on these programs' technical ability, access to funding, and the ability of the member communities to work together effectively to protect and manage common river resources.

## New York–New Jersey Harbor and Long Island Sound

The region grew up alongside the coastal estuaries of the New York–New Jersey Harbor and Long Island Sound. And these water bodies now reflect the past decades of industrial activity. Of the 70,000 acres of tidal wetlands that once lined the edges of the harbor and were part of a thriving ecosystem that once made the harbor the real "oyster bay," only 15,000 acres remain. Over 300,000 acres of open water have been landfilled, areas that today are occupied by abandoned industrial facilities that once helped build the growing metropolis but now prevent its citizens from reaching the shorelines.[31] Restoring these urban waters and waterfronts means meeting both natural and human needs— improving shoreline habitat and the estuaries' natural ability to cleanse themselves while at the same time expanding public access to these blue treasures in the very heart of the region.

The science of ecological restoration, while still in its infancy, is proving its viability in several places in both the sound and the harbor. The region can improve habitat and water quality by using the natural ability of streams, tides, and wetland vegetation to retain and process nutrients and other potential pollutants. While such created wetlands cannot duplicate the complexity of nature's own handiwork, they offer far greater benefits than the channeled flow, riprap edges, and other engineered conditions that now often characterize the tributaries and shorelines of these estuaries.

Several recent efforts are showing how these projects can work. New York City's Salt Marsh Restoration Group is using funding from fines paid by polluters to help create and restore wetlands along the Arthur Kill. The Fairfield Conservation Commission has restored tidal flow to wetlands along the South Pine Creek, a tributary to Long Island Sound. The tributaries to the Arthur Kill and Raritan Bay have been the subject of studies by the New Jersey Audubon Society and New Jersey Conservation Foundation. And the New York/New Jersey Baykeeper is in the process of creating a comprehensive plan for the restoration of habitat throughout the entire harbor estuary.

These efforts need to be fostered and encouraged. But their true value will be known only to a few scientists unless the public can have ready access to these water bodies. Both the sound and the harbor have been the focus of National Estuary Program studies that recommend spending billions of dollars to finish the job of the Clean Water Act to achieve high water quality—a laudable goal that seems within our reach. These substantial public investments will not be possible without vigorous public support. But improving water quality will

**Figure 56:** *Ecological restoration can improve habitat and water quality by using the natural ability of streams, tides, and wetland vegetation to retain and process nutrients.*

also require new behavior on the part of millions of coastal and inland residents. Polluted runoff, for instance, can only be controlled if people actively manage their own parking lots, farms, lawns, and waterfront property. Why should any of these people care if they cannot get down to the water they will soon be asked to protect?

Tens of thousands of people use and enjoy Long Island Sound every year and spend $5 billion a year to swim, fish, sail, and take motorboats out in the sound. The public beaches are so popular that on hot summer days they are often forced to turn away visitors. Mariners have made these waters one of the boating capitals of the world. Public and private nature preserves provide a number of opportunities to get close to a lively and complex estuarine ecosystem. Yet for the most part this access is limited at best to the residents of the towns that actually border the sound. Twenty percent of the Connecticut shoreline is publicly owned, but only 5% of the shoreline is deemed to be "publicly accessible recreation space," meaning that it can actually be used by any citizen of the state. The situation in New York State is about the same, with only five sites in the entire 340-mile shoreline open to the public at large, and two of these are located in eastern Suffolk County far away from the bulk of the demand. Only about one-third of the public fishing access sites in New York State on the sound are open to the public.[32]

In recent years Connecticut has taken a quiet approach to enhancing public access to Long Island

Sound. Slow but steady progress has been made in providing additional access and, just as importantly, in improving existing access points. This low-key success is the result of two main efforts. First, both local and state governments have continued to acquire and upgrade publicly owned access points. Second, local zoning officials and state coastal regulators acting under the state Coastal Management Act have required property owners to provide public access as a condition to a number of shoreline development approvals. Approximately 10 miles of coastline have been acquired in this way. Access gained in this fashion ranges from pedestrian walkways to boat launches and fishing piers. New York State recently prepared a draft Long Island Sound Coastal Management Program that recommends that similar strategies be undertaken.

These types of approaches are sensible and will make progress. However, they may not provide additional public access rapidly enough to generate new support for cleaning the sound, to enhance tourism, or to make the sound an attractive amenity to maintain and lure business and workers. Additional measures, perhaps even the creation of a new bi-state conservancy dedicated to Long Island Sound access, may be needed for the region to make the most of this extraordinary resource.

The New York–New Jersey Harbor, the region's most hidden biological treasure, is approximately 1,500 square miles of open waters, 770 miles of waterfront, and a direct drainage area of 3,000 square miles. The estuary is an important reserve for shorebirds and waterfowl. For example, the Arthur Kill waterway supports one of the largest heron rookeries in the entire Northeast. A great variety of fish live in the estuary and spawn in the upper portions of the rivers that feed it.

The harbor remains a vital economic resource for shipping and industry and continues to be the receiving water for much of the region's sewage. But increasingly, as water quality has improved, the harbor is also being seen for the tremendous wildlife and recreational resource it is and could be. As a result of the federal Clean Water Act of 1972, the harbor's waters are already cleaner than they have been for a century. Yet, ironically, the harbor's political future is far more perilous than the sound's because, as a lingering result of old industrial uses that years ago denied people access to the waterfront, the harbor has practically no constituency at

*Figure 57: The Long Island Sound is the region's "urban sea."*

all. But the waters are cleaner and many of the industrial uses have withdrawn. So, in fact, unparalleled opportunities now exist to create sensational new harborfront parks. Olmsted and Moses would have leaped at this chance to take on a third great round of city-scaping and urban parks construction.

Several bold new initiatives are already underway, including the Hudson River Park and the proposed park at Riverside South on the West Side of Manhattan; the Hudson River Waterfront Walkway in New Jersey; the federal disposition of Governors Island; and the proposed Brooklyn Bridge Park on the East River from the Manhattan Bridge down to Atlantic Avenue. Those are just some of the most notable examples of projects that need to continue to move forward. In addition, New York, New Jersey, and the federal government should do more to both improve Gateway National Recreation Area and to provide access to its shoreline. While substantial work is being done to improve public access around Jamaica Bay, as a whole the park remains under-utilized. One possibility is to tap the entrepreneurial spirit of the region's emerging ferryboat network to provide service to Sandy Hook, the Rockaways, and the Sandy Hook beaches.

### Atlantic Seashore

The Atlantic Seashore is one of the region's premier quality of life assets. The 200-plus miles of sand and dunes, the swimmability of the water, and, thanks to important public investments, the access of metropolitan residents to the beaches of Long Island and New Jersey shores make this area unique in the world.

The barrier beaches that line much of the seashore are shifting, ephemeral structures; ocean waves and tides are constantly eroding the beach in one area while depositing sand elsewhere. As a result, structures built in these areas are subject to flooding and the erosion of the sand beneath them. Virtually all are required to participate in Federal Flood Insurance programs, which guarantee coverage in exchange for homes being constructed to certain "floodproof" standards. While homeowners do pay premiums, this program is not self-sufficient and has required billions of dollars in years of severe flooding.[33] In addition, the state governments respond to erosion and flooding with grants for beach replenishment and disaster aid.

This problem is likely to be exacerbated in the future. An expected consequence of global climate change is an increase in sea levels and in the frequency and severity of coastal storms, including hurricanes.

New York, New Jersey, and the federal government need to ensure that as they address storm damage to barrier beaches and other coastal areas with public dollars, the public at large reaps some benefits. Limited tax dollars should be spent first to protect public beaches, heavily developed upland areas, public transportation facilities, or areas where past public actions have exacerbated erosion problems. In New York State the Governor's Coastal Erosion Task Force developed such a set of policies in considering responses to the winter storms of 1992–1993.[34]

**Figure 58:** *Barrier beaches are most suitable for park use, as built structures are subject to flooding and wave damage.*

Public entities should consider how to better connect federal flood insurance programs, local zoning, and open space acquisition strategies so that these public policies work together to limit the new construction in flood-prone areas and limit the liability of taxpayers for repairing structures built, and then rebuilt, with government-issued insurance. Nationally, the General Accounting Office has estimated that 2% of the federal policy holders have resulted in 43% of the claims paid by the National Flood Insurance Program.[35] New Jersey's "Blue Acres" program is part of the answer. This $30 million effort will use the state's open space program to buy-out property owners in flood hazard areas. A greater percentage of National Flood Insurance Act funds could also be used in this way. This would not only create new public spaces along the ocean and other waterfronts but would lighten what may increasingly be a major budget liability. In addition, the states, localities, and the federal government should consider ways to better tie local land use regulations with flood insurance provisions so that new homes and businesses are not built in flood-prone areas.

### Agricultural Lands

Protecting the region's 11th reserve, its agricultural land, poses a different challenge. Those concerned with farmland preservation know that it is not enough to be concerned with saving farmland—you need to save the farmer too. Land will only stay in agricultural production if it is economically viable for the farmer to continue to produce food and fiber.

Between 1964 and 1992 the number of acres of farmland in our 31-county region declined from 1.7 million acres to just under 1 million acres.[36] Most of the region's remaining farmland acreage is spread across the "great valley" that extends from Sussex County, New Jersey, along the Walkill River

***Figure 59:*** *Greenmarket Farmers in the Tri-State Region.*
Source: Council on the Environment of New York City.

Valley to Dutchess County, New York. However, some of the most economically productive lands are on the North Fork of Long Island and some of the most scenic are the rich, rolling farmlands of Hunterdon County.

The most direct techniques to retain both farmland and farmer are purchase of development rights (PDR) programs, where farmers sell conservation easements on the farmland to state or local authorities. While expensive, this strategy ensures that agricultural land will stay in production forever while giving the farmer funds that are often plowed back into capital improvements on the farm itself. Both Connecticut and New Jersey have active PDR programs. As of 1995 Connecticut has protected 24,250 acres on 161 farms. New Jersey's efforts have protected 22,085 acres on 148 farms. New York State just recently created a statewide program. Acting on its own, Suffolk County has developed a program setting aside 6,941 acres on 154 farms.[37] In addition to these public programs, a number of the region's land trusts, notably the Dutchess Land Conservancy, have actively worked with farmers.

Like other land acquisition programs, however, it is clear that the region cannot simply buy development rights on all the farms in the region. Keeping land in production will require revising or reducing property, inheritance, and income taxes so that these public policies do not force farmers out of business. It will necessitate that farmers develop new marketing strategies that tie the region's food producers directly to the region's millions of consumers through farmer's markets such as New York City's Greenmarket, the State of New Jersey's campaign for buying local produce, or the increasing number of "pick-your-own" operations. And it will necessitate developing land use and environmental strategies that help ensure that farmers and transplanted suburbanites can be good neighbors. New York State's Farmland Protection Program is one model of a county-based planning and technical assistance program that brings farmers together to address land use, marketing, and economic development issues.

### Creating the Regional Reserves

As described above, efforts in many of the reserve areas are well established with solid achievements already in place; others are just starting to define themselves and their mission.

While these initiatives involve a range of strategies, their success is predicated on achieving a delicate balance of regional focus and local control. Water quality, scenic resources, and the other natural resources in the reserves can best—and perhaps only—be managed on a regional basis. Moreover, the funding and technical assistance needed to manage these resources is generally not available at the local level. But maintaining local control is critical because none of these efforts will succeed without the active and willing participation of the residents of the reserve areas and, significantly, because local land use regulatory powers are the most comprehensive set of tools available for ensuring that regional conservation goals are met.

New development in the Regional Reserves should be designed to reinforce the character of existing communities, with the goal of maintaining the balance between man and nature that is the hallmark of these communities. Unfortunately, the conventional zoning currently in place in most Greensward towns will produce very different and more damaging patterns of growth, including large lot residential subdivisions and frontage lots and commercial strip development. Even modest amounts of this kind of development can damage water quality, generate excessive traffic, reduce opportunities for affordable housing, and obliterate the rural character that draws people to these communities.

In recent years, sophisticated new growth management tools that encourage appropriate development while safeguarding community character and providing for orderly patterns of growth have been created and tested in rural communities across the country. A number of these techniques have been described in rural design handbooks (including some written and published by RPA and its staff) that can be a source for planning board members.[38]

These techniques include:

• *Growth Rate Controls.* Fast-growing communities can regulate the rate of residential and commercial growth, limiting development to a rate commensurate with their ability to provide infrastructure, schools, and other services.

• *Open Space Subdivision and Zoning Bylaws.* Rural districts, particularly those containing significant agricultural, watershed, or wildlife resources, should be zoned for very low densities, preferably with provision for cluster development. Rural areas of King County (Seattle), Washington, for example, are zoned for 10-acre minimum sized lots; Marin County, California (just north of the Golden Gate Bridge), zones agricultural and hillside districts for 40-acre minimum lots. Most reserve communities zone similar areas for 2- or 3-acre minimum lots, producing large lot suburbs rather than rural places. The many residents of the region seeking rural life-styles should be given the assurance that the places in which they live will remain rural. Larger rural lot sizes and mandatory cluster can provide that assurance. Reserve towns can combine very large lot zoning with cluster provisions to produce outcomes that will sustain their rural character. Cluster bylaws are most effective when they include provisions for mandatory cluster, or strong incentives for cluster development (such as density bonuses). Cluster bylaws should also provide strong guidelines for protection of useful open spaces that can be managed for wildlife, recreational, farming, or other purposes.

• *Village and Town Centers.* Towns should adopt zoning that encourages higher density, mixed-use development in centers. All commercial and most multifamily development should be accommodated in centers, perhaps in conjunction with transfer of development rights provisions that transfer density out of districts containing important natural resources.

• *Improved Site Planning.* Towns should adopt site plan review, roadway layout, and other siting guidelines designed to produce new subdivisions and commercial development that "fit" the character of existing development in the community. Dimensional requirements, building massing, form and materials, signage, and other features of new development should closely match the traditional patterns of Greensward communities.

• *Traffic Control.* Towns should adopt subdivision roadway guidelines that discourage cul-de-sacs and encourage connected grids of roadways to spread traffic loads and allow pedestrian usage. Dimensional standards should produce village-scale streets, as opposed to the excessively wide streets required by many rural subdivision ordinances. Traffic calming measures, including zig-zag lanes, "neckdowns," and mid-block extensions at corners and pedestrian crossings, and other devices, should be employed to slow traffic in rural hamlets.

• *Affordable Housing.* Towns should promote year-round affordable housing in village centers and in new cluster subdivisions by providing density bonuses and other incentives.

• *Wastewater and Stormwater Treatment.* In reserve areas located in public water supply watersheds, aquifer protection areas, and adjoining important streams or estuaries, efforts should be made to provide advanced wastewater treatment systems. Central sewage treatment plants, in the context of a town-wide growth management strategy, can provide an incentive to locate new development in traditional village and town centers. These facilities can involve new treatment technologies, such as the solar aquatic treatment technology now being employed in a number of rural communities in Massachusetts. Stormwater management can be improved through regional districts that pool resources to create or restore wetlands and provide adequate maintenance of stormwater treatment systems.

We also need to ensure that these improved local land use plans and regulations are integrated with regional management goals and state policies.

• The most direct method of accomplishing this goal is through the establishment of regional commissions. These can be state-level programs like the New Jersey Pinelands Commission or commissions that are locally controlled, like the Long Island Pine Barrens Commission. The basic tenet is that localities must either revise their local plans to meet regional goals or cede some home-rule authority to the regional body. The commission may also provide incentives and technical assistance for communities complying with their guidelines. Local control of the commission can help reassure municipal officials who are concerned about ceding their authority to another layer of government.

• A broadly based approach is to use statewide planning mechanisms, such as the policy areas and designated centers defined in the New Jersey State Plan, as a framework for guiding state support for infrastructure and regulatory policies. Localities helped develop New Jersey's Plan through a "cross-acceptance process" and were thus encouraged to adopt corresponding local plans. State planning can provide a context for the reserve system. Current state plans in place in New Jersey and Connecticut do not have much influence on state or local policy. New York State has no such provisions in place, although its Open Space Conservation Plan does identify Major Resource Areas as being the foci of conservation efforts, including all of the proposed reserves.

• Another method involves inter-community compacts, like those being promoted by the Hudson Valley Greenway Communities Council. Local governments are encouraged to meet regional goals and to coordinate their actions through a system of rewards in the form of legal support, state adoption of corresponding policies, and/or implementation grants. These programs may be the most acceptable to local communities concerned about the erosion of their home-rule powers. Because they are strictly voluntary, their implementation may be slow as communities choose to focus on other priorities.

Making these programs work will require a commitment of new funding. There will need to be financial support for planning, for land and less-than-fee acquisition programs, and for supporting pollution prevention programs. The cost will be substantial. There are two recent, comprehensive programs in the reserve areas that can serve as gauges to the approximate dollar amount. New York City is directing more than $1.5 billion to finance land acquisition, sewage treatment plant upgrades, and pollution prevention programs in its 1,900-square-mile drinking water watershed.[39] About $75 million will be spent acquiring land and developing a management program to achieve the mandate of the Long Island Pine Barrens Commission. Based on the per-acre cost of these programs, implementing similar operations in the remaining reserve areas would be in the neighborhood of $6 billion. This does not include costs associated with meeting existing environmental mandates, such as implementing water pollution control programs outlined in the Long Island Sound management plan.

Some of these needs can and are being met by rethinking existing programs and redirecting existing funding:

• Drinking water protection programs can prevent pollution through land conservation. As noted, New York City has an ambitious program underway in the Catskills and Hudson Highlands. Funding from New Jersey water bond acts is being used for land acquisition while water quality regulatory programs are being reinvented to deal with issues on a watershed basis. There may be other ways of linking infrastructure and water treatment spending (or savings) to land conservation and planning.

• The use of transfer of development rights programs and other creative conservation financing techniques can also help reduce the public cost of these programs. The New Jersey Pinelands Commission has protected over 10,000 acres through its TDR program, in essence, using for conservation purposes the money that private developers "saved" by being able to build at increased density in appropriate building areas.

• All three states have ongoing land acquisition programs and all three have recognized, New York's most explicitly, the importance of focusing acquisition in the

11 proposed reserve areas. In recent years the financial resources of these programs—the Environmental Protection Fund in New York State, the Green Acres Program in New Jersey, and Connecticut's Recreation and Natural Heritage Trust—have fluctuated as state funding is redirected to meet other budget priorities. New Jersey is in the process of raising $340 million for land conservation using general obligation bonds. However, even in the Garden State there needs to be a concerted effort to find dedicated or at least consistent revenue streams to fund these programs.

• The federal Land and Water Conservation Fund has traditionally been a source of support for both federal and state-level acquisition. However, the revenues from oil and gas leases on federal lands that supply the fund have increasingly been siphoned off to pay for other federal programs. Moreover, this region has consistently received less than its share of the federal dollars. From 1987 to 1993 New York received an average of $9 million a year, far less than the 50-state average of $27 million and dwarfed by California's $248 million.[40] The region's Congressional leadership should take action so that in the short term more of this funding is directed toward the region and in the long term the fund is revised so that innovative partnership projects like Sterling Forest and the Long Island Pine Barrens can readily receive federal assistance.[41]

• Existing taxes, including those on property, inheritance, and capital gains, may need to be rethought to ensure that these programs do not send the wrong economic signal to private landowners or otherwise constrict conservation practices. In particular, RPA's proposal for education financing reform, if successful, would help rationalize the current property tax structure, a system that pushes many local officials into a no-win choice between schools or the environment.

Consideration of new sources of funding—either explicitly for the reserve areas or as part of larger statewide programs for open space—should stem from the "User Pays" argument promoted throughout this plan. The open lands and pure waters of the reserve areas are relatively finite resources, and their consumption should be taxed. In addition, any new revenues need to be derived in a way that is fair to both the residents in the reserve areas and to the residents in downstream urban and suburban areas.

Some possibilities include:

• A small surcharge on water bills could be put in place for urban and suburban communities that draw their drinking water from reserve areas. This fee would

CURRENT

CONVENTIONAL DEVELOPMENT

ALTERNATIVE DEVELOPMENT

*Plate 1C: Alternative planning and zoning can meet local needs without compromising the region's resources. Here, the future of a rural village is projected under conventional and alternative planning and development guidelines.*

# BUILDING A METROPOLITAN GREENSWARD

The Metropolitan Greensward is a vision of a system of protected open spaces, greenways and rural landscapes that distinguish the cities and suburbs of the New York/New Jersey/Connecticut metropolitan region. By implementing the Greensward, the Region will conserve its critical natural resource systems, its recreational opportunities and the working landscapes of farms and forests. Together, these protected open lands will help shape future patterns of growth in the Tri-State Region.

## REGIONAL RESERVES

To construct the Greensward, the Region must help communities manage change in nine special places, or "regional reserves," which encompass the Region's most important scenic, biological and water resources and which are now threatened by urban sprawl.

Catskill Park
Delaware River Valley
Hudson River Valley
Long Island Pine Barrens/Peconic Estuary

Long Island Sound
The Appalachian Highlands of New York, New Jersey and Connecticut
New Jersey Pinelands

New York-New Jersey Harbor
Shawangunk/Kittatinny Mountains
Atlantic Seashore
Agricultural Areas

## Greenway and Greenspace Initiatives

Building the Greensward also means weaving together a network of Greenways and Greenspaces that protects and enhances individual rivers, trails, ridgelines and urban open lands. Seventy-two of the most important public and private initiatives are listed below.

**NEW YORK**
1. Long Path
2. Route 28 Corridor
3. Mongaup River and Reservoirs
4. Neversink River and Gorge
5. Delaware and Hudson Canal/Ontario and Western Right-of-Way
6. Shawangunk Kill
7. Black Dirt Agricultural Area
8. Sterling Forest
9. Hudson River Shore Trails
10. Wappinger Creek
11. Stissing Mountain
12. Harlem Valley Right-of-Way
13. Nellie Hill
14. Putnam/Northern Tier Greenway
15. Great Swamp
16. Putnam Division Right-of-Way
17. Hutchinson River Parkway
18. Hudson River Waterfront Park
19. East River Esplanade
20. Harlem River Esplanade/Putnam Railroad Greenway
21. Bronx River Trailway/Soundview and Ferry Point Parks
22. East Bronx-City Island Greenway
23. Queens-East River Greenway/North Shore-Flushing Meadow Trail
24. Brooklyn-Queens Greenway/North Brooklyn Greenway/Piers 1-5
25. Cross Brooklyn Greenway
26. Shore Bikeway/Jamaica Bay-Forest Park Trail
27. Laurelton Parkway Greenway/Rockaway-Gateway Greenway
28. Staten Island Greenbelt
29. North Shore Esplanade/Staten Island Railroad Trail
30. West Shore Greenway
31. South Shore Esplanade
32. Oyster Bay Estate and Waterfront
33. Underhill Estate
34. Nassau-Suffolk Border Trail
35. Cross County Trail
36. North Fork Trail
37. South Fork/Montauk Trail
38. Dwarf Pine Barrens
39. Shinnecock Bay Tidal Wetlands
40. Robbins Island
41. Long Pond Greenbelt

**NEW JERSEY**
42. Paulins Kill Trail
43. Bear Swamp
44. Wallkill River Greenway
45. Delaware River Greenway
46. Lehigh and Hudson Right-of Way/Pequest Greenway
47. Morris Canal
48. Musconetcong River
49. Lamington/Black River
50. Lenape Trail/Patriots' Path
51. Passaic River
52. Pyramid Mountain/Turkey Mountain/Farny Highlands/Wyanokie Highlands
53. Ramapo Mountains and River
54. Lower Palisades Cliffs/Hudson Waterfront Walkway
55. Rahway River/Arthur Kill Tributaries
56. Kuser Mountain
57. Sourland Mountain Ridge
58. Bayshore Project
59. Manasquan River
60. Northern Barnegat Bay/Metedeconk River

**CONNECTICUT**
61. Robbins Swamp
62. Housatonic River and Tributaries
63. Mianus River
64. Merritt Parkway/Wilbur Cross Parkway
65. Bridgeport Hydraulic Lands
66. Pequonnock River
67. West Rock Ridge Trail
68. Boston and Maine Right-of Way/Farmington Canal
69. Farmington River
70. Metacommet Trail
71. Metabasset Trail
72. New Haven Water Co. Lands

*(map labels)* R. I. · Fishers I · Block Island Sound · Orient Pt · Gardiners I · Montauk Pt · Shelter I · Estuary · 41 · 37 · thampton · Bay · 6

This map was prepared with the assistance of the Mary Flagler Cary Charitable Trust, American Conservation Association, and the USDA Forest Service

10/95

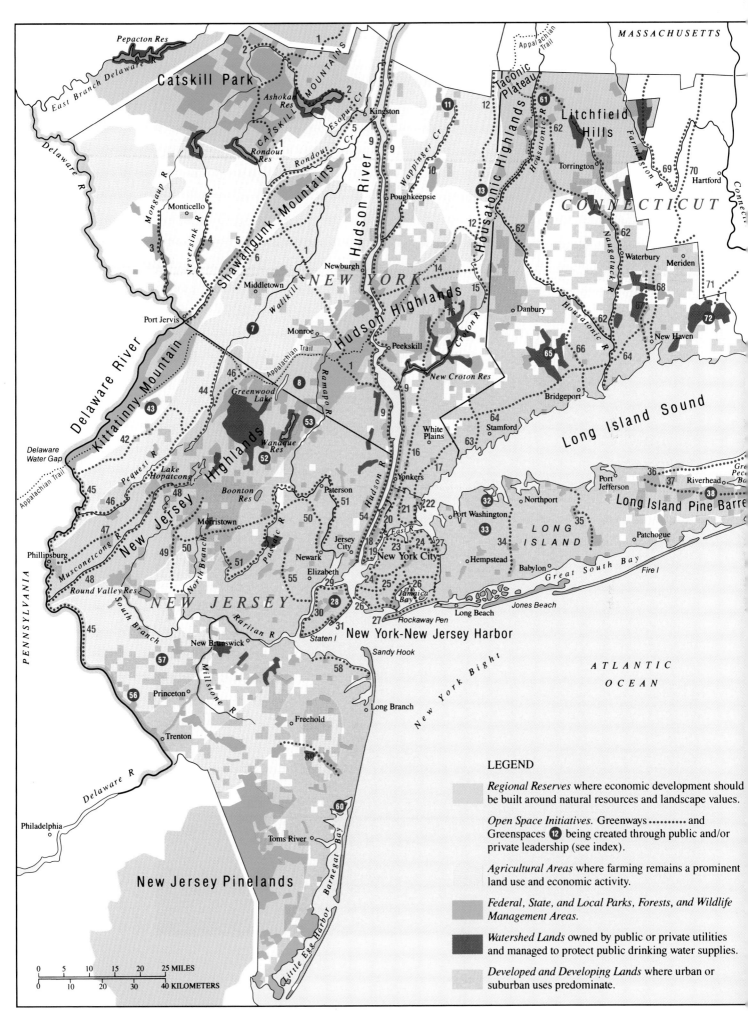

**Plate 1B:** *Greensward Summary Map (© Regional Plan Association).*

**Plate 1A:** *The New York–New Jersey Highlands form a green edge to suburban growth just 25 miles from New York City.*

help protect the quality of their drinking water today and help them avoid paying for more costly treatment systems down the road. It may also help encourage water conservation—saving authorities the need to increase capacity on downstream treatment systems. In essence, such a system is already in place in the New York City drinking water watersheds where sewer and water fees are helping finance their upstate program. As an estimate of the potential revenue, New Jersey derives about 1.2 billion gallons a day from public and private water purveyors; a tax of 0.001 cents on each gallon would create a revenue stream of about $40 million per year.

• A dedicated real estate transfer tax would provide funding tied directly to development activity. About 40 states have such provisions; the states of Maryland and Florida dedicate a percentage to open space acquisition. New York State's existing Environmental Protection Fund is scheduled to receive about $90 million in fiscal year 1996 from the state's existing title transfer tax of $2 per $500 of property value. Applying a straight tax of $1 per $1,000 region-wide would yield about $40 million annually.[42] This surcharge could be limited to large landowners and/or short-term transactions in the reserve areas. In addition, exemptions should be provided for title transactions completed solely as part of a property refinancing or inheritance.

• Property tax surcharges that would capture the rise in property value expected from adjacent conservation lands could be instituted. A number of municipalities in the region, notably in Morris County, New Jersey, are already taxing themselves in this way to support land conservation generally at a rate of one to two cents per $100 of assessed value. Based on a straight assessment of one cent per $1000 of assessed property value in the region as a whole, about $280 million a year would be generated.[43] This surcharge could be limited to the reserve areas only. To reduce the burden on individual homeowners, this surcharge is often not applied to the first $100,000 of value.

There are a number of smaller levies that can also help provide funding for the Reserve Program. However, none of these would be able to provide substantial revenue by itself:

• A tax on hotel and motel rooms or other tourism activity that will be enhanced through conservation of the reserve areas. The Hudson River Greenway Communities Council was funded through such a tax, levied at a rate of 0.2% on hotel/motel bills in the Greenway counties.

• A tax on billboards. Such signs detract from the scenic value of open space areas while they benefit from public investments in roads and road maintenance. A pro-

posal in New York State would dedicate such a revenue stream to community forestry programs.

• A tax on extractive industry operating in the reserve areas, such as mining and sand and gravel operations.

• A tax on sporting equipment, including boats, bicycles, and off-road motor vehicles, whose utility is directly affected by the availability of public spaces.

While new taxes are never popular, dedicated specialty taxes may be politically salable. RPA's 1995 Quality of Life Poll indicates that a majority of the region's residents are willing to pay more for greenery, clean air, and clean water, and that dedicated fees were the way to do it. Fifty-six percent of the region's residents said they would personally spend more money to preserve open space and parks, and 66% would spend more money to ensure clean air and clean water.

## Investing in Urban Open Spaces

Improving the delightful aspects of life in our cities and older suburbs, which include parks and other greenspaces, is essential to attracting and retaining businesses and residents. RPA's 1995 Quality of Life poll indicated that for 60% of the region's residents who had moved to the suburbs, outdoor recreation was a primary consideration. Very few citizens, whether urbanites or suburbanites, have yet awakened to the fact that within a generation the region's gritty centers could offer exactly comparable outdoor experiences. All the potential is there. It is a matter of restoring and re-greening urban parks, streets, and other public spaces and of capitalizing

*Figure 60: Urban parks help keep cities livable.*

on the region's greatest urban public spaces—the waterfronts adjoining the New York–New Jersey Harbor, Hudson River, and Long Island Sound.

There is a wealth of evidence that shows how open spaces help cities and towns:

- Well-managed and attractive open space can be a positive part of community and downtown redevelopment efforts. Numerous studies have clearly shown that adjacent parks, street trees and woodlots, and views of open space or water can significantly enhance rents, property value, and property taxes.[44] .

- Urban parks make it possible for all of the region's residents to have places to ride their bikes, play ball, or just relax in the sunshine. This is especially important for children and adults without backyards of their own or the means to reach countryside parks. Recreation programs can be important vehicles for education, especially for young people.

- Greening cities by planting and managing trees in streets, parks, and backyards can dramatically improve the environmental surroundings of urbanites. Scientists at the United States Forest Service have shown how street trees can reduce a city's peak summertime temperatures by 3 to 5°F, cutting the size of air conditioning bills and peak electricity demand and significantly reducing the formation of health-threatening, low-altitude ozone pollution.[45]

- Stream and wetland restoration techniques do not just re-create habitat—they often clean water more effectively and more cheaply than large-scale engineering solutions such as treatment plants. They can be an important way to reclaim urban waters for people as well as for the extraordinary fish and waterfowl populations that reside in these estuaries.

*Figure 61: Greening cities by planting and managing trees can improve environmental quality and save energy.*

Maintaining the quality and increasing the quantity of urban parks and public spaces is of paramount concern for cities such as New York, Newark, Trenton, Poughkeepsie, Bridgeport, and Stamford. This is also very much a regional matter: when centers can hang on to people, suburban sprawl loses much of its pull.

### Urban Waterfronts

The reclamation of the region's urban waterfronts offers opportunities to create extraordinary new public spaces. This means commuter ferries, restaurants, and water-enhanced commercial centers in addition to parks. By making public use an integral part of this waterfront redevelopment, developers and cities can spread the benefits of the waterfront inland as well. At the same time, new techniques of ecological restoration coupled with improved water quality and a greater appreciation of urban ecology offer the promise of improving the environmental quality and recreational potential of the New York–New Jersey Harbor, Long Island Sound, Hudson River, and other urban water bodies.

There are a number of citizen- and government-led planning efforts to help increase public access to the region's urban waterfronts. Proposals for the New Jersey Waterfront Walkway, Brooklyn Bridge Park, the Hudson River Park, and Riverside South are just some of the efforts that have galvanized community and political support for waterfront plans. Such programs need to be initiated and supported for all of the region's urban waterfronts.

To make these proposals a reality, it is essential that increased public access be combined with appropriate commercial uses. Both the Hudson River Park Conservancy and Brooklyn Bridge Park propose to pay for their own maintenance by incorporating just enough water-related development, such as marinas and restaurants, to raise the funds they need. The New Jersey Waterfront Walkway is to be built as developers complete their waterfront projects and is designed as part of the overall redevelopment—including a light-rail system—of the Hudson River coastline. While the public's interest in the waterfront is paramount, and the few remaining natural areas at the water's edge must be respected, it is important to understand that many of these former industrial areas will attract far greater numbers of year-round visitors if they are

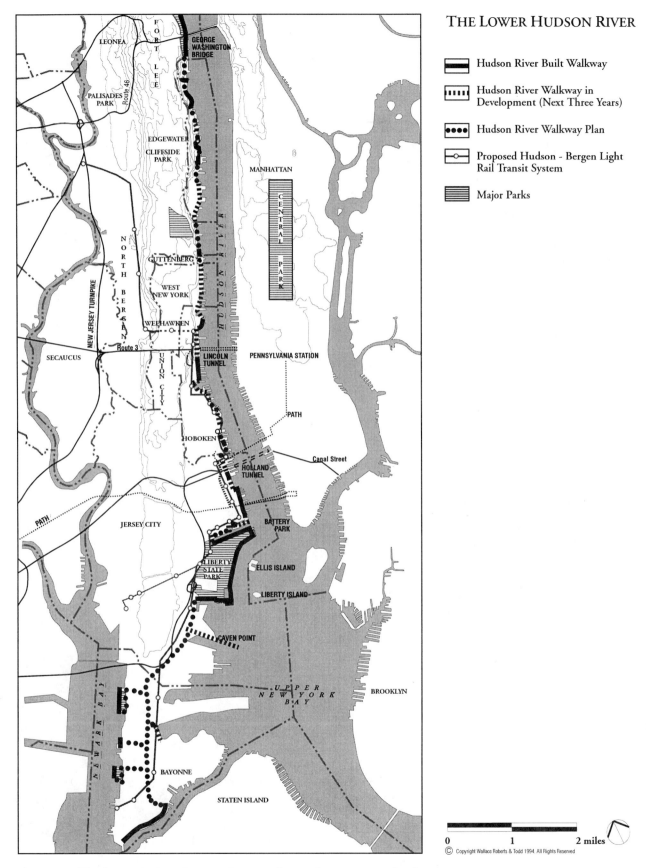

THE LOWER HUDSON RIVER

▬▬▬ Hudson River Built Walkway

▬▮▮▮▬ Hudson River Walkway in Development (Next Three Years)

●●●● Hudson River Walkway Plan

▭○▭ Proposed Hudson - Bergen Light Rail Transit System

▤▤▤ Major Parks

LEONEA

FORT LEE

GEORGE WASHINGTON BRIDGE

PALISADES PARK

Route 46

EDGEWATER

CLIFFSIDE PARK

MANHATTAN

NORTH BERGEN

HUDSON RIVER

CENTRAL PARK

GUTTENBERG

WEST NEW YORK

NEW JERSEY TURNPIKE

WEEHAWKEN

Route 3

SECAUCUS

UNION CITY

LINCOLN TUNNEL

PENNSYLVANIA STATION

PATH

HOBOKEN

Canal Street

HOLLAND TUNNEL

JERSEY CITY

BATTERY PARK

PATH

LIBERTY STATE PARK

ELLIS ISLAND

LIBERTY ISLAND

CAVEN POINT

NEWARK BAY

UPPER NEW YORK BAY

BROOKLYN

BAYONNE

STATEN ISLAND

0        1        2 miles

© Copyright Wallace Roberts & Todd 1994. All Rights Reserved

**Figure 62:** *The lower Hudson River is the site of several important redevelopment initiatives, including a waterfront walkway.*

combined with active and appropriate commercial uses.

Public agencies responsible for guiding waterfront development must realize that the region has a powerful way of spurring economic growth and improving its quality of life. Coastal zone management agencies should not shrink from their responsibility for safeguarding public access. This is the only way to ensure that redeveloping waterfront areas benefits upland residents, businesses, and property owners. Those public authorities and economic development agencies that hold waterfront properties should move forward on redevelopment plans and ensure that their own lands are open to public access, even on an interim basis. Based on the projected costs of creating the proposed 75-acre Brooklyn Bridge Park (a project on public land that includes limited development), creating 20 waterfront parks in urban centers around the region would require about $1 billion in capital costs.

### Neighborhood Parks and Recreation

The region needs a concerted effort to improve the quantity—and even more importantly the quality—of urban parks and recreational spaces. Many urban neighborhoods have less than 1.5 acres of park land per 1,000 people, far below the national urban standard of 8 acres. And many parks that do exist are under utilized due to poor maintenance, lack of recreational programming, and safety issues. These public spaces require additional care and resources. In a time of shrinking city budgets, park needs have often been the first and most heavily cut service.

Involving neighborhood residents through community management strategies can help meet the need. Having local citizens more directly involved in the stewardship of their local parks, on a volunteer or paid basis, can help meet management needs on a smaller budget. Maintaining an increased local presence in the park can also reduce vandalism and help make residents feel more secure when using parks.

Successful efforts to restore Prospect Park and Central Park in New York have shown that substantial private funds can also be raised to help. One special focus could be the dozens of Olmsted and Olmsted-tradition parks in the cities of the region. These parks, like Seaside in Bridgeport, Branch Brook Park in Newark, and Cadwalader Park in Trenton, are often the flagship open spaces in the region's cities. A special Olmsted Park restoration could help make this happen by galvanizing private (and public) support for these parks.

However, private resources are unlikely to meet all the needs of the system. New York City's Parks Council has estimated that creating 100 new park and recreation centers in under-served neighborhoods would cost $195 million in capital costs, plus an additional $20 million annually for maintenance. Enacting such a program in the region's 20 largest cities would cost around $1 billion over the 25-year life of the plan.[46] The most direct way of ensuring adequate park budgets is to make sure that elected officials understand the value of parks and make their management a priority at budget time. New sources of financing, as well as ways of dedicating these funds to park uses, have to be explored as well. The property tax surcharge and the real estate transfer tax described for the reserve areas could be used for urban parks as well. Potential sources that relate specifically to urban parks include special park improvement districts, similar to privately supported business improvement districts, as one possibility. As shown in Bryant Park, improvements paid for by these taxes can help pay for themselves by increasing property values and rents. However, these assessments are likely only to support parks in wealthier areas. Another possible dedicated revenue source is to ensure that concession revenues generated by park structures, places like Shea Stadium and Yankee Stadium, stay within the park system itself. A possibility for funding recreational programs is to assess a charge per professional sports ticket, as

***Figure 63:*** *The quality of urban parks and recreational spaces is essential to making cities livable.*

*Figure 64: In Bryant Park, improvements paid for by a business improvement district resulted in higher rents and property values in adjacent areas.*

is being done in San Francisco. Such a charge could be instituted in both New York City and the towns belonging to the Hackensack Meadowlands Development Commission.

### Managing Urban Natural Resources

Natural resource management in urban areas can be improved by rethinking how environmental mandates can be met by tying the restoration of "green" infrastructure into urban planning programs and funding sources that traditionally focused on "grey" infrastructure.

The "Bluebelt" project on southern Staten Island is one example of a creative public investment strategy. By constructing wetlands and otherwise improving the ability of the island's natural drainage network to handle the rainwater that pours off city streets, New York City has greatly reduced the number of expensive storm sewers it will have to build and has simultaneously provided wildlife habitat and public open space. Another example is the restoration of New York City's Jamaica Bay estuary, where an innovative water quality program is integrating planned treatment system upgrades and the protection and restoration of natural systems and habitat. The results will be improved wildlife and fisheries habitat, new recreational opportunities, and mandated water quality improvements at less than half of the costs of traditional water quality and wildlife management programs. A similar approach could be expanded to restoration of the rest of the region's estuary system. RPA believes

that this would significantly reduce the cost of cleanup during a time of lowered state and federal fiscal capacity—and produce a wide range of wildlife, sport and commercial fishery, and recreational benefits. If the region shifted 5% of its annual $750 million expenditures on coastal wastewater treatment to restoring natural systems, about 20,000 acres of wetlands could be restored in 25 years.

By planting and maintaining the region's urban forest of street trees and backyard woodlots, city streets and neighborhoods benefit in two ways: (1) Through the enhancement of property values and the amenity of public spaces; and (2) by improving the air quality in urban centers where the most violations are concentrated. Existing programs and community "ReLeaf" networks can be supported through direct support and by better connections between tree planting and maintenance needs to development decisions, energy and air quality, street repairs, and other public infrastructure programs. We need to explore other "smart infrastructure" solutions that can help restore the vitality of our community forests. One set of possibilities—reflecting the proven air and water quality and energy conservation benefits of urban forestry—involves using Clean Air Act mitigation funds, climate change programs, road repair, and energy conservation programs to help finance the planting and maintenance of trees in urban areas. A second set of strategies revolves around the possibility of better links between traditional urban planning programs and community forestry objectives. Even where they do exist, many of the tree planting and vegetation retention provisions of local ordinances are inadequately enforced. A major tree planting program in the region—one that helped green urban and suburban neighborhoods by planting 2 million trees and ensured their maintenance for 25 years—would cost about $1 billion.[47]

## A Regional Network of Greenways

Throughout the region, citizens groups, state agencies, and public commissions are planning, funding, and creating greenways. It is not hard to see why. Protected corridors of open space can provide for free flow of people, water, and wildlife—benefits that isolated tracts of land cannot provide.

Greenways are many things. They have trails, scenic roads, and bikeways for recreation and for nonmotorized transportation. They double and triple the value of existing public parks by linking them to neighborhoods and commercial centers that may lack open space. They buffer rivers, streams, and wetlands that cleanse runoff waters and retain floodwaters. They safeguard wildlife and biological diversity by providing continuous vegetative cover between core habitats. And they can help local communities grow smart by defining the open space corridors that should be protected.[48]

Making a greenways network a reality will mean building on the local, grassroots effort that has started more than 75 greenway projects already underway in the region's 31-county area. This can best be done by establishing and maintaining regional programs to help coordinate and link local projects. This type of work is already underway in all three states and New York City:

• Connecticut is helping to foster a statewide greenways network by inventorying local efforts and by encouraging technical assistance to community-based organizations undertaking these projects. Good examples of where towns have come together to establish greenways include the Housatonic River, the Farmington Canal right-of-way, and the Merritt Parkway. The state has recently created a permanent Greenway Council and authorized small capital and planning grant programs. Importantly, the legislation creating these programs mandates that locally designated greenways be recognized by future state agencies in their planning and policies.

• New York State has incorporated the greenways concept in its Open Space Conservation Plan and has recognized a series of state recreationways, including the Delaware and Hudson Canal corridor and the Long Path. The New York Parks and Conservation Association is launching a "Greenways New York" program to foster creation of local greenways. The State Department of Environmental Conservation is creating a handbook and video to encourage local open space planning, including greenways.

• The New Jersey Conservation Foundation is building on earlier efforts by the State Department of Environmental Protection and the Association of New Jersey Environmental Commissions by creating "Greenprint—A Greenway Plan for the State of New Jersey." When completed in 1996, the "Greenprint" will include an inventory of all conservation land in the state and a draft greenways vision that will be used to connect them.

• In New York City a greenway plan created by the Department of City Planning and others is focusing local spending of federal Intermodal Surface Transportation Efficiency Act (ISTEA) money. As a result, highway money is rebuilding a hiking and biking trail along the Shore Parkway in Brooklyn, adding key elements of the Brooklyn/Queens Greenway, and buying the abandoned North Shore Staten Island Railroad right of way. A Metropolitan Greenways Council led by the Neighborhood Open Space Coalition will promote and extend this citywide network.

To foster these citizen-led efforts, the ongoing state-level planning and coordinating initiatives need to be coupled with small grants to local organizations and municipalities. Connecticut has recently passed legislation to do just that. New York and New Jersey should undertake similar efforts. These small expenditures of funds can go a long way when coupled with the energy and efforts of grassroots activists.

Another way to help encourage local efforts is by providing technical assistance. The National Park Service's River and Trail Conservation Assistance Program is an excellent example of how government can help local organizations and municipalities to create and maintain greenways.

Greenways help provide an important alternative to not making the trip by car—important both to reduce congestion and air pollution and as a means of making our transit-friendly cities more livable. Many local greenways are already being built using transportation funding from the Intermodal Surface Transportation Efficiency Act (ISTEA). About $100 million of federal and local funds have been invested in bicycle and pedestrian improvements in all three states since the program's inception.[49]

**Figure 65:** *Greenways are being proposed throughout the region.*

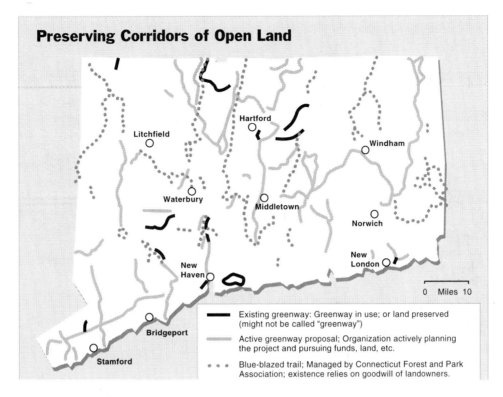

**Figure 66:** *Map of Proposed Connecticut Greenways.*
Source: Connecticut Greenway Committee.

Maintaining this level of support for planning and construction for ten years would require an investment of $1 billion.

## Next Steps

Realizing the Greensward vision will take a concerted effort on the part of thousands of the region's public officials, citizen activists, conservationists, and business leaders. It will take time and effort, political capital, and tough budget decisions.

These are choices that every generation of the region's leadership has had to face. And thus far, they have made them so that the next generation of residents would continue to have green open spaces and clean waters to play in, marvel at, and enjoy. We need only imagine Manhattan without its great green central playground to understand the value of these investments and thinking.

To help move the Greensward forward, RPA is starting three long-term efforts. The first is the creation of an expansive Greensward Network, consisting of representatives from business and the conservation community. The network will provide a vehicle for sharing information and technical assistance. It will work directly and through the media to help raise the region's consciousness about the importance of our green infrastructure. And it will engage public officials to work for the building of the Greensward.

The second effort is the long-term research needed to assess the region's ecological form and function across the range of urban, suburban, and rural landscapes that compose the metropolitan area. The Greensward concept needs to be buttressed by solid ecological and natural resource research about the ecological scarcity, diversity, and representativeness of habitat types within the Greensward areas; the "optimum" size and management policies for remaining patches of open space; and the relationship between the Greensward units and their surroundings. Working in cooperation with scientists at the Institute for Ecosystem Studies, Rutgers University, and the United States Forest Service, RPA will examine ways in which we can best manage and value the functions of this ecological system.

Finally, RPA will work with its partners—conservationists, business leaders, and local, state, and federal officials—to provide the leadership and planning expertise required to build the Greensward through demonstration projects and targeted advocacy.

## Notes

1. Population estimates based on U.S. Census Population data for 1960 and 1990. Land use data from 1962 is "The Tri-State Region and Environs," Regional Plan Association, 1965, and "Urban Land Use in the Tri-State Metropolitan Region," Regional Plan Association and the Center for Remote Sensing and Spatial Analysis, Cook College, Rutgers University, 1995.

2. For example, state park attendance in southern New York State has increased by 32% in the last six years according to the Office of Parks, Recreation and Historic Preservation.

3. USDA Census of Agriculture.

4. U.S. Census of Population.

5. USDA Forest Service, *New York–New Jersey Highlands Regional Study*, 1991. See also Richard Lathrop, *Landscape Ecological Analysis of the Sterling Forest*, Center for Remote Sensing and Spatial Analysis, Cook College, Rutgers University, 1995.

6. Central Pine Barrens Joint Planning and Policy Commission, *Proposed Final Central Pine Barrens Plan*, April 1995.

7. Report of the New York–New Jersey Highlands Work Group, Regional Plan Association, September 1992.

8. Ibid.

9. *A Brief History of the New Jersey Pinelands and the Pinelands Comprehensive Management Plan*, Pinelands Commission, 1989.

10. Annual Report, Pinelands Development Credit Bank, 1992.

11. Patrick Beaton, *The Impact of the Regional Land Use Controls on Property Values: The Case of the New Jersey Pinelands*, 1991.

12. Eagleton Institute of Politics at Rutgers University for the New Jersey Conservation Foundation, 1994.

13. U.S. Census of Population.

14. Central Pine Barrens Joint Planning and Policy Commission, *Final Central Pine Barrens Comprehensive Land Use Plan*, June 1995.

15. National Estuary Program, Peconic Estuary Nomination Document, 1993.

16. Benton MacKaye, *The New Exploration: A Philosophy of Regional Planning*, Harcourt, Brace and Company, Inc., 1928.

17. There are 145,000 acres of open space in the New York–New Jersey Highlands (Hudson to the Delaware River) according to the New York–New Jersey Highlands Regional Study, USDA Forest Service, 1991. There are 12,293 acres in Putnam County, New York; 20,357 acres in the Northwest Planning Region, and 17,000 acres in the Litchfield Hills Planning Region in Connecticut (from Regional Plan Association, *Where the Pavement Ends: The Open Space Imperative #1*, 1987). Nine million visitors includes numbers from major state parks only (from New York–New Jersey Highlands Regional Study, USDA Forest Service, 1991, and Robert Freedman, personal communication, Connecticut Department of Lands and Forests, 1994).

18. There are 4,243 sites where endangered, threatened, or rare plant and animal species are known to occur in the Tri-State region. There are 1,256 sites in the towns encompassing the highlands. Data from Connecticut Department of Environmental Protection, Natural Diversity Database, New York Natural Heritage Program, and New Jersey Natural Heritage Program.

19. The resources of the highlands, and the risks to them, are more fully documented in a number of other recent reports including: USDA Forest Service New York–New Jersey Highlands Regional Study, 1991; Skylands Greenway Task Force, *Skylands Greenway, A Plan for Action*, 1990; New Jersey Conservation Foundation, *The New Jersey Highlands: Treasures at Risk*, 1992.

20. U.S. Census of Population and RPA/NYMTCC Forecasts.

21. Report of the New York–New Jersey Highlands Work Group, Regional Plan Association, September 1992.

22. The trail is a project of the New York–New Jersey Trail Conference, the New Jersey Conservation Foundation, and the National Park Service Rivers and Trails Conservation Assistance Program.

23. Additional information on the Shawangunk and Kittatiny mountains can be found in Erik Kiviat, *The Northern Shawangunks: An Ecological Survey*, Mohonk Preserve, 1988; Peter Fairweather and George Schnell, *The Shawangunk Mountains: A Critical Environmental Area*, Institute for Development, Planning, and Land Use Studies, 1987; David Church and John Myers, *Shawangunk Ridge: Conservation and Design Guidebook*, Catskill Center for Conservation and Development and the New York–New Jersey Trail Conference, 1993; and Karl Beard and Eric Hollman, *The Shawangunk Ridge Trail: A Feasibility Study for Relocating the Long Path*, New

York–New Jersey Trail Conference and National Park Service, February 1990.

24. The Nature Conservancy, the Mohonk Preserve, and a number of state agencies in an effort to fully assemble the biological data and a management strategy needed to protect the unique biological diversity of the ridge in New York State.

25. U.S. Census of Population, 1960 and 1990.

26. David Church and John Myers, *Shawangunk Ridge: Conservation and Design Guidebook*, Catskill Center for Conservation and Development and the New York–New Jersey Trail Conference, 1993.

27. New York City department of Environmental Protection, "Key elements of Watershed Accord," November 1995.

28. Bucks County Conservancy, Delaware River Greenway Factsheet, 1992.

29. Conference of Upper Delaware Townships and the National Park Service, Final River Management Plan: Upper Delaware Scenic and Recreational River, 1986.

30. *Hudson River Estuary Management Plan (Draft)*, New York State Department of Environmental Conservation, September 1990.

31. D.F. Squires and J.S. Barclay, *Nearshore Wildlife Habitats and Populations in the New York/New Jersey Harbor Estuary*, University of Connecticut, 1990.

32. New York State Department of State, *Long Island Sound Coastal Management Program (Draft)*, March 1994.

33. Governor's Coastal Erosion Control Task Force Final Report, Volume II, p. 134, September 1994.

34. Governor's Coastal Erosion Control Task Force Final Report, Volumes I and II and Summary, September 1994.

35. Governor's Coastal Erosion Control Task Force Final Report, Volume II, p. 75, September 1994.

36. USDA Census of Agriculture.

37. All numbers from the American Farmland Trust.

38. Robert D. Yaro et al., *Dealing with Change in the Connecticut River Valley: A Design Manual for Conservation and Development*, 1988; Randall Arendt et al., *Rural by Design*, 1994; Randall Arendt, *Designing Open Space Subdivisions*, 1994; and John Feingold, Robert Pirani, and Graham Trelstad, *Managing Watersheds: Combining Watershed Protection and Community Planning*, Regional Plan Association and the New York City Department of Environmental Protection, 1996.

39. New York City, 1993, "Long Term Watershed Protection and Filtration Avoidance Program"; and New York City department of Environmental Protection, "Key Elements of Watershed Accord," November 1995.

40. John Samatulski and Eric Siy, *Shortchanged: New York State and the Land & Water Conservation Fund*, Environmental Advocates, Albany, NY, 1995.

41. One proposal for reform is contained in National Park System Advisory Board Land and Water Conservation Fund Review Committee, *An American Network of Parks and Open Space: Creating a Conservation Recreation Legacy*, National Park Service and Texas Parks & Wildlife, August 1994.

42. The estimated value of real estate transactions in the region is based on United States Census of Governments, Taxable Property Values for 1986 and Commercial Record, Inc.

43. United States Census of Governments, Taxable Property Values for 1986.

44. See, for example, Tom Fox, *The Value of Parks and Open Space*, Neighborhood Open Space Coalition, 1992.

45. *Urban Forests*, August/September, 1993; E. Gregory McPherson, David Nowak, and Rowan Rowntree, *Chicago's Urban Forest Ecosystem: Results of the Chicago Urban Forest Climate Project*, USDA Forest Service General Technical Report NE-186.

46. The Parks Council and Central Park Conservancy, *Public Space for Public Life*, December 1993.

47. Environmental Action Coalition, *New York City's Urban Forest*, August 1995.

48. See Jonathan Labaree, *How Greenways Work*, National Park Service and Atlantic Center for the Environment, 1992.

49. Rails-to-Trails Conservancy, Enhancement-Funded Projects, Categories 1 and 7, June 1995.

# Chapter 7

# The Centers Campaign

RPA STRONGLY REAFFIRMS the Second Regional Plan's commitment to strengthening the region's city and town centers. The plan's goal of redirecting much of the region's next generation of growth to centers is based on the principle that centers—places that provide housing, jobs, education, shopping, and recreation in close proximity—are the form of community that can deliver the largest number and greatest diversity of opportunities to the largest number and greatest diversity of people. By providing for efficient use of land, energy, infrastructure, and other resources, centers also provide critical benefits to the region's economy and environment. These places are a product of nearly four centuries of human habitation, and they represent the best of our civilization—arts, architecture, and culture. Finally, the region's hundreds of city and town centers provide a permanent organizing framework for future growth in the region. But unless we immediately begin to take concerted action to restore the region's centers, they will decline rather than prosper in the next 25 years.

## Issues

The population and economic growth trend of the last 30 years, and the projected trend into the next century, is away from centers. National studies project "exurbia" as the predominant urban form of the next century.[1] And in the short term, as the region's economy begins to resume some robustness, it is suburban offices, not traditional downtowns, that are filling up most quickly.[2] Earlier chapters have outlined how the region's centers continue to lose population, gain crime, and suffer much higher rates of unemployment than suburban areas. The trends are equally stark in office construction: at the beginning of the 1980s the suburban ring—the 31-county region excluding New York City and New Jersey's Hudson, Essex, and Union counties—accounted for 13% of the region's total inventory. By the 1990s it was at 35%, having tripled its share and added 173 million new square feet of office space in only 10 years.[3]

Centers provide the right balance of economy, equity, and environment that the region needs to fully prosper, but their success is far from inevitable. If we want centers, we will have to work for them. What follows is an action plan to reinvigorate and restructure centers, from Midtown Manhattan to Poughkeepsie, from Bridgeport to Morristown, and from central business districts to small town Main Streets. The arguments for centers are multifaceted, and the solutions to the dilemma are equally complex. So in order to focus the plan, RPA proposes four organizing goals:

- Locate a significant share of new jobs in centers rather than out on the suburban and exurban highways.
- Revitalize inner-city communities by reinforcing community-based organizations and linking them and the residents they serve with the regional economy.
- Reclaim bypassed and derelict brownfield sites for new commercial, industrial, and residential development.
- Attract an expanded share of suburban residential and commercial growth into transit-oriented centers.

Concentrating jobs in centers does not mean that the full economic, cultural, and environmental benefits of centers will automatically follow, but it is an essential start. The region benefits from a strong tradition of downtowns. Specific centers throughout the region may have lost employment and other downtown activities, but overall our cities have held on to almost half of the region's jobs—an impressive achievement considering the decline and collapse of centers in other American metropolitan areas. Vital downtowns have been one of the region's great strengths. But new jobs created during the past 25 years have gone overwhelmingly to suburban communities, which have gained almost 2 million jobs while the urban core has lost 300,000 jobs.[4] The region has the potential to gain 2.5 million jobs in the next 25 years, both in payroll employment and sole proprietorships. A critical issue to the success of the plan is where these jobs will be located.

Many of these suburban areas have begun to run out of room to grow, as traffic congestion and rising housing prices force new businesses to consider locating elsewhere in the region.[5] Which way will they head—back in, or farther out? That is a critical choice, one that thousands of regional businesses will face again and again over the next 25 years. And it sets up an overarching question for the region; whether it will choose to facilitate growth far away from the core and outside of regional downtowns, or find the leadership to redirect growth to centers.

It is time to set up a benchmark goal for the nearly 2 million new payroll jobs projected between 1995 and 2020. RPA proposes working toward putting 1 million jobs in newly strengthened regional downtowns. We must develop the initiatives and strategies to help regional downtowns keep their share of employment. Keeping their share is an extraordinarily ambitious goal and is in direct contrast to recent trends. If centers do not get half of the new jobs, they may lose the critical mass that still gives them a leading role in the region's economy. One broad goal is for regional downtowns to maintain as many as possible of the region's export industry jobs—employment that caters to national and international markets. Cities with regional downtowns certainly have the space to support another million jobs. There are about 50 million square feet of existing empty office space in downtown cores, room for 250,000 jobs, and this space can be supplemented by infilling and expanding existing successful centers and revitalizing others.

In addition, by defining regional downtowns by their municipal boundaries rather than by the smaller area of their mixed-use cores, the plan emphasizes the importance of centering a variety of jobs, not only downtown-type office jobs. While these other jobs may not directly contribute to maintaining and rebuilding a mixed-use center, they do fulfill economic, equity, and environmental objectives by focusing development on already urbanized land, locating new jobs near mixed-income populations, and bringing taxable income to municipalities that need it most.

The plan's priority is to focus new jobs in these regional downtowns. But it also recognizes that many new jobs will be located elsewhere. For one thing, many new jobs serve local markets apart from the region's downtowns. Yet this does not mean that the rest of the million jobs must inevitably locate on greenfield sites, consuming open land and leading to more congested roads. The plan proposes that emerging suburban centers, from Hauppauge to Parsippany, can be retrofitted, or made more town-like, if offices, shops, and parks are placed within walking distance of each other. More important, the region's existing constellation

| Year | Payroll | Proprietorships | Total |
| --- | --- | --- | --- |
| 1995 | 8,899,000 | 1,584,000 | 10,483,000 |
| 2000 | 10,743,000 | 2,235,000 | 12,978,000 |

*Figure 67: Projected Job Growth.*
Source: NYMTC Baseline Projections.

of compact communities should be built upon, from traditional mixed-use centers like New Rochelle, New York; Waterbury, Connecticut; or Elizabeth, New Jersey, to smaller residential centers like Madison, New Jersey, to compact communities within the Greensward like Hunter, New York.

## Implementing a Centers Strategy

Implementing this centers strategy will require coordinated efforts by every level of government, business, and community groups. Elements of a successful strategy should include:

- State growth management systems in all three states that discourage growth in rural areas and encourage growth in centers. These systems could implement urban growth boundaries, urban service limits, and incentives or requirements for communities to adopt plans and regulations consistent with these goals.

- Regional reforms designed to reduce inequities between urban and suburban taxes and to share social service and affordable housing responsibilities more fairly.

- Municipal plans and investments that improve urban quality of life and public service delivery, including schools and public safety.

- Increased efforts by businesses to locate or expand operations in downtown locations and coordinate development and redevelopment of these places.

## Regional Design Principles

RPA's Second Regional Plan pointed out the dangers associated with the emerging suburban patterns of retail strips and malls, office parks, and large lot subdivisions that even in the 1960s were seen as damaging to the character of landscapes and communities. The Second Plan also warned against abandoning older urban communities. These admonitions went largely unheeded here and nearly everywhere else in metropolitan America, as we built a new civilization around the interstate highways and the automobile and walked away from cities and older suburban neighborhoods.

In many places suburban highways have become choked with traffic. Air and water quality have deteriorated as vast areas of former countryside have been replaced with suburban sprawl. Communities that encouraged this growth to expand their tax rolls now face rising demand for services and infrastructure and revolts from hard-pressed tax payers. High housing prices, exacerbated by rising land values, command a larger share of everyone's resources. And these residents, who now must live with congestion and sky-high tax bills and mortgage payments, find their lives to be less convenient, less safe, and less connected to their neighbors and communities. Yet many of the cities and older suburbs they left have become even less attractive and safe as a result of urban neglect and concentrated poverty. Facing these trends, growing numbers of the region's residents seek refuge by moving even farther out into the suburbs and exurbs, threatening to repeat these patterns in outer rings of the region. Many residents choose to leave the region altogether, in search of greater quality of life and economic opportunity.

In response to these trends, a number of individuals, including Andres Duany and Elizabeth Plater-Zyberk from Florida and Peter Calthorpe from California, have come together under the banner of the Congress for the New Urbanism (CNU). CNU has begun to promote alternative models for suburban growth, generally based on the concept of building new, planned, compact, mixed-use village and town centers. Most of these models have emerged in parts of the country that do not share the region's tradition of compact, transit-oriented village and town centers. Many of these new town plans are based on older models of town planning—including the work of early 20th century British and American planners from the Garden City Movement, including Raymond Unwin, Frederick Law Olmsted, Jr., and John Nolen—which were first promoted in this country by RPA's 1929 Regional Plan.[6] These trends have formed an important movement in planning and architecture, and they have improved the design of new communities and brought contextualism back into urban design.

But today the Tri-State Metropolitan Region is a mature region and does not require the development of a significant number of new towns, since much of our built environment consists of literally hundreds of traditional towns, villages, and hamlets, many with access to the regional rail system, and with room for significant infill and expansion. For this reason this plan seeks more to refocus development and investment in existing centers than to create new development at the region's edge,

*Figure 68: The Tri-State Metropolitan Region has such a wealth of existing downtowns, such as Scarsdale, New York, that it does not need any new town developments in the suburban ring.*

even if new planning models are a significant improvement on post–World War II suburban sprawl.

Most successful centers evolve over generations, eventually forming a network of established communities. The challenge here, and in other metropolitan regions that developed around rail systems, is to revitalize, rebuild, round-out, and gradually infill the existing constellation of town centers. But where suburban sprawl already exists, or where brownfields are being reclaimed, the principles of the new urbanism could be applied to create new centers, retrofitting density onto sprawl. And in some Greensward areas, small, well-sited new communities could also be designed around these principles. These issues are summarized below and represent RPA's fundamental planning and design philosophy for centers, both here and in other regions.[7]

• *Design with regions in mind.* Regions must provide the organizing structure and context for all community plans and architecture since they embody the basic environmental, cultural, and economic unity within which we all live and work.

• *Build upon each region's natural and cultural structure.* Every region has a unique *raison d'être* and a natural setting, cultural tradition, and settlement pattern that must provide the foundation for new plans and designs. Pioneer regionalist Benton MacKaye declared

that the planner's responsibility is to reveal each region's inherent potential, not to impose his or her own solutions. MacKaye also asserted that people need access to towns, countrysides, and wilderness to be fulfilled as human beings, requiring that we make plans that maintain accessibility to all three of these settings.[8]

• *Rebuild and reclaim communities first.* We have a special responsibility to rebuild the cities and suburbs damaged by post–World War II development patterns. We must reclaim, infill, and expand existing communities before building on greenfield sites. This is, again, particularly appropriate in the Tri-State Metropolitan Region, where there is a well-developed network of traditional village, town, and city centers.

## Summary of Recommendations

RPA wants to see tremendous job growth in the region's existing centers over the next 25 years—with more than a million new jobs distributed across the Central Business District; among 11 regional downtowns within the region's larger core area; and throughout a constellation of compact, smaller, centered towns that are rail-served, walkable communities built around a main street or a mini-downtown. At the same time RPA also wants to see suburban edge cities, the expected recipients of perhaps another million new jobs, take on the characteristics of true centers and become vibrant, 24-hour-a-day communities.

The health of the region's Central Business District—which has recently outgrown its historic, high-rise, Manhattan origins—is fundamental to the well-being of the region. (The new CBD, still anchored in Midtown and Downtown Manhattan, has now spread across a state line and two rivers, and takes in Downtown Brooklyn and Long Island City, on the east side of the East River, as well as a stretch of Jersey City and part of the west bank of the Hudson.) The CBD is still the great engine that moves the region's economy and the great magnet that pulls in new talent from around the world.

But beyond bolstering the CBD, why should this region put so much energy into re-centering itself over the next 25 years? Because businesses, the arts, research, and learning all thrive in centers. Because centers are one of the transforming forces that make us distinctively human—places where ideas are sparked and prejudices can be shed.

RPA's regional re-centering campaign proposed four key actions:

1. Strengthen the region's Central Business District.

   • Transform Midtown Manhattan into a Crosstown District served by the Crosstown Light-Rail Loop.

   • Coordinate transit initiatives to connect Lower Manhattan to regional rail with an effort to guarantee the district's role as a global financial center.

   • Strengthen Downtown Brooklyn's civic identity by improving the quality of public spaces and by linking educational, cultural, commercial, and transportation assets.

   • Revitalize Long Island City with new *Rx* transportation links and development, including new offices for an expanded United Nations.

   • Develop a new mass transit system and better public access to the Jersey City and Hudson River waterfront.

2. Invest in 11 regional downtowns.

   • Attract the remainder of job growth to compact centers throughout the region.

   • Build on the region's natural and cultural structure of rail-served centers and connect to new infrastructure initiatives including *Rx*.

   • Rebuild and reclaim communities before building on greenfield sites.

3. Create incentives for new development and investment in transit- and pedestrian-friendly centers.

   • Implement planning techniques in the region's centers, from special improvement districts, to revising zoning to encourage higher density, to community-based jobs and development initiatives.

   • Work with municipalities and community groups to oppose anti-center development such as remote, free-standing office and retail development.

   • Implement mixed-use planning and design principles to guide development and redevelopment throughout the region.

4. Support new institutions and uses in centers.

   • Link urban and rural communities with the regional economy by encouraging "telematic" at-home businesses to locate in small towns, villages, and other compact centers.

   • Support arts, culture, and preservation planning as crucial techniques for stabilizing and building viable centers.

# The Region's Central Business District

Investments in the region's center must begin with an understanding of its importance—in particular New York City and Manhattan—to the economic, social, and environmental goals of the entire region. If the region's Central Business District falters, the results will be continued economic decline, social isolation, and spread development that further polarizes our society and ravages the last remaining open spaces in the region.

## Crosstown

RPA is proposing that we build a new identity, easier access, and new development opportunities in *Crosstown*—the Manhattan district between 32nd and 44th Streets, from river to river—that would serve an expanded role as the region's crossroads. RPA has worked with a committee of architects to suggest ways to integrate transit improvements (including new or renovated regional gateways at Penn Station, Grand Central Terminal, the Herald Square PATH terminal, the North River Ferry Terminal, and several new *Rx* rail stations) and a proposed Crosstown Light-Rail Loop with a system of civic design improvements. Already, six business improvement districts have significantly improved security, sanitation, and streetscapes in portions of the Crosstown District. And a proposal to build a light-rail system along 42nd Street from the East River to the Hudson River has focused attention on the issue of surface transportation improvements in the region's core. RPA proposes to build on this progress and generate a positive new identity for the district in much the same way that Paris integrated its new *RER* rail system with a set of *Grands Projets*—civic design improvements, new museums, public spaces, and refurbished avenues. Paris has seen extraordinary benefits in both image and vitality. Major opportunities exist in the Crosstown District for new commercial and residential development and the creation of new public spaces, particularly in areas west of Eighth Avenue that will become more accessible by the proposed light-rail system.

Central to the Crosstown concept is the creation of a light-rail loop that would serve to connect at street level all the elements of the existing transit system. In doing so it would also link most of the district's tourist attractions (see Plate 2D). The combined effect is a new service for tourists, residents, and commuters. As a street trolley it will become a recognizable, permanent, and positive presence and a unifying force for Manhattan. The route will extend a proposal by the 42nd Street Development Corporation to run a line from the United Nations Headquarters on the East River to the Hudson River and down past the Javits Center. RPA's proposed Crosstown Light-Rail Loop would extend this service from the Convention Center east past Penn Station and on to Herald Square. There it would turn northward up Broadway through the theater district to Columbus Circle and Lincoln Center. Broadway would be closed to through traffic to Columbus Circle. Between Columbus Circle and Lincoln Center, Broadway would run one-way northbound. The effect would be to unlock some of the most gridlocked intersections in Manhattan—Columbus Circle, Herald Square, and Times Square—and to open up the Duffy Square and Times Square area as one of the great public spaces in the world, befitting an entertainment district. The closing of traffic would be consistent with RPA's policy of limiting road capacity into and out of Manhattan.

The light-rail loop would be available with an all-you-can-ride ticket, serving everyone—tourists, residents, workers. Anyone entering Crosstown by any form of public transit—by commuter rail at Grand Central or Penn Station, commuter bus at the Port Authority Bus Terminal, PATH at 33rd Street, Amtrak at Penn Station, by every one of the 16 subway lines serving midtown, and even by ferry at the Hudson River and eventually the East River—would be just steps from the light-rail line. When access to the region's airports is provided via the two rail terminals (see discussion of airport access in *Mobility*), air passengers will also be served.

In 1994 RPA convened a panel of architects and urban designers, chaired by Robert Geddes, to consider potential transformations in the region's core that could be realized through Crosstown. The images in Plates 2E through 2K present some ideas about how different parts of Crosstown could be transformed by urban design initiatives that correlate to targeted investments and a new light-rail system. RPA presents this work as the opening of a new dialogue and a vision for the region's center.

### Lower Manhattan

RPA proposes the creation improved *Rx* rail links to Midtown, Long Island, the Hudson Valley, southwest Connecticut, New Jersey, and the airports, making the Lower Manhattan financial district one of the most accessible places in the region. These improvements would address perhaps the single most important reason for the decline of the region's second largest employment center—its inaccessibility from most of the region. But these transit improvements should be combined with efforts to preserve Lower Manhattan's special architectural character. Incorporating almost a century of notable towers, it is the world's foremost skyscraper district. Elements of this strategy are being proposed by the city, the Lower Manhattan Alliance for Downtown New York (the district's new business improvement district, or BID), and others. These include:

- Efforts by the BID and city to restore the concentrated downtown that attracts workers, residents, and tourists by reclaiming historic public spaces, adding pedestrian streets, and other improvements.

- The proposed Downtown Heritage Trails network and visitors' hub, which will secure the district's role as a major tourist and cultural destination.

- Proposals by the New School for Social Research and the New York City Planning Commission to create a special zoning district, preserving the area's historic character while permitting the creation of residential and mixed-use buildings and districts and to expand the ratio of workers to residents in the district to something approaching Midtown's 8 to 1 ratio.

- A proposal by the BID, the New York City Partnership, and a consortium of media and telecommunications companies to create incubator space for the city's burgeoning new media industry.

- A set of short-term real estate and tax incentives to rebuild confidence in the district and jump-start redevelopment.

Collectively, these strategies could position downtown to attract a stimulating new mix of industries, services, and residents that complement and reinforce the district's core finance and government sectors. Combined with a strategic plan for all the other significant downtowns in the region's Central Business District, which now includes Downtown Brooklyn, Jersey City, and Long Island City, the result could be the reemergence of Lower Manhattan as one of the most exciting and magnetic centers in the world.

### Downtown Brooklyn

RPA is following up on past work in helping to forge a powerful identity for Downtown Brooklyn, an integral part of the region's Central Business District that has the potential to become a new kind of modern metropolitan center.[9] To achieve this, RPA and the Downtown Brooklyn community have developed a comprehensive master plan for the area.

Downtown Brooklyn has all the ingredients of a great downtown: a ceremonial entrance, via the Brooklyn Bridge, to a civic park and an historic city hall; seven institutions of higher education; world-class cultural institutions; an active pedestrian-oriented retail area; a state-of-the-art office and acad-emic complex; headquarters of major government agencies and federal and state courts; a commuter rail system and excellent public transit access; a diverse population; and historic brownstone neighborhoods. Downtown Brooklyn boasts one-quarter of a million workers and visitors daily and serves a population of 2.3 million residents.[10]

But these ingredients need to be brought together through infrastructure connections, institutional cooperation, and other initiatives to help Downtown Brooklyn capitalize on its strengths, including its vital location at the center of the Tri-State Metropolitan Region and inclusion in the region's Central Business District. Despite the potential of Downtown Brooklyn to offer all the amenities an employee, student, and resident might want, there is considerable expression of dissatisfaction among these groups, mostly centered around the need to improve the image of Downtown Brooklyn. The problems of image have been traced

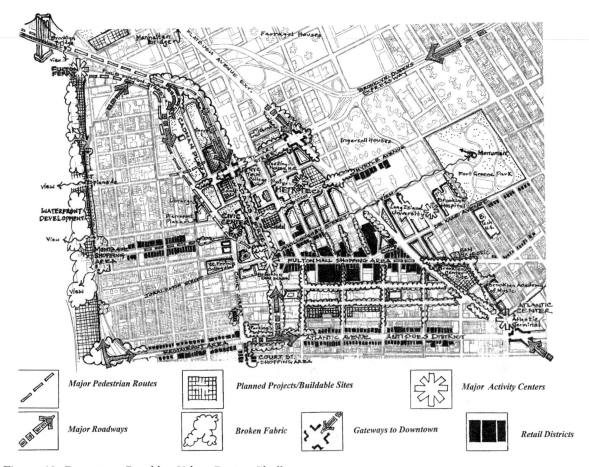

**Figure 69:** *Downtown Brooklyn Urban Design Challenges.*

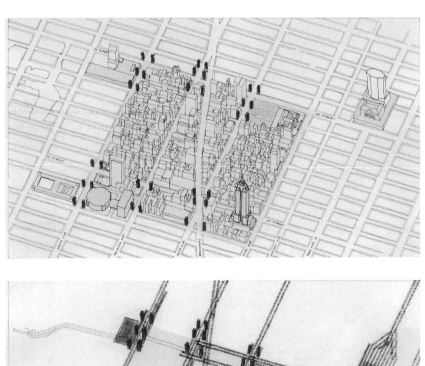

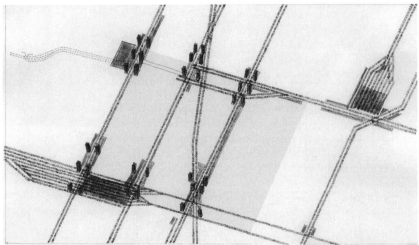

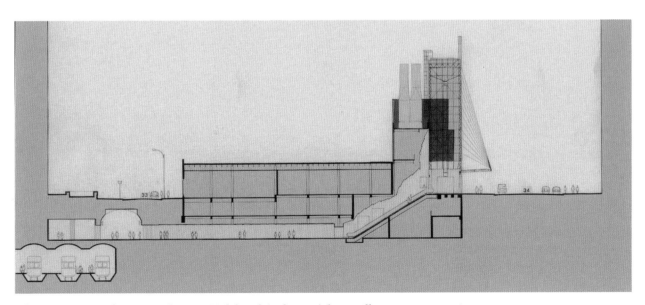

**Plate 2K:** R.M. Kliment & Frances Halsband Architects' design illustrates connections between subways, commuter trains, and the sidewalk grid. Crystal pavilions marking the presence of the vast subterranean transit network would be the real gateways to Crosstown, welcoming and sheltering travelers, bringing light into the tunnels, and providing orientation points at the entrances to the city.

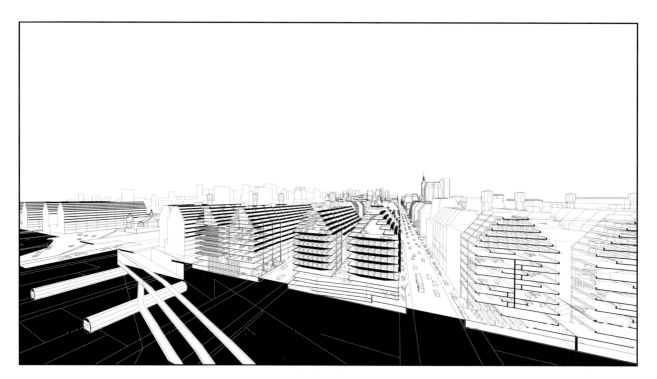

**Plate 2I:** *The extensive transportation system west of the garment center might easily support greater bulk than the current zoning allows, if it is made to serve an intensive 24-hour pattern of mixed uses. Colin Cathcart's design advocates flexible loft structure and use permits; the mapping of tolerance levels for noise, vibration, traffic, and other nuisances; and a new sunlight-derived building envelope.*

**Plate 2J:** *Jane Thompson (Thompson & Wood) would transform Pershing Square into a worthy facade to Grand Central Terminal, a forecourt that unites the two sides of Park Avenue with a square studded with shade trees, benches, and cafe tables. The arch under the viaduct bridge would be reopened, while Park Avenue would be closed to automobiles from 40th to 42nd Street and converted into a pedestrian park.*

Swimming Pool/ Pier

Light Rail Station

Hudson River Park

Existing Warehouse Converted to Entertainment Complex

Ferris Wheel

Potential Park Expansion

Amphitheater/ Outdoor Cinema

Running Track

Sports Complex

Park/ Sports Complex Entrance

Light Rail Port Authority Station

Existing Tunnel Ventilation Shaft

Light Rail Station

Convention Center

Reflecting/ Wading Pool

Park Entrance Ramp

Sunken Forest/ Tunnel Entrance

**Plate 2H:** *Wayne Berg's proposal for Clinton Park claims the space created by the Port Authority Bus Terminal's elevated road structure and right of way for public use without impeding transit. The plan would create an urban park by developing the space under and between the elevated roadways for public uses. The space above—elevated to allow continued vehicular circulation—would be a park running from 9th Avenue to the Hudson River, where it would tie into the planned Hudson River Park along Manhattan's waterfront.*

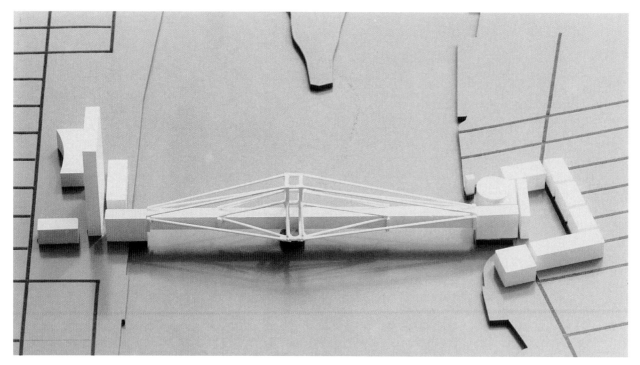

**Plate 2F:** *Robert Geddes' design proposes that the United Nations construct a bridge over the East River, connecting the existing UN headquarters at 42nd Street to a new United Nations Square on the Queens riverfront. The two-level pedestrian bridge would be a modern version of the Ponte Vecchio in Florence, with public cable-car and pedestrian promenades, meeting rooms, offices, shops, restaurants, and lounges for delegates and the public.*

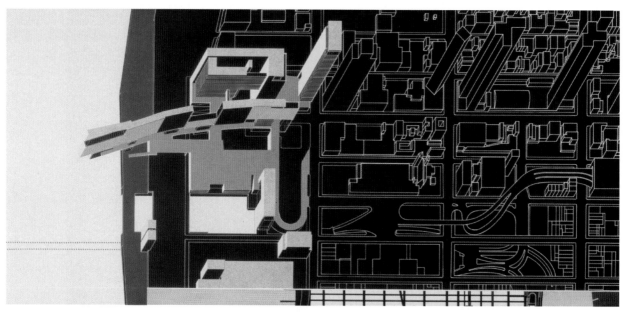

**Plate 2G:** *Keenen/Riley's schematic proposes multiple levels of public space, connected by pedestrian and automotive circulation, for a northern anchor to the Javits Convention Center and a westside locus along the Hudson River: a center with diverse functions, interior and exterior spaces, and building types including a hotel and ferry terminal, an extension to the convention center, a commerce center, a residential tower and a water treatment plant. The proposal is inspired by the urban elements of the surrounding infrastructure—tunnels, bridges, ramps, and exhaust towers.*

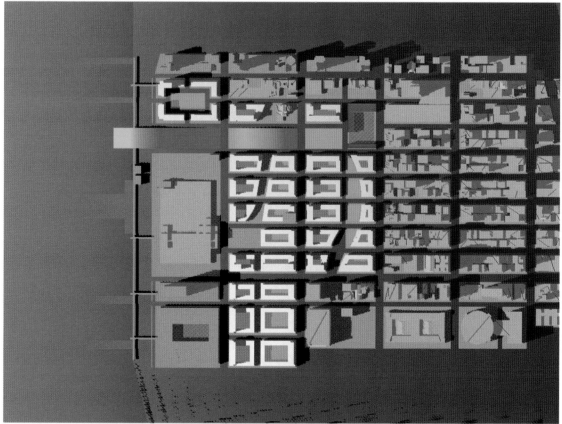

***Plate 2E:*** *Max Bond's design (with Navid Maghami) focuses on the empty lots and abandoned buildings west of 9th Avenue. To reinforce the fabric, strengthen the local street network, and create a neighborhood, positive elements are improved and missing ones introduced. Parks and buildings cover ramps (which are placed in tunnels), and a rolling park connects the Port Authority Bus Terminal to the Javits Convention Center.*

**Plate 2C:** *Two views of an urban industrial waterfront: at present a mix of working and derelict factories and dumps, and after reclamation.*

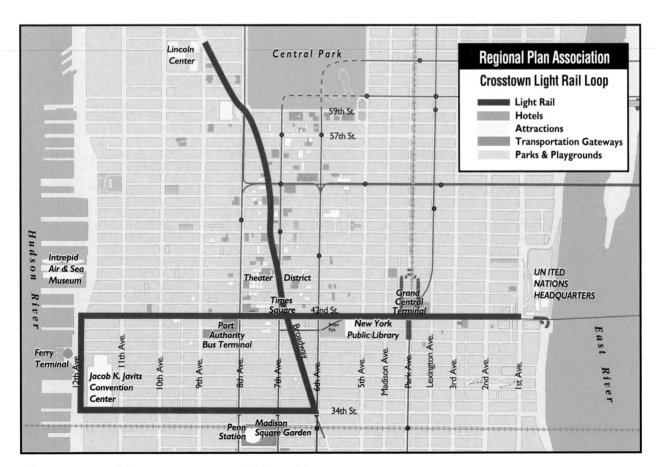

**Plate 2D:** *Map of the Crosstown area and light-rail line.*

**Plate 2B:** *Three views of an exurban highway cloverleaf interchange: at the present (upper left), as it will look with current development patterns (upper right), and how it could look if reoriented around its village center and rail station (lower left).*

*Plate 2A:* *Three views of northern New Jersey: at the present (upper left), as it will look with current development patterns (upper right), and how it could look if developed in accordance with regional design principles (lower left).*

to a perception of danger on streets at night, a lack of cohesiveness in the urban fabric, an undefined sense of place, and the unattractiveness of certain parts of downtown.

General goals and specific recommendations that have been identified for the revitalization of Downtown Brooklyn include:

- Make Downtown Brooklyn a vibrant, 24-hour community with an exciting mix of activities. Improve security and perceptions of safety by coordinating efforts of the local BIDs and the 84th Precinct; pursue development of a central university center or dormitory facilities shared by local campuses; and increase opportunities for after-hours entertainment.

- Improve the physical environment and appearance of Downtown Brooklyn, creating connections between activity centers. Improve the storefronts and facades of streets, encourage the development or temporary use of empty lots, improve the pedestrian environment and bicycle access, and examine the feasibility of a shuttle transit service.

- Provide stores and restaurants that better satisfy Downtown Brooklyn employees and residents of nearby communities. Foster retail development, particularly in the Willoughby Corridor and Myrtle Avenue, and encourage the development of the proposed BAM cultural district.

- Utilize Downtown Brooklyn's higher education institutions to improve the economy. Establish a consortium of higher education business programs, coordinate higher education and cultural institutions, and encourage local employees to take advantage of nearby educational and cultural opportunities.

- Persuade city, state, and federal leaders to continue substantial investment in Downtown Brooklyn. Fund capital projects, including renovation of the LIRR Terminal and subway station at Atlantic Avenue, and maintain the commitment of various government agencies to stay in offices and facilities in Downtown Brooklyn. Resist efforts to move current government functions away.

- Promote greater coordination of Downtown Brooklyn's communities and leadership to implement these and other recommendations.

## Long Island City

Recently, in response to consolidation of industrial uses, city officials and Amtrak have proposed to create an expanded office and media employment center in Long Island City, focusing on a new intermodal transit facility serving Amtrak, the LIRR, and NJ TRANSIT, as well as improved subway service. RPA's proposed *Rx* service to Westchester and Long Island could also improve service to this location. Building conversions and new construction would proceed within a well-defined district between Queens Plaza and the Citicorp Tower, and eventually on air rights over the Sunnyside Yards—all linked to a revitalized Queens West waterfront. Recent plans have the potential to strongly tie this district to Manhattan and to suburban residential and employment centers, offering the long-term possibility of making a renewed Long Island City another vital part of the region's Central Business District.

Revitalization of Long Island City may also play an important role in the future of the United Nations and the region. Recent studies have urged the UN to consolidate its globally dispersed operations to give more coordination and coherency to the organization. So if the United Nations is going to remain in New York, it is likely that it will have to expand. New development in Long Island City at Queens West and RPA's proposed Crosstown Light-Rail Loop would provide both room to grow and improved access to the entire region, better serving an expanded UN organization in the region.

## Jersey City and the Hudson River Waterfront

RPA's 1966 report, *The Lower Hudson*, presented the tremendous development and open space opportunities posed by abandoned industrial and transportation facilities on New Jersey's waterfront. Three decades later the promise of the New Jersey "Gold Coast" is just starting to be realized. During the late 1980s as many as 40,000 residential units and 33 million square feet were proposed for the waterfront from the George Washington Bridge to Bayonne. While many of these projects were never completed, major office, residential, and retail complexes at Exchange Place and Newport are now close to capacity.

There are two key issues that still govern the redevelopment potential of the area. First is the development of a mass transit system so that valuable waterfront land does not need to be dedicated to roadways or parking lots. A waterfront light-rail line linking Exchange Place in Jersey City with other waterfront development areas, with the NJ TRANSIT Station in Hoboken, and with Park and Ride lots in the Meadowlands will soon be under construction. The second is the need to ensure that redevelopment enhances the public's physical and visual access to the waterfront so that upland businesses and residents can share the value of this tremendous open space asset. The Hudson River Waterfront Walkway, a proposed 18-mile continuous pedestrian boulevard, has been completed only in sections. With construction contingent on the developers moving ahead on waterfront projects, the walkway has fallen victim both to the slowed market and to unwillingness of some developers to fulfill their obligation under New Jersey's coastal zone management regulations.

## Regional Downtowns

RPA believes that the region's 11 established transit-served downtowns could accommodate a significant portion of projected employment growth. And this employment growth could be supplemented by new development in the adjacent brownfields.

- *The Tri-State Metropolitan Region's Central Business District:* Incorporating Manhattan up to 72nd Street; consists of three other downtowns, including Downtown Brooklyn, downtown Long Island City, and Jersey City and adjacent areas on the Hudson River waterfront.

- *Eleven Regional Downtowns:* New Haven, Bridgeport, Stamford, White Plains, Poughkeepsie, Hicksville, Mineola, Jamaica, Trenton, New Brunswick, and Newark. These places have the necessary underpinnings of transit and mixed-use center infrastructure to rebuild and expand, with the potential of *Rx* service further tying them tightly into the regional economy and allowing them to take on hundreds of thousands of new jobs.

- *Brownfield Sites within and Adjacent to the Urban Core and Regional Downtowns:* The region, RPA estimates, has more than 50,000 acres of virtually abandoned urbanized land that could be profitably redeveloped with state and public–private initiatives, keeping jobs and revenues close to existing centers rather than dissipating them to greenfield sites.

RPA's 11 regional downtowns are defined according to whether municipalities had: (1) existing mixed-use centers with a strong share of area employment; (2) the building blocks needed for expanding and improving a downtown center; (3) good, high-frequency, two-way rail service; and (4) recent or upcoming significant transit or intermodal improvements. In other words, the infrastructure and the quality of life, or its potential, to support new jobs (see Figure 70). Regional downtowns need not necessarily fit some predetermined paradigm to prosper and attract new jobs; rather they will be municipalities that can muster the greatest combined public–private commitment.

Despite supply-side advantages of infrastructure and institutions, most regional downtowns require powerful and sustained strategies to attract new employers. Even though these centers have retained large numbers of jobs, many of these places remain less appealing, convenient, safe, and pedestrian- and transit-friendly than they must be to attract a significant share of projected employment growth. That downtown enhancement initiatives can work is demonstrated by the experience of Stamford, New Brunswick, Jamaica, and Downtown Brooklyn—where revitalization efforts have had important successes—and several of the region's business improvement districts. These districts are examples of how a partnership of interests can attract and keep jobs. Private initiative, community input, and the public tools of planning—zoning, incentives, and master plans—can be effective when they are part of a well-conceived and deftly carried out strategy.

Construction of the New Jersey Waterfront Light-Rail line is scheduled to begin soon, linking Jersey City and other New Jersey employment centers with PATH, NJ TRANSIT, and *Rx*. In Newark a new performing arts center is being built as a strong cultural anchor for the downtown's continued rebirth. Stamford is exploring ways to create pedestrian friendly links between its transportation center and expanding downtown employment districts. Bridgeport is working to revitalize its waterfront as a major recreation and tourism destination. And New Brunswick is expanding its cultural and residential/business districts.

RPA believes that if these and other downtowns are to succeed in attracting their fair share of employment growth, the concepts being developed and applied in Crosstown, Lower Manhattan, Downtown Brooklyn, and others—such as integrating transit and *Rx* accessibility with strong civic

| | Does the Center have... | | | | |
| Center | Existing mixed-use center with viable residential and high share of area employment? | Building blocks for expanding mixed-use center? | Two or more rail lines coming together? | Good high-frequency two-way rail transit? | Recent or upcoming major transit and/or intermodal improvement? |
|---|---|---|---|---|---|
| Regional Central Business District | yes 2,000,000 (3.7 million with all five boroughs) | yes | yes | yes | yes |
| New Haven | yes 86,227 | yes | yes | yes | moderate |
| Bridgeport | yes 62,492 | yes | no | yes | no |
| Stamford | yes 78,754 | yes | yes | yes | yes |
| White Plains | yes 59,711 | yes | no | yes | yes |
| Poughkeepsie | moderate 23,768 | yes | no | yes | no |
| Hicksville | moderate 24,107 | yes | yes | yes | moderate |
| Mineola | moderate 17,963 | yes | yes | yes | yes |
| Jamaica | yes (see NYC) | yes | yes | yes | yes |
| Newark | yes 152,585 | yes | yes | yes | yes |
| New Brunswick | yes 32,265 | yes | no | yes | no |
| Trenton | yes 57,808 | yes | yes | yes | yes |

**Figure 70:** *Regional Downtown Matrix.*
Source: Figures are from *Journey to Work,* U.S. Census Bureau, Washington, D.C., 1990.

design; building on strong arts and cultural institutions; providing pedestrian amenities; and other quality of life improvements—must be applied to all of these centers. And they must receive the continual support of state governments and business.

### Brownfield Sites

RPA sees the region's vast accumulation of abandoned industrial sites and trash dumps—brownfield sites—as a tremendous potential asset. Other world metropolitan regions, including Tokyo, London, Paris, and Berlin, have regional economic development efforts that recognize these assets: brownfields make better use of land that has already been urbanized. In New Jersey RPA has inventoried abandoned industrial sites and landfills in Union County (one of the core urban counties that has lost employment in the past 25 years) and reached the conclusion that reclaimed brownfields can accommodate that county's development needs for decades to come. RPA worked with a Danish devel-

oper to reclaim one of the largest of these sites, a former city dump and industrial area in Elizabeth between the New Jersey Turnpike and Newark Bay. This site is being recycled for a major retail development that would otherwise have ended up miles away on a greenfield site—never before developed and out on the edge of the region. It is estimated that this project will create 5,000 permanent and 1,700 construction jobs, and it will generate $3.6 million a year in taxes for the city of Elizabeth.[11]

The Union County inventory revealed several important issues. It identified more than 185 sites, totaling over 2,500 acres of redevelopable land in the county. One-tenth of this land would be sufficient to accommodate Union County's projected employment growth to the year 2010. The inventory also found that the sites were larger than expected, averaging 14 acres each, and cleaner than expected. More than half of them either do not require state-mandated cleanup, are now getting cleaned up, or have already been treated and are now available for development. The costs of devel-

*Figure 71: White Plains, New York, is a regional downtown that has grown through new investments in the last 30 years.*

Region includes hundreds of compact communities located on commuter rail lines, from exurban hamlets to bedroom communities to significant mixed-use centers. Most have the potential to be reinforced and expanded, to bolster their own economies and livability, and at the same time to more fully support the regional economy and the rail transit system.

What these transit-friendly communities offer the region is choice. RPA has no expectation that all of a community's working residents will walk to the train station and ride the train in the morning. There are too many alternatives and too many destinations for that scenario. Even in a functioning transit-friendly community such as Scarsdale, the percentage of work trips fulfilling the traditional

oping these sites compares favorably with those for suburban sites. Finally, the project generated a public–private task force of community leaders, the developer, and public officials. The presence of this group and the appointment of a state-level case manager gave everyone involved a sense that this was a priority project and helped push state permit applications to the top of the pile. A local coordinator did the same at the local level. As a result, all permits were issued in less than a year—record time.[12] A prerequisite for this successful experience was New Jersey's Industrial Sites Recovery Act, which clarified issues relating to owners' liability and tied reclamation standards to proposed new uses. These provisions should be adopted in New York and Connecticut.

## Transit- and Pedestrian-Friendly Centers

Many of the issues, principles, and solutions for the Tri-State Metropolitan Region's Central Business District and downtowns come down to a set of strategies that apply to a range of community types. These transit-friendly principles are dedicated to sustaining and enhancing communities in which the basic experiences of life, work, schools, commerce, and recreation are accessible without multiple automobile trips. Unlike most other metropolitan areas in the country, the Tri-State Metropolitan

*Figure 72: Brownfield sites, often located close to the region's center and existing infrastructure, offer new potential for development and growth in the region.*

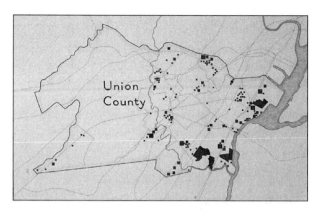

*Figure 73: Union County Brownfield Sites.*

pattern of a New York City rail commute rests at 30%.[13] But sustaining that option—whether in the region's commuter rail towns, along Newark's subway line, in the New York City boroughs serviced by the subway, or from center cities to the suburbs—is extremely valuable to the sustainability of air quality, mobility, and general quality of life. Most Americans have been given no choices at all of how to get to work—it is the private automobile or stay at home. But here in our region, we do not *have* to take a car to get to work.

Transit-friendly and pedestrian-friendly designs form a continuum. Any user of transit is inevitably a pedestrian, whether walking to the rail station in Mount Kisco, walking to the bus stop in Montclair, or walking from the subway station to the office in New York City. Inevitably, the transit user must move through public space, ranging from train stations to plazas to sidewalks, and if those public spaces are unsafe, dirty, ugly, or without any amenity, the strength of transit and the life of centers will decline simultaneously.

Zoning, design, and business changes can all have positive impacts on transit- and pedestrian-friendly communities. While each change should be considered on the merits of individual circumstances, RPA proposes the following strategies for promoting centers in the region:

1. Recommendations regarding zoning changes for buildings include:

   • Mixed-use development to reduce unnecessary travel and create lively environments.

   • Special transit zoning districts to encourage greater intensity land use near transit.

   • Reduced parking requirements for development near transit.

   • Ground-level activities that make walking more attractive.

   • Reduced building setbacks.

   • Transfer of development rights downtown to compensate developers for not building on land owned away from transit in return for higher densities near transit.

   • Incentives for infilling in urban areas and near transit stations.

   • Clustering of buildings to make transit more efficient.

   • Limitations on development adjacent to existing or new highway interchanges.

*Figure 74: New Brunswick's commuter rail stop has been the center of new development and resurgence for this regional downtown.*

- Limitations on strip development along highways.

2. Recommendations regarding changes in ordinances to improve design include:

- Elimination of dead-end cul-de-sacs by interconnecting streets to reduce trip lengths and make walking and biking less circuitous.

- Creation of continuous walkways and bikeways.

- Installation of pedestrian amenities such as lighting, seating, attractive pavement, and street furniture.

- Street and driveway designs that improve the operation of transit vehicles, such as bus pull-out bays to give buses places to wait and load away from traffic, and turning radii that buses can negotiate.

- Requirement for bus shelters at bus stops.

- Traffic calming techniques, including neck-downs and redesigning narrow streets to accommodate both pedestrians and cars.

3. Recommendations regarding changes in business practice include:

- Trip reduction ordinances that require developers and employers to reduce peak hour auto use (see *Mobility*).

- Requirement for a municipal circulation plan before state funding for transportation improvements can be authorized.

- Requirement that transit operators and municipalities coordinate their actions so that transit improvements can be made hand-in-hand with development decisions.

To the extent that these recommended items can be viewed as being unfunded mandates imposed by the states, the states should provide municipalities with a mix of technical assistance and incentives. It is an opportune time to pursue such objectives because scores of communities throughout the region are on the verge of greatly improved transit service as part of capital plans of regional transit agencies. New Jersey faces the most dramatic change: with the completion of the Kearny connection, Montclair connection, and Secaucus Transfer, thousands of New Jersey commuters will have faster and more direct options for rail travel. The challenge for these communities is to ensure that these improvements provide not only the additional parking that better rail service may require but encourage the types of development that will strengthen downtowns, including housing for residents who would choose to walk to the rail station.

## The Region's Central Business District

It is important to recognize that Manhattan, Downtown Brooklyn, Long Island City, and Jersey City, where so many of the region's transit trips begin and end, have proved to be remarkably resilient pedestrian environments against great odds. Yet they face a very real threat of decline, meaning both diminished size and loss of their role as the essential experience of the city. Ten percent fewer people come to Manhattan south of 60th Street today than in 1948 (from 3.7 million in 1948 to 3.3 million today), but twice as many now come by car (from 660,000 to 1.2 million).[14] The automobile's impact has hurt the pedestrian character of the city and as a result has hurt the viability of transit. In Midtown Manhattan, pedestrian spaces constitute only one-third of the available public spaces; the rest are devoted to motor vehicles.[15] Over the years streets have been widened at the expense of sidewalks, and available sidewalk space has been further reduced by the presence of dozens of obstructions, including newsstands and vendors, street furniture such as light poles and waste baskets, ventilation gratings, plantings and sidewalk cafes. Although some of these features serve as amenities at less congested moments, there is a delicate balance of uses that is often overwhelmed by the presence of automobiles.

### Concentration without Congestion

The following outlines a series of fundamental strategies for dense centers to avoid the fate summed up by Yogi Berra: "It's so crowded, nobody goes there anymore."

To strike a balance between concentration and congestion, we must limit the volume of vehicles entering and traveling within the region's Central Business District (CBD) while simultaneously making the walking experience more pleasant. The most effective policies for limiting vehicle travel involve either higher prices for driving or limiting the amount of space available to enter the CBD, circulate within it, and store vehicles there. Limiting space through a gradual reduction of street capacity into and within the CBD, or of parking spaces in the CBD, will have the long-term effect of reducing vehicle traffic to the CBD. With these options, people will choose either an alternate way of getting to the city, an alternate destination, or not make the trip at all. Objections that these strategies will damage the CBD's strength as a destination ignore the fact that those who would no longer drive into the city are marginal users of least value to the economy of the city. Those people whose livelihoods depend on driving into the city will continue to do so.

To reduce vehicle capacity entering and leaving the CBD, RPA proposes:

- Close Central Park north–south drives permanently to vehicle traffic. Central Park would be restored to its intended state, for use without the hazards of motor vehicle traffic.

- Close Broadway southbound, between Columbus Circle and 34th Street, in conjunction with construction of the Crosstown light-rail.

- Narrow 130-foot wide Adams Street, Tillary Street, and Boerum Place in Downtown Brooklyn to create slower moving (or "traffic-calmed") civic boulevards.

Reducing vehicle capacity for circulation simultaneously reduces the number of vehicles congesting the streets and opens up the potential for more space for pedestrians. Steps to be taken should include:

- Close selected streets to traffic, including streets that serve little through circulation or goods loading and unloading functions. Such measures have been opposed in the past on the grounds that they restrict access to customers. But few customers of retail establishments in Midtown or Lower Manhattan arrive by car or taxi. Vehicle diversions would not be a problem with proper signing, particularly where closings are made permanent. Delivery access could be provided through improved design and by limiting it to selected low pedestrian hours. Streets that are candidates for closing, because they serve little or no traffic circulation, would include 41st and 43rd Streets in Midtown, various street segments in Lower Manhattan, and (because it causes more congestion than it relieves) Broadway from Lincoln Center to Madison Square. Broadway both creates and intersects Columbus Circle, Times Square, Herald Square, and Madison Square, areas that are both the city's most vibrant and congested. Service vans would be permitted on closed streets during off-peak hours (10 A.M. to 12 noon, 2 P.M. to 4 P.M., and after 6 P.M.).

- Widen sidewalks on Madison, Lexington, and Fifth Avenues and along 42nd Street in Manhattan and on Adams Street, Tillary Street, and Boerum Place in Downtown Brooklyn. The effective available walking width of Madison and Lexington Avenues is eight feet and the sidewalks are the most crowded in the CBD. Fifth Avenue, the premier strolling street in the CBD, is

*Figure 75*: *Automobile congestion detracts from the quality of life in the region's Central Business District and delays buses and important service and delivery vehicles.*

crowded from Central Park to 42nd Street despite its 20-foot-wide sidewalks. Widen 42nd Street sidewalks from Second Avenue to Eighth Avenue as part of the installation of the midtown trolley.

- In Midtown ban street vendors near subway stations and intersections and from avenue sidewalks that are less than 15 feet wide.

- Reduce taxi cruising by banning cruising during midday and peak periods. Create more taxi stands to compensate. Taxis make up 40% of the moving vehicles and create about 50% of the vehicle miles traveled in midtown. Their low productivity stems from their low occupancy, which is caused by cruising. Taxis carry, on the average, only 0.74 passengers per mile traveled, the lowest of any mode.[16]

To reduce the storage space for vehicles in the CBD:

- Ban the use of sites cleared for office buildings from temporary use as parking lots.

- Reduce parking ratio requirements for new office buildings.

- Eliminate parking privileges for city workers, especially in the City Hall area and in Downtown Brooklyn's Civic Center and Courthouse area. Any serious attempt by the city of New York to reduce automobile travel into the CBD must begin with its own workers.

- Measures to reduce vehicles through pricing are discussed in the *Mobility* section of the plan.

New York's transit and pedestrian problems may seem to be the opposite of those in other communities—New York, suffering from an embarrassment of riches with its many pedestrians, while other regional downtowns have too few—but the issues are interrelated. Attractive, walkable mixed-use centers are one of the region's greatest assets, and for all the anecdotal recognition of these as places of value, from Carroll Gardens in Brooklyn to Summit, New Jersey, these places are still seriously threatened. There is no reason short of a cataclysmic change in attitudes, or the cost of gasoline or taxing policy, to expect that the conditions that inspired the trend of the past 30 years have been reversed: businesses and retail stores do not have to be downtown to survive. They *choose* to be there, and transit- and pedestrian-friendly design helps create the circumstances that make these choices logical. Businesses then have as much flexibility as residents, because the region can tell them: "You do not *have* to locate on a strip or in a campus office center to be successful."

### Regional Downtowns

A number of regional downtowns have already taken ambitious steps to revive their amenities and economies. In Yonkers, New York, RPA worked to ensure that the city adopted its own existing master plan calling for a mixed-use downtown built on the special character of a recreational waterfront and taking advantage of an excellent in-place transit service. By harnessing the downtown's role as a transit center and combining it with the great physical resource of the Hudson River waterfront, the strong cultural resource of a new Hudson River Museum, and the largely untapped human resources of the state's fourth largest city, Yonkers' waterfront downtown can become a renewed, accessible, and highly desirable urban center. South Norwalk, Connecticut, and Peekskill, New York, are continuing to implement successful revitalization strategies based on preservation of their special historic character, promotion of artists' housing and related activities, strengthened cultural attractions, and commuter rail access for tourists and residents.

The lessons from these cities can be applied throughout many of the region's older rail-accessible downtowns, including Port Chester, New Rochelle, Newburgh, and Hempstead in New York;

Elizabeth, Paterson, and Morristown in New Jersey; and Waterbury and Danbury in Connecticut. These techniques range from the public participation design workshop process to: (1) improving physical appearance and circulation in the downtown station area (with local, state, or federal Community Development Block Grants and funds from the Intermodal Surface Transportation Efficiency Act of 1991); (2) promoting community-wide activities and arts and cultural destinations downtown; (3) designing and installing pedestrian connections; (4) reviewing preexisting master plans and incorporating recommendations into municipal codes, including zoning and redevelopment codes.

### Suburban Centers

Beyond the regional downtowns, most suburban jobs are located in free-standing office buildings or office parks accessible only by car. One of RPA's suburban mobility strategies is to find alternatives to cars for some workers, to benefit both these individual drivers and others. Even a modest reduction in automobile use could unclog highways during peak periods. A number of suburban areas are already or could easily be well served by transit. One example is MetroPark, along the northeast corridor line of NJ TRANSIT and Amtrak, where a dense cluster of recent office buildings has been developed adjacent to the transit station. But the current layout and design of MetroPark requires rail commuters to walk long distances through unsafe, unattractive parking lots to get to their offices, making it a hostile place for pedestrians and transit riders. But even in a place like MetroPark, where walking is a hazard, retrofitting is possible. New parking structures at the station could incorporate commuter-friendly uses, from daycare to health clubs and restaurants, as well as complementary uses such as a movie theater.

The challenge is to create walkable, comfortable environments in which taking transit is every bit as attractive a choice as driving a car. Scores of smaller, transit-oriented communities throughout the region are looking at plans for greater density and mixed-use near rail stations. Many are moving toward planning and implementing such ideas, including the 30 station areas being examined by NJ TRANSIT as a follow-up to its *Station Area Handbook*. This effort was largely inspired by the fact that, with the completion of the Secaucus Transfer

**Figure 76:** *For a charrette sponsored by RPA, a scale model of downtown Yonkers was built by the New School for Social Research's Environmental Simulation Center. A camera was run through the model to create a videotape showing different plans for the area. This tape was used as a visual aid at public hearings and exhibitions.*

and Kearny Connection, in the next decade dozens of New Jersey rail stations will offer a far faster and more convenient ride to Newark and New York City. Other examples include the MTA's proposal for a "transit village" in Ossining, as well as RPA's own work in Patterson, New York, and Princeton Junction, New Jersey. The goal is not to urbanize the suburbs but rather to create compact districts, ranging from two- and three-story mixed-use commercial buildings in the vicinity of train stations, to small lot, single-family homes within a walkable, half-mile radius of the station. For many towns, all that is required is the promotion of sensitive infill

and replication of the fabric of existing villages in adjacent new development served by attractive sidewalks and public spaces. If these communities are to attract a significant share of the region's residential growth, these efforts should be systematically encouraged and regionally supported.

Cumulatively, these changes are a long-term proposition, but they will never have any effect if they are not begun soon. Since localities want to retain control over how their communities develop, and zoning prerogatives are jealously guarded at the local level, these changes can only occur if people in hundreds of communities can see them as a part of their own lives, strengthening their families and their neighborhoods. Public authorities, particularly transportation providers, will have to learn how to work with local communities throughout the region.

RPA strongly supports the strategies outlined in *Redesigning the Suburbs: Turning Sprawl into Centers* (a report published by RPA in partnership with the MSM Regional Council), that call for new municipal ordinances that will retrofit suburban employment centers into walkable, transit-accessible places. In addition to MetroPark, this approach could apply to Hicksville and Mineola (among the regional downtowns listed above) as well as Mitchell Field and Hauppauge on Long Island, or the Princeton–Route 1 corridor in New Jersey.

*Redesigning the Suburbs* presents a series of case studies about how to transform suburban commercial sprawl into centers, with special emphasis on highway strips, shopping centers, and office campuses. This project offered a "Kit-of-Parts" and a model ordinance that would allow suburban areas to retrofit themselves with the help of some basic guidelines: (1) layout—an interconnected network of streets; (2) alleys encouraged to accommodate narrower lots; (3) street trees, landscaping, street lighting and furniture; (4) 5-foot minimum sidewalk widths; (5) building setbacks—no minimum, can be right up to the sidewalk, no blank walls to sidewalk; (6) on-street parking encouraged and counted toward minimum parking requirements to accommodate the mixed uses and human scale needed to improve the quality of life in these places.

The model ordinance proposed use of the state of New Jersey's "redevelopment" law—normally applied only to "blighted" urban areas—to remedy suburban conditions, such as a strip mall with associated vacant lots. Using the redevelopment law,

*Figure* 77: Redesigning the Suburbs *presents alternatives to sprawl, using new computer simulation techniques to communicate the result of development and zoning patterns in existing communities.*

municipalities in New Jersey, and those in other states with similar legal frameworks, could develop a specific plan that supersedes general zoning criteria. This plan could achieve suburban center goals by offering density bonuses, for example, as a reward for providing commercial ground-floor uses. As a center in a less urbanized context, a municipality could require that 50% of the land in a large center district remain open, but it could fulfill this requirement by buying open lands outside the urbanized core area.

### Superstores

Across the country, retail activities are shifting to larger scale outlets that have come to be known as superstores or big-box retail. The superstore label covers a number of different retail types, including larger scale discount department stores; large single-product stores, called "category killers"; and collections of these stores, called "power centers." Each of these types has different markets, different siting and access requirements, and different relationships with established retail districts.

The region is one of the last areas in the country to experience this phenomenon. For decades, large discount chains and category killers have been locating outside established downtown retail districts, and in most cases undercutting the vitality of these

districts. In recent years as superstore chains have begun to enter the Tri-State Metropolitan Region they have caused similar dislocation to a number of Main Streets and older highway commercial strips.

The question now facing the region is not whether but how to accommodate big box stores and how to site, design, and operate them so that they reinforce rather than undercut the region's downtowns. The key is to distinguish between the majority of big box activities that can be incorporated into or can adjoin established downtown retail districts and those—such as building supply or home improvement stores—that due to size or product mix can be best located in isolated highway commercial or industrial areas.

In general, discount department stores and category killers should be located in an adjoining downtown and adapted to fit in and reinforce the districts. In a number of places this has already occurred. For example, in Stamford and in New York City's 14th Street, Chelsea, and Jamaica retail districts, chains that normally locate larger single-floor facilities surrounded by areas of parking have adapted to their new urban surroundings. Most of these are multifloor stores, some in converted industrial or warehouse structures or former department stores. They all rely on structured parking or public transportation and reinforce the surrounding retail district.

These examples demonstrate that big boxes can be adapted to reinforce established downtown retail districts. The region's cities and towns should:

- Zone for big box activities in or contiguous to downtowns and locations with transit access.

- Require siting, design, and operations that adapt these facilities to downtown (e.g., requiring appropriate, multistory development, structured parking, incorporation of smaller retail establishments in street-facing locations, and use of delivery services for customers using mass transit).

- Adopt zoning that precludes these activities in isolated highway and industrial locations, excepting big box building supply and other activities that are more suitable to these locations.

### A Habitable Region

Housing affects the way we live, the health of our natural environment, and the way our society functions more than any other element of the built environment. In response to economic, technological, and demographic changes, housing forms have led the evolution of land use and development patterns in the New York–New Jersey–Connecticut region over the last 200 years. This section reviews regional housing development, scopes current housing conditions and projects future housing needs, explores the current affordable housing problem, and offers an agenda for ensuring adequate and affordable housing for the region.

*Integrating New Housing in the Plan*

Housing, in conjunction with transportation and the location of jobs, has a cumulative effect on the region. Housing cuts straight across the three main themes of the Third Regional Plan: economy, environment, and equity. The housing industry is a critical component of the region's economy. For example, the value of new construction permitted in 1993 was $3.3 billion, and nearly $5 billion in 1986, the peak of the last housing boom.[17] Another $17.4 billion was spent on housewares and furnishings, building supplies, and heating oil in 1992.[18] And the total value of work done in the construction industry itself topped $40 billion in 1987.[19] Moreover, housing also gives people a wealth-building link to the economic mainstream; and without adequate housing, individuals are placed at an overwhelming disadvantage when trying to take part in the economy. Conversely, inadequate or unaffordable housing reduces the region's ability to attract and retain talented workers. The environmental consequences of housing policy and land use development are immense when considered at a regional level.

The need to create and protect the Greensward should compel the region to invest in centers of all sizes throughout the region. New housing, the dominant consumer of land, should be built in existing centers and transit-served suburbs as opposed to new greenfield locations, and renewed effort should be placed on rejuvenating and rehabilitating housing in existing centers and older suburbs. Such a development pattern takes advantage of existing infrastructure including roads, sewer and water services, and commercial areas, and it reduces the need for new highways to serve outlying areas. New and renovated housing must also be integrated with other environmental considerations. The cost of housing has risen over the last several decades for a number of reasons, not just rising costs of land. Environmental regulations on choice of materials and lead and asbestos abatement, for example, have caused construction and renovation costs to increase. It has been demonstrated that these additional costs have the greatest effect on those households least able to pay for them.

"Infill" development—building in bypassed urban areas with existing transit lines and near job centers—assures that all members of a community have equal access to employment and shopping centers. This concept was strongly supported by two-thirds of the respondents to a Fairfield 2000 housing poll. Other "infill" proposals endorsed in the poll include zoning changes to encourage more townhouse development and allowing the creation of accessory apartments within large homes. These housing approaches are important elements of transit-friendly development, a critical component of the Third Regional Plan.

The emphasis the plan places on sustainability further stresses the need to restore the existing stock, rather than building new. Rehabilitation of existing buildings has significant energy-efficiency advantages: less energy is spent on the creation of new materials when existing materials and structures can be re-used. Housing rehabilitation and restoration is a major portion of the total housing activity in the region: it accounts for nearly one-third of the total value of construction contracts and over $5 billion in sales of "do-it-yourself" retail lumber, landscape, and home supplies.[20] And reclaiming existing buildings for housing adds little cost to municipal service provision—indeed, it helps to stabilize communities.

Vast changes in the region's landscape were brought about by the growing use of automobiles a half century ago. Because greater distances could be traveled between residences and the central business district in nearly the same amount of time, more and more people began to push beyond the boundaries of the metropolis as defined by streetcar lines, into forested and open space now suddenly ripe for development. At the same time, city residents were outgrowing the existing crowded and under-maintained stock. Postwar economic recovery tools such as the GI Bill, Veteran's Administration, and existing Federal Housing Administration

**Figure 78:** *Many older public housing developments are being replaced with owner-occupied townhouses.*

home loan programs brought home-buying within reach of a far larger number of families.

As people moved out to the new development near new expressways, housing forms accommodated their changing circumstances. More emphasis was placed on the automobile as a central design principle of neighborhoods, and less thought was given to pedestrians—primarily because the new low-density environment offered few walkable destinations. This same late 20th century development dynamic is by no means extinct. In the 1980s two new forms of housing began to dominate the suburban landscape: relatively high-density condominiums and large luxury homes. Both forms tended to be sited on old agricultural land far from either centers or public transportation, so even larger stretches of the region became increasingly automobile-dependent.

Back in the cities, slum clearance and urban renewal projects conceived between the 1950s and 1970s produced "machines for living," new housing units in large tower complexes, improving the urban housing standards in the short term but having little regard for community design principles. At the same time, the suburbs were separating themselves even more from urban centers and their residents: new suburban zoning and design codes typically contained set-back, lot size, and unit size standards that drove up prices, reducing their affordability to low-income families. There were also countless instances of overt efforts to maintain income and racial segregation by both realtors and existing homeowners. These efforts served to further exclude poor and minority families from the

suburbs. The result was to further concentrate the disadvantaged in cities and adjacent areas ceded by the fleeing middle class.[21]

### Expectations of Future Housing Needs

Three indicators help in understanding the possible dimensions of the region's future housing needs:

1. *New Households:* Regional Plan Association estimates the region may need to create as many as 1 million new units for our growing and changing population by 2020, based on population forecasts discussed previously. As the average age of the population is expected to increase, there are more opportunities to form households and seek independent housing at a faster rate than population growth. In the short term, New Jersey's Council on Affordable Housing (COAH) estimates as many as 85,000 affordable units will need to be built or rehabilitated in that state alone by 1999.

2. *Income:* RPA projects a decrease in household incomes for many new households. Between 1990 and 2005 households with annual incomes below $17,500 (in 1982 dollars) will increase by 1 million to comprise 45% of new growth. By today's standards, these households cannot afford housing valued on the open market above $50,000.[22] RPA believes there is a considerable latent affordability demand: persons who would like to move into larger homes or from renter to owner but are blocked by increasing affordability difficulties.

3. *Household Composition:* Between 1980 and 1985 the expansion of nonfamily households accounted for 71% of the region's increase in occupied housing while families comprised only 29% of the growth. In addition, five of every six new families were formed by female heads of

household. RPA forecasts this pattern to continue into the early years of the 21st century.[23] While the size of today's housing units is getting larger on average (the typical 1950s "Levittown" home was roughly 800 square feet of readily adaptable space in comparison to new units consisting of over 2,000 square feet[24]), household size is decreasing.

## A Regional Housing Agenda

Affordable housing is a subject encumbered by misunderstandings and scraps of misapplied conventional wisdom. It is important to keep the region's housing needs clearly in focus.

- Affordable housing is not a welfare give-away program but an essential element of a community's vitality and the region's competitiveness.

- True poverty represents a unique challenge not well addressed by typical affordable housing programs. Providing satisfactory shelter for all is a key goal of this plan—and that will require a variety of programs that meet the needs of the various groups who live in the region. Impoverished households, for example, often may require, along with new housing, specialized assistance in job training and placement, daycare, and other programs, in order to secure and keep their homes.

- A vast inventory of space appropriate for new affordable housing units exists within the region's centers. A significant portion of housing activity is focused on rehabilitation and improvements to the existing stock, and this trend should continue. The region cannot afford large-scale construction of affordable housing at its periphery that endangers our environment and undercuts our existing infrastructure.

- A great many public sector and private sector policies and practices can nourish affordable housing. So far, most public approaches have been based on supply-side assistance; for example, purchase price and rent subsidies and subsidized mortgages. Many other methods, also highly effective, have an important place in this mix, including design, zoning, regulatory approval, construction materials/process, and labor changes.

- Building affordable housing for the 21st century does not mean reinventing the 19th century urban tenement. Attractive, affordable housing can now take many forms, including congregate facilities, condominiums, townhouses, duplex houses, zero-lot line single-family homes, garden apartments, accessory apartments, and rehabilitated structures.

- The region is burdened by its persistent racial and income segregation. Successful communities will include all races, ethnic groups, income groups, and age groups. If we allow present trends to continue, urban enclaves of poor and displaced persons in shoddy housing—or none at all—are likely to grow. This is a drag on the region, its competitiveness, and our spirits. Unless we see to it that everyone who needs such a house can afford one, we will have failed ourselves.

## What Is Affordable Housing?

What housing is truly "affordable"? The median household income for an area is typically used as a benchmark to determine which groups require the most assistance with their housing needs. Affordable housing is then often broken down into three sub-categories: "low/moderate income housing," "middle-class housing," and "special needs housing." Low/moderate income housing typically is earmarked for people with a household income between 50% and 80% of the median household income, which translates into a purchase price ranging from roughly $63,000 to $102,000.[25] Middle-class housing is defined as housing available to households earning 80% to 120% of the median household income, equaling a purchase price between $102,000 and $157,000 (special regional economic factors such as higher energy costs and property taxes need to be included in such calculations). Special needs housing is housing made available to groups of people requiring different levels of care and assistance, such as the developmentally disabled, the elderly, and single mothers.

What does an affordable unit look like, inside and out? Like a home. There is a profusion of designs for new affordable homes, and none of them is a slum or tenement. RPA and "Fairfield 2000" conducted an affordable housing design competition for a redevelopment site in Greenwich. This competition generated attractive designs reflecting various market-rate units in the town.[26] Design practices that take advantage of new construction techniques, such as modular construction or clustered development, reduce costs of housing without any decline in aesthetics. *Progressive Architecture* magazine held a design competition for an affordable house in Cleveland, its corporate base. The winning submission used modular construction that was adapted to be contextual with other houses in the neighborhood. Community and critical reception was extremely positive, yet preconceived notions of prefabricated construction often prejudice community attitudes.

The trend toward new larger units with more amenities has shifted the housing market away from more affordable units, driven in part by hidden subsidies such as the federal income tax deductibility of mortgage interest and local property taxes, which can encourage over-consumption of housing. Nationwide, in 1970, the "most typical" single-family house was under 1,200 square feet, had two bathrooms, and had no central air conditioning or fireplace. By 1991 this "most typical" home was over 2,400 square feet, had two and one-half baths or more, central air conditioning, and at least one fireplace.[27] Another measure of this trend is the shift in market share from smaller, "starter" homes to more luxurious homes. In 1986 houses and condominiums selling for under $100,000 represented 44% of total house sales in Connecticut. In 1990 that share fell to 14%. In the same time period the share of houses selling for over $200,000 in the total housing market increased from 16% to 27%.[28] We are constructing Cadillacs when many of us are really looking for a family sedan.

People face different housing needs during different decades of their lives: young families need affordable starter homes; families with teenage children need more rooms; single-parent families need access to daycare or other social services; "empty-nesters" need smaller, more carefree homes; and many elderly people need housing that offers the option of health or social support. Strategies to address affordable housing needs at the state, county, and local levels must be comprehensive enough to include different solutions for each affordable housing market sector. Creating a mix of housing types in a community allows residents to stay in their neighborhood as their life circumstances change. In fact, most affordable housing is for a community's residents—teachers, firefighters, police officers, and others—who want to stay in the town where they grew up or now work but cannot afford to live there.

### Creating Affordable Housing

Affordable housing has traditionally been associated with federal and state subsidies or housing programs, as well as nonprofit and community-based development groups. Some private developers have sought to provide affordable housing as a

**Figure 79:** *Jennifer Deanne Fier and Warren Temple Smith's Winning Design of Affordable Housing in Fairfield County.*

way to balance their "product-line" of more luxurious housing. Nonprofit organizations, from the Phipps Houses in the 1920s to recent projects by the New York City Housing Partnership, have had a long history of advocating and providing low-income and middle-income housing. Each of these groups works toward the same goal by using different tools. Nonetheless, there are many pockets of affordable housing activity, using, in some combination, a broad continuum of strategies for implementing affordable housing programs. The task is to expand, encourage, and replicate their efforts that address the following regional housing goals:

- Provide acceptable housing for all residents of the region regardless of race or income.
- Build what is needed and can be paid for; avoid housing excesses that consume large amounts of natural and financial resources.
- Integrate all housing markets for all racial and economic groups.
- Focus new housing in existing centers.
- Reduce the cost of "least-cost" housing—make affordable housing truly affordable.

A combination of approaches will help improve affordability, reduce segregation, and increase regional competitiveness. The four generic approaches to solving our regional housing problems include planning for affordability, providing incentives to development, providing subsidies to residents, and building on the regional network of public–private housing partnerships. To be sure, individual efforts throughout the region have mixed and matched these elements with considerable success, but in these times of limited resources, a region-wide housing partnership and network needs to be developed. The following section reviews the four approaches and how they can be applied in the region.

*Plan for Affordability.* There are many ways to "plan for affordability," that is, for the public sector to take a proactive stance in the creation of affordable housing. The first is the elimination of exclusionary zoning and development standards that tend to raise housing prices above the means of most new families. The second is to reduce excessive development regulation and reviews by government agencies that add to a developer's carrying

costs before his or her units are even built and sold. Eliminating segregation will be the hardest work, but it can be accomplished by using all these tools in concert with the new enforcement provisions in the federal Fair Housing Act.

Exclusionary local zoning codes typically mandate excessive minimum lot sizes or prohibit multi-family dwelling units on any lot. As land development costs have assumed a larger portion of the total development costs of housing, larger lot sizes mean both greater acquisition costs and greater development costs, which translates into, as those who would promote exclusionary zoning hope, fewer less-well-off residents who are reliant on public services.

Affordable housing simply cannot be built on large lots due to higher land acquisition and infrastructure development costs. Many elements of municipal site plan and subdivision ordinances could be modified to cut costs, such as reducing excessive set-back, lot size, building coverage, and frontage requirements, as well as street right-of-way and pavement widths. Further modifications, such as allowing "zero-lot-lines," where the dwelling may be built against the side property line, can also cut land needs and therefore costs. For example, a one-acre square-shaped lot would have a street frontage of over 200 feet, compared to less than 70 feet for a home on one-eighth of an acre. Cutting minimum lot sizes would reduce the cost of basic infrastructure—streets, curbs, sidewalks, sewer and water lines, utilities—by two-thirds. All these savings in infrastructure and development costs can then be passed on to the buyer.

These changes not only help create more affordable housing by removing excessive development costs, they create a more compact neighborhood in which walking and biking becomes not only feasible but pleasant, enhancing a sense of community. Providing transit services become cost-effective, and with narrower yet safe residential streets, cars travel more slowly and safely. And potentially more open space can be saved around the neighborhood to provide a sense of nature.

It has been estimated that the costs of regulatory compliance add as much as one-quarter to the price of a new home. Local governments must develop policies and programs to streamline the planning, permitting, and implementation of new affordable housing construction. A recent study of New York land development found that 11 out of 13 projects reviewed were delayed one to five years, due to a combination of regulatory problems and public opposition. As the profit margin for privately constructed affordable housing is slim enough in the best of circumstances, construction delays seriously hinder private developers.

A potentially powerful tool in reducing delays and redundant reviews is to combine local and regional master planning with a generic environmental impact statement (GEIS). In essence this combination sets forth both the development and conservation goals of the community, as expressed in its master plan and accompanying zoning and development ordinances, with a GEIS "pre-review" of the environmental impacts of development that could occur. This would give a developer who proposes a project that conforms to the master plan and GEIS "as of right" approval to proceed, bypassing a potentially long and risky approvals process. In addition, such projects would also skip the long and costly EIS process; a more targeted "supplemental" EIS would be used in cases where the proposed development was beyond the scope of the GEIS.[29] The community receives the development it planned for, and the developer can keep costs, and hopefully home prices, to a minimum.

Further, overly rigid standards might be replaced by performance standards that allow using alternative methods to achieve the same goals. New Jersey is in the process of developing statewide uniform site standards that may reduce development uncertainty by streamlining site development plans, though critics have charged that it may also reduce both design options and local control over development. Moreover, local governments might remove a layer of review by allowing developers to self-certify plans, if they have been prepared by professional engineering and architectural consultants. Lastly, New York City has revised its building codes regarding renovations to better reflect the needs of building rehabilitation, which differ from the needs of new construction. New Jersey is presently creating a "rehab code" as well.

*Provide Incentives for the Creation of New Affordable Housing.* Many innovative measures exist to spur the market to provide more affordable units, including tax credits, development funds, and zoning and density bonuses. A key subsidy to building affordable units is the federal "Section 42" tax credit program. Federal tax credits are available to eligible contractors creating low-income rental housing through the Low-Income Housing Tax Credit Program, adopted as part of the Tax Reform Act of 1986, and codified in Section 42 of the Internal Revenue Code. By selling low-income tax credits to an investment pool, builders can acquire the necessary funds to fill the gap between the amount of their mortgage and the actual costs of constructing housing for low-income tenants.[30] In many cases, even when a municipality has made a gift of the land where the apartments will be built, developers could not afford to move forward with the project without the gap financing that these tax credits provide.

Connecticut has a subsidy program to encourage low-income units. A developer must set aside a minimum percentage of units in a subdivision for low-income residents and must maintain that percentage throughout a designated compliance period, usually at least 30 years, to be eligible for state tax credits. At a minimum, 20% of the units must be set aside for tenants with incomes of 50% or less of the area's median income, as established by the United States Department of Housing and Urban Development; and at least 40% of the units must be set aside for tenants earning 60% or less of the area's median income.

Connecticut municipalities are empowered by the state to encourage affordable housing through zoning bonuses, housing trust funds, and transfer of development rights programs. Due to a low level of participation in such programs, new methods for achieving adequate levels of affordable housing were sought. Legislation passed in 1989 (PA 89-311) establishes the affordable housing appeals procedure. This procedure shifts the burden of proof from a developer of affordable housing to the town to establish that a substantial public interest in health and safety clearly outweighs the need for the proposed affordable housing. Towns in which at least 10% of the existing housing stock is affordable are exempt from this appeals provision. In addition, towns that are active participants in either a regional fair housing compact pilot program or other partnership programs are exempt from appeals for a period of one year. After this period ends a town must meet the 10% threshold; if not, the exemption is lost and developers can file appeals. The appeals procedure has come under close scrutiny from many groups and is the subject of weakening leg-

**Figure 80:** *Renovation of existing housing provides a multi-billion dollar boost to the regional economy, preserves open space, and strengthens centers of all types.*

tablish that municipal zoning that does not give due consideration to regional housing needs may be held as invalid. In particular, the "Continental" decision of 1991 found that municipalities must permit their share of regional affordable housing needs to be constructed. The state Advisory Committee on the Preparation of a Land Development Guide recommended that in the context of strengthened municipal planning and zoning, local officials should be required to justify denial of permits to a development of affordable housing. Unless public health and safety would be jeopardized by the project, an appeals court judge could overrule the municipality's decision. This concept is similar to Connecticut's new program. It was further recommended that new planning and zoning requirements reflect regional affordable housing needs.[31]

The state of New Jersey uses an artful and successful combination of developer-initiated projects and state-mandated objectives to provide affordable housing in each of its communities. New Jersey's affordable housing program developed out of a series of judicial decisions by the State Supreme Court (the Mount Laurel decisions) passed down between 1975 and 1986, as well as the Fair Housing Act, passed in 1985, which created the state's Council on Affordable Housing (COAH).

The first two Mount Laurel decisions—*Southern Burlington County NAACP v. Township of Mount Laurel* (1975) and some exclusionary zoning cases considered jointly, and now commonly referred to as Mount Laurel II (1983)—stated that municipalities have an obligation under the State Constitution to provide a realistic opportunity for low- and moderate-income housing. They also provided guidance in determining the "fair share" of affordable housing in each municipality. In the absence of any legislatively created body to administer a housing program, a three-judge panel was assigned to implement these ideas.

Initially, developers were encouraged to file suit against towns with exclusionary policies to obtain variances for sites they intended to develop. The developer had to include one low- or moderate-income unit for every four market-priced units built. Developers responded quickly to this idea and over 100 suits were filed against municipalities with exclusionary zoning codes. This approach, the so-called "builder's remedy," created a great deal of discontent among municipal officials and planners faced with the challenge of finding space for an

islative proposals each session. While the 1989 act remains intact in statute, its existence in Connecticut has, unfortunately, not resulted in greater participation in the provision of affordable housing. RPA advocates strengthening the legislation by providing strong incentives for communities to zone for a wide range of housing types, prices, and densities.

New York City and the state of New York have been developing new regulatory incentives to spur affordable housing. These are in addition to many creative programs, particularly in New York City, of tax incentives, property donation to owner-occupied rehabilitated rental units, and zoning incentives. Planning and zoning changes elsewhere in the New York portion of the region are of particular interest. Recent court cases have begun to es-

enormous amount of new market-priced housing units to subsidize the affordable units. As a result, pressure was placed on the state legislature to create a method that would let municipalities handle their fair share of affordable housing locally.

The Fair Housing Act of 1985 (N.J.S.A. 52:27D-301 *et seq.*) created the Council on Affordable Housing (COAH) to replace the judicial panel created by the Mount Laurel decisions. The act recognized that "the interest of all citizens, including low- and moderate-income families in need of affordable housing, would be best served by a comprehensive planning and implementation response" (N.J.S.A. 52:27D-302(c)). The third Mount Laurel decision, *Hills Development Corporation v. Bernards Township*, in 1986, affirmed the constitutionality of the Fair Housing Act and recognized COAH as the administrative body to handle all housing litigation then pending in the courts.

Under the Fair Housing Act, any municipality may submit a plan to COAH that outlines how it intends to fulfill its fair share obligation. COAH is then responsible for certifying the plan and determining that the municipality has established a "realistic opportunity" for fulfilling its housing obligation over a six-year period. The COAH process is voluntary. Although every municipality has a fair share obligation, each town has the option of coming under COAH's jurisdiction or being vulnerable to an exclusionary zoning lawsuit. In addition, a municipality may adopt a plan and then may ask that the plan not be reviewed for a two-year period unless the town is sued by a developer. The two-year period can be used by municipalities to engage in informal review of the plan by COAH. Interestingly, the Fair Housing Act does not require municipalities to construct affordable housing, only to adopt zoning that will create a realistic opportunity for affordable housing. The act assumes that the market will respond and the housing will be constructed by a willing developer.

COAH's other responsibilities, besides certifying local housing plans, are the creation of housing regions and the establishment of guidelines to determine the fair share of affordable units in each municipality. An innovative concept—the Regional Contribution Agreement (RCA)—allows a municipality to transfer up to 50% of its housing obligations to another municipality within the same housing region. Typically, under these agreements, suburban towns transfer a portion of their obligation to an urban town by making a minimum $20,000 cash payment to the receiving community. The transferring community is still obligated to fulfill the remaining part of its fair share. These RCAs are overseen and certified by COAH. The New Jersey Supreme Court has recently ruled that municipalities under COAH's jurisdiction may also adopt mandatory development fee ordinances to finance affordable housing activity.

The many benefits conferred on municipalities by the Fair Housing Act and COAH encourage local involvement and planning for new housing. Towns with certified housing plans are given priority access to sources of housing subsidies including the state's Balanced Housing Program funded through the real estate transfer tax and the federal Low-Income Tax Credit Program. In addition, the "mitigation instead of litigation" concept induces many municipalities to submit plans to COAH for certification. Towns have often found innovative and prudent ways to meet their obligation for affordable housing without having to spend municipal funds or zone for higher densities. The arrangements provided in New Jersey's approach create an optimal environment for public and private interests to work together to create housing for all ranges of incomes.[32]

*Provide Direct Federal/State Subsidies to Households.* Another possible way of ensuring adequate housing is to provide direct government subsidies to families so that they spend no more than a certain percentage of their income for shelter. This could be modeled after existing "Section 8" programs that help poor families pay their rent. An affordable housing subsidy program would allow families to live where they choose and to make housing decisions based on the quality of schools or other quality of life concerns. Such a program would further help eradicate residential segregation and allow new suburban residents the same access to job opportunities that current suburbanites already enjoy.

A contemporary issue is whether the federal government should combine housing assistance with welfare funding into one large "block grant" made to states. Advocates argue that by bundling these funds, states can best decide how to deploy the resources and also eliminate federal housing "red tape." However, there is considerable concern that this approach dilutes, if not eliminates, the federal commitment to housing the poor. Inasmuch as this region is home to a considerable number of poor families, continued federal assistance in their housing needs is important. While a "direct subsidy" approach would presently appear to be interventionist, expansion of current federal housing subsidies would still represent only a small fraction of the estimated $425 billion the federal government forgoes every year in indirect subsidies to home ownership—in the form of local property tax and mortgage interest deductions from federal income taxes.[33]

Finally, while many areas have residential energy bill assistance programs, an across-the-board effort to cut the operating costs of housing must be made by government agencies, utilities, and civic and business groups. Rising energy costs and sewer and water rates have increased operation expenses of households; as a group, residences are the largest energy consumers in both New York and Connecticut—greater than industry or transportation. Urban units are older; less well insulated; have older, less-efficient furnaces; do not have water-conserving plumbing fixtures; and are thus likely to have the highest utility costs. RPA's work in the Bronx found many prospective residents would have difficulty with utility bills, even if the rent or mortgage were subsidized. One "win-win" approach between the New York City Department of Environmental Protection and developers was to encourage use of water-saving plumbing fixtures in renovated units, serving both DEP's need to conserve water and the need to cut operating costs for low-income tenants. These efforts need to be continued and expanded.

*Replicate and Expand the Work of the Third Sector.* With continuing federal and state retrenchment in housing programs altogether likely, local and regional government agencies must take a more active role in providing affordable housing and developing a national urban housing agenda. The "third sector" is made up of thousands of community, business, environmental, religious, and neighborhood groups that have become effective participants in the region's decision-making processes. This third sector of private nonprofit and community-based organizations can and does play a critical role in this campaign. What is different is that

these groups have taken on new and additional roles.

Community-based development organizations have included social service provision and community empowerment roles in addition to home building to create more successful neighborhoods. New Community Corporation (NCC) in Newark set out to create a planned community within an existing city center. Nationally known, leading urban developers and town planners came to Newark to train community members in planning and architecture so that local citizens could be involved in every level of decision-making. Because the residents then eloquently expressed their needs, the assembled architects and planners were able to steer away from accepted, sterile, and confining models of low-income redevelopment. In nearly 30 years of work, NCC has over and over again transformed seemingly hopeless Central Ward blocks into livable and safe homesites. More than 3,000 units of housing have been built or rehabilitated, and NCC is now beginning to take on projects in other Newark neighborhoods and in Paterson. NCC has no doubts that its programs can be successfully replicated in any of the region's hard-pressed centers.

Inadequate provision of social services has often been cited as a principal reason why past low-income housing projects have so often failed.[34] To be of use to people, services have to be on site, and coordinated with the schedules and needs of residents. The Third Sector, particularly the community-based development organizations, has led the housing industry in seeing to it that their building programs include innovative, on-site, hands-on, and ongoing social support services for tenants and owners. These groups do not just build homes, as they like to say, they build communities. And the communities they build endure.

"Intermediary" groups—such as the New York City Housing Partnership, Local Initiatives Support Corporation, and Enterprise Foundation in New York City, and Long Island Housing Partnership on Long Island—help developers and community-based organizations navigate the bureaucratic mazes, cut through "red tape," and assist in developing project financing from multiple sources. They have formed in response to new fiscal and development complexity and regulations, acting as community empowerment facilitators and brokers to shepherd projects to completion. Another force leading to their creation is the reduced ability of government agencies to produce new or rehabilitated units. The New York City Housing Partnership in particular brought together civic-minded businesses, lenders, labor, and community organizations to work with government agencies on the production of thousands of new units and is one of the nation's largest intermediaries. The four groups above have created or plan to create well over 20,000 units.

In Connecticut, Fairfield 2000 Homes Corporation (F2HC) brings together the experience of a 16-member, nonsalaried board of directors and a paid professional staff to act as an affordable housing developer, sponsor, builder, consultant, management agent, or mortgagee, depending on the nature and scope of a particular development. Because its purpose is "least-cost" housing, F2HC works either independently or in conjunction with other nonprofit or private sector developers on a joint venture basis. It also cooperates with state and federal housing agencies and serves as a resource for local municipalities. F2HC can identify land that is appropriate for development, and it can secure nontraditional, below-market-rate financing and grants.

Both types of groups often have great expertise and the warm relationships with specific communities that can lead to highly successful programs. Replication of their programs can be a great timesaver when the alternative is reinventing housing programs as the need arises. For example, RPA has helped network a Bridgeport community group with New Community Corporation to share ideas rather than "reinventing the wheel." As public housing dollars seem to shrink, further networking of these groups with others, as well as banks and civic-minded businesses, becomes more critical.

## New Institutions and Uses

For centers to remain viable in an uncertain future, they need to nurture new and emerging uses and institutions. Urban and rural communities can be linked to the regional economy by attracting new economic activities, such as businesses that thrive in smaller areas and industries that maintain connections through "telematic" at-home employees. Furthermore, supporting resources such as the arts and cultural activities offers the potential for new growth and vitality. By adapting to new demands and meeting new needs, centers remain a major part of sustainable development patterns.

### Communities and the Regional Economy

Fundamental economic shifts now underway and expected to accelerate in the first decades of the 21st century could create new opportunities for currently isolated urban and rural communities to become integral parts of the regional economy. RPA is opposed to unplanned exurban development but recognizes that given the changes described below, more jobs may be located outside of regional downtowns. Only with strong planning and implementation initiatives will this out-of-downtown growth ultimately be beneficial to the character and quality of life in communities.

Among the shifts that will affect where people live and work are:

- The "de-layering" (removing layers of management and production) of *large* corporations and the related process of outsourcing (or farming out of) activities to outside contractors.

- The expected dramatic increase in sole proprietorships and small businesses, expected to produce 866,000 of the more than 3 million new jobs that will be created by 2020.

- The trend toward home work, whether as payroll jobs or proprietorships, in which people will work at home and communicate with offices, clients, and colleagues via phone, fax, e-mail, and the internet; on any given day in 2020, perhaps up to 10% of the total workforce will not commute, compared to roughly 2% today.

Many of these enterprises and jobs could be located in relatively isolated urban and rural centers. On the one hand, this represents a "de-centering" force; on the other, it could tie small towns and smaller compact centers into the growing regional economy, reduce traffic congestion, and better enable the region to offer an even fuller range of housing and life-style choices. Home workers, for example, should be encouraged to locate or stay in urban and rural communities with marked quality of life attributes (convenience, safety, diversity, beauty, sense of place) that also provide a variety of services, ranging from office supplies to daycare to cappuccino-to-go. At the moment, however, some of these quality of life and convenience attributes may not yet be present. Rural as well as urban communities that want to seize the economic opportunities presented by at-home work will have to clean up and green up their centers and improve their schools and other public services. Such investments could pay off handsomely: If they succeed in attracting new workers and enterprises, communities can link and broaden their tax and employment bases, expand retail activities, and share services.

Community groups throughout the region have begun local initiatives in sharing services, supporting enterprise, cutting living costs, and generating economic activity. Farmers' markets in Manhattan and beyond enable farmers from surrounding counties to sell fresh produce directly to city customers. Establishing a direct connection between producers and consumers has saved many family farms and provided a greater variety of products to city residents. The New York State Board of Cooperative Educational Services provides grants to school districts that collaborate on educational programs, stretching limited funds and initiating new activities. Now, incentive grants of up to $20,000 will enable school districts to explore the possibility of cutting costs by collaborating in functions such as purchasing and transportation.

Across the region communities can also encourage new forms of residential, employment, and retail development in ways that reinforce centers, and they should anticipate changes in economic structure and patterns in living, working, and travel. Rural and suburban communities should discourage development of new free-standing office and retail developments and instead focus these activities in centers. Communities should also prohibit new commercial strip development to reduce congestion on arterial highways and to reinforce traditional village and town Main Street retail districts, possibly by developing a "just-say-no" checklist for their master plan and project reviews that will automatically alert them to development proposals and transportation projects that would jeopardize community character. And urban centers should prohibit the development of isolated "big box" retail developments because they often undercut ex-

isting downtown retail centers, increase highway traffic, and reduce transit use.

## Cultural Resources: The Arts, Transit, Urban Design, and Historic Preservation

As has been emphasized throughout this chapter, the future success of centers depends on their becoming places that people choose to live and work in for better opportunities and quality of life. Because so much contemporary activity—work, shopping, recreation, and living—no longer must take place in centers, successful centers will have to further emphasize the positive characteristics that continue to distinguish them from suburban and exurban locations. Extraordinary cultural resources have long been among the greatest strengths of centers in this region.

Increasingly, the arts are being considered a key element in successful downtown revitalization strategies. As an outstanding contributor to human fulfillment, the arts should be seen in this context not as a luxury, but as central to the identity, viability, and attraction of urban areas. The use of the arts as part of an overall and sustained commitment to renewal presents practical alternatives or complements to other revitalization efforts, such as convention centers, casinos, festival marketplaces, or high-technology centers.

Practically speaking, the arts are attractive elements in revitalization efforts because they are often already onsite or nearby—through the presence of individual artists, cultural institutions, community arts programs, and service organizations. Urban centers are often the natural home for artists and cultural institutions; it is where they have historically congregated, both yesterday and today. Reinforced by mass transit systems and pedestrian access, downtown areas provide proximity to other artists, numerous possibilities for presentation, and access to diverse and large audiences—all of which might not be possible in isolated rural and suburban areas.

While providing a destination and sense of place to those who live outside of centers, the arts also offer opportunities and benefits to the centers themselves—to residents and communities that may not have the mobility and choices available to others. These benefits may include training and job opportunities, arts education linkages in local schools, and community-building aspects that are difficult to quantify but essential to healthy urban neighborhoods.

Models of how to strengthen the role of arts in centers need to be tailored to the aspects and needs of each community. For example, public art programs that make public spaces more inviting may be sponsored by partnerships of governmental agencies, nonprofit curators, community-based institutions, or local schools. Space for performance and exhibitions may be provided by both public and private hosts. Local zoning codes may be revised to attract and accommodate artists in need of live/work studio space.

Historic centers such as Manhattan's Times Square, the city of Peekskill in the Hudson Valley, and the downtowns of Newark and Brooklyn have undergone periods of decline and renewal. In each of these centers, a variety of programs and initia-

tives emerged to highlight the arts as a practical component of revitalization efforts.

• Working from a strong employment and retail base downtown, the Fund for the Borough of Brooklyn has sought to act as a community facilitator, connecting adjacent communities of artists and cultural institutions to the daily users of the central business district and the broader community beyond. The fund has played a role in creating venues for the arts throughout the downtown area—sponsoring events, gallery space, and exhibitions throughout the year. Reopening the historic Kings Majestic Theater was the result of a successful partnership between 651 Kings Majestic Corporation and the nearby Brooklyn Academy of Music. The theater and its environs will be used cooperatively with the surrounding diverse communities as a place of music, dance, discussion, public art, and education.

• In Peekskill an entrepreneurial spirit was evoked in the Artists Spaces Program. The program identified a community of artists looking for live/work space with

*Figure 81: The New Jersey Performing Arts Center has created new activity and excitement in downtown Newark, allowing the city and the arts to reinforce each other for the benefit of all.*

easy access to New York City and was able to match them with a surplus of commercial loft space in the downtown area. Essentially treating the artists as a small business they wanted to attract, Peekskill developed a public–private partnership that resulted in a growing residential community of artists, bringing new life and activity to the street—absent since the departure of Main Street–type retail from the downtown. Since 1991 some 75 loft conversions for artists and related businesses have resulted from the program. Changes to the downtown area since the program was initiated include new retail businesses such as a local art supply store, cafe, gallery, and performance and exhibition spaces. A satellite arts program of Westchester Community College has opened downtown, and the presence of artists downtown has benefitted the arts education programs of local schools. Plans are currently underway for new construction of artist live/work space on an urban renewal site with design funding in part from the National Endowment for the Arts and the New York State Council on the Arts.

• In Manhattan the 42nd Street Development Corporation has embraced public art as an agent to reclaim the long-blighted street and to make it a truly public destination again. Utilizing a lively array of theaters, marquees, lobbies, and the sidewalks themselves, Creative Time mounted the 42nd Street Art Project. These properties became the backdrop for provocative and engaging artist installations that ultimately involved local colleges, the tourism information center, businesses, and residents of the area. While the art project is one component of a larger redevelopment plan for the entire area, it was responsible for creating one of the first and most visible signs of improvement in the most famous, and infamous, street in the United States.

• The New Jersey Performing Arts Center in Newark, now under construction, represents a major financial and philosophical commitment to the arts as a revitalizing force for the core of the city and the region as a whole. Building on the presence of the Newark Museum downtown, the center will provide the first permanent home for the New Jersey Symphony Orchestra, expanding later to include other groups and forming an entertainment and cultural district. Significantly, the arts center is leading a redevelopment effort that will ultimately include office towers, shopping, and dining along a main boulevard.

Bringing the arts to bus and rail service is a sign that public agencies recognize that they are custodians of public spaces and public experiences—and that the arts are a part of winning back the public's trust. Just as New York City's Interborough Rapid Transit Corporation, almost a century ago, required the inclusion of decorative elements such as mosaics "to uplift the spirits of riders," mass transit agencies in the region increasingly view the inclusion of the arts as an opportunity to enhance the overall commuter experience.

Recent efforts to integrate the arts and transit were led by the Metropolitan Transit Authority's Arts for Transit program in 1985, in which 1% of core capital construction costs were set aside for permanent and temporary public art, exhibitions, music performances, and poetry posters. The Port Authority of New York and New Jersey's Arts Committee seeks opportunities to include artwork in all the public spaces they operate, from the PATH System to the airports and bus and train stations. NJ TRANSIT's Transit Arts Committee has reached out to artists for ideas and projects while in the planning stages of the proposed 20.5-mile Hudson-Bergen Light-Rail Transit System, a $1.3 billion project.

The built environment is an expression of the arts that often gets overlooked. But the physical plant we have—in our architecture and urban planning and the buildings, plazas, residences, and gardens that shape our society—is an expression of artistic ideals and philosophies. This region has excelled in architecture and planning for over 200 years, from Central Park to Hyde Park, from Park Avenue to Jones Beach. Some communities insist on design excellence—through architectural review boards, design guidelines, or other regulatory procedures, or through a basic demand for and attention to aesthetic sensibility—while others have allowed the quality of their built environment to decline.

Several programs are available nationally and regionally to help communities identify and encourage good design, from the American Institute of Architects' Regional/Urban Design Assistance Teams (R/UDATs), to American Planning Association–sponsored interventions, to educational and nonprofit institutions looking to teach and organize community design workshops. For example, the Mayors' Institute on City Design, sponsored by the National Endowment for the Arts, has provided forums for American mayors to attend urban planning and design workshops and candidly debate local design and planning issues with a team of design, development, planning, and preservation professionals. The Tri-State Metropolitan Region also boasts over a dozen excellent schools of architecture, urban planning, and design that are often involved in local community design projects and present a powerful resource for fostering excellent design in communities.

Many of our region's centers, towns, and villages possess unique buildings and distinctive historic environments that contribute directly to the character, value, and desirability of their communities. Reflecting periods from colonial through the present, these resources may include classic residences, civic and religious buildings, historic theaters, and parks, as well as the rich qualities that arise from an ensemble of buildings or a historic district such as a traditional main street.

The failure of many citizens and local governments to build public support for a system, process, or local law that promotes excellence in urban design and protects historic buildings and resources has resulted in great losses to the region. For instance, the destruction of New York City's glorious Pennsylvania Station helped, in the end, to catalyze support for the nation's most advanced landmarks law—which was upheld by the U.S. Supreme Court and in turn protected Grand Central Terminal from demolition. The Grand Central Terminal area is now the functional and visual focus of an enhanced Midtown Manhattan.

Historic landmarks that serve as the centerpiece of community identity are at risk because actions to protect them are uneven. Threats to these historic resources may include demolition, neglect, alteration, or insensitive use, as well as the unintended consequences of rezoning and road widening, among others. Nevertheless, notable examples do exist throughout the region where development and preservation goals have been considered jointly as a part of a larger plan to retain community identity and allow appropriate growth at the same time. In Westbury, the proposal for a Long Island Performing Arts Theatre seeks to spur cultural activity and economic development by renovating a theater built in the 1920s.

Help is available from both government and nonprofit organizations to assist communities in identifying historic resources and planning for their preservation. There are state and national designations, such as the National Register of Historic Places. Though no guarantee against demolition of a building, these designations may provide access to tax incentives or grant money, or they may entail additional review of proposals to mitigate negative impacts.

However, local governments and the use of their powers are seen by many as the most effective way to ensure the protection of buildings, sites, or historic environments. Many communities have integrated preservation goals and requirements into their overall systems of planning and development. This may take the form of a local landmarks law with a commission to govern it or a landmarks advisory committee to the planning board. The state of New Jersey has passed enabling legislation to make it easier to create local preservation ordinances. When established properly, these commissions or committees may research, review, and designate sites of significance, and comment or rule on changes or additions that affect the landmark. Tools such as the transfer of development rights may be employed to provide flexibility and additional economic incentives for appropriate development.

Several New York examples of these approaches can be found in the master plan in the town of Pawling and the local laws in Mamaroneck, Rye, and Roslyn. In Plainfield, Haddonfield, and Princeton, New Jersey, as well as in Greenwich, Westport, and Stamford, Connecticut, local commissions have been established.

## Arts and Culture of the Tri-State Region

The presence of a vital arts community in the region provides substantial economic and other quality of life benefits, such as retaining and attracting business and corporations, improving the quality of our public realm, and reinforcing neighborhoods and centers. Yet for all of these strengths, the health of the arts and culture community is vulnerable, placing a host of crucial benefits at risk.

The harsh economic environment is leading to the loss of artists, performers, and other creative individuals. Incremental disinvestments and neglect of both public and private institutions result in a decline of both established and new arts and cultural assets in the region.

To sustain the arts community, continue the region's national and international leadership, and maintain a thriving tourism industry, six primary challenges must be met:

1. *Maintain the region as a destination for creative people.* Above all else, the region's primacy in the arts depends

on its ability to attract and nurture artists and creative individuals. As this region is a place where talented people often arrive with few resources and formal pathways to a career, the ability of the region to meet the "start-up" requirements of creative individuals is crucial to the continued influx of talent. It is also an opportunity that needs to be protected by maintaining a healthy "incubator" environment that allows new talent to emerge from small and experimental venues. To some extent, the issue for artists is the same as for other professions that the region needs to attract and develop—do the professional opportunities and life-style choices available in the region outweigh the high costs of living and the problems of crime, congestion, and inconvenience?

*2. Integrate the arts into the basic institutions and resources of the region.* Changes in government funding prospects and in the economics of the entertainment industry have increased the importance of integrating the arts more closely with the activities and agendas of business and government in the region. The challenge for the arts and culture community is, therefore, to identify and build alliances based on those common issues that enhance the arts and the region as a whole.

*3. Meet the financial needs of the arts.* Arts and culture are frequently treated as a luxury by government and industry, despite their central importance to the economy and quality of life. Moreover, many critical research and development aspects of the industry are not as connected to market forces as commercial products. The viability of many small cultural organizations often hinges on relatively modest sums of public subsidy and private support. Profitability or success for nonprofit or commercial institutions does not necessarily mean that the initial makers of the creative ideas have been rewarded or that a favorable atmosphere exists for new ideas. For instance, in the 1994 to 1995 season there was much discussion about why theaters and producers of Broadway plays brought to the public only two new musicals. Critics noted that the industry as a whole is becoming increasingly characterized by revivals. There is clearly a need for innovation in connecting new ideas and content more closely to market forces and in developing more support for public subsidies.

*4. Ensure leadership in arts training and education.* This region is a center for arts training and for the development of talented artists and performers for local, national, and international audiences. However, without a conscious and coherent program to foster continuing development of its own arts and culture talent base, the region will invite decline as a global center of the arts. Paradoxically, arts education has become one of the areas most vulnerable to cost-cutting in contracting school budgets. The decline of arts education coincides with a changing population with different cultural backgrounds

*Figure 82: The arts are a critical resource to the quality of life of the region.*

and priorities than previous generations. Both the development of these new audiences for the arts and the training of another generation of artists requires a new commitment and dedication to arts education.

*5. Meet the physical needs of the arts.* Arts and culture, and the tourism that they attract, are significantly influenced by the physical conditions under which they operate. If size and diversity of the region's arts and cultural resources are a major asset, developing full access and presentation venues are major challenges. The region's size, density, and congested transportation systems impose a difficult hurdle for both residents and visitors to attend cultural events, particularly those located outside the region's core. While our mass transit system is a major asset, it is oriented toward the hours and locations of employment centers, not cultural and recreational destinations. As congestion and costs of operating facilities increase, physical access and opportunities decline. Greater consideration of the needs of arts and culture in transportation planning and cooperative efforts to disseminate information on the full range of activities in the region would expand access as well as tourist activities.

*6. Provide all communities with better access to and participation in the arts.* Although the increasing cultural diversity of the region is a great asset for creativity and innovation, there is also a gap developing between many communities and traditional arts and cultural institutions. Increasing access to and participation in the arts for new populations and low income communities strengthens both the arts and local neighborhoods. Arts and culture are a major channel for shaping and expressing the identity of individuals and communities within a diverse metropolis. The arts provide opportunities through which new generations of consumers and participants can be developed. Ensuring both institutional leadership and audience development in larger institutions that represent the region's diversity is another key factor in developing a regional arts community that fully benefits from, and returns to, the richness of its community resources.

## Notes

1. "The New 'Burbs: The Exurbs and Their Implications for Planning Policy," Judy S. Davis, Arthur C. Nelson, and Kenneth J. Dueker, *Journal of the American Planning Association*, Winter 1994, Vol. 60, No. 1.

2. "Edge Cities Dominate Office Market," Kim Kennedy, *AIA Architect*, November 1994.

3. "The New Geography of Service and Office Buildings: A Rutgers Regional Report," James W. Hughes, K. Tyler Miller, and Robert Lang, Rutgers, The State University of New Jersey, New Brunswick, 1992, p. 13.

4. Bureau of Economic Analysis.

5. "Transportation Choices 2020: Executive Summary," p. 2.

6. For examples, see Peter Calthorpe, *The Next American Metropolis*, Princeton Architecural Press, 1993; or Peter Katz, *The New Urbanism: Toward an Architecture of Community*, McGraw-Hill, Inc., New York, 1994.

7. These principles are adapted from Armando Carbonell, Harry Dodson, and Robert D. Yaro, *Expanding the Ahwahnee Principles*, unpublished monograph, February 1995.

8. Benton MacKaye, *The New Exploration: A Philosophy of Regional Planning*, Harcourt, Brace and Company, Inc., 1928.

9. For previous work in Brooklyn, see RPA's *Downtown Brooklyn Report*, 1983.

10. Regional Plan Association, *Downtown Brooklyn: Strengths and Challenges Report*, June 1995.

11. Linda P. Morgan et al., *Union County Model Site Redevelopment Project: Final Report*, Regional Plan Association/New Jersey, June 1994.

12. Ibid.

13. U.S. Census of Population, 1990, *Journey to Work*.

14. RPA, "Transportation Needs of the Manhattan Central Business District," unpublished report prepared for NYMTC, 1992.

15. Boris Pushkarev and Jeffrey M. Zupan, *Urban Space for Pedestrians*, MIT Press, Cambridge, MA, 1975.

16. Ibid.

17. U.S. Census Bureau, "Housing Units Authorized by Building Permits," selected years.

18. U.S. Census Bureau, "Census of Retail Trade," 1992.

19. U.S. Census Bureau, "Census of Construction Industries," 1987. Note this is most current year available. It is likely that this amount has declined since the peak construction years of the 1980s.

20. U.S. Census Bureau, "Census of Retail Trade," "Census of Construction Industries."

21. Regional Plan Association analyses in the 1960s and 1970s forecast housing shortages and upward price pressures, as well as increasing segregation, as a result of exclusionary zoning requirements enacted by municipalities at that time.

22. Regional Plan Association, *Household Formation in the Tri-State Region & the Demand for New Housing, 1980–2015*. Working Paper No. 3. Prepared by Regina B. Armstrong for the Metropolitan Transportation Authority, September 1990.

23. Ibid.

24. Average new unit size from "Statistical Abstract of the United States, 1993."

25. Computed by adjusting the regional median income by the income range criteria and multiplying by 2.5, a rough factor of income to mortgage value, assuming a 5% down payment.

26. RPA and Fairfield 2000, "Affordable Housing for Connecticut: the Results of the Greenwich Affordable Housing Competition," 1989.

27. U.S. Bureau of the Census, "Statistical Abstract of the United States, 1992," Table 1213.

28. State of Connecticut, Conservation and Development Policies Plan for Connecticut, 1992–1997.

29. For more information about this process in New York State, see "Recommendations for Improving the Land Use and Development Approval Process in New York," prepared by the New York City Housing Partnership, 1993.

30. This program was reauthorized and permanently extended by the Revenue Reconciliation Act of 1993. The tax credits are distributed by the Internal Revenue Service to designated state agencies. In New Jersey the Council on Affordable Housing (COAH) is the responsible agency. In Connecticut the Connecticut Housing Finance Authority (CHFA) distributes the funds.

31. NYC Housing Partnership, 1993.

32. For more information on New Jersey's affordable housing programs, see State of New Jersey, Council on Affordable Housing, *The COAH Handbook...getting through the maze*; Housing New Jersey, "Mount Laurel II—10 Years Later"; and Art Bernard, "Affordable Housing Seen as a Constitutional Obligation," *Trends in Housing*, Vol. 26, No. 6 (April–May 1988), p. 2ff

33. Total U.S. property tax receipts were $155 billion in 1990. Total outstanding mortgage debt for homes of one to four units was $2.7 trillion in 1990. Assuming 10% of the total mortgage debt ($270 billion) is deducted, plus the $155 billion local property tax deduction equals $425 billion. The 1990 HUD budget for lower income housing assistance was $7.37 billion (from U.S. Bureau of the Census, "Statistical Abstract of the United States, 1992").

34. Thomas Fischer, "Low-Income Housing: Avoiding our Past Failures," *Progressive Architecture*, May 1994, pp. 49–55.

# Chapter 8

# The Mobility Campaign

TRUE REGIONAL MOBILITY, the free-flowing movements of people and goods, has three principal components, all of them achievable:

1. Improved transit service available to a larger number of the region's citizens.
2. A highway network largely freed from congestion.
3. A transformed freight transportation system.

Transformation is indeed a central theme of this section of the plan. And at this point, urgently needed new services can be achieved more quickly by embracing new thinking about how transportation works.

## Issues

The difficulties of meeting many of the region's transportation needs are compounded by inherent limitations within the system. Some of these limitations are physical, others are institutional, and some seem almost beyond belief. We have all heard about overcrowded trains, even if we have not ridden on one, but how many people realize that parts of our transit system are underused, unused, or have never even been hooked together? The 63rd Street tun-

nel under the East River was built with two levels—one for rapid transit, the other for commuter rail. The upper level, for rapid transit, is in service, although it operates far short of capacity and is so poorly connected that it does far less than it should for under-served residents of Queens. No trains have ever run through the lower level. After a generation of delay, tracks have yet to be threaded under Manhattan from the end of the tunnel at Second Avenue to Park Avenue and into Grand Central Terminal. The Hell Gate Bridge, part of a vast Pennsylvania Railroad system, is the railroad equivalent of an Interstate highway, with vast unused capacity capable of serving regional needs. Yet it sees less service than a private driveway, carrying only a handful of intercity Amtrak trains. Other transit lines, such as the Atlantic Branch of the LIRR and the Broadway BMT in Manhattan, have a ghost-like quality and operate far short of their capabilities.

### Commuter Rail

The three regional commuter railroads have seen their ridership growing due to significant investments over the past 15 years in new equipment, station rebuilding, and track and signaling. Getting to the trains, however, remains a particular problem. Some people can walk from their homes to a commuter rail station, but low-density zoning near many stations limits that potential. Many people drive to the train station when there is adequate parking—itself a problem. Additional parking facilities are often resisted by local communities because they bring added traffic and consume land that could support tax-paying businesses. And some people take buses or shuttle vans to the train stations. These "feeder services" are expensive to provide and, for most people, represent an intolerable additional inconvenience. Making transit attractive means finding the right mix of access methods, while avoiding the negative impacts of parking—not an easy combination.

Lack of direct and unimpeded access from suburbs to major employment centers in Manhattan can diminish the economic well-being of both the centers and the suburbs. Lower Manhattan is in particular jeopardy. It is inaccessible by rail without at least one transfer, whether a person is coming from New Jersey, Long Island, Connecticut, or upstate New York. Long Islanders can only easily reach west Midtown. Both Metro North and Long Island riders are faced with crowded subways, expensive taxis, or long walks if they are going from their rail terminals to Midtown locations. The former group has trouble reaching the west side, the latter group the east side. Only three NJ TRANSIT rail lines presently come into Manhattan, and then only to Penn Station in west Midtown. Riders on all other NJ TRANSIT lines must transfer, while still in New Jersey, to PATH trains or ferries. As a result, New Jersey residents have a difficult time reaching east Midtown.

Use of the commuter rail network is further inhibited by:

- Low frequency of service in the "reverse peak direction" that could bring city workers to suburban jobs, and by the fact that suburban offices are almost always well beyond walking distances from suburban train stations.

- The absence of through-services—say, from Long Island to New Jersey, or from New Jersey to Westchester and Connecticut.

- Limited service in off-peak hours and on weekends in many areas. On the LIRR the West Hempstead and Oyster Bay lines suffer in this regard, as do Metro North's Waterbury and Danbury branches, and NJ TRANSIT's Gladstone, Boonton, Montclair, and Pascack Valley lines. The last three have no weekend service at all.

Moreover, much of the region simply has no commuter rail service. Most new suburban growth is either beyond or between existing lines. Closer to the center, many residential areas at the edge between urban and suburban transit services typically have lost commuter rail service without urban transit improvements. The suburban areas farthest from rail lines, yet relatively close to Manhattan, include the eastern portions of Bergen County in New Jersey and Rockland County in New York.

Solutions to these problems have often been proposed. The continuing availability of creative thinking has never been a barrier to progress. Planning for new rail services in the region has gone on unslackened for the last 70 years, but with few tangible results in the last half-century. The amount of new rapid transit track provided can be measured in yards, and commuter rail lines have been dropped rather than added. Elevated rapid transit lines have been torn down but never replaced. Certainly, inadequate public funding has had a great deal to do with retarding appropriate actions. But the region's planning talent is scattered among half a dozen subregional transit agencies, each with its own agenda. No one has a mandate or a mechanism to focus on either long-term or regional perspectives. Transit agencies, filled with dedicated officials, are aware of the problem and have begun in very real ways to reach out to each other. But we still need a new way to build a truly regional network of rail services.

### Subways

The New York City subway system is the center of the rail transit system. It carries more than 3 million people each day—a billion a year—over 280 miles of track, stopping at 469 stations. The system is old, but in the last 15 years $10 billion has been spent to bring the system back from devastating deterioration caused by years of neglect. Derailments, fires, stuck doors, and graffiti, once all too common, have been virtually eradicated, and all cars are now air-conditioned.

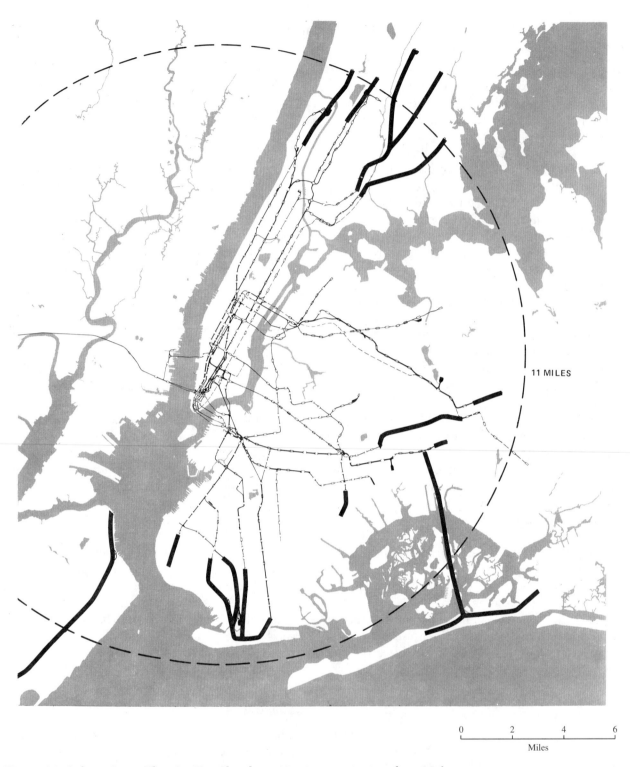

11 MILES

```
0        2        4        6
|--------|--------|--------|
         Miles
```

**Figure 83:** *Subway Lines That Are Too Slow [over 30 minute train time from Midtown (42nd Street and 6th Avenue) or Downtown (Fulton Street/Broadway Nassau)].*

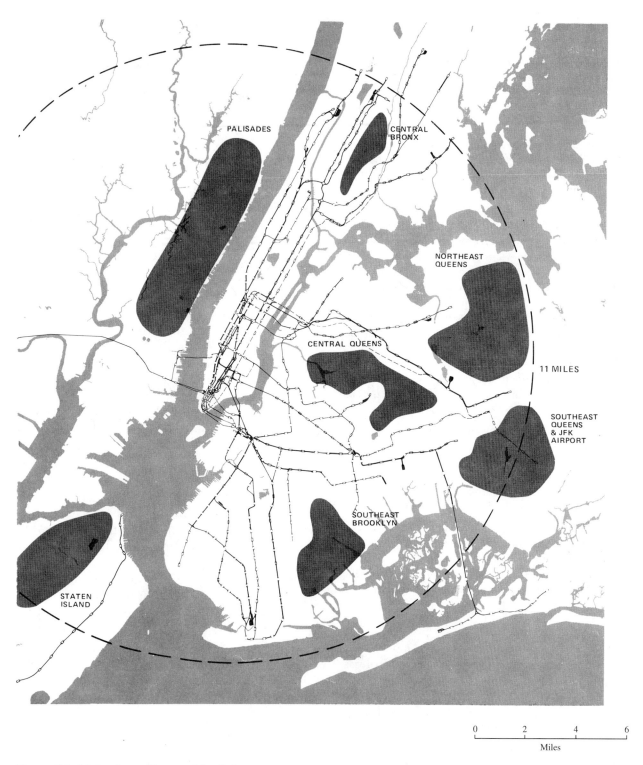

**Figure 84:** *Major Areas Unserved by Subway.*

But the subway rescue operation is far from complete:

- Despite a few glowing exceptions, station conditions are poor.

- The system is slow, averaging only about 20 miles per hour. Many of the outer portions of the outer boroughs of the Bronx, Brooklyn, and Queens are up to one hour away from Manhattan.

- For all their vast numbers, subway stations are far beyond walking distance throughout many parts of the four boroughs in which the subway operates, so people have to get on a bus (and pay another fare) just to reach a subway line that can take them to work. Over one-quarter of New York City residents live more than one-half mile from a subway station. They are concentrated in southeastern and northeastern Queens, parts of southern Brooklyn, the upper east side of Manhattan, and neighborhoods of the central and northeastern Bronx. Only a small minority of Staten Island residents live within a reasonable walking distance from the single south-shore Staten Island Rapid Transit line.

- Crowding reaches inhuman proportions on many lines and in many stations. Among the worst are the Lexington Avenue lines and the E and F trains from Queens. Crowding creates dangerous backups and long waits to leave platforms. Most notorious of all is the 53rd Street and Lexington Avenue station.

- In addition, there are still 70 miles of elevated lines in the subway system, all built before the Depression, with some dating back to the Civil War era. These lines are an eyesore and detract from surrounding neighborhoods. And they require an inordinate amount of upkeep.

Perhaps the subway's greatest problem is the continued perception on the part of the public that it is unsafe, augmented by the lack of control passengers feel over their circumstances. This feeling comes despite a 50% drop in the crime rate over the last five years and discouragement of panhandlers and fare-beaters. This perception problem is a generation old and dates back to the disinvestment that transformed the subway into a sour and dim environment in the 1970s and early 1980s. Now the perception lingers dangerously, mocking billions of dollars of constructive reinvestment. The subway is a public treasure, yet many people still shy away from using it, particularly in late night and early morning hours. The irony, of course, is that by any measure the chance of deaths and injuries from motor vehicle accidents is much higher than that of being victimized in the subway. But drivers, who actually face greater danger, believe that they can control, at least to some degree, the risks they face. And until the subway provides simple amenities such as adequate lighting and well-kept restrooms, it will continue to reinforce these perceptions.

### Buses

The bus network is more flexible than the rail network because it can be more easily deployed to respond to new markets. But buses, with few exceptions, must travel on the same congested roads that automobiles and trucks use, rendering them so unreliable that riders may arrive home on time one day, 20 minutes late the next day, and 45 minutes late the day after that. Bus ridership in New York City has continued to decline as more residents take local jitneys or buy cars. Within New York City, declining revenues have brought cutbacks in service, which in turn have led to a further loss in ridership. It is the now-familiar downward spiral. And in less dense areas, where there are fewer potential customers to begin with, it is even harder to justify frequent and extensive service.

Express buses operate from the outer boroughs in places that the subways do not reach, but they add to the traffic and pollution within Midtown and in the neighborhoods they pass through. Express buses from the suburbs are largely confined to New Jersey and the New York counties west of the Hudson River. They benefit from the Route 495 exclusive bus lane—the busiest in the world—but that lane is reaching its capacity. Moreover, buses must use other crowded highways, especially in the evening peak period. The use of the Port Authority Bus Terminal is also a deterrent, since it is distant from many workers' employment locations.

### Ferry Service

Since the mid-1980s ferries have seen a rebirth in the region. They serve markets that were poorly served by conventional ground transportation modes and where boarding points are accessible, either by being in easy walking distance, connecting with other modes of transportation, or providing parking facilities. The Hoboken-to-World Financial Center, the Weehawken-to-West 38th Street, and the Atlantic Highlands-to-Lower Manhattan ferry services successfully meet these criteria and have been helped by public investments in docking facilities or strong private sector efforts. New York Waterways has been particularly successful in these first two markets because they have provided premium amenities and convenient parking in New Jersey with bus services in Manhattan. The absence of these features explains the failure of other ferry service experiments. The abundance of waterways in the region suggests that we should continue to search for the market niches where ferries can meet these criteria.

### *Highways*

Throughout the 1950s, '60s, and '70s, highway construction continued explosively. New toll roads were constructed (New York State Thruway, New Jersey Turnpike, Garden State Parkway), the Interstate system was largely completed, and a number of state highways were widened and upgraded into limited access facilities. The rate of expansion of regional road capacity has now slowed, from 62 miles per year in the 1950s to only about 7 miles per year in the last 10 years. It will never again reach the earlier pace. The last Interstate highway in the region has now been built. Remaining highway expansion proposals are already mired in controversy. Highway budgets now focus on maintenance of the aging highway infrastructure network and on management systems to gain greater productivity.

Meanwhile, increases in highway travel also appear to be flattening, but it is too early to know if this is a temporary or permanent trend. If highway usage does not grow strongly, we will not need much more highway capacity. And if stronger growth appears, we must redirect it toward centers where transit, walking, and biking can take the place of auto travel. The bottom line is that we should not be building, on a wholesale basis, more road capacity. That era is over. If we revive it, it will bring us choking new congestion and millions of acres of new sprawl. Local suburban development projects, which seem to be in a particular town's best interest, draw ever more cars onto already crowded streets. When this happens again and again, the cumulative regional effect is crippling traffic congestion, a diminished quality of life, impaired air quality, and decreased productivity.

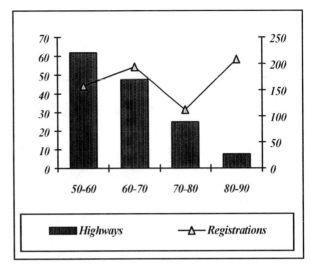

**Figure 85:** *Annual Miles of New Highways and Thousands of New Auto Registrations, per Decade, 1950–1990.*

Other factors have also been pouring more and more cars onto the region's roads:

- Most parking in the region is free. And even when it is not, many employers provide it to their employees. The federal tax code allows a nontaxable fringe benefit of up to $150 a month that reimburses drivers for parking charges. A mid-1980s survey of trans-Hudson auto commuters into Manhattan found that over half were being subsidized by their employers. But by law, employers can only provide a tax-free fringe benefit of $60 per month to workers who take transit, even if their out-of-pocket costs are comparable to those of drivers, which translates into a government-sponsored 60% penalty to transit users.

- Gas prices have continued to dwindle compared to the rate of inflation and the price of transit. Gasoline prices are lower today than at any point in the last 75 years, after adjusting for inflation.[1] Gas is the cheapest liquid you can buy, cheaper to buy than milk, beer, Coke, or even bottled water. But unlike these other liquids, it is nonrenewable.

- More people are able to drive, and the number of workers and the number of registered autos are now almost identical in many parts of the region. During the 1980s the youngest of the baby-boom population became old enough to drive, and shortly thereafter they "arrived" in the workforce, fueling the large increase in driving during the decade.

- Current toll policies are absolutely backward. They reject the fundamental market principle of charging more for a scarce resource. Instead, tolls are discounted for commuters who use the roads during the most crowded times.

While the region can take some small comfort in not being the most congested major metropolitan area in the nation—Los Angeles tops the list by far—our congestion levels are not improving, and they impose a competitive burden we cannot afford to live with. Moreover, there are significant congestion costs that further reduce our competitiveness. According to one 1991 estimate, congestion costs the region $6.6 billion a year in lost time and extra gas, or nearly $1,100 per year per vehicle—compared to $900 per year per vehicle in Dallas, and only $650 in Atlanta.[2]

### Freight

Freight transportation in the region is marked by many weaknesses. Much of the infrastructure needs renewing. It has gaps where key connections have yet to be built and it is crippled by congestion. Commercial truck traffic both creates congestion on major routes and river crossings and is itself hampered by congestion. In response, trucking firms charge premiums to deliver in the New York area. It costs as much to move a truck from New Jersey to Long Island as it does to move the same truck to Pittsburgh—400 miles away. And shipping firms are moving their own trucking and warehousing facilities away from the urban core and out to greenfield sites at principal interchanges along the region's Interstate highways, for instance, in Middlesex County and at the intersection of the New York Thruway and I-84 in Orange County. This, on balance, causes more traffic, because now home-base is a longer drive away from shipping destinations. And this solution will work only as long as fuel remains cheap.

Freight railroads have a tough time competing with trucks in the region for several reasons. There is not much expansion space near existing urban rail freight terminals, which makes it hard for existing carriers to grow and for potential carriers to enter the market. Much of the rail freight track in the New York City area has overhead clearances that are too low to permit double-stack container trains. And there are no trans-Hudson rail crossings south of Albany, which creates circuitous routings and

slow service. The small short-line carriers in New York City and Long Island, the Long Island Rail Road freight division, and the New York Cross-Harbor Railroad are, despite several new initiatives, continuing to lose market share due to a combination of high costs and a lingering perception of unattractive services. Further, it has been estimated that heavy trucks do not pay their total travel and infrastructure cost in user fees, leading to both unfair modal advantage and infrastructure maintenance burdens being shifted onto others.[3]

Our position as one of the nation's premier air cargo hubs is undermined by the condition of our airports, poor highway access to these airports, and limited expansion room nearby. Moreover, continued financial instability and bankruptcy and the resultant integration and retrenchment of the aviation industry can lead to myriad combinations of carriers and routes with differing impacts for the region. A merger of major airlines could easily result in redistribution of flights, carrying with it a redistribution of airlift capacity supplied by passenger airliners. For instance, a USAir and British Airways union could have the effect of consolidating many of New York's interline flights into USAir's Pittsburgh hub.

Collectively, the region's marine terminals are the largest on the Atlantic Coast and some, in New Jersey and Staten Island, have room to expand and good links to major railroads and key highways. The port's market share is declining, however, in part from a perception of high costs and security concerns. While total tonnage imported and exported to and from the port has remained fairly steady since 1967, the region's share of North Atlantic trade has fallen from roughly three-fifths in 1967 to two-fifths in 1990. Meanwhile, global trade patterns have become dominated by Pacific Rim trade, which partly explains why the port's share of total U.S. trade has dropped from nearly 20% in 1967 to less than 8% in 1990. In addition, our channel depths are relatively shallow, and dredging to deepen them has caused environmental concerns.

## A New Vision of Regional Transit

With more and more drivers on the road, transit now has to be made attractive enough to hold on to

| Operator | Vehicles Used in Maximum Service | Route-Miles | Stations | Annual Passengers (in thousands) |
|---|---|---|---|---|
| **Commuter Rail** | | | | |
| NJ Transit | 589 | 398 | 158 | 47,552.1 |
| MTA-LIRR | 979 | 312 | 134 | 90,534.0 |
| MTA-MNRR | 702 | 268 | 108 | 57,398.6 |
| Total | 2,270 | 978 | 400 | 195,484.7 |
| **Rapid Rail** | | | | |
| MTA-NYCTA | 4,877 | 247 | 469 | 1,325,706.5 |
| MTA-SIRT | 36 | 14 | 22 | 5,355.2 |
| PATH | 297 | 14 | 13 | 60,107.8 |
| Total | 5,210 | 275 | 504 | 1,391,169.5 |
| **Light Rail** | | | | |
| NJ Transit | 16 | 4 | 11 | 3,283.1 |
| **Bus** | | | | |
| CT Local | 200 | 585 | na | 43,828.3 |
| NJ Transit | 1,551 | 1,443 | na | 113,449.9 |
| NJ Private | 991 | 2,337 | na | 67,507.1 |
| MTA-NYCTA | 2,963 | 2,337 | na | 656,105.2 |
| NYC Private | 983 | 757 | na | 80,009.7 |
| MTA-LI Bus | 261 | 447 | na | 26,376.3 |
| NY Suburban Local | 29 | 16 | na | 36,550.6 |
| Total | 6,978 | 7,922 | na | 1,023,827.1 |
| **Grand Total** | **14,474** | **8,201** | **915** | **2,613,791.4** |

*Figure 86*: *Extent and Use of the Regional Transit Network, 1991.*

the riders it already has while at the same time gaining a large new following. Maintaining the system is more than just a physical task, because it is measured by whether improvements can maintain, or regain, people's trust. In this context, repair no longer means replacement in kind. It means upgrading to higher standards that can attract people who have never ridden transit or who stopped riding years ago. This is particularly true in the case of the subway system—by far the largest element of the network, claiming half of all transit riders, where significant reinvestment has yet to overcome slow speeds, crowding, and too many under-served or unserved neighborhoods. The region's commuter railroads have already dramatically improved many services. Making it easier to get to stations is the next step. This means more opportunities for

walking and biking to stations in pedestrian-oriented village and urban centers, clustering new development near stations, and more parking facilities sensitively located. The commuter rail network also needs easier access to centers of commerce in the region's core. And new links between the three existing railroads are needed before it can be called a true network.

After the subway system and much of the commuter rail system came close to physical collapse in the late 1970s as the result of a generation of under-maintenance, the massive rehabilitation program set in motion by 1982 necessarily focused on bringing the system to "a state of good repair." Although such a program was necessary given the desperate state of affairs, little attention was paid to major improvements to or reconfiguration of the network. But today we must reach beyond the rescue mentality of the early 1980s. While bringing the system back to a state of good repair was critical over the past 25 years—and remains essential—a dollar spent to replace track on an existing route generates no benefits beyond those already in place. A dollar spent to put that track on a new alignment or create a totally new service can improve value by providing a string of new benefits. New alignments, for instance, can attract more passengers by reducing crowding and offering a faster ride and better service to under-served neighborhoods. It can also improve operating costs through higher speeds, better station spacing, and more sensible routing that reduces duplication of services with a new low-maintenance roadbed. And Victorian-age blight can be eliminated by replacing ancient and maintenance-intensive elevated lines with subway or surface routes. It is in this spirit of making every dollar work harder and smarter that RPA addresses the physical transformation of the region's rail system.

Today, more emphasis must be placed on improving dreary and decrepit stations. In addition to necessary cosmetic work such as replacing tiles, repairing leaks, and removing clutter, we need to undertake reconstruction at major stations, as has been done at the triumphant new Penn Station LIRR concourse and the 57th Street/Carnegie Hall stop on the old Broadway BMT line. New station work also needs more emphasis on security and clear and accurate subway information. As for overcrowding, a minimum space standard of four square feet per passenger should be the target for system upgrades.

Feeling unsafe is a problem that can be improved with better lighting, redesign of unattended corridor spaces and passages, and creation of expanded access to stations through light wells opening up the stations to light and air. Also needed are more stairways inside buildings, reducing conflicts between people trying to exit a subway and people walking along a street, and wider, shallower, and easier-to-climb stairways. More escalators would also improve the flow between streets and platforms. Stations that should receive priority in improving access are 72nd Street and Broadway; Times Square at 42nd Street; the joint New York City Transit/Long Island Rail Road stations at Atlantic Avenue and the DeKalb Avenue stations in Brooklyn; the Jamaica Center and Roosevelt/74th

Street stations in Queens; and Pelham Bay and the two 161st Street stations in the Bronx, among others.

The commuter rail network can similarly become a more attractive transit option by the provision of heated station buildings with ticket sellers and rest rooms, high-level platforms for easier boarding, and expanded parking in selected locations (see *Centers*).

Service can be improved with higher speeds that are not only more attractive to train riders but make the transit system more efficient by making better use of rolling stock. Greater rail speeds and comfort can be achieved through improved signal systems and switches, upgraded rail beds, continuously welded rails, universal cab signaling, and more skip-stop and express service. These improvements also make it possible to carry greater numbers of passengers. In off-peak hours and on weekends, more frequent service can be provided by using shorter but more frequent trains. The added labor costs can be offset by introducing one-person train operations and a system of off-vehicle or self-service fare collection on commuter rail trains.

Faster bus trips can be achieved by creating more express and skip-stop services—keeping in mind that there is a trade-off of longer walking distances to reach stops—or less frequent service at any one stop. Care must be taken to prevent inequities in service by neighborhood. Additional express bus services should supplement existing local routes. Where it can be provided and enforced, preferential treatments for buses to bypass traffic congestion can work, especially in corridors where rail service proves unfeasible, such as the Route 9 corridor in central New Jersey.

Finally, providing immediate and convenient information about the transit system is critical to attracting and maintaining ridership, particularly for the occasional rider. A rider who cannot easily find out when the train arrives, or where the bus stop is, or how to get the ticket or token required for the trip is unlikely to struggle to get questions answered if the family car is sitting in the driveway. Information systems can be improved in many ways: by informing customers about delays and alternatives, and about emergencies on the transit vehicles and platforms; by providing route and fare information in advance of transit trips; and by furnishing schedules, fares, "vicinity" maps, and route options at stations and stops to help customers find their way. Automated information services, accessed through telephones, can be put in place now, as is being done on Amtrak and the airlines. In time, emerging interactive computer-based techniques can expand the accuracy and timeliness of travel information for transit riders who call in for information or seek it at transit stations.

## Summary of Recommendations

The First Regional Plan proposed a massive campaign to reshape the region by building hundreds of miles of new highways and rail lines. The current plan has a bolder aim: because of a superb series of separate transportation projects already accomplished by previous generations, it is now possible to bring the region together and put nearly all of it within almost everyone's reach by building only a handful of miles of new rail lines, along with a second handful of miles of new highways.

We already have seven good subregional railways and subways—which often come tantalizingly close to each other. The few new miles of track, which would bridge the gaps between the existing systems, would give us, for the first time, a single, cohesive, coherent, region-spanning, and (in many places) high-speed rail line—*Rx*, or Regional Express Rail. Completing the region's rail network will make it as easy to get around much of the region by train as it already is by car—so the proposed new miles of track are also a key part of RPA's new highway campaign. Because what would otherwise have been the next generation of increased congestion on the roads will instead be accommodated by effortless train rides.

In the reshaped region people will leave home in the morning with car keys in one pocket and a rail pass in another. RPA's congestion busting is also bolstered by a separate plan for accelerated freight movement—because people can move around far more freely if they don't have to keep getting out of the way of slower moving "things," whether parcels, beer barrels, compact discs, steel beams, or any of the other goods we need to have at our fingertips.

### Sixteen Transportation Objectives

Today, there is no collective vision of what this region wants and needs most from its transit system.

RPA believes that such a vision must embrace the following 16 objectives:

1. Increase access to labor markets for employers of the region.
2. Connect the suburban transit network with all the major concentrations of activity at the heart of the region—specifically, Long Islanders to east Midtown and Lower Manhattan; northern suburbanites to west Midtown and Lower Manhattan; and New Jersey residents to all of Midtown and Lower Manhattan.
3. Improve service to the region's major urban centers in Downtown Brooklyn, Jamaica, and Newark.
4. Link the suburban sectors of the region.
5. Link the outer boroughs of New York City with one another.
6. Decongest the most crowded parts of the New York City subway transit system, including the Lexington Avenue line and the E and F lines in Queens.
7. Add to transit capacity into Penn Station from New Jersey in anticipation of added ridership from NJ TRANSIT improvements in the Meadowlands—the Kearny Connection, the Montclair Connection, and the Secaucus Transfer.
8. Expand coverage of the rail and subway network in areas that are poorly served today—the central Bronx, eastern Queens, and eastern Bergen and Rockland counties.
9. Speed up Manhattan-bound service from the outer reaches of the Bronx, Brooklyn, and Queens.
10. Create reinforcing internal Midtown Manhattan circulation systems in the subway and on the street.
11. Relieve the overloaded exclusive bus lane (XBL) on the approach to the Lincoln Tunnel.
12. Access the two Port Authority airports in Queens with rail transit service.
13. Establish a universal transportation fare payment system for all of the regional transit lines.
14. Break the barrier of the Hudson River for rail freight.
15. Free up capacity for essential truck traffic between New Jersey and New York.
16. Remove substantial volumes of nonessential motor vehicles from the streets and highways of the inner parts of the region.

Recommendations in the mobility campaign address each of these objectives. These recommendations fall into four major categories. First is the upgrade and state-of-good-repair of the elements of the existing transit system to attract more riders and keep the existing ones. The second category is the transformation of the existing rail network into a truly regional system, *Rx*, to overcome the system's inability to compete effectively in the global marketplace. Third is the implementation of highway congestion relief measures to increase its reliability and reduce the costs of delay. Finally, the mobility campaign calls for the upgrade of the goods movement network to reduce the cost of moving goods and services in the region. The individual elements in these four areas are summarized below:

1. Transit upgrades.

   - Shorter and more frequent trains to add off-peak frequency.

   - More skip-stop and express service.

   - Clear, accurate, current information systems.

   - Universal regional "smart card" with "self-service" collection system.

   - Subway stations with better lighting, redesigned to expand access and eliminate unattended areas, with wider, shallower, and easier-to-climb stairways and more escalators to improve flow.

   - Meet space standards on subways to relieve most overcrowded lines.

   - Heated commuter rail stations with ticket sellers and rest rooms.

   - High-level platforms for easier boarding at commuter rail stations.

   - Expanded commuter rail parking where access on foot is impractical.

   - Improved signals for higher speeds.

   - Upgraded rail beds and continuous welded rail for comfort.

   - Universal cab signaling.

   - Self-service fare collection to reduce costs.

   - Faster bus services with expresses and skip-stops.

   - Preferential treatment for buses to bypass traffic congestion.

   - New high-speed ferry services to fill the market niches where they can provide more direct and efficient services than can buses or rail transit. This is especially true for shore communities and locations such as Staten Island.

2. Create a Regional Express Rail (*Rx*) System and build new rail routes.

   - Construct the Long Island Rail Road into Grand Central Terminal connection.

   - *Broadway Rx* from Port Washington to JFK Airport via west Midtown, Lower Manhattan, and Downtown Brooklyn.

   - *Downtown Rx* from the Hackensack Meadowlands Sports Complex through east Midtown to Grand Central Terminal and to Lower Manhattan and on to Jamaica, Queens.

   - *Midtown Rx* from Secuacus and possibly from Paterson, New Jersey, to Great Neck via east Midtown.

   - A new Second Avenue subway line into the Bronx, with one branch starting in Co-op City and the other from the Grand Concourse, extending to Lower Manhattan and Downtown Brooklyn.

   - *Tri-State Rx* from Stamford to New Brunswick via Penn Station.

   - *Triboro Rx* connecting Brooklyn, Queens, and the Bronx.

   - Extension of the subway from Jamaica to Laurelton, Queens.

   - Restoration of the West Shore rail line to West Nyack.

   - Crosstown Light-Rail Loop.

   - Newark–Elizabeth Rail Link.

   - Cross-Nassau Light-Rail Link.

   - Staten Island Light-Rail.

   - New LIRR station in Sunnyside Yard in Long Island City.

   - Replacement of elevated line—McDonald Avenue (1.7 miles) and Canarsie line (2.8 miles).

3. Congestion busting through physical changes and market approaches.

   - Widen certain roads.

   - Finish only the missing highway links that support region's centers.

   - Fix notorious highway bottlenecks.

   - Oppose new highways that act as land-development "can openers."

   - Manage the highways better with demand- and supply-side tools.

   - Create employer-based incentives such as transportation vouchers and "cashing out" of free parking to encourage transit and carpooling.

   - Eliminate discount tolls during rush hours to ease peak congestion.

   - Establish tolls on free East River bridges.

- Establish differential tolls with electronic toll collection systems by time of day and congestion levels.

4. Improve commercial transportation's competitiveness.

- Build a rail freight line with any new trans-Hudson passenger crossing.

- Move long-haul solid waste by rail to help finance infrastructure improvements.

- Do not cut congestion by discriminating against trucks.

- Establish an equitable truck toll structure at the Hudson and East River crossings to encourage use of less-crowded facilities during less-crowded times.

- Deploy new technologies to minimize congestion and keep trucks moving.

- Cut freight's noxious impact on the environment.

## Regional Express Rail (*Rx*)

RPA's *Rx* plan accommodates most of the commuter markets that are projected to experience substantial growth over the next generation. RPA projects that more than 230,000 new trips to work will be made to Manhattan daily in 2020. This growth will have to be accommodated by rail—only 5 more sets of tracks would do it, while over 80 lanes of highways would be required. About 56,000 new trips are projected to come from Queens and Brooklyn; another 32,000 from Nassau and Suffolk counties; about 70,000 new trips into Manhattan are projected to originate in New Jersey, mostly from Hudson, Bergen, Essex, and Middlesex counties; and another 13,000 from the neighboring New York counties of Orange and Rockland.

For travel within the boroughs, over 40,000 new work trips will be made among the other four boroughs of New York City, with an additional 50,000 new work trips to be made completely within Queens and another 48,000 within Brooklyn. In New Jersey, the counties closer to New York City will also experience an influx of new commuter travel, with Essex, Hudson, Union, Passaic, and Bergen counties leading the way. Without the construction of *Rx* or other projects to provide for this growth, it is almost certain that it will not occur. The *Rx* proposals will bring substantially more service into the core of the region and will meet these needs, using the 63rd Street tunnel, a new tunnel under the East River from Brooklyn to Lower Manhattan, a new line from the Bronx and Upper Manhattan, and a new tunnel under the Hudson River from New Jersey. *Rx* will also serve substantial parts of the surrounding city and inner suburbs with new intra-borough and inter-county services.

Our existing rail system can be transformed into a truly regional rail network serving the diverse needs of the entire Tri-State Metropolitan Region. Such a regional rail network, called *Rx*, would be created not by building a brand-new rail system but by modifying the way the existing one operates and by adding critical new links. The resulting network would be the backbone of the region's transportation system, operating at higher speeds and more frequently to attract more riders, augmented in capacity to provide more comfortable rides for more people, interconnected to eliminate wasteful transfers, and reoriented to serve new travel markets. Working toward this metamorphosis, the region would create a transit system that can help strengthen its threatened core, repair the torn urban fabric, connect multiple centers of activity, preserve communities and open spaces, and offer equality of access for citizens in an economically efficient and environmentally sensitive manner.

A regional rail system can become the springboard to launch the next wave of development in the metropolitan region. This system can spur redevelopment just as earlier rail transit opened up new land opportunities in the early part of this century and as the automobile did in the second half of this century. Today, with environmental, social, and capital costs of new highways becoming prohibitive in much of the region, rail transit improvements should be the catalyst for economic growth in central areas.

Regional rail can be fast, comfortable, and convenient, actually rivaling the qualities of the private automobile. And rail is an option for all citizens. The region's existing rail system hands us, perhaps for the last time, the opportunity to save, rebuild, and re-create communities that have been losing out to the ravages of the automobile culture. Moreover, if designed and properly coordinated with land use decisions, a truly regional system would effectively serve many medium-density portions of the region now not served by rail, while providing new opportunities for economic development in suburban centers.

Today, the Tri-State Metropolitan Region faces competition from other existing or budding world cities. Each of our rivals already has developed or has ambitious plans to create its own regional rail system. Paris, Tokyo, London, and the major cities of Germany have completed theirs. Berlin's transit network, long divided by the Cold War, is being re-connected. And even Los Angeles has launched a multi-billion-dollar effort to create from scratch a rail network, that if completed as planned will only be a fraction of ours. Regional rail's productivity gains would make more effective use of public funds and fares through more efficient use of labor, rolling stock, and other infrastructure. Further, by regionalizing rail systems—breaking down artificial barriers between the three states and between the urban and suburban areas of the region—transit operators can make broader appeals for capital and operating funds and region-wide revenue sources, particularly after citizens of the region have come to view the entire rail system as "their own."

For these reasons, attracting more travelers to the region's rail is crucial. In the future, auto travel is likely to be increasingly constrained for environmental reasons, while revitalization of the traditional urban fabric, usually accessible by rail, will gain in importance. In many suburban areas of the region, transit use to the region's core is disproportionately low, since these areas have no trains at all and are served only by slow, traffic-delayed buses.

### Current Regional Transit Studies

Manhattan East Side Access (NYC Transit)

- To examine options for north–south transit on the east side of Manhattan
- Underway, completion July 1997

East River Crossing (NYC Transit)

- To examine options for East River transit crossings between Brooklyn and Lower Manhattan to reduce reliance on Manhattan and Williamsburg bridges
- Underway, completion Spring 1996

Access to the Region's Core (Joint MTA/PA/NJT)

- To examine options in the east–west Midtown corridor between New Jersey and Queens
- Underway, completion June 1997

LIRR East Side Access (LIRR)

- To examine options for access for the LIRR to east Midtown
- Underway, completion July 1997

Airport Access (Port Authority of New York and New Jersey)

- To examine how best to use the passenger facility charge to provide transit access to the two Queens airports
- New options being considered, given the rejection of the original, unaffordable, 22-mile automated system

Lower Manhattan Transportation Access Economic Benefits Study (Empire State Development Corporation)

- To examine the economic impacts of improved Lower Manhattan transit access
- Underway, completion Spring 1996

Long Island City Transportation Needs and Opportunities Study (MTA)

- To examine the alternatives for improved transit services in and to Long Island City
- Underway

To achieve all these purposes we must recognize the limitations of our current system, consider the options available to us to remove those limitations, and make some logical choices. The region's transportation agencies are already hard at work examining a range of alternatives in their distinct areas, as shown by the above list of transit studies. RPA applauds their work and wants to see it continue. Choosing new projects is never easy, particularly when dozens of other choices are simultaneously being made in so many separate agencies. Each alternative should be fully informed about all the other alternatives under examination, so that the region develops a clear vision of the future region-wide rail transit network. Then, we can work together to achieve it.

There are undoubtedly many ways of achieving at least some of these objectives for the regional rail network. RPA has concentrated on developing one plan, Regional Express Rail, or *Rx*, which we believe can accomplish them all. The concept is presented for active consideration by the citizens of the region and by the transportation agencies now planning particular portions of the rail network's future. Regardless of the fate of the *Rx* concept and its components, these issues—of ameliorating poor travel conditions and accommodating potential growth—must be faced. Ignoring them will result in declining regional competitiveness, a deteriorating quality of life, and ever-increasing transit irrelevance.

## What Is Rx?

*Rx* consists of a few critical projects, totaling only 25 miles of new transit lines added to the existing 1,250-mile rail network in the region—a 2% increase that makes possible a multitude of new services. Many of these concepts build on projects previously proposed or now actively being studied by transit agencies. Other concepts seek to capture the unrealized and ultimately abandoned investments made in previous generations, such as the 63rd Street tunnel connections, the Second Avenue subway, or the extension of the Archer Avenue subway in Jamaica.

What is *Rx*? It is a new rail network spliced together from the existing system by constructing a few critical links that are now missing. Some parts would be no different from commuter rail as we know it, others would remain just like rapid transit (the New York City subway or PATH), and still others would operate as frequently and with the acceleration of rapid transit but with the comfort of commuter rail. This last "hybrid" service would operate with *Rx* trains, redesigned from vehicles having the dimensions and power capabilities of the most modern rapid transit vehicle (like the ones in operation on the Washington Metro) so they can operate in existing tunnels, but with seating arrangements of the most comfortable commuter rail vehicles. *Rx* services would, where necessary, break down the artificial barriers among rail properties that had their genesis in the 19th century, when private rail companies competed with one another.

The proposed phasing of *Rx*, described in the following pages and illustrated in Plates 3A through 3D, is merely one possible sequence. The precise sequencing is an open issue, to be decided by available funding and the political process.

## Phase I of Rx

• *Tri-State Rx*, or through trains from Connecticut to New Jersey (e.g., Stamford to New Brunswick or Trenton), can run today without any new construction. These trains would make use of the nearly empty Hell Gate Bridge and could offer new stops in the Bronx at Co-op City and at the Bronx hospital complex in Eastchester near Hunts Point, where transfers to and from the Pelham Bay subway line would be possible, and perhaps in Queens at Northern Boulevard, where subway transfers could also be made. Connecticut, eastern Westchester, and eastern Bronx residents could also use *Tri-State Rx* trains to reach Penn Station and Newark Airport. Other through-routing among the three commuter railroads is possible. But it would require either changes in power sources or new vehicles and may not warrant the changeover. If through-service between Connecticut and New Jersey is very successful, however, other possibilities should also be considered, including: Hudson Line to Penn Station to Long Island, including Amtrak services; and NJ TRANSIT Northeast Corridor Line to Long Island.

• The long-awaited Long Island-to-Grand Central Terminal (GCT) connection would be completed. The project's "missing links"—short sections of track in Long Island City and between Park and Second Avenues—would be constructed, connecting the unused lower level tunnel under the East River at 63rd Street and giving Long Island Rail Road trains access to GCT by making use of available capacity on the terminal's lower level. About one-half of LIRR riders would switch to Grand Central–bound trains, saving up to 30 minutes per day. This connection would also shift some 8,000 Long Islanders from their automobiles. This would relieve congestion on the crowded roads of Queens and Nassau County, on the Queensborough Bridge, and in the Queens–Midtown Tunnel.

• Simultaneously, the LIRR's Port Washington line would be connected to the 63rd Street's upper level subway tunnel. This line would then be transformed into a high-frequency service, the *Broadway Rx* line, providing access to West 57th Street, Times Square, Herald Square, 14th Street, and City Hall, near the World Trade Center and municipal government buildings.

• Simultaneously, a rail link would be built from JFK Airport to LIRR's Jamaica Station, funded by the existing air passenger facility charge (PFC). This link would give LIRR riders one-transfer (by escalator) access to JFK, as well as setting up direct service to the airport from Downtown Brooklyn via the Atlantic line of the LIRR (converted to an *Rx* line), and the abandoned, city-owned ex-LIRR Rockaway Line, provided that the loop on JFK Airport was built to support the *Rx*-type vehicles. A new line would also be built from the present LIRR stop in Woodside, Queens (to be renamed LaGuardia), also using PFC funds. This transfer too would be easily accomplished via escalators.

• The old Farley Post Office across from Penn Station should be redesigned for Amtrak service, opening up more space in Penn Station for the expanded commuter rail operations and services expected there. This project, funded in part by the federal government through the efforts of Senator Daniel Patrick Moynihan, would once again establish a proper New York City gateway for intercity rail travel.

The first two projects in Phase I open up more frequent service into Penn Station. Currently, about three dozen LIRR trains enter or leave the station to and from the east in a peak hour: seven of them are Port Washington trains. The LIRR's current capacity expansion project will increase this number to 42 trains per hour. With some riders shifting to trains into Grand Central Terminal and with the Port Washington trains running in the 63rd Street tunnel, the LIRR will be able to bring more trains directly into Penn Station without the century-old change in Jamaica. There will also be more room for the other trains that use (or will use) Penn Station: high-speed Amtrak Northeast Corridor trains to Boston and *Rx* through-service between New Jersey and Connecticut. A total of 81 trains into Manhattan in the peak hour from the current LIRR lines operating through Queens would be provided (compared to 36 today), opening up many new opportunities for commuter rail–like services for Queens residents. Construction of the Grand Central Terminal link makes construction of the proposed Sunnyside Intermodal Terminal possible. For Port Washington line riders, the *Rx* link provides both increased service coverage in Manhattan and greater frequency of service, which can attract many new riders from northeastern Queens now relegated to the overcrowded Flushing subway line. This, in turn, could reduce traffic congestion in downtown Flushing caused by subway-bound commuters. Finally, these projects give all the region's suburban areas, east and west Midtown, and Lower Manhattan easy one-transfer access to JFK and LaGuardia, using either the new *Rx* or the existing LIRR.

### Phase II of Rx

• The long-stalled Second Avenue subway would be built from the Bronx to the Lower East Side. Starting at the Grand Concourse at 161st Street and heading south down Second Avenue, one new service would turn down the west side at 63rd Street in an existing tunnel under Central Park, while the other would continue down Second Avenue and end—temporarily—at New York Plaza

on Water Street. An added bonus is that with the Second Avenue subway in place, some Queens Boulevard trains that already use the 63rd Street tunnel could turn down Second Avenue to 34th Street.

• With the Midtown portion of the Second Avenue route completed, the already transformed Port Washington line would inaugurate a second *Rx* service known as *Midtown Rx*, through the 63rd Street upper level tunnel and down Second Avenue. This would serve east Midtown destinations before turning west to a new station under the lower level of Grand Central Terminal at 43rd Street. From this new station, *Midtown Rx* would be poised to continue west under 43rd Street and the Hudson River to New Jersey (see Phase IV).

• A *Downtown Rx* would run from the new Grand Central "under" station used by the *Midtown Rx*, south down Second Avenue to Nassau Street in the heart of the financial district. It would accommodate transferring Metro North riders at Grand Central Terminal who would have an easy escalator transfer to a high-speed, high-amenity, and frequent express service to Lower Manhattan. A second *Downtown Rx* service would operate under Second Avenue to Water Street and then to Brooklyn.

• Subway service would be extended from Jamaica Center beyond the current Archer Avenue station to provide coverage in southeast Queens equivalent to that provided in northeast Queens by the intensified Port Washington line. Most of this construction was completed in the early 1980s and then simply abandoned. Completing a short ramp to the surface would extend the Queens Boulevard subway service three miles east on the Atlantic Branch of the LIRR to Laurelton and Rosedale. The limited LIRR service now on that line would be shifted to the parallel Montauk LIRR mainline through St. Albans, where a third track could have been constructed during Phase I to provide capacity for the added service. As another bonus, LIRR Jamaica Station operations would be simplified and a blighting elevated trestle in Jamaica Center removed.

• A new station of the LIRR at Sunnyside Yard would be constructed to provide new rail access and make it possible to develop above this site in Long Island City. The construction of this station would be made possible once the LIRR connection to Grand Central is in place. Stopping trains at such a station now would actually reduce capacity and make service between Penn Station and Jamaica worse.

The *Downtown Rx* creates a high-amenity service from Grand Central to Lower Manhattan, making it possible for Metro North commuters to avoid the overcrowded Lexington Avenue subway line. Phase

II affords significant relief to the overcrowded Lexington Avenue subway and provides better east side coverage and faster speeds from the Bronx to Manhattan. Sending some Queens Boulevard trains down Second Avenue further relieves congestion on the 53rd Street line and gives convenient access to east side destinations. Moreover, it eases the particularly overcrowded transfer point at Lexington Avenue and 53rd Street. The Woodside station serves as a useful transfer point to allow LIRR riders to transfer to Port Washington *Rx* trains, giving them six new access points for Midtown Manhattan. Completion of the southeast Queens extension provides subway coverage into southeast Queens, thereby reducing the bus, van, and car traffic into Jamaica Center, and it provides new development possibilities for Jamaica and York College. Finally, the new Sunnyside station, along with improved transferring capabilities constructed at Queens Plaza, would create a development opportunity accessible by transit from most of Queens and Long Island, and via Amtrak to more distant locations from New England to Washington.

### Phase III of Rx

• The *Broadway Rx* service already reaching City Hall would be extended in a new tunnel under Broadway, stopping farther south to serve the financial district and then operating in a new tunnel under the East River to Brooklyn and under Atlantic Avenue and into the Atlantic Avenue terminal of the LIRR. This tunnel, which might be unnecessary if the BMT Montague Street tunnel were sufficiently freed up by subway improvements affecting the Manhattan Bridge, would also carry the *Downtown Rx* operated under Water Street. The two *Rx* services would continue along the *Rx* route on the converted LIRR Atlantic Branch east toward Jamaica, with one turning south down the Rockaway line to JFK and the other continuing to Jamaica to meet the LIRR.

• The new Manhattan–Brooklyn tunnel under the East River would be capable of receiving many Brooklyn trains that now operate over the unreliable and often-closed Manhattan Bridge, thereby reducing the reliance on the subway level of the bridge, which was never designed to carry such loads. These trains would operate along Water Street in Lower Manhattan, connecting to Sixth Avenue routes at Chrystie Street and providing subway coverage for the eastern edge of Lower Manhattan.

• Already established Second Avenue service in the Bronx would be extended north to Co-op City, replacing obsolete elevated sections of the White Plains Road subway line with a joint-service tunnel under Boston Post Road and on the surface along the existing Dyre Avenue IRT subway line.

Once Phase III is completed, LIRR riders will have a higher frequency of trains and two-stop service to Lower Manhattan from Jamaica. Midtown and Lower Manhattan will have direct service to JFK. Extending the Second Avenue subway north will bring the Bronx closer to Manhattan by slashing travel times. The replacement of slow, trouble-prone Manhattan Bridge subway service with a reliable route along Water Street will benefit Brooklyn subway riders enormously. And for those destined to the eastern edge of Lower Manhattan, including South Street Seaport, it will provide access not currently available.

### Phase IV of Rx

• Two *Rx* lines would operate west from the new station under Grand Central Terminal to the Secaucus Transfer site in New Jersey, where all ten existing NJ TRANSIT lines converge and where reactivated service on the West Shore rail line to West Nyack would also be available. The Secaucus Transfer station would then give all New Jersey rail riders the option of transferring to *Rx* service across 43rd Street to the east side at Grand Central Terminal, either on the *Midtown Rx*, which would take them up Second Avenue, stopping in the 40s and 50s, or to the *Downtown Rx* service, which would turn down Second Avenue to Lower Manhattan, as detailed in Phase II.

• The two *Rx* lines could extend farther into New Jersey by using the restored West Shore rail line at least as far as the Meadowlands Sports Complex and possibly to Paterson via the Main Line.

In this final phase New Jersey riders gain either direct or easy-transfer rail service to all of Manhattan's business and cultural districts, as well as to Downtown Brooklyn and Kennedy and LaGuardia Airports. Also, service along the West Shore line would establish rail service in eastern Bergen and Rockland counties for the first time in decades and substitute for slow bus services. These improvements would significantly ease the increasing congestion in the exclusive bus lane leading to the Lincoln Tunnel, making room to speed up vehicle traffic into the Lincoln Tunnel.

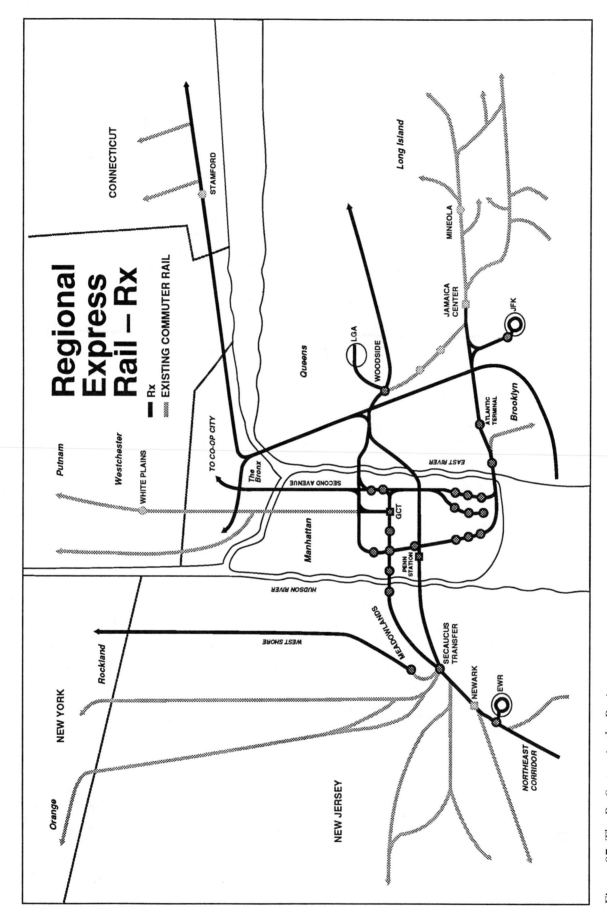

Figure 87: The Rx System in the Region.

The bulk of the subway system was constructed to reach out radially from Manhattan to the outer boroughs of the Bronx, Brooklyn, and Queens to enable mass commuting to jobs in the Manhattan central business district. The high-density construction that these early subway lines made possible also generated many travel needs within the outer boroughs and between them. But the subways never catered to these needs that they had themselves created. A new transit line, the *Triboro Rx*, running essentially perpendicular to the existing radial subway lines, would attract many outer borough transit riders, and by crossing existing lines would provide countless new intra- and inter-borough options. Twenty-three subway lines would be intersected at least once, with six others intersecting twice. Fortunately, most of the right-of-way is already available, in the form of the LIRR Bay Ridge freight line in Brooklyn (mostly 4-tracks wide), the New York Connecting Railroad in Queens, the lightly used Hell Gate Bridge between Queens and the Bronx, and the St. Mary's Park Tunnel in the Bronx,[4] which would allow Triboro trains to reach across 161st Street to Yankee Stadium.

The *Triboro Rx* could be constructed independently from the rest of the *Rx* system described above. It would be constructed in stages. The place to start is Brooklyn, replacing the 2.8-mile-long existing Canarsie elevated line and reusing the Bay Ridge right-of-way, in conjunction with the construction of 1.7 miles of tunnel south of Church Avenue to replace the slow-moving McDonald F elevated line.

Collectively, these subway projects would provide subway access to much of southeastern Brooklyn, eliminate antiquated elevated structures, fill underused express tracks on the IND F line, speed travel times from the Brighton Beach area, and begin the circumferential Triboro line.

The complete *Rx* system is shown in Figure 87, where the *Rx* services are indicated in gray with the commuter rail network depicted in black. Where there is an overlap, as on the Northeast Corridor in New Jersey and on MetroNorth's New Haven line, the *Rx* shading is used. RPA's *Rx* system:

- Uses both the upper and lower levels of the 63rd Street tunnel under the East River far more effectively.

- Makes maximum use of both major rail terminals in Midtown Manhattan.

- Makes maximum use of now underutilized subway and commuter rail lines.

- Breaks down the artificial barriers between the commuter rail network and the subway system, taking advantage of the best features of both.

## New Light-Rail Transit Routes

NJ TRANSIT is about to construct, using a private-sector turnkey builder and operator, a new *Hudson-Bergen Light-Rail* system to link many of the new and revitalized urban centers along the Hudson River waterfront to longer haul transit lines at Hoboken and PATH stations and to park-and-ride lots at either end of the line. This project can pave the way for the construction of other light-rail lines. NJ TRANSIT is at the same time planning to expand the Newark city subway—actually a light-rail system, to connect with major railroad stations and existing and potential office and shopping centers—and a line to Newark International Airport and Elizabeth.

These New Jersey initiatives, well underway, fulfill efforts that have been made east of the Hudson. In Manhattan, the long-proposed 42nd Street Trolley may be moving forward. It should be built and extended to Herald Square and up Broadway to Lincoln Center, as described in *Centers*. This system will connect all the major transportation portals in Manhattan—Grand Central Terminal, Port Authority Bus Terminal, Pennsylvania Station, PATH, and NY Waterway ferries—to key business and tourist destinations, as well as all north–south subway and *Rx* lines in Midtown Manhattan. This project should also follow the private operator "design–build–operate–maintain" model used for the Hudson-Bergen Light-Rail Line.

On Staten Island, the lightly used and inefficient Staten Island Rapid Transit rail line could be converted to light-rail to provide access to the ferry terminal at St. George. Extending a new line westward from the existing SIRT in the median of the Staten Island Expressway to Route 440 and the teleport will give residents of the north side of Staten Island reliable access to the ferry system, which should be expanded with high-speed services directly to Midtown Manhattan. It will also make transit travel within Staten Island easier, particularly to jobs and educational opportunities in the Staten Island Expressway corridor.

Specific centers on Long Island should also consider light-rail projects. The Oyster Bay and West Hempstead lines of the Long Island Rail Road should be converted to *Cross-Nassau Light-Rail Link* service to provide higher degrees of access along a north–south spine through Nassau County. A 3.3-mile-long connection between the existing Oyster Bay and West Hempstead lines through downtown Hempstead would not only help revitalize Hempstead but would also provide a much more frequently served cross-county transit spine connecting to LIRR trains at Mineola, Valley Stream, and Hempstead. Ultimately, three services could be developed: Oyster Bay to Mitchell Field via Mineola; Oyster Bay to Valley Stream via Mineola; and Mitchell Field to Valley Stream via Hempstead. Operated by MTA-Long Island Bus with single-operator crews, and with self-service fare collection, these light-rail lines could produce huge savings over the current LIRR operation, eliminating the need to replace old diesel trains on the Oyster Bay branch and simplifying the Main Line's costly third-track and grade crossing elimination project. It too could be ripe for a private–public partnership approach similar to the Hudson-Bergen LRT.

While the *Cross-Nassau* proposal provides an opportunity to convert a low-frequency, high-cost commuter rail operation to high-frequency light rail, similar opportunities in the suburbs of the region are few, either because there are too few potential riders or because no suitable rights-of-way are available. Furthermore, any light-rail service requires a downtown anchor, even one as modest as Mineola or Hempstead, and is ill-suited for circumferential trips or for areas dominated by strip commercial highway development.

### Barriers to Regional Transit Solutions

The greatest barrier to achieving the vision of *Rx* is self-perpetuating pessimism. Many people believe that we cannot afford to spend the kind of money required to put *Rx* in place. But if the region does not make this investment, it is guaranteeing that it will never again have the resources to even consider building such a system, since our ability to compete globally will decline and our economic base will erode.

The barriers to fulfilling this regional transit vision are institutional and financial, not physical or geographical. Many of the *Rx* phases require close and ongoing cooperation between operating agencies, mostly within the MTA organization. RPA's vision requires six barriers to fall:

1. Conflicts exist even within the same transit organization. Metro North, for instance, is wary of allowing LIRR trains into Grand Central Terminal, and LIRR is concerned about running Metro North Trains into Penn Station. And at the Port Authority, planning for airport access has proceeded without any serious consideration of alternatives that would involve cooperating with other transit systems.

2. Each agency continues to make its choices based on its own mandate. This is understandable in the absence of coordinated planning but unacceptable for the region. For example, at NYC Transit, the examination of subway options to relieve the burden on the Manhattan Bridge casts aside the interests of the LIRR in bringing Long Islanders to Lower Manhattan. Also, the Access to the Region's Core study is not examining options that have benefits to Lower Manhattan, because its mandate is only to look at the Midtown corridor. Sub-optimal choices are inevitable in such an environment.

3. Following directly from item 2, there is no universally agreed upon set of evaluation criteria proceeding from a shared value system to apply to alternatives. How, for example, do we weigh capital costs against operating deficits? How much are we willing to trade off in community impacts to gain some transportation benefits? How much are we willing to spend to remove motor vehicles from the roads to make our cities more livable or reduce air pollution? Or to give a transit rider a seat during the peak period?

4. Because responsibility is scattered among many entities and across many jurisdictions, there is no overall process for decision-making. Federal legislation theoretically puts this process in the hands of the official Metropolitan Planning Organizations (MPOs) in each metropolitan area, but in this region there are separate MPOs in each state. Moreover, even within each state the MPOs do not now have clear control over the process of prioritizing projects as intended by the legislation. A decision-making bridge across jurisdictions is needed.

5. Regional funds are not apparent. Moreover, federal funding for capital projects is directly assigned to each transit operator. It is difficult for individual agencies

to give up funding for projects beneficial to their operations and constituencies for projects whose benefits will be shared with other political jurisdictions. Current funding mechanisms must be changed to accommodate the regional funding of worthy regional projects.

6. Finally, the public in each state needs to see the entire regional transit system as their own. The system needs to present itself as a seamless whole to a public whose fundamental interest is in moving around freely. One way of doing that is through a universal fare system, one that integrates tokens, Metrocards and paper tickets, with highway, bridge, and tunnel tolls.

There are certainly many ways to improve the regional rail network for the benefit of the entire region. RPA has concentrated on developing a single plan, Regional Express Rail (*Rx*), which incorporates the best advantages of them all. Because the *Rx* system provides benefits to so many parties, it should be possible to build a consensus around the full plan. But this will happen only if the region's separate constituencies are able to agree to support elements of the program that do not directly benefit them, understanding that they will receive mutual support from others. The range of interests that will benefit from the system must not be forgotten—benefits for employers and employees, realtors, developers, unions, New York City subway riders, suburban commuter rail riders, and airport passengers and employees. The benefits also cast a wide geographic net—including Long Island, New Jersey, the Hudson Valley, Connecticut, and each of the boroughs of New York City. *Rx* works to strengthen the region's centers, most notably Lower Manhattan, Downtown Brooklyn, Long Island City, Jamaica, the Hudson River Waterfront, and Newark. And *Rx* gets cars and trucks off the road, easing congestion on the region's highways and benefiting even those people unable to take advantage of the new system directly.

## Congestion Busting Through Physical Changes

The highway system does need expansion, but only by a very small amount. Five kinds of projects are needed to attack congestion, rather than encourage it: (1) the widening of existing roads with high-oc-

cupancy vehicle lanes; (2) completion of relatively short missing links of the network; (3) short bypasses of critical points of congestion; (4) new highways extended into new areas; and (5) parkway upgrades.

### Widening

Because the widening of existing highways is constrained by the Clean Air Act Amendments (CAAA), such projects must show that they will result in no net increase in vehicle miles of travel (VMT). To try to move highway expansion forward and still comply with the CAAA, highway agencies have proposed widening projects that add high-occupancy vehicle (HOV) lanes. Segments of Interstate 287 in Westchester and in Morris and Somerset counties, and Interstate 95 in Connecticut, and the Long Island Expressway have been proposed for widening with lanes reserved for vehicles with two or more occupants. On 10 miles of the Long Island Expressway and on I-80 in New Jersey such HOV lanes have been put in place with only mixed results. Given past experiences, new HOV lanes are likely to generate increased VMT without encouraging much carpooling or transit use. In the long run their result is likely to be only a wider highway carrying more vehicles moving at slower speeds, thereby opening up more land to sprawl development and adding to air pollution problems.

One obvious remedy would be to require more people per car, but it is hard to guarantee that enough properly filled cars would turn up. Carpools have to travel by indirect routes, are dependent on the kindness of strangers, and generally lack flexibility in their starting times. Without some other strong incentives to carpool or use transit, these lanes are likely to be underused. When low demand results in empty lanes, pressures rise to open them up to single-occupant vehicles, and HOV lanes become a euphemism for highway widening. One new concept is to allow single-occupant vehicles and trucks to buy their way into the HOV lane (as is now being done on Freeway 91 in Southern California), thereby increasing the lane's productivity and raising revenue. But this can raise fairness and equity issues.

Competing interests are clearly at work here. Widening projects need to be judged by a variety of criteria, such as "people throughput," VMT growth, delay reduction, and cost—and in the case of HOV "buy-ins," revenues. These projects also need to take note of policy changes regarding pricing of transportation recommended later in this plan. Until they can be subjected to this kind of comprehensive review, any widening projects using HOV lanes should not proceed.

### Missing Links

The completion of so-called "missing links" in the highway system should depend on whether they serve existing centers or otherwise directly assist the economy of the region. Projects that open up undeveloped greenfield areas to sprawl should not proceed. RPA recommends the completion of the following missing links in New Jersey: NJ 21 through Passaic to US 46 to relieve traffic; and the Interstate 280 connector into Newark to provide improved downtown access. The extension of Route 34 outside New Haven in Connecticut would complete another missing link.

### Bottlenecks

There are numerous long-standing and even legendary traffic bottlenecks in the region that will not be cured by even substantial shifts in travel demand. Each part of the region has notorious favorites. These problem areas, which are not amenable either to pricing changes or to other solutions, should be fixed. In New Jersey, examples include the interchanges between Routes 4 and 17 in Bergen County or Routes 3 and 46 in Passaic County.

### Substantial Capacity Upgrades

Certain projects, all in low-density undeveloped areas would act as "can-openers" to sprawl development. For this reason, RPA opposes the following current projects in New Jersey: Route 92 between the New Jersey Turnpike and Route 1, and the extension of NJ 18 in Monmouth County. Extension of Connecticut's "Super 7" expressway between Danbury and Wilton should proceed only if it is built to parkway standards, has no intermediate interchanges, and is accompanied by strong land

use controls to prevent new sprawl from sprouting along the route.

### Parkway Upgrades

Parkways hold a special place in the history of the region. There have been successful upgrades that have brought the Hutchinson River Parkway and parts of the Saw Mill River Parkway closer to modern standards. Plans to do similar work on the Bronx River Parkway in Westchester County and the Southern State and Northern State on Long Island should not proceed because of the absence of significant adjacent rights-of-way. The Taconic Parkway's southern segment can be reconstructed sensitively, however, and should go forward. The Merritt Parkway should only be upgraded to improve safety and provide bicycle opportunities; it should not be widened.

### Managing the Road Network Better

While there are only a limited number of expansion projects for the highway network, there are many ways of "tweaking" the system to get more productivity out of it by either managing the system better or by dampening demand. The latter refers to how the system is priced, and it is discussed in the next section. (Pricing actions are indicated with a double asterisk below.) Responsible actions to manage highways better (called supply-side here), as well as appropriate approaches for controlling driving demand (called demand-side here) are summarized in the accompanying box.

The current program in the Clean Air Act Amendments to reduce vehicle travel to work—the Employee Trip Reduction Program—created a bureaucratic mess both for employers and for government oversight agencies. It should be replaced by a simpler, less-burdensome program that is based on a point system. Possible actions appropriate to employers would be assigned points in proportion to their effectiveness in reducing pollution. Employers would simply select any set of actions totaling a prescribed number of points and self-certify that they are being implemented. This approach is designed to reduce bureaucratic headaches while at the same time ensuring that the most effective pollution and congestion reduction tools actually get used.

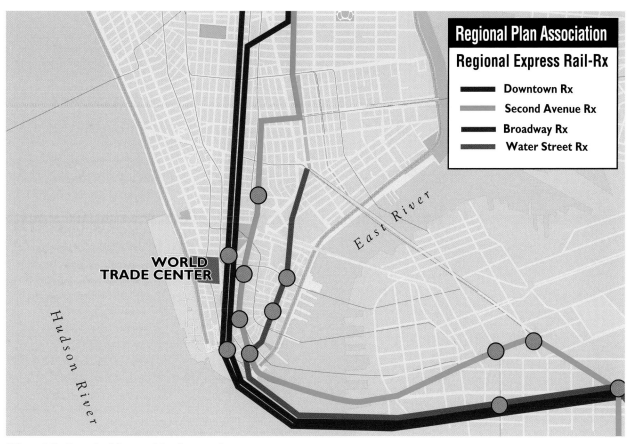

**Plate 3G:** Detail of Lower Manhattan Rx projects.

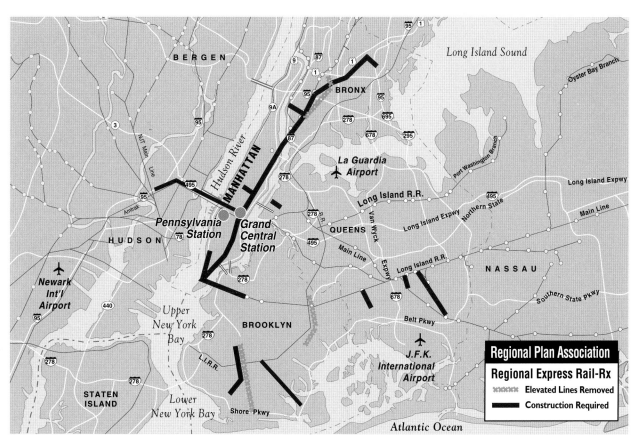

**Plate 3H:** New construction required and elevated subways removed by Rx.

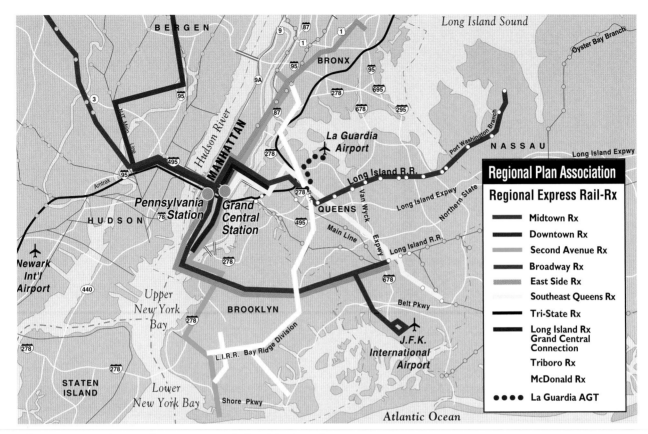

**Plate 3E**: *Completion of Rx system, including Tri-Boro Rx.*

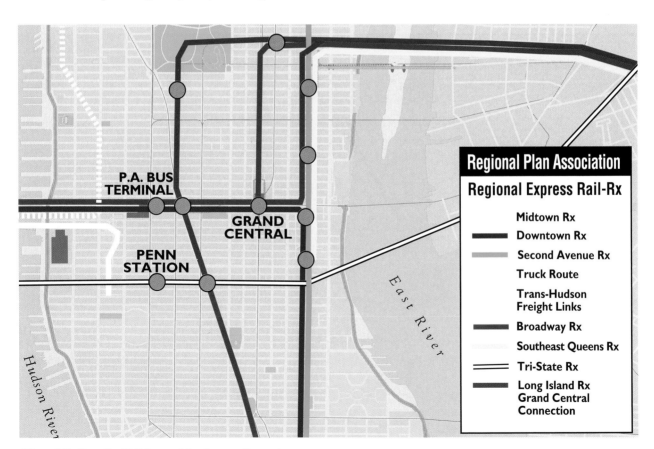

**Plate 3F**: *Detail of Midtown Manhattan Rx projects.*

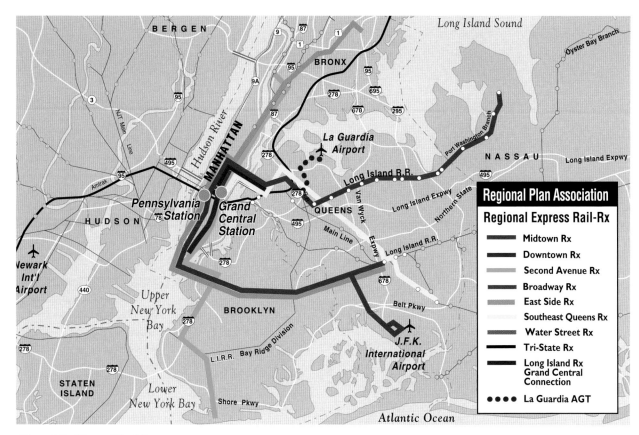

**Plate 3C:** *Phase III of Rx construction.*

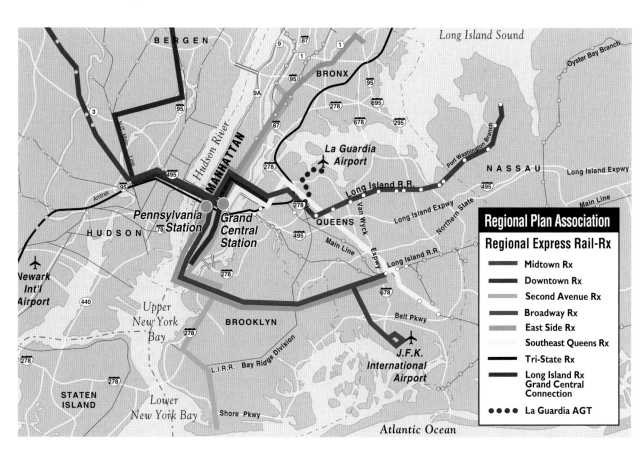

**Plate 3D:** *Phase IV of Rx construction.*

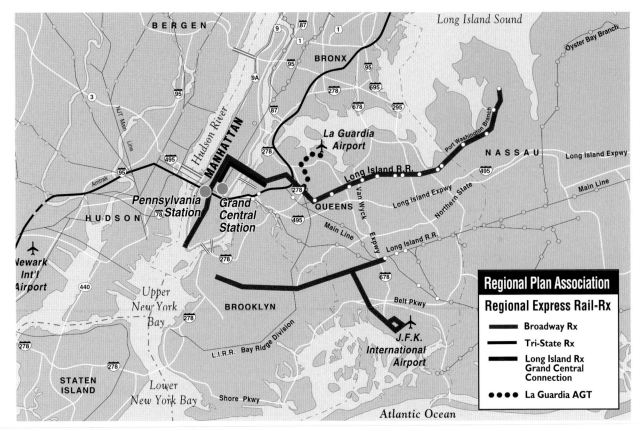

**Plate 3A:** *Phase I of Rx construction.*

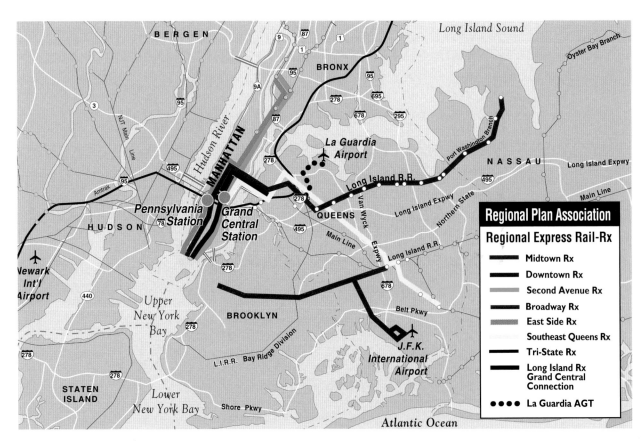

**Plate 3B:** *Phase II of Rx construction.*

**Supply-Side Tools for:**

*Incident management plans*

- Electronic toll collection**
- Intelligent Transportation Systems (ITS) instant traffic information for vehicles
- ITS pre-trip driver information
- Use of truck weigh-in-motion devices to speed up goods movement
- Truck and HOV priorities at toll approaches and lanes
- Ramp metering

*Localities and highway agencies*

- Access management plans to limit curb cuts
- Improved community design patterns (see Centers)

*Employers*

- Employer pick-up of employees at transit stations

**Demand-Side Tools for:**

*Highway agencies*

- Road pricing

*Localities*

- Trip reductions ordinances

*Employers*

- Working arrangements that encourage flexible times and fewer workdays in the week
- Promotion of home telecommuting
- Subsidized transit passes and checks**
- Transportation vouchers**
- Cashing out of free parking**

## Congestion Busting Through Market Approaches

Market-based pricing incentives can be a powerful tool to overcome congestion that results from the marked imbalance in the pricing of transportation that currently promotes excessive automobile and truck use. But any pricing measure that attempts to exact an added price from travelers or freight handlers (without guaranteeing benefits which in their

eyes warrant the added costs) or fails to provide an incentive to take transit or rideshare and a counter-incentive not to drive alone will have a short political life. While this plan is not oblivious to the political reality of the moment, it can also see beyond it. Pricing proposals for transportation outlined here are made in the spirit of finding a palatable mix of honey and vinegar, without compromising the principles on which the transportation elements of the Third Regional Plan stand.

These pricing methods could either be revenue neutral or be designed to gain new revenues for transportation purposes. If the intent of the measure is to be revenue neutral, the political burden is somewhat less than if it is intended to raise revenue. But pricing transportation and funding it are, of course, inexorably intertwined.

Accordingly, pricing measures recommended in this plan are designed to provide measurable benefits to individual transportation users and to the region as a whole. For example, if road pricing is calculated to encourage drivers to travel during less-congested, off-peak hours, then it must be demonstrated that this will lead to reductions in delays in the peak hours, and possibly to avoidance of further construction of new facilities. If transportation vouchers or the "cashing out" of free parking by employers are instituted, then there must also be a gain for employers, perhaps in lower parking costs or more punctual and satisfied workers.

Countless research studies have shown that three tools—transportation vouchers, "cashing out" of free parking, and variable tolls and road pricing—can substantially reduce single-occupancy driving and resultant congestion. Vouchers and "cashing out" are implemented by employers as an act of taking control of traffic congestion in powerful and direct ways that the public sector seems unwilling or unable to do. If enacted in unison in a particular area, employers—using the same market pricing mechanisms they use internally—could begin to free themselves from the crippling congestion and burdensome red-tape that is diminishing the quality of life for both employer and employee.

With *transportation vouchers* employers provide each worker a set amount each month for transportation, and at the same time charge them that amount or more if they use parking spaces supplied by the employer. Those who decide instead to take transit, carpool, bike, or walk can pocket the voucher. Those who continue to drive come out no worse if the parking fee equals the amount of the voucher and slightly worse if the parking fee is larger. And the employer can consider leasing out any surplus parking space that becomes available.

*Cashing out* of free parking is a similar idea. It is based on the notion that free employer-provided parking is in fact an employee benefit, and that if an employee chooses not to use a parking space that has been set aside, he or she is still entitled to the full value of the benefit—whatever an employer has spent on the parking space. Thus, transit users, carpoolers, and bikers and walkers get the same benefit as those given a free parking space. Employees can then make travel choices without having their judgment biased by either having to cling to or jettison a valuable employee benefit—a fringe benefit that costs business an estimated $30 billion nationwide each year.[5]

Behaviors do change, and employers can easily meet their CAAA requirements with either system. Programs like these create a "win-win" situation for employers, employees, and the regional transportation system. They fulfill a number of worthy aims, such as complying with the CAAA, reducing the amount employers have to spend on parking, and easing local traffic congestion. While these are still new concepts and therefore generate skepticism in *this* region, "cashing-out" has been used in Southern California for a number of years. After studying 18 examples of parking fees, RPA has found that single-occupant driving has been cut on average by 25%. The benefits of these tools are so apparent that RPA supports them as a cost-effective way of relieving peak-period highway congestion. There is another point here as well: if the CAAA can be complied with, and without pain, and it results in cleaner air, swifter commutes, and more productive employees, then it is a valuable and worthy piece of legislation, not an arbitrary and capricious one.

*Variable prices* to match service supply with available demand are very common with most if not all private companies. The most common examples include offering discounts for using electricity and telephones at night or on weekends; "super-saver" airline tickets bought for nonpeak travel periods; "early-bird" specials at restaurants; matinee prices at theaters; and lower prices in the off-season at resorts. "Road pricing" is alluring to economists and theoreticians. Yet the public agencies that provide

the foundation for our entire economy—our highway agencies—have shown only minimal interest in these tools. Instead, we are forced to rely on a "first-come, first-served" highway system as inefficient as a bread line at an old Soviet market. And we slash productivity rather than congestion, diminish our quality of life rather than boosting it, and foul our air instead of cleansing it.

It is the last, or marginal, vehicle entering a congested traffic stream that imposes the most delay on all the others. Maximizing one's own needs—in this case, insisting on traveling on a particular road—diminishes the convenience of everyone else already on the road. So cutting the volume of traffic by a small amount as it approaches the congestion level can increase speeds substantially, as drivers who see the fall-off in congestion during summer vacation months can attest to. Charging motorists for the privilege of driving during the most congested hours of the day will allow those for whom the trip is most important—commercial vehicles, vehicles on long trips, or multi-occupant vehicles—to move with little impediment, while encouraging those who can to switch to another mode or defer their time of departure.

Present-day electronic toll collection systems, as recently instituted on parts of the New York Thruway, including the Tappan Zee Bridge toll plaza, allow prepaid nonstop toll collection and solve past objections to toll barriers as the cause of still more congestion. But one factor is still unknown: how much must prices go up before they have a moderating influence on peak hour auto use? Variable toll structures are fairly rare in the United States, but European experiences seem very positive. Beginning in 1992, tolls on a highway outside Paris were raised by 25% during a congested period and cut by the same amount for two hours before and after the congested period. This cut traffic by 5%. While this may seem small, it can increase average speeds by more than 20%.

Road pricing in this region would best be instituted where:

- There is a serious congestion problem that is well known to the traveling public.

- There are no expectations of significant additions to highway capacity.

- Alternative options to single-occupant auto use exist or can be created.

- The new pricing system will either break even, or the

funds it generates can be earmarked for improvements to the existing facility.

- Success will reduce or eliminate the need for an expensive highway construction project.
- The peak period is relatively short.
- Existing tolls are in place.

Congestion charges, set sufficiently high, represent a solution to highway overcrowding. There are five distinct advantages to variable pricing, including:

- Those who pay receive a direct benefit in reduced congestion.
- Total auto travel demand is reduced.
- Diversion to transit is encouraged.
- A large sum of money can potentially be generated to spend on better upkeep of highways and public transportation.
- Congestion is solved without regulations.

Yet there are some hurdles to overcome, such as:

- Uncertainty over public acceptance of the principle "instead of waiting, you pay."
- The poor might be priced off the road.
- The need to install metering systems both in the road and on the cars.

A logical place to institute a pricing demonstration in this region is at the Tappan Zee Bridge. This might avoid a $450-million HOV widening project on Interstate 287 in Westchester, since two-thirds of the traffic on I-287 comes from the Tappan Zee Bridge. Some limited improvements on I-287 to reduce excessive weaving on the highway along with a combination of new transit services; an HOV lane on the bridge in the morning; and employer-sponsored peak-period pricing and parking, flextime, and telecommuting pricing measures can reduce the congestion on I-287 in Westchester, preventing the need for this expensive project.

Other road pricing measures can be instituted during the next round of toll increases at the six Port Authority crossings and on the New Jersey Turnpike. In the case of the Port Authority, the first step would be to eliminate the commuter discount. Although not revenue neutral, these funds can be used for parallel transit alternatives—for example, restoration of the West Shore rail line for Bergen County and high-speed ferries from Staten Island.

On the turnpike, lower tolls at night or midday, particularly for trucks, could relieve congestion in the peak hours.

Once electronic toll collection proves itself and is commonplace—which is likely to happen soon—tolls should be put in place on the "free" East River bridges—the Queensboro, Williamsburg, Manhattan, and Brooklyn. Funds raised would be directed to improving transit service, particularly the corridors in Brooklyn and Queens leading to the Central Business District, and to rehabilitating these bridges and others. This could clear Downtown Brooklyn of drivers seeking out the free Manhattan and Brooklyn Bridges to avoid tolls at, for example, the Brooklyn-Battery Tunnel. We realize that this is a politically difficult issue, but it is clear to any observer of the New York City budget scene that maintenance of these and other bridges will take a back seat to other pressing needs. A funding source derived from the system's users is a logical means to move bridge maintenance costs "off budget," while ensuring that resources will remain available for their perpetual maintenance needs. See the accompanying box for an example of one such approach.

Ultimately, a more complete road pricing system for the region, involving all of the crossings with tolls and without, such as the bridges over the East River, can even out congestion, create a pool of revenue to repair decaying bridges, and encourage transit alternatives. RPA intends to devise such a system as part of its action plan.

## Improving Commercial Transportation

Overall, the region's commercial transportation system—moving some 700 million tons of freight each year—is driven by the extraordinary strength and unusual diversity of the region's economy. Because so many people do business here, freight handlers have traditionally been inventive, and there is always strong competition for this rich market. The freight system still has expansion room, particularly in New Jersey and parts of the Mid-Hudson and Long Island, where cheap land is available for terminals, warehouses, and distribution centers. The region also benefits from strategic public infrastructure investments in ports and aviation. Another plus is a critical mass of fast-growing, innov-

*"Psst! Want to buy a bridge?"*

That old joke may have a new punch line. The central question of the current NYCTA "East River Crossing Study" is whether transit service on the Manhattan and Williamsburg Bridges can be continued in the future. The tentative answer is a definite maybe—provided the city properly maintains the bridges, something it hasn't done over the last generation. RPA believes that privatizing the four East River Bridges could ensure their proper maintenance, reduce commute times, create new transit opportunities, and let the city receive a share of the profits.

New York City could lease the four East River bridges for 50 or more years. The winning company or public authority would:

- Install tolls on the bridges, in exchange for assuming operation and maintenance responsibilities.

- Share a portion of the profits with the city.

- Design, build, and maintain new parallel transit infrastructure.

RPA estimates that the private firm would have nearly $5 billion in bonding capacity to create desperately needed new parallel transit infrastructure, such as completing the LIRR to Grand Central Terminal link that would remove 6,000 cars from the roads; fixing the IRT Nostrand Junction in Brooklyn permitting expanded IRT service; connecting Downtown Brooklyn to Lower Manhattan; and constructing the Sunnyside Intermodal Station to spur commercial growth in Long Island City.

What are the benefits of this privatization?

- The bridges are taken off the city capital and operating budgets.

- The city receives roughly $50 million in annual rent in the short term (growing with inflation and traffic volumes).

- Key pieces of 21st century transit infrastructure are built, providing superior airport access and commutes to Midtown and Downtown.

- Remaining drivers are assured the bridges will be properly maintained and at full capacity.

- Traffic volumes are reduced over the bridges, thereby speeding traffic.

- The city can try a bold experiment in privatization while still retaining ownership of the bridges.

ative support businesses, including logistics firms, insurance agents, import/export firms, and customs brokers, many located in New York City. On balance, these firms may be more substantial direct employers than the trucking companies, railroads, and steamship lines.

Yet the region struggles with antiquated infrastructure, missing highway and rail links, limited urban expansion space and crippling congestion. Some of these problems stem from inadequate public infrastructure investment or uneven tax and regulatory structures, which tend to favor autos over trucks and trucks over railroads. But some industry practices may also aggravate the conditions the region seeks to remedy. For example, the new business practice of "just-in-time" deliveries requires goods to be delivered precisely as they are needed, thereby cutting out intermediate warehousing costs. This otherwise admirable practice can also produce more truck trips on roads that are already congested.

The goods movement system relies heavily on the public sector, even though the public perception is that government agencies have greater involvement in auto travel and transit. Public policies and actions in commercial transportation have had varying levels of effectiveness and impact. Public capital investment specifically earmarked for freight infrastructure has been generally successful, such as the Port Authority's investments in ports and airports. But trucks are primary users of highways built for cars. Public agencies seem to give less attention to freight operations, perhaps because they are a completely private enterprise. Moreover, freight seems less easily understood than passenger transportation. From the other side, most private freight firms are leery both of public regulation and of subsidies, perhaps out of fear of becoming beholden to public agencies.

Nevertheless, a regional agenda to improve the flow of goods is needed. This agenda requires a partnership between public and private parties, as well as coordination between jurisdictions. While there are many public agencies with varying responsibilities for commercial transportation, interjurisdictional cooperation is very rare, as it is with highway and transit systems. Goals for the regional goods movement system agenda should:

- Build a flexible, robust commercial transportation system that allows the region to compete effectively in the national and global economy, both now and in a variety of future scenarios.

- Develop new logistical tools to make the flow of goods and relevant data throughout the region seamless, timely, and cost-effective.

- Provide equitable access for key commercial transportation to the regional network.

- Reduce the adverse environmental and social impacts of commercial transportation, and try to use less resource-intensive transportation to help solve other environmental problems.

The following section discusses each goal and recommendations to achieve them.

### Build a Flexible Commercial Transportation System

Changes in the freight industry are taking place very rapidly as new business relationships, both spatial and financial, are developing. Technology, regulations, and business practices are comletely different from those of even 20 years ago. Some technological changes include "double-stack" railroad container services; "RoadRailer" intermodal highway trailers that can also be pulled in a train; overnight package delivery services like Federal Express; and communications and computer systems that allow companies to have much greater control over their shipments, trucks, and trains. These technologies have transformed the flow of goods in the Tri-State Metropolitan Region. The majority of the region's Pacific Rim trade is conducted by sea and rail, rather than just in ships, and by a double-stack container train pipeline that brings Pacific Rim freight across the nation by railroad, which sharply cuts costs and transit time to and from Asian and West Coast shippers.

The virtual elimination of federal regulation of trucking, railroads, and airlines is a significant regulatory change. Some firms have thrived, particularly the railroads, while many trucking and airline companies perished from the resulting intense competition. Revolutionary changes in business practices have altered both the structure and nature of commercial transportation. Many firms have farmed out their transportation and distribution functions to independent companies, spawning new practices and partnerships. Others have closely integrated their manufacturing, planning, transportation, and distribution functions with key customers.

This reduces product cycle and delivery time, thereby cutting costs and improving quality.

Given the rapid and ever-increasing pace of technological and business practice changes, this region needs the most flexible transportation system possible. We cannot assume things will be the same even five years from now, so it is no use extrapolating either yesterday's or today's trends.

During the last decade most railroads made great strides nationally in improving quality, competitiveness, and service. Innovation in management and labor practices, cost containment, targeted capital investment, and deployment of new technologies, such as double-stack and RoadRailer intermodal services, made railroads true competitors after a generation of disinvestment and decline. The renaissance of freight railroads has spawned new truck–rail intermodal partnerships where, for

*Figure 88: Large "double-stack" container trains (top) are the region's primary link to Pacific Rim trade. Highway trailers can be loaded on trains (bottom) to take advantage of the best characteristics of railroads and trucks. Neither of these technologies is available east of the Hudson River.*

example, a trucking company picks up trailers or containers from the customer, but instead of that truck driving long distances to deliver the trailer, it is loaded onto a train and travels thousands of miles by rail before being picked up again and locally delivered from the rail terminal by the trucking company. This process uses the strengths of each partner—truck flexibility in pickup and delivery and rail's ability to have a few locomotives and two crew members move hundreds of containers long distances—to serve the demands of an increasingly difficult marketplace and heighten carrier profitability. These partnerships are expected to become even more commonplace in the future.

The freight system in New York, however, remains archaic. The east-of-Hudson market does not possess a modern rail system that can accommodate large double-stack trains from all parts of the nation. Intermodal services to New York typically consist of an intermodal train that arrives in New Jersey, where trucks haul the trailers and containers across the Hudson. New York City and Long Island trailer–train intermodal rail access from the north should improve with the completion of the Oak Point Link, but it cannot accommodate full-size, double-stack trains.[6] Though the Cross-Harbor Railroad can bring double-stack trains to the Brooklyn waterfront, it cannot move them inland across Long Island.

### Infrastructure Improvements

Some regional transportation agency planning studies are examining rail freight improvements.[7] All of these studies should posit a double-stack facility that could allow direct access to a national rail system, particularly to the Southeast—two functions the Oak Point Link cannot provide. Any new rail crossing should be designed to allow easy access from a multitude of routes and carriers.

The preferred clearance for a double-stack route is 22.5 feet; the Oak Point Link route is fully three feet lower, and even smaller clearances exist in Brooklyn, Queens, and Long Island. The "Access to the Region's Core" study may consider a joint passenger–freight line from New Jersey, straight across under Manhattan to Long Island City, to connect with LIRR lines. This idea is attractive but could be very expensive. An alternative trans-Hud-

son route could be built in conjunction with *Rx* passenger service, which would connect routes west of the Palisades in North Bergen to the West Side Line in Manhattan. The line would swing east after crossing into the Bronx, connecting to the Hudson Line and Oak Point Link (rebuilt to higher clearances). This alternative could be more cost-effective and could be completed faster. New intermodal rail freight terminals east of the Hudson would also be needed in places such as 65th Street in Brooklyn and Deer Park or Republic Airport in Suffolk. Another candidate terminal, the abandoned Cerro Conduit factory in Syosset, could also be the subject of a brownfields reclamation project.

Generating westbound back-haul loads is critical to the success of any regional rail system, particularly east of the Hudson. For any transportation company to remain competitive, equipment should be carrying revenue-producing loads as frequently as possible. This region has always consumed more transportation services than it produced, an imbalance that has increased over time largely due to the regional decline in manufacturing. Yet a new back-haul commodity may be emerging. New York's waste disposal systems are reaching a critical condition, as the city will soon be shutting down the Fresh Kills landfill. And incineration is increasingly problematic, while sewage sludge can no longer be dumped at sea. RPA is studying waste management systems, including recycling and resource recovery, and whether the existing or improved rail system can be put to use in the efficient movement of these materials between sorting, reprocessing, and disposal facilities. If this approach is effective, it could serve as the foundation for westbound shipments, leveraging considerable capital to further upgrade the regional rail facilities.

New opportunities for the regional ports may include opening new all-water trade routes from the Far East via the Suez Canal now that manufacturers are seeking out new low-cost production sites in Southeast Asia. Since the port's obvious orientation is with European ports, increasing trade with emergent economies in Eastern Europe and the expansion of the Western European economy may also increase demand for port facilities. But the region's ports struggle with relatively shallow channel depths that constantly require dredging, and they face increasing difficulty in disposing of dredge materials. Three forces are converging: new Southeast Asian/Suez routes, port capacities, and the future replacement of older ships.

All sides agree that the New Jersey berths and channels require ongoing maintenance dredging simply to remain navigable. But the manner in which dredge spoils are disposed of has caused near-gridlock. There is also a question of whether berths and channels should be deepened (e.g., beyond the 32 to 40 feet depth around the port) to safely accommodate larger ships in the future. A review of relevant literature is inconclusive. There is a close relationship between ship design and port capacities, as ship owners, possessing an asset with a 25-year plus life span, want to be sure that they can operate their vessels in as many ports and time-saving canals as possible. For many years the dimension limitations of the Panama Canal governed ship sizes, and our ports could accommodate those vessels. But new ships bigger than these are now in use for Pacific trade that does not require use of the Panama Canal.[8] Further, many oil tankers today cannot reach their berths in New Jersey and Staten Island, instead transferring their cargo in the Upper Bay or Sandy Hook Bay to barges for the final leg of the journey. Not only is this practice inefficient, it also carries the considerable risk of an oil spill near many precious recreation and natural areas.

As noted, new routes from Southeast Asia to the region via the Suez Canal are already being established. Given the Suez Canal's much larger size, larger vessels could be used on this route to New York. However, such large ships only make sense if there is enough traffic volume to justify their huge capacity and if ports can physically accommodate them with sufficient channel and berth depths and widths, larger cargo loading cranes, and more dockside space. It has also been speculated that further deepening of the Kill Van Kull separating Bayonne and Staten Island would be very complex and costly—if possible at all—due to the presence there of bedrock rather than silt. Competing North Atlantic ports, such as those in Baltimore and Norfolk, are more likely to accommodate larger ships immediately, while additional channel and berth increases would be required here. Unloading such "superships" in these locations would likely require trucking the cargo up I-95 since the goods still need

to get to consumers here, thereby decreasing our competitiveness, and damaging infrastructure and increasing truck traffic all along I-95. A "port survival" plan needs to be drafted that considers these factors and develops workable contingencies that meet the equally important needs of economic growth and environmental quality.

Even if new port facilities are developed, we should not expect significant employment increases. Direct port employment has plunged over the last generation, the result of containerization and mechanization of the ports. But new avenues for direct maritime employment growth can be explored. This port contains many inactive ship repair and maintenance facilities on both sides of the Hudson, despite thousands of ship calls each year. Putting these facilities back to work competitively could generate a considerable number of well-paying skilled jobs, perhaps more than the current number of direct on-dock jobs.

Trucking could be improved by targeted implementation of IHVS/ITS to reduce congestion and detect and clear congestion-spawning accidents more rapidly. "EZ-Pass" automated toll collection systems would be particularly effective in reducing truck congestion. New information systems can help keep trucks moving by electronically managing shipping documents as the truck crosses state lines. A related improvement would be the installation of "weigh-in-motion" truck systems, to reduce truck delays at truck scales and to discourage overweight trucks which severely damage pavement and bridges. Simply enforcing existing weight and safety rules will go a long way in making trucks appear as good neighbors on the roads.

Yet it is doubtful that these improvements will significantly reduce traffic congestion in key commercial corridors unless we first ease auto congestion. For example, much of the growth in Hudson River traffic over the last generation can be traced to rapidly increasing automobile traffic, not to truck traffic. And highway congestion is nearing epidemic proportions. Literally billions of dollars of productivity are lost each year in the region as traffic sits in accident- and construction-related delays. A typical large truck costs about 55 cents per minute to operate, not including the additional cost of spoilage or missed sales opportunities when the delivery is late. If one truck sits in a half-hour traffic jam each day, it loses a minimum of $4,200 each year. Again, the most effective way to cut congestion is through a pricing system. If the system costs a truck $500 out-of-pocket per year but cuts the amount of traffic congestion in half, the owner would receive a threefold yield on that investment. Cutting traffic congestion for trucks through road pricing is clearly beneficial to corporate and regional productivity. Importantly, any pricing scheme, such as one that might be introduced on the Tappan Zee Bridge, should not penalize trucks, particularly during the off-peak hours.

### New Logistical Tools

The regional logistics chain is quite complex and, in many cases, typically extends beyond the bounds of the region. Firms are engaged in nationwide production, distribution, and logistics activities. This is particularly true for direct merchandise companies that have spun off their own warehousing and distribution to third parties. For example, many computer retailers use Airborne Express to warehouse and distribute from their air cargo hub in Ohio, while keeping control of the sales and customer service functions at the home office. This type of system thereby guarantees next morning delivery of any product to any location in the nation and leads to high levels of customer service and responsiveness by the retailer.

There are many nontransportation aspects to this new logistics chain, however, most of which involve reliable information transmission via many types of telecommunication technologies and, of course, sophisticated computers and software. Indeed, pure travel time might become less of an issue within the total order delivery cycle. It has become clear that many failures in the chain occur at the interfaces and typically involve poor information transfer, such as between customer and order receiver, between supplier and hauler, or between hauler and supplemental haulers. A part of the final travel time to the customer may include some "fudge factor." If previous delays cause the shipper to rely on "fudge time," local traffic congestion delays can consume the last of this cushion, thereby causing the shipment to arrive late.

Contemporary logistics are clearly far more complex than moving trucks or trains: our competitive position also depends on information. These new requirements indicate a need for transportation and telecommunications and information service companies to jointly develop advanced logistics information systems to improve the "information interfaces" in the regional logistics chain.

### Equitable Access to the Regional Network

The region's road, rail, airport, and seaport network probably now contains almost all of the physical fixed capacity we can count on for the foreseeable future. Congress has declared the Interstate system to be finished, and I-287's completion from Morris County to Rockland County was probably the region's last new highway. Assuming both commercial and personal travel demand will continue to grow, how should travel priorities be established? The *de facto* policy seems to be that everyone has equal priority and everyone has the equal opportunity to sit in a traffic jam. Trains are delayed as Amtrak, commuter, and freight trains all compete for space on rail lines such as the Northeast Corridor, the Lehigh Line in New Jersey, and the Hudson Line in New York. When one private railroad owned and operated all services in a given corridor—intercity, suburban, and freight—dispatching decisions were made with a view to the success of the entire network. Today, the line owner's trains move first and "foreigners" go last. Strong rail freight and passenger services both need equitable access to the regional rail infrastructure.

An equitable access policy makes sense if it is based on market principles. Well-intended regulatory policies, such as the Southern California rule that banned peak-period truck deliveries so as to improve air quality, tend to spawn many unintended consequences. In that case, drivers and shipping clerks needed to be paid overtime. It also raised late-night security questions for companies making or accepting late deliveries. An alternative approach could be implemented through the congestion pricing systems described in the preceding section.

Trucks are banned on many portions of the regional highway system, particularly the parkways. While there may be reasonable engineering reasons to do so, such as low clearances, inadequate bridges, or narrow lanes, other prohibitions seem to be more historical. For example, while many of the New York City parkways were envisioned as touring or recreational routes, it is not representative of their current uses—commuting to work by car. These parkway prohibitions force all trucks destined for Kennedy Airport, regardless of size, to use only the Van Wyck Expressway, a highly congested highway. Regulations should be modified to allow appropriately sized commercial vehicles, such as pickup trucks and small vans, on certain city parkways to provide alternative access to JFK cargo terminals. In addition, urban commercial transportation would be improved by allowing appropriate commercial and service vehicles to use parking garages in New York City, thereby freeing up curbside loading areas for larger delivery trucks.

Separate commercial and passenger routes are needed in some parts of the region. For example, Conrail's Jersey City to Albany West Shore line is a critical freight link that should not be forced to accommodate commuter rail without additional passenger tracks. Another critical freight link is the New Jersey Turnpike. Some of its lanes are reserved for cars, but cars can also use the truck and bus lanes, in turn slowing down the trucks. Careful thought should be given to reserving the truck lanes for just trucks and buses during peak periods. Finally, an Exclusive Commercial Lane on I-495, Lincoln Tunnel, and southbound Dyer Avenue/34th–31st Street connection, similar to the existing Exclusive Bus Lane, could potentially save truckers

*Figure 89: Trucks are banned on many parkways in the region, particularly leading to JFK International Airport, despite the fact that many commercial vans are virtually the same as their passenger counterparts.*

as much as 30 minutes of delay during the morning rush.

## A Good Neighbor

Air pollution, particularly carbon monoxide and particulates, is generated by trucks and locally intensified by prolonged truck idling and congestion. In addition, residential areas are disturbed by the noise and traffic caused by through-trucks on local streets. Diesel particulates—soot—are carcinogens. In New York City alone, trucks, buses, and other diesel-powered vehicles produce over 3,000 tons of particulates per year. The federal Clean Air Act Amendment mandates have reduced diesel particulate emissions, although the deadlines for trucks lag several years behind those for buses. The effect of these mandates will be limited by the fact that truck engines can be kept in service for decades, and the regulations for trucks only apply to new engines.

Highways, water mains, and other subsurface infrastructure are damaged and fail at a faster rate as a result of heavy truck use on the surface. One pass of a large delivery truck weighing nine tons on typical pavement is equal in impact to 9,600 passes of an automobile. The region's Congressional delegation should work to develop a national truck weight/size limitation that recognizes the condition and design limitations of older infrastructure. Loopholes in the current regulations allow tacit overloading, and many competing areas exploit these loopholes. Failure to enact and strengthen such regulations would allow larger and heavier trucks than currently permitted. Many key highways would be unable to accommodate the larger vehicles, and this would accelerate the decay of the region's infrastructure.

Shifting more freight to rail would make a difference, but this should be accomplished rationally by a market-based system and not by bureaucratic fiat. One method is to let the various modes compete on a level playing field, each paying all its true costs. A key question is whether the transportation market is skewed by direct and indirect public subsidies and taxes. Data developed by the Tri-State Transportation Campaign suggests that trucks pay a small share of their total public costs. On the other hand, New York railroads have a very heavy local property tax burden. Conrail estimates that it pays more property taxes in New York than in all the other states in which it operates combined. A detailed review of the appropriateness of taxes and fees paid by the freight community, and whether each is covering the public costs it generates, is needed. Once all the information is available, the public can decide how or if it should support or subsidize commercial transportation.

## Notes

1. American Petroleum Institute, *The Cost of Motor Gasoline to Consumers: 1994 Annual Review*, 1995.

2. Texas Transportation Institute, 1994.

3. U.S. General Accounting Office, 1994.

4. Considerations for expanded freight service along this route must also be made. Where the route is four tracks wide, such as in parts of Queens and Brooklyn, sharing the right-of-way is obvious. In areas where only two tracks exist, additional right-of-way may be required, or "gauntlet" tracks could be used if the Triboro line frequency permits. It is assumed that the St. Mary's Park tunnel in Port Morris would be largely surplus once the Oak Point Link route is completed in 1995.

5. Consortium for Regional Sustainability, "Market-Based Initiatives for Controlling Emissions from Motor Vehicles," 1993.

6. Published data suggests that larger freight trains are too wide to pass along most of the MTA commuter lines. This is because typical double-stack cars are wider than passenger cars and may strike high-level passenger platforms built to minimize the "gap" between the platform edge and the door of passenger trains and third rail power conductors that supply electricity to the passenger train.

7. The Port Authority's "Access to the Region's Core" study will examine the feasibility of a freight link from New Jersey to Manhattan and possibly on to Queens. Studies by Metro North and the New York City Department of City Planning and Economic Development Corporation will also examine freight rail lines across the Hudson in the Tappan Zee corridor and across the Upper Bay, respectively. The latter study may also investigate new forms of rail-float services that could be introduced.

8. The Panama Canal can accommodate ships with a maximum 38 feet of draft and 106 feet wide. "Post-Panamax" ships, larger than the canal, include vessels such as American President Lines C-10 class container ships, which require 42 feet of draft and are 129 feet wide.

# Chapter 9

# The Workforce Campaign

FROM THE GARMENT WORKERS and designers who made the region's fashion industry world famous to the artists, writers, and computer analysts who are currently making the region a new media center for CD-ROMs, interactive videos, and virtual reality programs, the region has always depended on its tremendous concentration of brainpower and skills to generate new sources of prosperity. Now that information—acquiring it, processing it, and disseminating it—has increasingly become the currency of the world's new economy, development of our human resources is more critical than ever to the region's continued success. Making the region beckon the best minds and talent in the world is one-half of our human resource challenge, the part that can be addressed with quality of life improvements described elsewhere in the plan. But of equal importance is developing the full potential of people already here who have not yet acquired, or are prevented from using, the skills demanded by the new economy.

## Issues

The argument for a focused workforce development strategy becomes stronger as evidence of the benefits of investment in human resources accumulates. It is already well documented that investment in education and skills increases the incomes of individuals, perhaps by as much as 8% for each additional year of schooling. A recent study by the National Center on the Educational Quality of the Workforce indicates that a 10% increase in the education level of a company's workforce improves its productivity by nearly 9%, a larger increase than that caused by comparable increases in hours worked or investments in computers, machinery, or other equipment.[1]

In the 1980s over 1 million jobs were created in the region for workers with college degrees, while jobs for those without a high school diploma shrank. The education requirements of the workplace will continue to rise in most occupations and industries, even though the majority of jobs will still require less than a college degree for many years to come. Currently, 68% of the region's employed workers have less than a college degree, compared to 74% for the country as a whole.[2] Lab technicians, computer maintenance and repair workers, health and child care providers, skilled industrial workers, and other nondegree occupations will be critical to productive growth in the region's economy, but these jobs will still require strong lit-

*Figure 90: A workforce with diverse skills and cultures is central to the region's strength in the global economy.*

eracy, quantitative, and technical skills. Community colleges, vocational training, and other sources of post-secondary education will assume greater importance in maintaining a quality workforce. At the same time, a large proportion of young people growing up in our cities never finish high school, possibly as many as one-third in some cities.[3] Employers report the need for increasing communication, reasoning, and technical skills at all occupation levels, yet as many as 3 million adults in the region are estimated to be functionally illiterate.

The value of a well-educated, highly skilled workforce extends beyond immediate benefits to productivity and incomes. The ability of the economy to adapt to rapid changes in technology and world markets, and to develop new industries and innovative products and services, will depend on our collective creativity. Too large a gap between a

high-skill intellectual class and the rest of the workforce will increasingly limit the flexibility and inventiveness of organizations, as well as exacerbate social tensions that threaten to undermine the region's quality of life.

Neglect of our human resources not only threatens the skill base required to compete in the global economy but also contributes to a deepening equity crisis, propelling the well-off and the left-out on increasingly divergent paths. Even during the booming 1980s, incomes grew rapidly for the affluent but only minutely for the poorest households. Differences in skill levels are the largest, although not the only, cause of the "hourglass" economy, an economy that is creating increasing numbers of high- and low-income households while the number in the middle declines.

Earnings, which account for two-thirds of personal incomes, have been growing for high-skill jobs but are declining in terms of constant dollars for lower-skill jobs. Nationally, in 1979 a 30-year-old male with a high school diploma could expect to earn 88% as much as a worker with a bachelor's degree. Ten years later, in 1989, a high school graduate was only making 68% of what a college graduate could earn.[4]

Real income for people in the region with a high school diploma or less declined during the 1980s while growing for those with at least some college. People who never completed high school saw their incomes drop most sharply. Wage differences are only part of the explanation—for many it has become a question of whether they can find any work at all. Less than half of locally born African-American males aged 25 to 34 without high school diplomas, for example, had jobs in 1990.[5]

It is not just skill differences that deny people access to opportunities. Geographic isolation from centers of job growth and persistent racial and cultural biases add their own overlapping effects. At all education levels, African-Americans, Asians, and Hispanics have average incomes substantially below those of whites. In addition, tax changes over the last decade have exacerbated rather than eased income disparities, and public assistance payments have gone down, if measured in constant dollars.

### Three Fundamental Transformations

This building crisis for the region's competitiveness and cohesion is driven by three transformations—

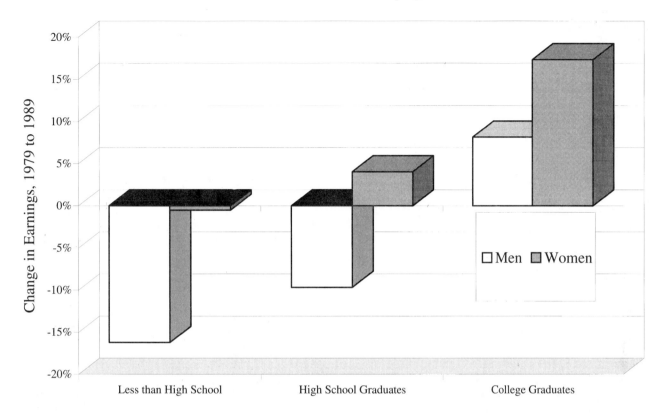

*Figure 91*: *Change in Real Earnings by Level of Education, U.S. Workers, 1979 to 1989.*
Source: U.S. Department of Labor, *Report on the American Workplace,* 1994, Table 2-5, p. 67.

technological, demographic, and geographic. Each of these is a global force overwhelming outmoded local institutions. While all three represent phenomena that regions are attempting to cope with worldwide, in several respects they are hitting the Tri-State Metropolitan Region earlier and harder. Part of our burden as a leading global center is to be in the forefront of economic and social change.

These transformations are the fundamental challenges that must be addressed to insure that the region's human resources are up to the demands of the next century:

1. Continuous changes in production and communications technology are leading to a relentless escalation of the cognitive and technical skills required by the economy.

2. The surge in immigration that has continued since the early 1970s is both supplying an essential source of skills and vitality and enlarging the region's sizable number of under-employed, low-skill workers.

3. The low-skilled and the poor are increasingly isolated in communities with declining access to jobs, quality schools, and services.

Each of these transformations can also be seen in terms of its challenge to local, state, and regional institutions. Rapid technological change has left education and training institutions increasingly out of sync with the requirements of the global economy. The largest share of the region's new jobs will require at least some college or post-secondary training, yet even among those with high school diplomas, many do not read or compute well enough to enter the job market. National studies, as well as anecdotal evidence from the region's business leaders, indicate that employers have little confidence in the ability of schools to produce work-ready graduates. According to one study, employers often do not even bother to look at grades and school evaluations when making hiring decisions for entry-level workers.[6]

The nearly 3 million immigrants who have come to the region since 1970 provided labor and skills that were essential to the region's job growth in the late 1970s and 1980s. This surge, however, has out-stripped the capacity of local services and institutions, from schools that must use hallways and restrooms as substitutes for overflowing classrooms, to adult English-as-a-second-language courses that can serve only a fraction of what is needed. In addition, regulatory structures have limited our ability to make full use of immigrants' skills. Professional certification requirements often unnecessarily disregard foreign accreditation, and many business regulations prevent viable, but officially unrecognized, business activities from becoming part of the mainstream economy.

The concentration of low-skilled workers and impoverished families in older working-class neighborhoods and racially segregated inner cities physically isolates them from centers of suburban job growth. Declining tax bases lead to the deterioration of the local services and institutions that develop human potential, particularly public schools. In addition, social networks and community institutions, important supports for individual development as well as sources of job contacts, are often weakened in communities where poverty becomes concentrated. Transportation systems were generally built either to provide transit access to the region's core or auto mobility within the suburbs, and they often connect these communities poorly to distant or even nearby suburban job centers. Telecommunications networks and new information technologies have the potential to reduce the isolation, but in most neighborhoods there is currently too little infrastructure, equipment, and expertise.

### State, Local, and Private Initiatives

The scope of these transformations requires coordinated action on a scale far exceeding our current efforts. Business, labor, civic leaders, and citizens, as well as all levels of government, must be part of the solution. The business sector, in particular, needs to take a leadership role in devising, managing, and financing innovative solutions. As beneficiaries of a work-ready labor force, as "clients" of education and training services, and as skilled managers, employers need to become far more deeply involved in the transformation of our current system of learning.

Numerous state, local, and private efforts in the last decade have made strong attempts to reform our approach to education and workforce development. The Connecticut Business and Education Coalition, the New Jersey Employment and Training Commission, and the New York City Workforce Development Commission are among the more prominent examples. Lasting results, however, have often been slowed by political resistance and bureaucratic inertia as well as by the enormous complexity of what is being undertaken.

In spite of these obstacles, the region is bursting with local success stories. For example, the Greater New York Hospital Foundation's "Walks of Life" program has developed innovative partnerships between nine public schools and a consortium of city employers. Newark's New Community Corporation's Center for Employment Training is implementing a promising program of comprehensive employment services for low-skilled, unemployed residents. And in both New York and New Jersey a number of local school-to-work alliances have been formed with funding from the federal School to Work Act to create a comprehensive school-to-work system. In New York City, for example, the New York City Partnership, Board of Education of the City of New York, United Federation of Teachers, New York City Department of Employment, and others have joined forces in a city-wide School-to-Work Alliance to implement full-scale systemic change in the way young people are prepared to enter the workforce.[7]

These and other successful approaches provide guidance in how to reconnect work and education with a system of lifelong learning. However, to sustain and link these efforts and overcome the formidable obstacles to success, the region will need to mount a campaign that addresses human capital needs on an unprecedented scale. In the race to keep pace with the economy's accelerating demand for an educated, informed, and flexible workforce, the region cannot allow inertia, political resistance, or competing priorities to divert our attention. If we continue to provide only part of the region with the resources to succeed, then we will eventually be unable to sustain industries that require more than an elite group of high-skilled professionals. Because the solutions require new ways of thinking, a restructuring of institutions and scaled-up investments in a time of tight resources, a region-wide mobilization of local, state, and private initiatives is needed to create strong constituencies for sustained, coordinated actions.

The actions described below are designed to expand and coordinate existing efforts and move the region toward three goals that address the transformations in the region's industrial, demographic, and geographic structure:

- Reconnect work and education with a system of lifelong learning.

- Connect the new workforce to the mainstream labor market.

- Connect communities to jobs with physical and social infrastructure.

RPA's recommendations will not only allow the region to keep pace with a changing economic landscape. If fully implemented, they will reverse the trends of an ever-widening gap between the workforce and workplace, and between the skilled and unskilled. While many causes of poverty and social division must be dealt with on a national scale, many of the institutions responsible for workforce development and outcomes are under state and local control. Even more importantly, the private sector, including business, labor, and civic organizations, must be engaged in this effort on a local and regional level. By expanding economic opportunities we may begin to break the cycle of poverty and hopelessness that is at the root of so many other social problems in our cities and communities.

## Summary of Recommendations

New investments and policies are necessary to make the region's workforce more competitive in a global economy and to allow all the region's citizens and communities to benefit from a growing job market.

1. Reconnect work and education through a system of lifelong learning.
    - Invest in early childhood development, child care, and arts education to nurture creativity and learning skills.
    - Increase performance levels in poor school districts through a more equitable distribution of education resources, administrative efficiencies, and

an environment that allows successful innovation to flourish.
    - Expand the capacity of post-secondary schools, literacy programs, and comprehensive employment services to address the needs of adult workers.
    - Build on the network of high-quality universities and community colleges to provide greater resources for continuous learning by adult workers.
    - Implement individual training accounts for employees.
    - Increase private sector training by assisting small firms to pool resources and expertise.
    - Establish a Tri-State council of business, labor, education, and civic leaders to guide the transition to a regional system of lifelong learning.

2. Connect the new workforce to the mainstream labor market.
    - Seek federal reform of immigration admission requirements to achieve improved balance between admissions based on skill levels, family reunification, and other criteria.
    - Enable affirmative action programs to assist a larger number of small firms and low-income workers.
    - Recognize and develop the informal sector of the economy.
    - Strengthen institutional supports to help immigrants assimilate, including promotion of naturalization and voter registration by schools and ethnic community organizations.

3. Connect communities to jobs.
    - Expand successful support programs for community-based organizations to develop alliances with regional employers and institutions.
    - Utilize new technologies to expand job information networks in low-income communities.
    - Improve transportation links between low-income communities and job centers with bus and van services.

## Reconnecting Work and Education

The goal of reconnecting work and education recognizes that we are educating our workforce under rules more appropriate for a previous era than for today's knowledge-based service economy. School hours have been largely unchanged since this country had an agricultural society, and they lag behind those of most developed countries. Education standards are often inadequate for entry-level skill requirements, and neither employers nor educators are providing sufficient, ongoing skills-upgrading required by rapid changes in the workplace. As a result, employers are not getting workers with the abilities they need out of our education system; workers have limited options for keeping up with changing skill demands; and people who have left the labor market or the education system face increasingly limited employment prospects.[8]

"Lifelong learning" refers as much to a change in our collective thinking as it does to institutional changes. It recognizes that education is not something that happens in school between the ages of 5 and 25, but a process that begins at birth and continues throughout life. The work site must provide an environment for learning and classrooms must provide an understanding of the workplace. A system of lifelong learning would have the following attributes:

- Home, preschool, and school environments that nurture creativity and learning skills in early childhood and beyond.

- Well-functioning elementary and secondary schools in all communities to provide the foundation skills required for successful career development.

- Coordination of high school, community college, and university programs to provide a rational progression of skill development in specific occupations.

- A substantial, ongoing role for business and labor in developing academic and training programs, establishing academic standards relevant to the workplace, and assisting students and workers with the transition from school to the workplace.

- Substantial investment in employee skills upgrading by employers, and an expansion of adult career development programs by community colleges and universities.

- Employee involvement in designing on-the-job training programs and work processes.

- Comprehensive employment and training services for school drop-outs and displaced workers.

The following recommendations highlight areas where the region is seriously under-investing in human capital or failing to integrate phases of learning and workforce development effectively.

## Childhood Development

*Invest in early childhood development, child care, and arts education to nurture creativity and learning skills.*

In an economy where workers will need to adapt their skills continuously, the ability to learn is more fundamental to success than the attainment of any specific set of skills. Schools obviously play an important role in teaching learning skills, providing self-confidence, and in fulfilling the promise of an inquisitive, creative child. The aptitude for learning, however, is well-shaped long before a child enters school, and it is affected throughout childhood by care and education that occurs outside the school. As stated in *Starting Points*, a seminal report on young children in the United States by the Carnegie Corporation of New York:

> The importance of the first three years of life lies in the pace at which the child is growing and learning. In no other period do such profound changes occur so rapidly: the newborn grows from a completely dependent human being into one who walks, talks, plays, and explores. The three-year-old is learning and, perhaps more important, learning how to learn.[9]

Substantial benefits from investment in early child development have been documented in a number of studies. Among the most well-known is the Perry Pre-School Project, a longitudinal study that followed a sample group of children who completed a quality preschool program and a control group through their 18th year. While controversial, it found a lifetime return to taxpayers of $23,700 in reduced welfare expenditures, crime reduction, and increased taxes for the $4,800 cost of the program. A review of different studies of the results of quality child development programs for at-risk children by the Family and Work Institute found "strong evidence that model preschool programs improve children's IQ for the short-term and reduce their placement in special education" and "moderate evidence that they decrease grade retention and increase the likelihood of graduating from high school."[10]

The importance of promoting creativity, confidence, and intellectual curiosity, in and out of school settings, continues beyond early childhood. The need for child care for working parents, particularly the poor, is receiving increasing attention. Less recognized is that child care is an important learning environment that needs to be considered part of our learning system. Also in danger of being lost in the emphasis on educational standards is the importance of engendering creativity, learning skills, and confidence in school settings. For example, arts education has demonstrated its effectiveness in improving education outcomes by enhancing confidence and creative thinking. One indication of the relationship between arts education and general education is a 1991 Harris poll that found significantly lower high school drop-out rates among students who take arts courses.[11]

The implication for the region's states and localities is the need to find ways to substantially increase funding for early childhood development, quality child care, and arts education. As importantly, these need to be considered core parts of our learning system, rather than segmented support systems or enhancements.

### Public Education

*Increase performance levels in poor school districts through a more equitable distribution of education resources, administrative efficiencies, and an environment that allows successful innovations to flourish.*

Regardless of how other institutions perform, elementary and secondary schools remain the bedrock of lifelong learning and worker preparation. No remedial efforts can pick up the pieces if our public schools continue to fail as many of our young people as they currently do. Reform of education is a complex topic, much of which falls outside the scope of this plan. Specific education reforms are being developed and implemented in all parts of the region, from alternative high schools to school-based management. Bold innovations in teaching methods, as well as continued improvement in management and fiscal stewardship, must remain at the highest level of priority for states and localities.

A look at just one aspect of public education, the physical condition of school facilities in New York City, indicates both the magnitude and urgency of the problem. A report by the recent Commission on School Facilities and Maintenance Reform opens with a dire warning:

A generation of inadequate funding by the State and City of New York and flawed management by the Board of Education of routine maintenance have combined to bring the condition of New York City's school buildings to a state of imminent calamity. Unless a comprehensive "Marshall Plan" for the schools is put in place immediately—including both improved management and dedicated new money—not only will the schools be essentially unrepairable, and their cost of replacement impossibly high, but children, teachers, principals, custodial workers and the public will be in danger.[12]

In every area of the region, there is a high correlation between poverty and poorly performing schools. Low-income school districts in New York City, Newark, Jersey City, Bridgeport, New Haven, and other communities are characterized by low academic test scores, high drop-out rates, and poor performance in post-secondary education and the job market.[13] The relation between income and performance can be seen from the results of the Connecticut Academic Performance Test, which tested 10th graders statewide and compared the scores of districts grouped by their socioeconomic characteristics. Figure 92 shows a sharp decline in test scores as income declines.

Income affects education outcomes in several ways, beginning with lower than average birth weights for poorer children and extending to home and community environments that do not prepare for or reinforce classroom learning. As a result, schools in poorer districts have larger problems to face than those in more affluent districts, including a larger number of children with learning disabilities and special needs, additional security needs, and difficulties in attracting qualified teachers.

Unfortunately, conditions in the schools themselves generally exacerbate, rather than ameliorate, conditions that inhibit learning. Class sizes tend to be larger than in affluent districts and materials are in shorter supply. For example, the average kindergarten class in New York City had 26 students in 1992–1993, compared to 21 in the suburbs. While suburban districts had over 20 books per student, city districts had less than 10. There was one computer for every 11 students in suburban districts, compared to one for every 17 in New York City.[14]

While academic performance is clearly related to income, there is a continuing imbalance between education resources and need. Since education is a locally provided service, affluent districts can fund

| | Median Family Income | Average Score in Mathematics | Average Score in Language Arts* | Average Score in Total Science |
|---|---|---|---|---|
| Group I | $40,425 | 31.6 | 84.2 | 44.9 |
| Group II | $28,114 | 29.0 | 77.1 | 42.5 |
| Group III | $24,431 | 27.0 | 74.8 | 41.1 |
| Group IV | $22,609 | 25.4 | 71.8 | 38.7 |
| Group V | $21,920 | 24.5 | 67.6 | 37.8 |
| Group VI | $20,325 | 21.5 | 68.1 | 35.0 |
| Group VII | $15,240 | 13.3 | 57.9 | 25.5 |

* Two language arts test were administered. Results refer to the "Response to Literature" test.

**Figure 92:** *Results from Connecticut Academic Performance Tests, Spring 1994.*
Source: Connecticut State Department of Education.

education from a much larger tax base than poorer districts. Each state provides some compensatory funding to poorer districts, but formulas vary considerably and wide gaps between need and adequate funding levels remain. Again, the findings of the Commission on School Facilities and Maintenance Reform are instructive for broader education funding issues:

> Finally, we note that we started our work as a Commission with the belief that the problem facing our schools was a management problem...We now believe that management was in fact inadequate, but in the final analysis it was only a small part of the overall problem. We now believe that management of the Division is on the road to improvement although work remains to be done. The money to maintain our schools is still wholly inadequate. Therein lies the problem.[15]

Data on gross spending per pupil indicates considerable differences within the three states. Average expenditures in New York City are far lower than in more affluent districts. For the 1992 to 1993 fiscal year, spending per pupil for New York City's 1 million students was $7,900, compared to $10,500 in the New York suburban counties in the metropolitan area. Spending per pupil in other major cities in the region ranges from $7,200 in Bridgeport to $10,700 in Newark. In some cases, average spending per pupil in New Jersey and Connecticut cities is on a par with or even exceeds that of the state as a whole.[16]

Gross spending per pupil is only a partial indicator of resource allocation. Since it includes expenditures for all purposes, districts with high administrative, security, debt service or other costs can have relatively low expenditures for instruction even if total expenditures per pupil are high. Both differences in fiscal management and differences in service needs can lead to wide variances in the ratio of instruction expenditures to total expenditures. In general, however, poorer districts have larger needs for both classroom instruction and support services. These include high numbers of special education students, maintenance or replacement of older buildings, and costly building security.

Raising student achievement levels in poorly performing schools will require a number of structural changes in our system of funding and delivering education services:

• Funding for public education needs to be much more closely aligned to need than it is currently. To significantly improve the distribution of education resources, the states will need to assume a larger role in both collecting revenues and allocating funds. A proposed restructuring of school financing, with the state assuming primary responsibility, is described in *Governance.* Along with funding reallocation, school administration will need to be continually scrutinized to insure that resources are being used with maximum effectiveness. In most cases, however, a substantial increase in resources for schools in low-income areas is required.

• Successful innovations in the teaching and the learning process need to be adapted to schools throughout the region. Even among schools with similar student needs and expenditure levels, there are considerable differences in academic performance. Applying successful innovations widely is the joint responsibility of local schools and the states, with meaningful involvement from parents and teachers and support from business, civic groups, and labor. To provide an environment for innovation to flourish and lead to system-wide improvements, school governance structures need to balance the goals of clear accountability, continuity of leadership, and active participation from teachers and parents as well as administrators.

• Over the long term, education equity cannot be completely addressed without changing the housing and development patterns that perpetuate the concentration of low-income, largely African-American and Hispanic, populations into isolated communities. In addition to easing the problem of inequities in the tax base to fund education, decreasing the concentration of poor students will give them a better chance of receiving the individual attention and learning environments necessary to overcome other learning disadvantages. The planning and land use recommendations in *Centers* and *Governance* are designed to provide both greater efficiency and equity in the use of the region's resources, and to protect our natural assets for long-term, sustainable prosperity. In addition, these recommendations will encourage the development of mixed-income communities throughout the region and the economic development of low-income urban centers.

## Adult Education

*Expand the capacity of post-secondary schools, literacy programs, and comprehensive employment services to address needs of adult workers.*

The third leg of life-learning is refocusing post-secondary schools, adult education training programs, and employment services to address the changing needs of the workforce. This is a two-faceted issue. For all workers, lifetime employment with a single employer is largely a thing of the past. With it goes not only job security but also some of the incentive for employers to invest in their workers, an area where under-investment appears to be prevalent. The second aspect of adult learning is improving the employment prospects for low-skill workers. The issue of illiteracy has already been cited. For others, the issue can be outmoded production skills or a lack of labor market experience of any kind.

One strong resource that the region possesses to address this issue is its wealth of quality institutions of higher education—from Columbia, NYU, Yale, and Princeton, to extensive state university and community college systems, to technology and specialized institutions such as New York Polytechnic, Stevens Institute, and the New Jersey University of Medicine and Dentistry. These institutions not only provide trained professionals, but they are also important contributors to the economic development of their communities. They attract resources from a broad financial base, they can have a catalytic effect on investment patterns and neighborhood development, and they can be involved in the educational needs of elementary and high school students.

Extending the role of universities and community colleges in both community development and adult learning represents a significant opportunity. Specifically, colleges and universities should be encouraged to provide technical assistance to their local communities, especially to elementary and secondary education and small business. Secondly, partnerships with unions or industry associations should be encouraged to expand retraining services, occupational development, or adult education. For example, CUNY and SUNY have partnered with NYNEX and the Communication Workers of America in instituting a "universal technician" training program, whereby workers can volunteer for a two-year, one-day-a-week program to broaden technological knowledge and skills.

Other recommendations to encourage continual worker and adult training include:

• Implementation of Individual Training Accounts, which set aside tax-exempt payroll deductions for training. Federal commitment to education tax credits is in doubt, and state legislation will be important as either a substitute for or supplement to federal action. A proposal has already been made by Governor Whitman's Economic Masterplan Commission to implement Individual Training Accounts in New Jersey.

• Educate employers on the productivity advantages of on-the-job training. Even though employees who receive on-the-job training show an average productivity improvement of 30%, training is only 1.4% of payroll expenditures in the United States, and only one in six workers with no more than a high school education receives training. This education effort could be undertaken by employer associations or by public economic development agencies.

• Assist small firms in forming training consortiums to pool resources and expertise. As one example, the Garment Industry Development Corporation uses in-

**Figure 93:** *The Garment Industry Development Corporation exemplifies labor–business cooperation to increase manufacturing productivity and competitiveness. Many GIDC programs focus on upgrading worker skills and increasing their productivity. Improved skills also increase the ability of workers to move up into higher paying jobs. Here, a sewing machine operator is instructed in pattern-making.*

dustry-wide resources to upgrade skills of apparel workers in an industry dominated by small firms.

Funding for programs to upgrade the literacy and skills of low-skill workers falls well short of the region's need. There is, admittedly, difficulty in designing and sustaining programs that attempt to address issues of this severity and complexity. There are, however, program areas in which increased funding can be expected to yield benefits in terms of a more work-ready population. Adult literacy and English-as-a-second-language programs can effectively remove the major impediment barring the way for many potential workforce participants, but such programs currently meet only a fraction of demand, perhaps as little as 5% of the eligible population.[17]

Employment programs for adults have also shown positive, if modest, gains in employment and earnings. Studies of welfare-to-work programs by the Manpower Demonstration Research Corporation have shown that the success of different types of programs depends on the objectives, such as reducing welfare rolls or maximizing earnings. However, it does appear that comprehensive programs that combine remedial skills training, job place-ment assistance, support services, and follow-up counseling are effective models for bringing the disadvantaged into the mainstream labor market.[18]

## A Tri-State Council

*Establish a Tri-State Council of business, labor, education, and civic leaders to guide the transition to a regional system of lifelong learning.*

On state, regional, and local levels there appears to be a scaling up of efforts around the country to bring about systemic reform of education.[19] Although efforts are already occurring in this region on the state and local level, there are compelling reasons to address these issues on a regional level as well. Employers draw their workers from communities throughout the region, giving them a stake in the quality of the workforce in municipalities within commuting distance of their work sites. Many institutions and programs serving a single community can benefit from ties to employment opportunities in a larger area, or even just from having improved information about successful programs and innovations in other parts of the region. States and localities could also benefit from coordinated development of specialized education institutions, such as technology centers, to avoid unnecessary duplication and cost in some program areas, while neglecting others.

Therefore, although states and localities need to remain the primary service providers in education and training, a Tri-State Council would address two important needs for a challenge of this scope and complexity: Coordination of state, local, and private efforts, and a larger leadership role for the private sector.

Structured as a private organization representing a coalition of business, labor, civic, and education leaders, a Tri-State Council would act as a strategic planning entity for the region as it develops a system of lifelong learning. It would provide a forum to address issues of institutional coordination, help the region's states and localities maintain their focus on lifelong learning, and provide a broader base to argue for future federal support. For example, a coalition of business, labor, education, and civic leaders from all three states could be a strong voice to maintain and expand federal support for school-to-work initiatives.

The functions of a council could include:

- Responsibility for assessing the region's institutions of learning and workforce development as a system and identifying needed actions.

- Establishing benchmarks for achievement of institutional reform by states, localities, business, and labor.

- Organizing employers and unions on an industry level to support school-to-work alliances and developing training consortiums, apprenticeships, and other industry-based initiatives.

- Developing standards for educational degrees and professional certification that meet employer requirements and establish some uniformity of standards throughout the region.

Ideally, the council would be given specific areas of responsibility by the three states, initially in an advisory capacity. Eventually, it could be empowered by the states to establish benchmarks and standards in designated policy and program areas.

## Connecting the New Workforce to the Labor Market

Early in the next century, the majority of the region's workforce will be African-American, Asian, or Hispanic. Immigrants and their children will provide most of the region's labor force growth. Even if we are successful in upgrading education and skill levels throughout the workforce, we must remove regulatory rigidities and lingering cultural biases that block full participation in the job market and prevent the economy from taking full advantage of existing skills.

Connecting the new workforce to jobs will build on methods that immigrants and minorities have already successfully created for themselves. "Ethnic enclave" economies that build enterprises serving and owned by particular ethnic groups, immigrant employment networks, and informal economic activity operating without legal sanction provide the region's economy with considerable capital, labor, and entrepreneurial energy. These methods are often self-limiting, however, preventing workers and entrepreneurs from enhancing their economic status and keeping an enormous source of potential growth from reaching the mainstream economy.

Clearly, many of the barriers to full participation in the workforce and economy involve deeply held racial and cultural biases that are not easily changed either by public policies or by private actions. Diversity, however, is the greatest underlying source of the region's economic strength, a fact that is worth repeating until it is understood and recognized as an opportunity, rather than a limitation. In addition, several of the legal and regulatory issues involve federal statutes that are outside of the region's complete control. Therefore, developing a participatory labor market must involve a spectrum of actions ranging from grassroots efforts on the community level, to changes in state and municipal regulations, to influencing national debate on issues of immigration and federal assistance programs. A long-term strategy can be built around these actions.

### Immigration Policy

*Seek federal reform of immigration admission preferences to achieve an improved balance between admissions based on skills needed by the economy, family reunification, and other criteria.*

Immigration to the region has been a primary reason behind our success in the global economy, and it must remain an important part of the region's future. However, current federal admission criteria are weighted disproportionately toward family-related visas and cannot flexibly respond to changing conditions in the labor market.

Over half of the region's immigrants have been admitted under family reunification criteria, while less than 10% were admitted with employment-related visas. The former tend to be lower skilled, increasing the number of low-skill workers in an era when shrinking numbers of low-skill jobs are creating enormous pressures in the region's labor market. Because they often work at below-minimum wages for long hours under poor working conditions, some immigrants are drawn into sweatshop economies, while others displace native-born workers formerly employed at considerably higher wages.

A more rational policy would regulate entries on a year-to-year basis, in accordance with labor market conditions in the national economy, and give greater priority to the skills and intellectual capacities most needed at the moment. Such an approach would better balance multiple goals of immigration policy: reuniting families, improving skills in the economy, and reducing unemployment among low-skilled workers.

### Affirmative Action

*Enable affirmative action programs to assist a larger number of small firms and low-income workers.*

Affirmative action programs have been instrumental in creating a substantial core of successful minority-owned firms. These firms hire proportionately more African-American, Hispanic, and Asian workers than do nonminority firms. At a time when the burdens of downsizing in corporate America are falling heavily on low-income and minority workers, it is more important than ever that assertive steps are taken to expand employment opportunities for these workers. This can be achieved through the continuation of affirmative action programs that assist low-income workers, including programs targeted to empowerment areas, programmatic efforts to assist start-up firms in minority and low-income communities, and voluntary actions from large corporations and from established minority-owned businesses. The latter could include mentorships of young entrepreneurs and increased outsourcing to less-established minority firms.

### The Informal Economy

*Recognize and develop the informal sector of the region's economy.*

While it cannot be accurately measured, unlicensed and unregulated business activity—including small manufacturers, home-based service operations, street vendors, and van services—represents a sizable, and probably growing, portion of the region's economy. These businesses are especially important in providing point-of-entry work opportunities within immigrant networks, but by their nature are less likely to provide credentials, skills, and opportunities for advancement in the higher income formal sector. Violations of health, safety, and labor laws are obviously more prevalent in unlicensed businesses, but these could be better addressed if more of these businesses were integrated into the formal economy.

A productive strategy—one that would expand job opportunities by encouraging expansion of local economies, provide more influence over health and safety conditions, and open procurement links to the mainstream economy—would reverse attempts to ignore or delegitimize informal economic activities. Rather, it would recognize their important role in the economy and provide incentives for them to develop into fully legitimate businesses. A set of actions to start this process in motion could include the following:

- Legalize activities that do not threaten health and safety, such as small, home-based businesses in areas zoned for residential use.

- Increase enforcement of health, safety, and child labor codes among both licensed and unlicensed businesses, while lowering other business thresholds, such as the unincorporated business tax.

- Provide zones or bazaar space where street vending is not only permitted but encouraged.

- Develop support programs for unlicensed businesses as part of small business assistance programs, with particular focus on obtaining legal status and developing a broader market. For example, incubators for start-up operations in sectors with large numbers of unlicensed businesses could provide centralized accounting, marketing, advertising, and other services.

- Give greater recognition to foreign accreditation in professional occupations. Certification requirements in many professions needlessly screen out talented professionals with foreign certification, even though foreign training may meet our own standards for rigor and quality. Reforming requirements to include this highly trained segment of the workforce would, without diminishing standards, unlock a large source of needed skills. It would also ease pressures in lower skill job markets, where uncertified professionals who cannot practice their trades instead compete for nonprofessional jobs. Where foreign credentials do not meet accepted standards, supplemental training and accelerated certification should be considered.

### Assimilation

*Strengthen institutional supports to help immigrants assimilate.*

Compared to prior waves of immigration, a lower proportion of today's newcomers seek citizenship or cultural assimilation. This has given the region thriving enclave economies and a vibrant multiculturism, but it has also further isolated many communities from wider economic opportunity and limited the synergy of immigrant and mainstream popular cultures. Accelerating the economic assimilation and civic participation of immigrants and their children, while respecting their traditions, would have important benefits both for immigrant communities and for the region's economy. Their skills could be more fully used and additional sources of income would open to them. They would gain greater access to services and civic functions, and the political process would be enriched by their participation. Popular culture would gain new dimensions and shadings with greater contributions from ethnic communities.

Specific steps to encourage assimilation efforts include actions both within and outside immigrant communities:

- Rapid acquisition of fluency in English should be a primary objective of elementary and secondary school education for immigrant children. Without this proficiency, opportunities for education and economic success are limited, and early participation in civic life is curtailed. Similarly, acquisition of a second language by native born children should be strongly encouraged. Success in the global economy requires that we be able to communicate with other residents of the region and with other cultures around the world.

- Ethnic community organizations can provide greater civic awareness among immigrants and promote naturalization and voter registration. With lower rates of citizenship, voting levels are lower among current immigrants than they were during previous waves of immigration, limiting access to public life, as well as many services, while at the same time restricting the responsiveness of local politicians, who are less likely to take actions on behalf of "invisible" constituents.

- Universities and community colleges are key institutions for developing the potential of the children of immigrants. These institutions can be more proactive in encouraging voter registration and participation in civic life.

## Connecting Communities to Jobs

Skill deficiencies, regulatory barriers, and cultural biases are primary obstacles to full participation in the economy, but the physical isolation of impoverished communities not only decreases access to jobs but also perpetuates skill gaps and cultural biases and misunderstandings. Education attainment is thwarted by the low tax base of poor communities, as well as by unstable and discouraging neighborhood environments. Continued residential segregation perpetuates discriminatory attitudes and practices that reduce economic opportunities.

The most effective long-term solutions to this isolation are addressed elsewhere in the plan:

- Creating jobs in downtowns that are accessible to most low-income residents is addressed in *Centers*. Closely aligned with these actions are the strategies to improve mass transit access to employment centers for both urban and suburban communities, as outlined in *Mobility*.

- Improving the availability of affordable housing and reducing residential segregation is addressed in *Centers*. Central to this effort are strong controls on zoning and land use development by the states.

In addition, however, actions must be pursued to improve technological and interpersonal networks between low-income communities and employment centers. These actions, described below, can provide more immediate benefits, as well as create a more effective base for investing in long-term infrastructure and human capital.

### Community-Based Organizations

*Expand successful support programs for community-based organizations to develop alliances with regional employers and institutions.*

The success of dozens of established community-based housing and development groups, such as Newark's New Communities Corporation, the Mid-Bronx Desperadoes, the Greater Jamaica Development Corporation, and ISLES' housing and re-greening efforts in Trenton, have demonstrated the fundamental value of locally initiated community and downtown revitalization. Still other success stories are even more recent, from effective crime-fighting in Bridgeport's East End to community-initiated affordable housing developments in Harlem and Red Bank, New Jersey. And the privately initiated work of groups such as the New York City Partnership and Phipps Houses has demonstrated how groups can leverage private and public dollars to build, renovate, and manage thousands of units of low- and moderate-income housing.

Many of these organizations, however, lack the connections to mainstream economic, social, and political networks that they need to obtain access to capital, expertise and information about employment and business opportunities. Successful models of strengthening CBOs already exist and provide a basis for improving community links to outside resources for job training and enterprise development, as well as for housing and social services. For example, the Local Initiatives Support Corporation has provided financing and technical knowledge to community development corporations, linking them with outside resources through local advisory committees and national program support. Through these support structures and through national fundraising, LISC has enabled local organizations to leverage more than $2 billion locally, build or rehabilitate 57,000 affordable homes, and develop 10 million square feet of commercial space.

By working through existing support institutions, or by establishing their own "Committees of Cooperation" that build on these models of success, community residents and businesses can improve their access to regional employment and business opportunities. These committees, composed of business, labor, civic, and political leaders from both within and outside the community, would provide a wider base of knowledge, resources, and access. They could provide the basis for regional compacts around specific objectives, such as the following:

- Creating job compacts between employers and community organizations to establish hiring programs, transportation services, and employment and training services that improve opportunities to obtain suburban and downtown jobs.

- Improving financing for community businesses by brokering services with financial institutions and developing consortiums to pool resources and share risk.

- Identifying outsourcing and procurement opportunities with regional industries and providing technical expertise to successfully develop these opportunities.

- Creating support networks among CBOs to enhance their political influence and provide opportunities to learn from successful experiments elsewhere.

### Job Information Networks

*Utilize new information technologies to expand job information networks.*

Lack of access to information about job openings has long been a major barrier to employment in low-income communities. Residents lack both the informal connections to employers outside of their immediate community and the literacy and job-hunting skills needed to pursue employment through conventional channels. The widespread use of computer networks to disseminate information about everything from consumer products to government contracts adds a new dimension to this issue. With an increasing number of employment opportunities likely to be advertised via the Internet and other interactive media, access to on-line services and acquisition of computer literacy are additional hurdles to overcome in entering the job market. This technology, however, also provides an opportunity to open information networks more widely, even for low-wage jobs that frequently now are not advertised at all. To insure that communities can take full advantage of these developments, there are number of public and private actions that should be pursued:

- All communities should have the telecommunications infrastructure needed for full access to the information highway. Providing access should be a priority for development of the communications industry.

- Community employment services should provide hardware, training, and assistance to connect residents with multimedia sources of job information.

- State and local employment services should develop partnerships with employers and community organizations to devise means of disseminating employment information more widely within low-income communities.

### Transportation Links

*Improve transportation links between low-income communities and job centers with enhanced bus and van service.*

The Regional Express Rail system proposed in *Mobility* would greatly expand the job opportunities accessible to low-income communities. For example, *Tri-State Rx* would provide direct rail service for residents of Newark, Elizabeth, Bridgeport, and New Haven to a larger number of suburban job locations, and the extension of subway service in southeastern Queens would significantly reduce commuting times to Manhattan.

In addition to improving rail connections and service, other modes of transportation are essential to linking low-income communities to jobs. Currently, both buses and vans, often unlicensed, perform this function. Occasionally, employer-sponsored van service from communities to specific job sites fills a gap in the public transit system. Improved bus service is needed in many neighborhoods, but privately operated van service is a transportation mode that deserves increased attention from policy-makers, community organizations, and employers. Vans are a major part of the informal economy, responding to a demand for inexpensive, flexible service. Regulatory and enforcement policy should attempt to encourage this type of service while minimizing the safety and traffic hazards they sometimes cause, such as by providing more opportunities for vans to operate legally. In addition, employer-sponsored transportation to low-income communities can be an important component of training and employment programs, providing the physical link once skill issues and institutional connections are addressed.

## Investment Needs

The plan's recommendations with the largest implications for increased public investments in human capital are increased funding for urban schools, investments in early child development and quality child care, and investments in adult literacy, retraining, and employment services. Of these, only schools are funded largely by state and local funds. Child care and adult learning have larger portions funded by federal or private sources.

The full cost of the region's shortfall in workforce investments has yet to be determined. However, there are some indications that provide rough orders of magnitude. If we raised spending per pupil in New York City to the suburban average, we would be spending an additional $2.5 billion annually. Even with substantial administrative savings, a large part of this difference would need to be bridged to bring service levels up to suburban standards.

Estimates of need for child care and early childhood development are equally difficult to ascertain. However, in 1990 the three states combined spent $350 million on all types of child care and early childhood education, and all three had extensive

waiting lists for subsidized child care. New York State, which spends approximately $70 per child under 14 on child care, served only about 14% of low-income families who were eligible for assistance. If all eligible families were covered, the state could have spent over $300 million, rather than the current $46 million, on low-income child care.[20] If we define need as low-income families who lack subsidized care or early childhood programs, and the difference between the amount spent on custodial care and what is needed for quality care, then the unfunded need in the region could easily exceed $1 billion.

The cost of literacy programs vary widely and the best estimate of illiteracy and program capacity is several years out of date. However, if we assume that 2.5 million illiterate adults do not receive any training, an outside estimate of need for literacy alone could be over $1 billion. Unemployed adults in need of retraining and employment services are another large population with no real way to estimate total costs.

Based on need alone, several billion dollars in additional workforce-related expenditures annually could be justified. Clearly, we need to challenge ourselves to use current expenditures more efficiently and wisely, and we will need to prioritize new expenditures as we strengthen our economy and tax base. However, we also need to challenge ourselves to identify means of increasing our level of investment in our future human capabilities.

The choices for competing needs are obviously difficult, but human capital investments should receive high priority for revenue captured through efficiencies in other areas of governance. Over the long run, these investments will reduce the costs of governance for social services, welfare, health services, and criminal justice. They also lay the foundation for a more prosperous and equitable region.

## Notes

1. National Center on the Educational Quality of the Workforce, *The Other Shoe: Education's Contribution to the Productivity of Establishments*, 1995, p. 2.

2. U.S. Census of Population, 1990.

3. Drop-out rates vary widely depending on how they are measured. For example, New York City's drop-out rate for a given year is around 6%. Over a four-year period, however, 18% of the original class of 1994 dropped

out (New York City Board of Education). In Newark only two-thirds of the class of 1993 graduated on time (New Jersey Department of Education). Single-year drop-out rates for Bridgeport and New Haven were 10.4% and 8.0%, respectively (Connecticut Department of Education).

4. David A. Brauer and Susan Hickok, "Explaining the Growth in Inequality in Wages Across Skill Levels," *Economic Policy Review*, Vol. 1, No. 1, January 1995, p. 62. Data from U.S. Current Population Survey.

5. U.S. Census of Population, 1990.

6. National Center on the Educational Quality of the Workplace, *First Findings from the EQW National Employer Survey*, 1995, pp. 4 and 14.

7. *New York Citywide School-to-Work Alliance*, an application to the New York State Department of Education, March 5, 1995, by the local partnership of the Board of Education of the City of New York, the New York City Partnership, City University of New York, United Federation of Teachers, New York City Central Labor AFL-CIO, Citywide Parents Leadership Group, Students, New York City Department of Employment, Advisory Council for Occupational Employment, and the Office of the Mayor.

8. See the report of the New York City Workforce Development Commission, "The New Workforce: Investing in New York City's Competitiveness," December 1993.

9. *Starting Points: Meeting the Needs of Our Youngest Children*, Carnegie Corporation of New York, abridged version, August 1994, p. 5

10. Ellen Gallinsky and Dana F. Friedman, *Education Before School: Investing in Quality Child Care*, Scholastic, Inc., 1993, pp. 72–79.

11. Richard S. Gurin, *The Arts Education Standards: A Payoff for Business*, from Perspectives on Implementation: Arts Education Standards for America's Students, Music Educators National Conference, 1994.

12. *Report of the Commission on School Facilities and Maintenance Reform*, June 1995, Executive Preview.

13. *Statistical Profile of Public School Districts*, New York State Department of Education; *New Jersey School Report Card*, New Jersey Department of Education; *Connecticut Academic Performance Tests*, Connecticut State Board of Education..

14. Community Service Society, *Separate, Unequal and Inadequate: Educational Opportunities and Outcomes in New York City Schools*, 1995.

15. *Report of the Commission on School Facilities and Maintenance Reform*, June 1995, Executive Preview.

16. *Statistical Profile of Public School Districts*, New York State Department of Education; *New Jersey School Report Card*, New Jersey Department of Education, 1993 Statewide Summary; and *Connecticut Public School Expenditure Report*, Connecticut Department of Education.

17. *Urbanomics*, "Illiteracy in the Tri-State Region," January 1989.

18. Judith Gueron and Edmund Pauly, *From Welfare to Work*, Summary, Manpower Demonstration Research Corporation, 1991.

19. See the Conference Board report "Business and Education Reform: The Fourth Wave."

20. Gina Adams and Jodi Sandfort, *State Investments in Child Care and Early Childhood Development*, March 1992; and Nancy Ebb, *Child Care Tradeoffs: States Make Painful Choices*, January 1994. Both reports of the Children's Defense Fund.

# Chapter 10

# The Governance Campaign

THE NUMBER of local governments, commissions, special districts, and authorities in the Tri-State Metropolitan Region is estimated to now be over 2,000. RPA's 1961 report *1400 Governments* remains a vivid portrait of the region's governance, and in many respects describes the regional management situation today. While some of RPA's significant recommendations, such as the creation of the Metropolitan Transportation Authority, did come to fruition, much of what RPA described in 1961 remains valid. The Tri-State Metropolitan Region now encompasses 31 counties, not 22.[1] The deconcentration of traditional urban functions, such as employment and housing, over the last 40 years has caused an increase in previously unnecessary government services throughout suburban and exurban areas. At the same time, urban flight has meant an increased need for government-assisted social services for those left behind.

Governmental fragmentation and redundancy has led to increased expense, inconsistency and inequity between places, reduced accountability, and often fragmented delivery of services. The revenue base supporting the region's governments is stretched beyond its limit, as demonstrated by municipalities reducing services and tightening expen-

ditures. This revenue base is largely derived from local property taxes, which are among the country's highest, and, to a lesser degree, from state aid, federal aid, and user fees such as bridge and tunnel tolls.

## Issues

Underlying nearly all of the problems and issues facing the region is a fundamental lack of coordination and consistency among the region's units of government. Each of the three states has its own transportation, housing, environmental, and economic development policies, and within each state are hundreds of individual municipalities, authorities, districts, and other units of government delivering services according to their own programs and sets of objectives. Further, several bi-state or tri-state regional functional authorities overlie portions of the region.

This governance system creates two fundamental obstacles to achieving the best use of land and financial resources in the region:

1. Reliance on the local property tax to finance public education forces municipalities to encourage inappro-

priate, impractical, and environmentally insensitive development.

2. Uncoordinated planning provides no mechanism for measuring the cumulative effects of local development decisions, which can overwhelm resources and infrastructure serving the region.

### *The Lack of Land Use Coordination and Consistency*

Over the past 60 years major improvements have been made in the coordination and consistency of regional, state, and local public services. And standardized procedures and criteria have been developed and applied to certain basic functional areas such as public safety, building and fire codes, infrastructure development, and minimum school curriculum standards.

Yet in other areas that are equally important to the region's ability to compete and sustain itself, little or no structure is provided for local government decisions. Connecticut, New York, and New Jersey all have long histories of granting the lowest levels of government the authority to manage land and land use with little oversight from outside government authorities. This failure of state governments to institute any meaningful land use regulations lies at the root of many fundamental environmental, economic, and social problems the region is facing today.

The region's largely nonprofessional, volunteer land use commissions make thousands of decisions each month that affect the region's quality of life, cost of living, access to opportunity, and integrity of the environment.

Until very recently, none of the three states in the region had meaningful statewide development or land use plans to guide local land use decisions. Connecticut was the first state to develop such a plan, but its function is purely advisory. Connecticut's 169 municipalities are not bound to it as they develop local comprehensive plans. In 1992, after a prolonged public and legislative process, New Jersey adopted its statewide land use and development plan that promotes valuable planning and land use principles, such as focusing new growth in designated centers. Compliance with New Jersey's State Plan is completely voluntary for the municipalities, counties, and state agencies it encompasses; however, there are incentives to do so. New York has

failed to enact any form of state planning reform. In fact, local plans and zoning laws are still optional in New York State.

As a result, throughout the region each municipality continues to act independently, making development and growth decisions that are largely locally focused, market-driven, and have no relationship to broader programs of transportation, environmental protection, job location, or economic development. In fact, there are important parts of the region, such as New York City's upstate watershed area, in which growth and development is completely unguided by even local planning initiatives.

The failure of the region to coordinate land use decisions promotes suburban sprawl, abandonment of centers, automobile dependency (and the resulting congestion, air pollution, and infrastructure expenses), consumption of the region's green infrastructure, racial and economic separation, inequity of jobs and housing choices, and increased costs of living and doing business. This system is a major obstacle to the region's economic competitiveness and sustainability.

### *Local Taxation*

Local taxation and distribution of government revenues has two primary faults. The reliance on local property tax revenues requires local governments to try to attract certain types of uses in a "race for ratables" that does not consider long-term and regional issues. And education finances are distributed inequitably, depriving many communities of quality education, the basic tool they most need for personal and professional success.

#### *Property Taxes and Land Use*

Municipal government works to provide services and to keep costs in check. Towns feel compelled to increase revenue generation through the local property tax system not by increasing the tax rate but by luring new taxpayers into the system. With state and federal program cutbacks, municipalities will be increasingly dependent on local tax revenues to maintain adequate levels of service, with urban centers facing the greatest struggle due to already eroded tax bases and state aid for education formulas already stacked against them. The net result will be an increasing chasm between inner-city and suburban communities.

Connecticut, New York, and New Jersey's municipalities maintain control over their tax base through the land use control authority vested in them by their three state governments. Insofar as a government is able to induce land uses that generate high property tax returns, they do so. Over the past 40 years, region's cities, towns, and villages have attempted to maximize property tax receipts by managing zoning and land use decisions to generate favorable property tax assessments. The "race for ratables" by municipal governments leads them to attract development without full consideration of whether growth will have unanticipated effects or whether it fits into a long-term plan for the community's well-being. The myth that commercial or industrial growth on the outskirts of town is good because it generates tax revenue without sending children to schools is a fallacy, ignoring costs induced in the form of traffic congestion, water pollution, secondary growth for new homes, wear and tear on existing infrastructure such as roads, and additional public services to provide public safety, among others.[2]

An associated suburban mythology holds that rental housing generates pupils and expenses for school districts disproportionate to the property tax revenues generated. Consequently, suburban communities rarely welcome rental housing for fear that it will escalate school costs beyond the local tax base's ability to support quality education. Ironically, in New York City and Nassau County a regressive tax policy taxes rental properties at higher rates than single-family homes, co-ops, and condominiums in exact contrast to the system in place elsewhere in the nation.

More apparent than the suburban tendency to discourage rental housing are suburban land use and zoning trends that favor large lot residential uses, resulting in higher land valuations and larger, more expensive homes that are, in turn, valued highly for property tax purposes. Similarly, zoning for strip commercial uses induces low-cost yet high property tax–generating businesses into an area. The tendency for local—and particularly suburban—governments to favor these two land use forms as positive tax-generating land uses has fed the region's deconcentrated pattern of growth.

Large lot residential subdivisions and commercial strip development along arterial roads or on stand-alone campuses, parks, or malls are generally thought to require little infrastructure investment and to generate few service requirements. Since spreading development patterns permit lot sizes large enough to accommodate on-site wastewater treatment systems and individual wells, expensive water and sewer works are not required. However, few zoning laws and subdivision and local health codes protect larger regional systems, such as New York City and Newark's drinking water supply watersheds, from being degraded by improper septic system placement and inappropriate land use impacts.

Since shopping centers and commercial office parks do not send children to school and low-density residential suburbs do generate fewer children per classroom than their higher density counterparts, there may be a savings as a result of these land use patterns. However, if other variables are included in the equation, such as school transportation costs, police and fire services, and road maintenance and snow removal, the scales tip away from cost savings and demonstrate that even on a local level, more compact forms of development are cost-effective.

Born out of a desire to cut costs and still finance expensive local government systems, suburban communities' sprawling development patterns have actually failed to accomplish what they intended: open space and farmland have been consumed at alarming rates; large-lot zoning policies encourage expensive and exclusive housing; automobile dependency is mandated due to separation of homes from each other and from employment and retail centers; and transit relevance is reduced, if not nonexistent.

The negative effects of job migration and middle class flight from the urban core are compounded by the concentration of new immigrant populations arriving in urban centers and the inability of the poor to migrate out. The region-wide effects of this concentration of poverty in urban areas are:

- Reduced tax revenues in urban centers.
- Declining levels and quality of basic services.
- Increased disparity between the "haves" and the "have nots."
- Large inequities in school finance between urban and suburban areas.

*Figure 94: The region's fragmented and inefficient system of governance has resulted in many communities' curbing services that they sorely need.*

The net result of this property tax–based and highly fragmented system is a region in which the cost of living is among the highest in the nation and the quality of life it offers its citizens is declining. Also, as a result of these trends, unsustainable growth and development patterns are established; the future workforce is inadequately educated and unprepared; low-density, automobile-dependent sprawl is encouraged; centers of all sizes are emptied of residents, jobs, and retail establishments; and open space and natural resources are consumed.

It is imperative that the pervasive problems of the region's fragmented and uncoordinated governance system be addressed. Coordinated land use decision-making is essential to establish the Greensward and protect the region's drinking water supplies; to build the *Rx* Regional Rail system; and to

ensure that new employment and affordable housing opportunities are created in our region's centers, building on infrastructure investments already made.

But reforming the region's governance system must move forward under several basic guiding assumptions:

- Local land use plans should be guided by regional and state goals. We need a shared regional vision and an understanding of what choices are available and what their effects will be.
- We need a coordinating framework within which individual units of government can work toward achieving shared goals.
- The home rule–based governance system should be improved and refocused rather than dismantled.
- We need to move away from local property tax–driven decision-making.
- We need to promote sustainable and effective ways of doing things by making the right choices the easy ones.

Improving the region's governance will require fundamental changes to the context in which municipal-level decisions are made. How, for example, can municipal governments be encouraged to consider the larger, long-term effects of their decisions? How can contentious land use decisions be made among towns and cities working together rather than individually?

*Education Finance*

Local school districts rely on locally collected property taxes for the bulk of their revenues. In New York State, for example, 57% of the cost of local schools is covered by property tax revenues; state aid pays for 39%; and the remaining 4% comes from federal and other sources. These school taxes make up at least 60%—and in some cases as much as 80%—of local property tax bills. Property taxes comprise 32% of all state and local tax revenues in New York State, including sales and income taxes.[3]

Current federal and state trends toward reducing spending, including local aid programs and intervention, indicate that these locally derived revenue sources will be increasingly relied upon to finance schools, local services, and capital needs. In addition, these same trends suggest an abrogation of federal and state responsibility for certain services and an involuntary and unfinanced devolution of responsibility to local units of government. These factors, combined with historically upward-spiraling local government costs associated with, among other factors, higher labor costs, have driven local governments to seek ways to reduce the cost of government and to increase property tax revenues.

Paralleling local government's increased reliance on property tax revenues has been the growing disparity between communities with rising property values and those with stagnant or decreasing real property values. Since property taxes rise or fall according to property valuations, the region's cities and inner suburbs are hardest pressed to raise sufficient tax revenues to fund adequate local services and schools. Conversely, outer-suburban school districts have largely done well as they have attracted commercial growth and property values have risen over the past few decades.

This trend, described in *Workforce*, has helped create a two-tiered public school system, with higher educational achievement emanating from the outer-suburban schools while urban and inner-suburban school districts experience proportionately higher levels of drop-outs and lower achievement scores and college entrances.

## Summary of Recommendations

To successfully implement the Third Regional Plan, new, better-coordinated, and refocused public institutions and public finance mechanisms will be needed. The first four proposals address government coordination to provide better government services. The next three proposals outline new public institutions that would provide new services to the region. The final proposals challenge current decision-making processes that fail to accurately reflect environmental costs.

1. Coordinate governance in the region.

   • Improve state growth management systems to create incentives for community plans and regulations needed to promote development in centers and create effective urban growth boundaries needed to protect the regional reserves and other Greensward areas.

   • Promote service sharing by municipal governments to "right-size" bureaucracies and to achieve economies of scale while maintaining accountability and local control.

   • Reform education finance to provide equity in the finance of urban school systems and to remove incentives for fiscal zoning.

   • Promote opportunities for decent housing for all residents.

2. Create new public institutions to finance and provide regional services.

   • Create a new Regional Transportation Authority.

   • Restructure the Port Authority to focus on its core mission.

   • Create a Tri-State Infrastructure Bank to direct funds to priority capital projects, with a set of dedicated taxes and fees.

3. Improve both public and private decision-making processes.

   • Incorporate the principles of sustainable economics into capital budgeting and tax and regulatory systems to build economic incentives into industrial and development processes that will benefit both the economy and the environment.

   • Reduce the cost of infrastructure investments by utilizing smart infrastructure concepts that promote multiple uses and objectives and employ alternatives to end of the pipe treatment facilities.

## Coordinated Governance

### State Growth Management Systems

For more than 65 years RPA has advocated improved local planning and zoning and other land use regulatory mechanisms. In the early 1930s RPA promoted the creation of local planning boards and helped develop the widespread adoption of municipal zoning as a means of implementing the First Regional Plan. By the 1970s, however, it became clear that the region's decentralized land use regulatory system was actually promoting sprawl, limiting housing opportunities, and exacerbating income and racial segregation. Each of several hundred municipalities administers zoning without regional or statewide guidelines and, in some cases, without even a municipal comprehensive or master plan.

In addition to being uncoordinated and not geared toward addressing regional issues, the existing planning, land use regulatory, and development approval systems of the region create an uncompetitive and hostile investment climate. While many communities use zoning—or a lack of zoning—to induce business location and residential and commercial development, few of the region's municipal plans actually articulate a vision for their communities that clearly lays out what sort of development is wanted and where it would be best located. This equivocacy often results in contentious development approval processes in which developers and neighborhood, environmental, or special interest groups, lacking clear ground rules, wrangle at length. The result is often frustrating delays, higher costs, and inappropriately sited and designed development.

A more rational planning and land use regulatory system would spell out where and to what degree a community agrees development should occur and where it should not occur. Further, local land use regulatory programs—zoning, subdivision regulations, and environmental protection ordinances—should be consistent with a community's comprehensive plan. In addition, a rational planning system should address regional needs at the local level and coordination between adjacent municipalities should be required to ensure that cross-jurisdictional matters, such as housing markets, transportation systems, and environmental resources, are consistently addressed.

Fundamentally, the goal of an effective land use system should be to identify appropriate locations for needed development and to provide citizens, businesses, and developers with reasonable assurances that land use decisions will be predicable, speedy, and open.

Across the country, concerns similar to those facing this region have prompted states to create new state-level planning and growth management systems. Hawaii's adoption of a statewide zoning system in 1961 initiated a phenomenon that came to be known as the "quiet revolution in land use regulation." In the 1970s Oregon, Florida, and Vermont adopted statewide growth management systems. And a decade later Georgia, Washington, Maine, and Rhode Island adopted similar systems. A total of ten states have adopted new planning systems in the past three decades. The experience of places such as Oregon strongly suggests that statewide growth management strategies can expand economic, transportation, and housing opportunities and reinforce community character while reducing land consumption and damage to the environment.

Except in Hawaii, these programs do not involve zoning by the state government. Instead, they provide state policy guidance for improved local planning, including the following techniques:

- A set of guiding principles or goals, often including promotion of compact patterns of growth.

- A requirement for consistency between municipal plans and regulations and state goals.

- A requirement for state agency functional plans to be consistent with state goals.

- Some kind of state certification process for municipal plans and regulations.

- State funding for municipal planning.

Creating systems for more effective growth management is essential to the implementation of many Third Regional Plan recommendations, including rebuilding the region's centers, promoting transit use, protecting the Greensward, and establishing regional growth boundaries. Since the 1980s RPA has promoted the creation of effective state growth management systems in this region. RPA is committed to continuing this fundamental initiative.

RPA is promoting reformed state growth management programs in New York, New Jersey, and Connecticut that incorporate the following principles:

1. Develop state or regional growth, development, and resource protection goals and policies through an open public process. These policies should:

   - Promote the kind of infrastructure investments that result in desired growth patterns—including transportation, water supply, wastewater treatment, and other facilities.

   - Promote economic development and improved opportunities for employment.

   - Create opportunities for affordable and decent housing for all residents.

   - Promote growth that complements the natural environment, preserving and protecting watersheds, wetlands, aquifers, floodplains, estuaries, river corridors, ridgetops, forests, and agricultural lands.

   - Protect and preserve cultural, historic, and archaeological resources.

   - Promote the protection of open space resources, including improved access to water bodies and better integration of open space features into communities.

   - Incorporate long-term environmental and social benefits and costs into economic analyses.

2. Require that local comprehensive plans and land use regulations be consistent with state and county policies. Local comprehensive plans should identify specific growth, economic development, quality of life, and preservation objectives. Local land use regulations should be designed to carry out these plans and provide predictable permitting for all activities that are consistent with the plan.

3. Make state agency plans and programs consistent. Agency plans, regulations, and investments should be consistent and should reflect state goals and municipal plans.

4. Provide assistance for local compliance. This assistance could include making technical help available for local planning; targeting discretionary state spending to municipalities with complying plans; and offering state indemnification of localities against challenges to regulations developed under complying planning programs.

5. Institute statewide planning entities. An existing or new state agency or arm of government should develop state goals and agency consistency and should coordinate development permitting and local comprehensive plan incentives.

6. Streamline environmental and land use regulatory processes. Approved local plans should function as generic environmental impact statements, "prequalifying" all development that is consistent with local plans and takes place within specified development areas.

7. Provide a financing mechanism. Funds to offset most of the cost of preparing and administering local plans and regulations should be available. Funds could either be made available as a small percentage of the state capital budget or be generated by new development review fees. In return for higher fees, sponsors of compatible projects in designated growth areas would benefit from a streamlined permitting process.

8. Create partnerships between state and local governments and private stakeholders to develop and implement strategies to protect important resource areas and to meet other shared goals. New regional entities—state-created but locally controlled—are one approach that allows large inter-municipal regions to cooperatively protect special resource areas and achieve common objectives.

## Municipal Government Service Sharing

Inter-municipal service sharing and coordination agreements can be instituted between the region's cities and towns to create economies of scale and generally reduce the extent to which there are costly redundancies and duplication.

In many functional areas, the region's governments already cooperate or use consistent regulatory standards. For example, standardized procedures and criteria have been developed and applied to public safety, building and fire codes, waste management, infrastructure development, and minimum school curriculum standards.

Despite movement toward consistency in some areas, local governments across the region independently provide a wide array of services, creating inefficiencies and adding unnecessary costs to their operations. Costly redundancies are created when adjacent cities, towns, and villages each must provide for health, police, fire, criminal justice, water, sewer, human and social services, solid waste, library, road maintenance, parks and recreation, and myriad other services to only their residents. To be sure, municipalities may take occasional advantage of cost savings through combined purchasing agreements for items such as police vehicles, but such savings through cooperation do not pervade either municipal purchase or service delivery programs. Highly localized home rule traditions combined with local property tax–based finance systems reinforce the cost-center nature of local government and impede coordination with neighboring municipalities.

### Current Service Sharing

Legislatures in Connecticut, New York, and New Jersey recognize the inefficiencies inherent in the locally centered governance system now in place. In Albany legislation to enable municipal governments to enter into inter-municipal service-sharing agreements with county governments has been enacted. In addition, municipalities are authorized to cooperate in developing health benefit plans. In the Albany capital region special legislation has been enacted to encourage inter-municipal cooperation in the areas of bulk purchasing, solid waste, police communications, public works, and other areas. Similarly, the Long Island Pine Barrens Commission has cooperatively prepared a land use and management plan for a three-town region that will guide the constituent towns' land use and development decisions.

Voluntary efforts to share services and coordinate among municipalities are underway in several places. Most of these are outside the metropolitan region, but the lessons are valuable. In the upstate New York Tug Hill region, a dozen towns have formed a joint planning board, pooling resources to retain professional planning assistance and coordinating their land use decisions among themselves rather than individually within their own town halls. In northern Westchester County three towns have established joint water works to save on the cost of drinking water filtration and to share in the savings of joint purchasing, equipment sharing, and composting.

Such inter-municipal agreements are, however, not standard operating procedure for municipal government. Consequently, cost-saving opportunities and economies of scale are not fully realized. The increasing cost of government reflects this failure.

The Somerset Alliance for the Future studied the potential for service sharing in Somerset County, New Jersey and determined that there are opportunities for sharing services in every community. Among those that could be effectively shared are composting, criminal justice, data processing, senior citizen transportation, police emergency dispatching, public works sharing, and solid waste management. In addition, the Somerset Alliance identified several local service areas that could be assumed by higher levels of government, such as environmental health, social services administration, and planning. This study echoed the findings of the SLERP Commission, which recommended that certain local functions should be assumed by the state, including trial courts and public assistance programs.

Even rarer than inter-municipal service-sharing agreements are cases of inter-municipal or regional tax base sharing. The local property tax, being the primary source of local government support, is held closely by municipal governments and drives local decisions. Decoupling the property tax from these decisions could significantly affect how local land use and development occurs. New Jersey's Hackensack Meadowlands Commission is but one example of regional tax base sharing in which property taxes are collected at an other-than-local level—by the Commission instead—and are allocated to the individual municipalities on a fair share basis.

### Right-Sizing Government

Reducing the cost of government through service-sharing arrangements is not the panacea, but it is one proven approach that needs wider application. A broader approach can be termed "right-sizing." The right-sizing approach acknowledges home rule traditions and the existing fragmentation and divisions among governments but seeks to place service delivery at the most appropriate and effective level of government. Right-sizing also builds on existing models of new regional entities, such as the Hackensack Meadowlands Commission, the Long Island Pine Barrens Commission, and the MTA.

The inefficiency of governance in this region is demonstrated by the dramatic rise in government revenues and expenditures. In constant dollars, and including public authorities, the region's governments have grown from total revenues of $70.9 billion and total expenditures of $61.8 billion in 1977 to revenues of $85.9 billion and expenditures of $90.7 billion in 1993. These increases, of 21% in revenues and 42% in expenditures over just 16 years, came during a period in which the region's population only grew by about 2%.

Right-sizing, sharing, and shifting responsibili-

| | General Revenues | | | | General Expenditures | | | |
|---|---|---|---|---|---|---|---|---|
| | 1967 | 1977 | 1987 | 1993 | 1967 | 1977 | 1987 | 1993 |
| 31-County Region | 39,780,299 | 63,765,158 | 67,700,111 | 76,955,456 | 38,095,179 | 57,221,990 | 60,555,223 | 83,892,437 |
| Public Authorities | | 7,127,838 | 9,648,343 | 8,969,229 | | 4,615,837 | 6,839,346 | 6,761,189 |
| Total | 39,780,299 | 70,892,996 | 77,348,454 | 85,924,685 | 38,095,179 | 61,837,827 | 67,394,569 | 90,653,626 |

*Figure 95: General Revenues and Expenditures for Government in the Tri-State Metropolitan Region. (All numbers adjusted to 1993 dollars, in thousands.)*

ties among existing and new governmental units will be required to implement the Third Regional Plan. Reorganizing the Port Authority, establishing new regional commissions to implement Greensward recommendations, and restructuring the collection and allocation of property taxes for school finance are all examples of right-sizing trends that must occur to retain the region's economic and environmental edge into the 21st century.

### Education Finance Reform

RPA strongly endorses the goal of reducing the growing disparity between urban and suburban school funding levels. Lawsuits have been filed in all three states arguing that these disparities violate state constitutions. In New Jersey the State Supreme Court has ordered the state to redress funding inequities, highlighting the need for structural solutions in all three states.

The goal of education finance reform is to more effectively direct public resources to improve academic achievement throughout the region's education system. Increasing resources for poor, primarily urban schools is essential if the region is going to prepare its future workforce to meet the demands of industry and if it is going to successfully accommodate the existing and anticipated resident and immigrant populations in the region's culture and economy. Insofar as the quality of the region's schools and the achievement levels of school children are linked to the inequitable distribution of real estate taxes, the tax revenue allocation system needs to be reevaluated and restructured to even out school finance.

The disproportionate number of poverty-level, minority, and non–English language proficient pupils in urban school districts hampers the delivery of basic education programs. This challenge is exacerbated by a narrow and diminished property tax base that is inadequately subsidized by state aid.

RPA understands that reducing the dependence of school finances on local property tax revenues is a complex issue. But it is essential that it be done to build a school system that can meet the standards of an increasingly demanding economy and to provide equitable funding of basic education for all of the region's children. RPA recommends that state government finance education, allocating funds to local school districts to serve all children in accordance

with local needs rather than local economic circumstances.

### State Assumption of School Finance

Shifting school finance upward, from local school districts or municipal levels, will require states to levy and collect taxes in place of locally collected taxes for school use. In addition, this shift will require the establishment of new and equitable distribution formulas to equalize funding on a per pupil basis, regardless of the property valuation base within that particular district. Further, the redistribution system must take into consideration compensatory funding to address special needs of the school population with respect to poverty conditions, special needs requirements, and English language proficiency.

Currently, no real property taxes are collected by states in the Tri-State Metropolitan Region. States do, however, establish equalization criteria and administer school aid distribution programs, however fair or unfair they may be. One option for state funding is to collect the proportion of local property taxes now dedicated to local school districts, as is done in Washington State. Other models involve mixing tax revenue sources. Michigan has recently tried this option, with an increased state sales tax (from 4% to 6%), new cigarette taxes, and a new "partitioned" property tax aimed at new high-end residential construction.

Under state finance assumption plans, consideration has to be given to the functional divisions between state and local responsibilities. One recommendation is for the three states to assume primary responsibility for funding the basic educational services provided in schools and gearing funding allocation to ensure that all school populations attain at least minimum education standards according to standardized achievement tests administered by the states. Doing so will likely mean that the distribution formulas will, in fact, contain compensatory and special education allotments for urban and inner-suburban classrooms above and beyond those needed for outer-suburban situations with fewer at-risk and special-needs pupils.

The objective of state funding is not parity per se, but improved performance for under-funded districts. Redistribution of current expenditures without productivity savings or new revenue will not be sufficient to improve performance in poor districts, and it could lower achievement in suburban communities. The first source to scrutinize is the efficiency of the school systems themselves. Secondly, education should receive a high priority for any savings achieved through efficiencies in other parts of the public sector. Ultimately, funding for education will reflect the degree to which we recognize its role in shaping our future prosperity.

### Regional Tax Base Sharing

Spreading the property tax revenue base of school districts over broader geographic areas has also been recommended as a means to equalize the gap between wealthy suburban schools and poorer inner-city school districts. This is already being done to some extent in the region. In New York City, for example, the city's 33 community school boards are financed by property taxes collected throughout the five boroughs. Likewise, but under very different circumstances, many sparsely settled suburban areas have established multi-town school districts supporting a single middle and high school for as many as five or more separate towns, among which may exist significant median income differences.

Under current conditions, however, the household income and real property tax base discrepancies and the school population needs are so divergent that existing tax base sharing schemes do not address the larger regional issues of inequitable school finance, even though they may ameliorate local differences. The basic problem is that current experiments in school finance tax base sharing in the region do not spread the base over a large enough geographic area to account for and equalize differences. In response to this pattern, in the 1970s the Minneapolis–St. Paul region adopted a metropolitan tax base sharing system in which 40% of new commercial and industrial tax revenues went into a regional pool for redistribution to communities on the basis of need. In recognition of continuing tax inequities, legislation is currently pending in the Minnesota state legislature to add new, wealthy districts to the regional pool. The Greater Toronto Area Task Force also recommended early in 1996 that the region adopt a tax base sharing system similar to the Twin Cities model.

In 1985 New Jersey created the State and Local Expenditure and Revenue Policy (SLERP) Commission to conduct a systematic review of the state's municipal fiscal structure and to develop recommendations for reform, focusing on reducing the fiscal burden faced by communities.[4] Among its recommendations were: change the nature of local school finance; guarantee a tax base formula that ensures that no municipality will receive less than its current allotment; reduce county, school district, and municipal spending caps to account for the increased fiscal relief from the state; and create a new agency with county-based offices to administer property taxes. The SLERP Commission also recommended implementing the New Jersey State Development and Redevelopment Plan as a means to save local governments money. The recommendations of the SLERP Commission have not been acted upon, but it is significant that the State Plan was viewed as a cost-saving initiative.

The increasingly high cost of local government—including schools—and the fact that municipal governments and schools are almost entirely financed by property tax revenues is the basis for "fiscal zoning" and the "race for ratables." This tendency for local land use decisions to be made on the basis of tax revenue generation can be addressed by disconnecting school finance from the property tax, as discussed above, and by simply reducing the cost of municipal services and improving the efficiency of their delivery.

## Regional Institutions

For most of this century the Tri-State Metropolitan Region led the nation in creating the regional institutions needed to finance, build, and manage metropolitan infrastructure, including the Port Authority of New York and New Jersey, the New York Thruway and New Jersey Turnpike Authorities, and, more recently, the Metropolitan Transportation Authority, Metro-North Railroad, and NJ TRANSIT. In the past two decades, while the region has stopped innovating, other regions around the country have been inventing and setting up new forms of metropolitan authorities. Portland, Oregon's Metropolitan Service District, or "Metro," as it is known, is perhaps the most ambitious of these, with a governing board directly elected by the voters. Metro, now a real government in many ways, has been given responsibility for regional growth management, including administration of the state-authorized urban growth boundary, water supply, waste management, and other activities serving the entire metropolitan area.

Advanced transit, freight, and other transportation systems have long been among the region's fundamental economic assets. As recently as the 1960s the region planned and developed a highway network that provided access throughout the region. But in more recent decades we have settled for fragmented planning and management and mid-20th century service levels for transit and freight movement systems, while our competitors across the country and around the world have been expanding theirs to serve 21st century needs. Tokyo, Paris, London, Los Angeles, and other metropolitan regions are building or planning integrated regional rail systems, while we have added virtually no new capacity to our system in decades.

Our fragmented transit system is now the responsibility of multiple planning and operating authorities. Most of these public authorities were created to take over management of failed private railroads that had once been bitter rivals, and it sometimes seems as if they have inherited old acrimonies along with the rolling stock. Serious consequences of this fragmentation are experienced daily throughout the region; poor commuting connections, inconvenient scheduling and ticketing, and other time-wasting deficiencies. Until recently, among the world's great centers, we shared this distinction only with Berlin. But since the fall of the Berlin Wall, that city has unified management of its system and is planning expansions to meet the needs of a healed and growing region.

In addition to fragmentation, the region's transportation authorities have too often diverted their attention away from their own core missions. For more than a decade the governors of New York and New Jersey have directed the Port Authority and other authorities, often against the advice of their professional staffs, into commercial real estate, waste management, and urban revitalization activities. Most of these projects meet important public needs but diminish the resources and management focus needed to fulfill the authorities' fundamental responsibilities. The Port Authority, for example, has directed hundreds of millions of dollars into such projects as a new legal office building in downtown Newark, waterfront redevelopment projects in Queens and Hoboken, industrial parks in the Bronx and Yonkers, a waste-to-energy plant in New Jersey, and a new academic building for Rutgers University in New Brunswick. Authorities have also been used to provide "one shot" payments to close annual state budget deficits, such as when the New York Thruway Authority and the New Jersey Turnpike Authority "purchased" highways from the states. Thus highway users in the 21st century will still be paying to close budget gaps from the early 1990s.

As a result, airports and other transportation facilities have been starved of capital and operating funds needed to maintain them in a good state of repair. Redevelopment of existing facilities and construction of new ones have been postponed or canceled. When the Port Authority canceled the proposed new central terminal at JFK Airport, citing a shortage of funds, the region's principal international gateway was doomed to remain substandard and continue to lose market share. JFK is often ranked by international air travelers as one of the worst international airports in the world.

Some of these authorities have become increasingly isolated both from the public and from the realities of the global marketplace. Consequently, they have lost public confidence, making it difficult for them to obtain necessary political and financial support for essential activities. At the MTA virtually all of the proceeds from subsidy increases since 1970 appear as increased payroll costs, weakening public confidence in its ability to deliver services efficiently. The Port Authority has not built any new infrastructure systems in almost three decades and seems to have lost sight of its primary mission. These institutions have also been hobbled by short-sighted political interference—for example, in setting tolls and fares too low to support necessary capital investments or to improve service levels, creating a downward spiral of declining service, ridership, and public support.

While existing institutions have failed to meet current needs, the region also has failed to create the institutions needed to respond to emerging challenges and responsibilities. When the Tri-State Regional Planning Commission collapsed in the early 1980s, it was replaced by several metropolitan planning organizations (MPOs), the agencies that are now responsible under the federal Intermodal

Surface Transportation Efficiency Act (ISTEA) for developing long-range transportation plans. This region is nearly alone in the country in having more than a dozen MPOs, none of which coordinates across state boundaries. This balkanization of responsibilities has contributed to the often parochial and short-term outlooks and the narrowly defined political and economic interests of groups that were intended by federal law to have broader, longer term perspectives. In addition, MPOs in this region do not have the authority to adequately address transportation-related land use and air quality issues, as called for in ISTEA.

### Potential for Interagency Cooperation

Meeting regional transportation and environmental goals will require a reexamination of the structures and mission of our regional authorities. In Paris and Tokyo regional rail systems have been built and operated through cooperative agreements between existing agencies. In greater London the government is breaking up the public rail system into a network of privately managed services to be operated on publicly owned routes, with coordination of schedules, fares, and connections. *Rx* rail could be developed through new forms of interagency cooperation, but only if the existing authorities fully integrate their transportation services and revenue streams. The fee revenues from the Port Authority's bridges and tunnels should be dedicated to support interstate elements of *Rx*, such as a new trans-Hudson *Rx* commuter rail and rail freight tunnel. Discrete dedicated accounts to finance *Rx* projects will reinvigorate public confidence and protect funds from being turned to nonessential projects or raided to fill sudden gaps in state budgets.

Recently, the Port Authority, NJ TRANSIT, and MTA agreed to cooperate on planning for improved access to the Midtown Manhattan core, indicating that they sometimes work together. But the experience here and in other regions suggests that voluntary models for cooperation between authorities will not produce the long-term collaboration needed to plan, build and operate major new investments. Although there has been some improvement in recent years in interagency cooperation, interstate projects almost always assume a lower priority within each agency than projects wholly within their control. The result has been the continued deterioration of the region's basic transportation infrastructure, contributing to declining public confidence in the region's future.

Los Angeles, Boston, and Chicago have created region-wide authorities to manage subway and regional rail construction and operations. All of these metropolitan regions have significant governing advantages in that each is located within one state; the Tri-State Metropolitan Region, as the name says, comprises parts of three states. A tri-state transit authority—structured differently from existing authorities in both geography and responsibilities—represents the best solution for delivering the region's transit needs for the 21st century.

### Models for Institutional Reform

This region's governance system is not the product of any grand vision or comprehensive design but of hundreds of years of evolution and accretion on a foundation dating back to the colonial period. A visiting British civil servant reflected on the venerable nature of this system upon meeting a group of selectmen, freeholders, supervisors, councilors, and aldermen. He remarked that the villages, towns, hamlets, boroughs, cities, and counties that they governed represented the last intact English medieval system of government anywhere in the world. Virtually everywhere else similar systems have been reformed, sometimes several times, in response to economic and social change. Here we have created public authorities and tax districts and new municipalities, but with few exceptions—notably the creation of Greater New York in 1898 and Connecticut's decision in the 1960s to eliminate county government—this region has never had any kind of comprehensive reform of its governance system.

However, we are not alone among the world's metropolitan regions in having a decentralized and uncoordinated system of government. Throughout the industrialized world, metropolitan regions have expanded beyond political boundaries established over a half-century ago. Even places that established metropolitan governments as recently as the 1960s and 1970s are now growing beyond their fixed borders. Only a handful of places—notably in the growing sunbelt regions of the U.S. south and southwest—have "elastic" borders that can expand as these regions grow.

When Greater New York was established in

1898, its five boroughs encompassed what was then the entire urban region, making this the world's first truly metropolitan government. As early as the 1920s, however, the region began expanding beyond these boundaries. No one today proposes that New York City should expand to encompass the 31-county region. The general trend in the country is toward deregulation and fewer levels of government over new institutions and additional layers of authority. But can we create a better system of governance to better manage and develop region-sustaining and region-shaping infrastructure, manage growth, and protect environmental systems?

The experience of other metropolitan regions suggests some options. In Tokyo no official ties bind the city with the suburban prefectures. The Ministry of Construction operates a National Capital Planning Agency to coordinate major infrastructure planning, but this agency provides few opportunities for local input and does not deal with the larger set of social, economic, and land use issues facing the area. The shortcomings of this system—manifested in excessive congestion, duplicative infrastructure investments, and deteriorating environmental systems and quality of life—are now becoming apparent.

As London has grown to encompass most of southeastern England, the region has had various forms of metropolitan government, beginning with the London County Council and subsequently the Greater London Council (GLC). By the early 1980s, however, the GLC no longer represented much of the growing region, and it was abolished. Since then, a series of service districts and advisory agencies have assumed many planning and infrastructure management responsibilities, including the London Research Centre and the London Planning Advisory Council. But the region lacks any organization with strong powers to shape growth or to coordinate investments and policies among local governments.

Closer to home, two other metropolitan regions, Portland, Oregon, and Toronto, Ontario, provide models that could be adapted to the needs of this region.

In Portland voters have established a metropolitan service commission, called Portland Metro, that is responsible for land use and infrastructure planning and major infrastructure systems, including parks, solid waste management, the convention center, and other facilities. Metro's governing council is elected directly by the voters, giving it democratic legitimacy and broad public support. In 1994 voters gave Metro authority to require that municipal plans and regulations be consistent with its new long-range regional plan. This power, when combined with Metro's existing authority to designate and enforce a regional urban growth boundary, makes this a national model for effective control of urban sprawl and provision of affordable housing and infrastructure.

Toronto has long been a laboratory for new approaches to metropolitan governance. In 1954 Toronto created a metropolitan government that encompassed the region. But since then, the Greater Toronto Area has grown and deconcentrated—it now includes parts of four suburban "regional municipalities," producing many of the same governance problems that Tokyo and this region face. In response to these concerns, in 1994 the provincial government created a Greater Toronto Area (GTA) Task Force to develop new proposals for reform.

The GTA Task Force proposes to replace the existing government and those of four suburban municipalities with a new Greater Toronto Region (GTR). The GTR would function as a regional service district similar to Portland Metro, assuming responsibility for regional infrastructure systems, metropolitan growth management, economic development, environmental protection, and other region-shaping services. The GTR proposes formation of a regional council representing mayors and communities. Major goals of the proposal include reduction in overlaps between local, regional, and provincial governments, reform of the property tax system, and transferal of specific powers from the province to the region.

### Implications for the Tri-State Region

It would be very difficult to replicate these kinds of sweeping reforms in the Tri-State Metropolitan Region. The borders of New Jersey, Connecticut, and New York cannot change under our federal system, and the states would be reluctant to surrender any power or taxing authority. In addition, most of the region's residents and business and political leaders are suspicious of distant government, and thus may oppose any proposals that significantly weaken home rule traditions of local services, schools, and land use controls. For these reasons,

RPA's governance recommendations reform existing regional authorities; create region-wide, single-purpose authorities; promote voluntary cooperation between the states; and reform state tax, infrastructure finance, and planning systems. They are modest in comparison with Portland's reforms and those being proposed for Toronto.

But if the Tri-State Metropolitan Region were to establish a new metropolitan service commission, the experiences of Portland and Toronto could provide insights into how a new entity might be governed and structured. The states could transfer authority and taxing powers to the region through the service commission. Municipal governments could retain most of their existing authority, although their land use controls and infrastructure spending would have to reflect policies established regionally. And a number of existing public authorities could be abolished, restructured, or privatized. A metropolitan service commission could be structured to assume some or all of these responsibilities:

- Administration of a regional urban growth boundary and oversight of a regional land use planning system in which municipal plans would become consistent with regional goals.

- Transportation planning and capital budgeting would be consolidated, assuming responsibility for owning highways, bridges, and rail corridors, and contracting for operation and maintenance of these systems with existing public authorities or private operators.

- A metropolitan service commission could assume responsibility for funding land acquisition in the proposed regional reserves and control of state and regional parks, parkways, and greenways.

- A metropolitan service commission could assume responsibilities from the states for environmental planning, regulation, and even operation of solid waste, wastewater treatment, and public water supply systems.

- The states could transfer environmental, land use, and other regulatory responsibilities and taxing authorities.

Creating a metropolitan service commission would represent a significant departure from existing governance systems, and its creation would require a fundamental shift in public attitudes and past practices. In Oregon, the impetus for creating Portland Metro came from the region's voters, eager to better manage growth. In Toronto, the drive for reform has come from a provincial government eager to cut costs and from business leaders and concerned citizens eager to reform economic development, growth management, and tax systems.

This region's citizens and leaders could be motivated by the recognition that the region needs a system of governance that can bolster its quality of life and competitiveness. But the prerequisite for these reforms will be bold and persistent public leadership. Even if this leadership materializes, it may take decades for it to yield structural changes in our governance system. For these reasons, this plan proposes a more modest and incremental set of reforms in how we finance, build, and manage infrastructure, finance public education, and coordinate land use planning. The plan also calls for voluntary cooperation between the states to coordinate economic development, transportation, land use, environmental protection, and other policies. These reforms would significantly improve the region's governance in the near term and could build the confidence and sense of regional identity needed to create an even more effective system of metropolitan governance in the future.

### Restructuring Authorities

The spirit of the times demands that government be accountable, results-oriented, and cost-effective. All three states have a long-standing and healthy skepticism about new layers of government and super agencies. As previously noted, creating a general purpose regional government or regional service district would probably not be politically feasible in the foreseeable future.

The more likely approach to creating more effective regional institutions would appear to be the reform of the existing multistate institutions, literally "re-forming" these agencies, shaping them anew to meet a new generation of needs. This would be the least disruptive, most acceptable, and lowest cost approach, and it would keep government closest to the people being served. No previous approach has attempted to think about all of these agencies simultaneously. Since all of the problems facing the region are interconnected, both across political boundaries and functional areas, we are now required by new realities to think simultaneously about the shape of all of the regional institutions that manage these issues.

A comprehensive approach to achieving this goal—creation of a Tri-State Regional Transportation Authority (RTA)—would involve a fundamental restructuring of the major transportation authorities, the Port Authority and the MTA, and a new relationship between them and the Connecticut and New Jersey Departments of Transportation and NJ TRANSIT.

## A Regional Transportation Authority

At present The Metropolitan Transportation Authority operates only in New York and Connecticut. Commuter rail and bus services in New Jersey are the responsibility of NJ TRANSIT, and trans-Hudson bridges and tunnels and the PATH system are controlled by the Port Authority. Consolidation of these transit and toll road, bridge, and tunnel services would create a unified Regional Transportation Authority.

This new organization would integrate the region's current seven separate rail systems into an integrated Regional Express, or *Rx* Rail system. The goal of *Rx* is to support the region's new and more deconcentrated settlement pattern by improving interstate and inter-suburban commutes, expanding service to a variety of destinations in the Manhattan core, and improving reverse- and intra-regional commutes. This goal cannot be achieved without consolidation of transit planning, funding, and management across the region.

The new authority should reform work rules, pay scales, and staffing patterns in all of the central office and operating divisions. The feasibility of privatizing operations, ranging from maintenance and terminal operations to bus and train operations, should also be systematically examined. One option would be for the authority to own the fixed assets (rails, roads, stations, etc.) and contract out the operations and maintenance. The MTA's current management structure of a centralized capital budgeting and financial control function and decentralized operations could be adopted by the new RTA. Under this structure, commuter rail services operated by NJ TRANSIT, Metro-North, and the Long Island Rail Road would retain significant operating autonomy. Connecticut could also transfer operation of its Shoreline East commuter service to

Metro-North. Bus operations could be operated in a similar manner, and the RTA should study ways to improve the operations of bus systems, including new technologies and vehicles that expedite implementation of dial-a-ride, van, and other flexible, customer-oriented services. Again, privatization of these services should be strongly considered. Management of the Port Authority Bus Terminals and Manhattan's Pennsylvania Station should also be transferred to the RTA.

To gain and retain public confidence, it will be important to design the RTA's governance structure to maximize its accountability to the people it serves. But there will almost certainly be a tension between the governors, state, county, and local officials, and other groups in defining who speaks for the public. And there will also be a tension between making the RTA responsive to immediate political needs and insulating it from daily political interference.

One way to provide voters with a sense of connection to the RTA would be to have at least part of its board directly elected by the voters. Portland, Oregon's Metro has certainly gained broad public support through its elected board. Reflecting the strength of public support for this metropolitan service district, in 1993 voters gave Metro significant oversight over municipal plans and regulations through referendum. Board members should have "hold-over" appointments to ensure a degree of independence from the day-to-day politics of the region.

A sound financial base will be critical to the new authority. One way to ensure sound fiscal footing would be to transfer the Port Authority's trans-Hudson bridges and tunnels to the Regional Transportation Authority, to provide "cross-subsidies" for transit services in much the same way that the Port Authority now subsidizes PATH service out of surpluses from bridge and tunnel tolls. Under this model, New York City's East River Bridges should also be transferred to the RTA and electronic toll collection systems installed, to help provide for their maintenance as well as to cross-subsidize transit improvements that would reduce congestion on these crossings. A share of tolls from existing toll roads, such as metropolitan segments of the New Jersey Turnpike and the New York Thruway, or the proceeds from congestion pricing fees on other highways could also be directed to the RTA. The concerns of bondholders would have to be addressed in these transfers, as would the impact on other remaining Port Authority operations—particularly the seaport.

### The Port Authority

The proposed transfer of trans-Hudson crossings to the RTA would also argue for transferring PATH and bus terminal operations to the RTA and restructuring remaining Port Authority responsibilities. The Port Authority should refocus on a core mission of maintaining high-quality gateways to the world at its airports and seaports, and wherever possible it should sell, lease, or privatize other operations. Recommendations to restructure the Port Authority include:

- Transfer PATH, bus terminals, and bridges and tunnels to the RTA.

- Contract airport and seaport operations to private operators where this can achieve greater efficiency (as has been done at London, Los Angeles, and Pittsburgh airports). Private operators would be responsible for administering capital investments, with surpluses being reinvested in improved airport and seaport facilities or operations.

- Sell or lease the World Trade Center and other non-port activities to private operators.

The restructured Port Authority would concentrate on the mission of improving the region as an international gateway for people and goods by building and operating world class airport and seaport facilities. It would oversee administration of these facilities and have the flexibility to operate facilities directly or under lease management agreements. The proceeds from sale or lease of Port Authority facilities would be reinvested in airports and seaports, as would any annual surpluses.

### A Tri-State Infrastructure Bank

RPA proposes that a Tri-State Infrastructure Bank be created to administer a long-range capital program for the region's transportation and environmental investment needs. This capital program would finance new systems, such as *Rx*, as well as maintenance of existing capital assets. RPA's recommendation is adapted from successful models in other states and from proposals to create a national infrastructure bank, such as Felix Rohatyn's suggestion for a bank that would be financed by a dedicated gasoline tax. Several rationales have been put forth for such a bank.

- An infrastructure bank is needed to develop and implement a long-term infrastructure investment program required to keep the metropolitan region competitive in world markets.

- Increasing the gas tax to pay for a significant proportion of the costs of transportation investments would help meet national energy, air quality, balance of payments, and other goals, and it would be directly related to the services being provided.

- Construction jobs resulting from these investments would provide much needed training and employment to relatively low-skilled residents during a period of economic transition.

The region does not have a coordinated long-range capital budget process or the assured financial means to support an ongoing transportation and environmental investment program. New York City and New York State's proposed 1996 budgets have jeopardized the MTA's five-year capital program, placing the transit system's recovery at risk and underscoring the need for assured funding. Similar cutbacks have been proposed in Connecticut's transportation programs, including the total elimination of Shoreline East rail service. Only New Jersey has managed to maintain a long-term transportation trust fund and the dedicated revenue sources needed to support it, although the state has also resorted to budget gimmicks to avoid increasing motor vehicle fuel taxes, tolls, or fares.

Moreover, funds that could be dedicated to the region's capital needs are being diverted to balance state budgets or to finance other economic development programs that do not help meet the region's infrastructure needs. For example, the estimated $1 billion per year that the three states and New York City devote to the "border wars"—tax incentives to attract businesses across state lines—could be better used. Consequently, the authorities and state governments do not have the funds needed either to maintain existing transportation and environmental systems or to make capital investments that would improve or expand them. Threatened federal cutbacks in capital grants for transportation and environmental projects make it more important than ever that the region have the financial will and organizational means to deliver on the infrastructure investments identified in this plan.

The bank's goal should be to ensure that the region has a financially stable institution that can guarantee that infrastructure requirements are met and that the system is kept in a state of good repair. The bank would channel a dedicated revenue stream toward capital projects that benefit the region, providing significant improvements in transportation, environmental protection, and other services. To qualify for bank funding, agencies would have to prepare capital plans that identify both maintenance requirements and new long-term investments.

The bank will only achieve public support and political viability—in a time of public dissatisfaction with government and taxes—if it can provide broad public participation and accountability in its investment decisions, produce high standards of stewardship and maintenance, improve agency capital budgeting, and ensure long-term financial stability while meeting the region's infrastructure needs. The state of Washington Public Works fund, established in the 1980s, has gained broad public and political support by achieving these principles—particularly its accountability to the public.

The Tri-State Infrastructure Bank could be established and governed in a number of ways. One option would be to create separate state infrastructure banks in all three states, but provide mechanisms for coordination or interstate infrastructure investments. Alternately, the three states could create a single tri-state institution focusing only on the 31-county metropolitan region. As an initial step, the three governors should appoint a special commission of state officials, legislators, and financial leaders to develop a detailed proposal.

A first step to creating a regional infrastructure bank was initiated in 1991 as part of the Intermodal Surface Transportation Efficiency Act (ISTEA). This act allowed state infrastructure banks to be established to guarantee loans with federal money where localities have difficulty establishing credit.

The likelihood of moderate employment growth for the next decade and continued high unemployment in urban communities underscores the need for investments that provide immediate jobs while also setting the stage for sustainable, long-term growth. An additional $75 billion in infrastructure spending over the next 25 years would produce a significant number of jobs for the region.

To ensure that these jobs help improve the skill levels and incomes of poorer communities, a proportion of bank funding should be set aside for training and apprenticeship programs in the construction trades. Funds should be channeled to effective employment agencies in low-income communities, with specific numbers of job slots made available to workers who successfully complete these programs.

RPA proposes that the Bank's activities and other transportation and environmental investment recommendations of the plan be financed through a "user pays" system similar to those employed in most industrialized countries. Under the current system many of these costs are borne by taxpayers. A recent study estimated that municipal governments in New Jersey spend more than $1 billion per year in property tax revenues to subsidize the costs of automobile use.

Shifting these costs to transportation-related taxes and fees is consistent with the findings of RPA's 1995 Quality of Life Poll, which determined that a majority of the region's residents would support the use of dedicated taxes and user fees for certain quality of life improvements, while they opposed increasing income or property taxes for these purposes.

The transit and highway improvements outlined in the plan will reduce congestion and delays, reduce energy use and air pollution, and provide other benefits as well. While conventional political wisdom dictates that we cannot afford to make these investments, if our concern is the region's future prosperity, we cannot afford not to. In constant dollars, gasoline is cheaper than at any point in history, and costs one-third or less of what it costs in other industrialized countries. For this reason, the Third Regional Plan calls for increases in gasoline taxes and other fees related to highway use, as well as tax increment financing, so that the burden of these expenditures can be shifted away from property taxes and other broad-based taxes.

*User Fees*

In RPA's 1995 Quality of Life Poll, two-thirds of the region's residents said they would be willing to personally spend money to ensure clean air and water—most between $25 and $100 annually. But when questioned about how they would be willing to have that money collected, only 15% selected the option of higher income, property, or sales taxes. Instead, 68% said they would like the new taxes to come either as user fees, such as service charges, or dedicated specialty taxes, such as gasoline or energy taxes. The significant finding of the poll was that, in an era of cost cutting and government cutbacks, people would be willing to pay for increased services as long as the new fees are directly and visibly tied to the production of public services.[214]

RPA has investigated a broad range of potential revenue sources that could be used to finance transportation investments, including the motor fuel sales and excise tax, various motor vehicle fees, parking and congestion pricing fees, and tax increment financing. Further, RPA has assessed the revenue potential, progressivity, job impact, border effects, ease of administration, and political acceptability of each potential source. Preliminary discussions with freight haulers and other highway user groups indicate an increased willingness to consider adoption of transportation demand management measures, such as congestion fees for highway or bridge use during peak travel periods. RPA has also developed and tested a new computerized economic model to predict the property value and travel impacts that proposed transportation service improvements would have on residential and commercial property, and it is now applying this model for the MTA in the Hudson Valley.

Revenues generated from dedicated taxes and fees established for this purpose would be received and distributed by the Tri-State Infrastructure Bank. The bank would then distribute funds for priority projects to those agencies that prepare long-range capital investment plans, particularly those that served both local as well as regional needs. Agencies wishing to divert funds to pork barrel projects not identified in capital investment plans would receive lower priority for infrastructure bank support.

Revenue sources for transportation improvements could include a mix of these dedicated taxes and fees, including:

- A dedicated regional gasoline tax.
- A vehicle miles traveled (VMT) fee assessed as a sur-

charge on automobile registrations reflecting mileage driven each year.

- Congestion fees charged for use of highways, bridges, and tunnels during peak congestion periods.

A 20 cent per gallon regional gasoline tax would produce approximately $1 billion a year, enough to finance *Rx* and priority highway improvements. A 1.5 cent per mile VMT charge would create a comparable revenue stream. By combining these two—for example, a 10 cent per gallon gas tax and a half cent per mile VMT charge, perhaps in conjunction with a 10 cent per mile congestion fee for peak period travel—all of the region's unmet transportation capital needs could be met while simultaneously reducing congestion time for automobiles and trucks. Lost time costs the region an estimated $7 billion a year in direct, out-of-pocket expenses. Just by reducing congestion alone, or even by avoiding increases in congestion, the region could finance the costs of *Rx* and other priority transportation improvements.

Environmental costs could be met through a parallel set of fees on water and sewer use and impact fees on development in Greensward areas (see *Greensward*).

## Decision-Making Processes

### Sustainable Economics

By fully integrating the costs and benefits of environmental management into our economic decision-making through changes in price structures and natural resource values, we stand a better chance of preserving our natural wealth and quality of life assets that future generations will need. But reaching the point where market mechanisms internalize the "externalities" will require new ways of thinking, changes in producer and consumer behavior, and public implementation of strategic actions that will help "get the prices right."

The Rio Declaration on Environment and Development proposed the adoption of integrated systems of environmental and economic accounting. These new accounting systems adjust national measures of gross domestic product (GDP) for depletion or enhancement of, or damage to, the value of our renewable and nonrenewable natural resources, including assets like clean air and water which lack a direct market value. To date, nearly 20 nations, including the United States, are developing environmentally adjusted measures commonly known as "green GDP." When fully implemented on an industry-specific basis, they will reveal more accurate measures of the value of production and profitability by sector, given differences in use of natural resources, and a more accurate basis for full-cost pricing of goods and services to maintain their environmental value.

At the regional policy level, the full-cost accounting principles of sustainable economics can be incorporated into capital budgeting, tax, and regulatory systems. Such a policy would encourage adoption of pricing methods that will conserve our natural resource systems, as well as reflecting the true value of renewable and nonrenewable resources.

A multiyear regional capital budget should be developed for the proposed Tri-State Infrastructure Bank, identifying planned and required infrastructure investments, alternative funding sources and mechanisms, and costs for new compliance with environmental legislation. To achieve more sustainable development, the projects proposed for the regional capital budget would be subjected to cost–benefit analysis with an economic valuation of natural and environmental resource usage. The regional capital budget would be designed to identify priority investments from the net present value of environmentally adjusted societal benefits. In addition to resource accounting, a "green" regional capital budget would consider depreciation based upon life-cycles of fixed investments, alternative funding options that include "green fees," and public policy incentives and investments that internalize environmental externalities.

The use of "green fees" will be explored as a way to restructure fiscal systems for sustainable development and fund a Tri-State Infrastructure Bank on a resource-conserving basis. The objective is to raise funds for the protection of the environment through charges or taxes on pollutants and polluting behavior—that is, on products and processes that contribute to unsustainable development—at the same time tax relief is provided to individuals or activities that encourage work, savings, and environmental investments. Thus, through strong positive and negative incentives, a cleaner environment and more viable economy can be promoted in tandem. Substantial public revenues and environmental gains can be realized from such green fees:

- Congestion pricing or rush hour tolls will yield less traffic on urban highways.
- Carbon taxes on fossil fuels with carbon dioxide emissions will encourage energy efficiency in homes, factories, and vehicles.
- Household refuse charges on per-bag collections will reduce solid waste disposal.

State planning principles have been formulated in Connecticut and New Jersey, and both state plans recognize conservation of natural resources and protection of the environment as vital to their quality of life and economic prosperity. But neither plan, nor the state of New York, adequately addresses the maximum carrying capacity of the environment, given existing development trends, or establishes the full value of public, private, and environmental costs incurred. Regulatory systems should determine the costs of sprawl to households, business and government arising from a build-out of future growth under current development patterns. These full costs should then be reflected in the development permitting process. An accounting of the costs of sprawl will include:

- Incremental costs of roadway, stormwater control, electric and gas utility, and telecommunications capital and maintenance costs to serve dispersed development.
- Relative economies of sewer and municipal wastewater treatment versus individual septic and community-scale facilities.
- Costs of defensive environmental expenditures to control impacts on air, water, and land quality from sprawl.
- Opportunity costs of lost natural resources and open space.
- Direct impacts on government efficiency levels of lower density service workloads.

### Smart Infrastructure

Remaining competitive and reducing the expense of government can also be accomplished through investments in the region's environmental infrastructure that are designed to avoid or replace investments in "hard infrastructure," such as water filtration or wastewater treatment plants. Similarly, there is a need to reduce the excessive cost of environmental protection, permitting, and administrative processes associated with infrastructure projects, which add years of delay and an estimated $1 billion a year to the cost of capital facilities in the region. RPA's smart infrastructure concept calls for rationalizing and expediting these review processes and finding opportunities for "creative piggybacking," which means, whenever possible, allowing one dollar to accomplish two or more purposes.

The "Bluebelt" project on southern Staten Island is one example of a creative public investment strategy. Instead of building hugely expensive storm sewers, the city lets the island's natural streams handle the rainwater that pours off city streets. This provides wildlife habitat and public open space and parkland as well as drainage. Because the streams are also helping to decontaminate the storm water, the city avoids the cost of constructing treatment plants.[6]

Another example is the restoration of New York City's Jamaica Bay estuary, where a smart infrastructure approach replaced a proposed "end-of-the-pipe" treatment plant with a plan that will achieve the same water quality improvements by protecting and restoring natural systems and habitat. The results will be improved wildlife and fisheries habitat, a range of new recreational benefits, and a nearly 50% reduction in the clean-up budget.[7] A similar approach could be applied to restoration of the region's other major estuaries, including three that are now the focus of national estuary studies: the New York–New Jersey Harbor, Long Island Sound, and the Peconic Bay system. RPA believes that this would significantly reduce the cost of clean up—a critical issue at a time of lowered state and federal fiscal capacity—and produce a wide range of wildlife habitat, sport and commercial fisheries, and recreational benefits.

Another example of a smart infrastructure approach to waste management is the potential for increasing use of recycled materials by developing new markets for them. In 1995 a group of representative recycling managers convened to develop

*Figure 96: In Jamaica Bay, a smart infrastructure approach is achieving water quality improvements by protecting and restoring natural systems and habitat.*

and implement a coordinated, proactive marketing strategy for mixed-color glass cullet. RPA estimates that a shift away from disposal-based management will increase the volume of recovered materials by 430% between 1995 and 2015, also expanding markets that may generate significant revenues for public sector waste managers—up to $230 million a year.[8]

## Notes

1. These 31 counties include Fairfield, New Haven, and Litchfield counties in Connecticut, whose county functions are limited to the court system.

2. *Impact Assessment of the New Jersey Interim State Development and Redevelopment Plan*, Executive Summary, prepared by Rutgers University Center for Urban Policy Research for the New Jersey Office of State Planning, February 1992.

3. U.S. Census of Governments, "Compendium of Government Finances."

4. New Jersey State and Local Expenditure and Revenue Policy Commission, *Final Report*, 1988.

5. Regional Plan Association and Quinnipiac College Polling Institute, *Comparative Quality of Life Poll*, 1995. The poll also found that 56% of the region's residents would be willing to pay for preserved open space and managed parks, and 24% were willing to spend money to eliminate traffic congestion.

6. New York City Department of City Planning, *South Richmond's Open Space Network: An Agenda for Action*, October 1989.

7. New York City Department of Environmental Protection, *Jamaica Bay Comprehensive Watershed Management Plan*, December 1993.

8. Regional Plan Association, *Existing and Future Solid Waste Management Systems in the Regional Plan Association Region*, RPA Working Paper #16, 1992.

# *Part IV*

# From Plan to Action

THIS PLAN calls for a reversal of trends that have undercut our economy and environment and limited opportunity for many of our citizens. These trends have resulted in a *de facto* plan in which the region unthinkingly subsidized sprawl development, creating an uneconomic use of the landscape and infrastructure and dissipating the region's unique communal synergies. At the same time, we have drastically under-invested in cities large and small—the region's traditional foundations. We got what we asked for, a sprawling suburban landscape. But we also got the logical if unintended consequence of congested highways, decaying cities, sky-high housing prices, growing racial and social divisions, deteriorating air and water quality, and the country's most expensive tax burdens. These trends have diminished the region's quality of life and undercut its economic competitiveness.

The bill for these mistakes has now come due. And those who promise quick-fixes or scapegoats are offering at best palliatives that only put off the inevitable. We now find that in many cases we cannot buy our way out of these problems or find acceptable technological solutions. Our drinking water could soon require expensive filtration, which will incur enormous capital expenses to simply get us back to acceptable conditions. Our highways are increasingly congested and will require additional lanes and new construction, but again the costs will be enormous and the benefits only temporary. Housing will become increasingly unaffordable, and property taxes will continue to climb. Continuing with the *de facto* plan will squander our remaining competitive advantages, in particular our quality of life. If we take the easy route of feel-good rhetoric or simplistic solutions, the region will continue to drift and provide diminished opportunities for the current and next generation of citizens.

The region is poised to take advantage of new technologies and emerging global markets to create a bright and more prosperous future, if we are able to make the tough decisions and investments needed to seize these opportunities. The conventional wisdom is that we are no longer capable of bold leadership. Government officials are too focused on the next poll or election. Business leaders are too focused on the bottom line or competition. And civic leaders are too focused on narrow local issues. We are becoming a place that never seems to miss an opportunity to miss an opportunity.

But the work of pioneer planner Frederick Law Olmsted provides an inspiration for our generation in how we can build public support for controversial policies and expensive public works. More than a century ago, Olmsted suggested a range of justifications for building the region's great 19th century parks and parkways, including Central, Prospect, Bronx, Branch Brook, and Seaside Parks, and the Ocean, Eastern, and Pelham Parkways.

For those motivated primarily by economic advantage, Olmsted pointed to the parks' potential to raise property values and enhance a community's image. To those concerned about social welfare, Olmsted detailed the parks' role in providing people with fresh air, recreation and contact with their fellow citizens. To those concerned about potable water, public health, storm drainage or improved highways, Olmsted underscored the advantages the parks would offer in meeting these goals. The result was the creation of broad coalitions of individuals and groups, each motivated by their own concerns but sharing a common rationale for investments that could provide broader public benefits.

As in Olmsted's day, officials, business leaders, and citizens continue to be motivated by different concerns. Therefore, the Third Regional Plan's recommendations must provide a broad range of justifications for each proposal. Such a broad range of benefits includes:

- Improving quality of life and the natural environment.
- Expanding education and cultural opportunities.
- Expanding choice and affordability in housing, and amenity and safety of communities.
- Reducing road congestion and expediting travel and goods movement.
- Increasing opportunities for work and entrepreneurship.

Continuation of the existing *de facto* plan, on the other hand, will produce diminished opportunity and quality of life and virtually no real growth, since increased congestion, a relatively unskilled workforce, continued high housing prices, and other impediments will severely limit the region's economic potential.

RPA has prepared an ambitious plan that targets new policies and investments necessary for sustained growth and continued prosperity in an uncertain future. The plan calls for radical changes in the status quo and bold initiative on the part of citizens. Some of the recommendations carry significant price tags, but the Tri-State Metropolitan Region cannot afford *not* to make these investments. Projections and analysis demonstrate that we are reaching the end of credible short-term solutions and must begin to look at the fundamental causes of our mounting problems. At their root, these issues are all regional and will require comprehensive approaches for meaningful improvements.

The Tri-State Metropolitan Region is only just beginning to learn to think like a region, or to find a regional response to fundamental issues that affect the lives of all of us. There is no single regional government and probably never will be. It is a region of many leaders and many voices. They are effective leaders and eloquent voices, but without much practice over the years at uniting people to focus on regional issues, or even regional aspects of local issues.

RPA is promoting a new approach to building leadership on public issues—one that mobilizes the capable leadership already in the region. RPA's approach is based on putting together coalitions of civic organizations, gathering the leadership of the region's *third sector*, an enormous force of an estimated 50,000 community, business, environmental, religious, and neighborhood groups. Under RPA's model, third sector coalitions will be convened to promote actions on specific issues that will bring us closer to important goals of the plan, such as legislative or regulatory reform, new production practices, or critical public capital investments. By reducing the isolation of government agencies and the business community, this approach carries with it the potential to strengthen leadership by encouraging elected officials to take bold actions on critical issues.

The plan has identified five major action initiatives that can rebuild the region's quality of life, competitiveness, fairness and sustainability. Third sector leadership will be critical to each of these initiatives if they are to have lasting results. RPA will lead *action campaigns* around each of these issues and will work to establish third sector coalitions that can further each initiative. Each coalition would necessarily vary in size and working arrangements from all others, reflecting the strengths, focus, and knowledge of membership organizations. A coalition for education or tax reform in Connecticut, for example, could proceed differently from a coalition organized to promote preservation of the New Jersey Highlands.

A tradition of strong business community leadership was for most of this century a great strength of the region's civic life and helped bring it through earlier periods of economic, political, and social crisis. In the first part of the century business leaders like George McAneny and Charles Dyer Norton led campaigns to plan and build the region's highways and parks. When the Depression overshadowed New York City's economic future, John D. Rockefeller, Jr., looked far ahead and made the decision to build Rockefeller Center. Three decades later his son David did the same, building Chase Manhattan Plaza to bolster confidence in Lower Manhattan's future. And when the fiscal crisis of the mid-1970s again threatened confidence in New York City's finances, Felix Rohatyn, Walter Wriston, and others led efforts to reestablish fiscal responsibility and the public trust.

In recent years, however, this tradition has waned, contributing to a widespread sense of drift. It is not hard to see why there has been such a fall-off in business involvement in public issues. Many executives are distracted by the intense competition they face, and corporate restructuring has forced them to focus on short-term earnings, not long-range prospects. For others, globalization has made them feel more like citizens of the world, and not just of New York, New Jersey, or Connecticut.

Yet here they are being mistakenly short-sighted. As a growing consensus of experts has concluded, metropolitan regions are the key building blocks of the future global economy.[1] The right motto for the businesses of the future must be: compete globally, act regionally.

Even as energy from business and government has waned, grassroots leadership and initiative have resulted in profound changes in communities throughout the region. In the South Bronx, both sweat equity and persistent advocacy by individuals and civic organizations have generated investments that have rebuilt and stabilized entire neighborhoods. Similar renewal has occurred in neighborhoods of Newark, Trenton, Bridgeport, and other communities. In other places, coalitions of parents, teachers, and community leaders have revived declining schools.

Focused action campaigns involving established third sector coalitions can give business, labor, and community leaders an important new forum for confronting challenges.Building third sector coalitions is something RPA has been doing on a number of issues for a long time. But coordinating them around a series of regional initiatives and engaging strong leadership will take innovative new organization. RPA expects to be a catalyst to this process. In the following areas, third sector coalitions could immediately be brought together to focus on the initiatives articulated in the Third Regional Plan: promoting a Tri-State Business Council; building a Tri-State Compact; coordinating annual Tri-State Governors meetings; organizing a Tri-State Congressional Caucus; arranging summit meetings of commissioners in the region; and monitoring implementation of the plan.

## Note

1. "Papers of the World Bank," Habitat to Urban Finance Conference, Washington, D.C., September 1995.

# Chapter 11

# Paying for the Plan

IF FULLY IMPLEMENTED, the plan's five campaigns will yield a range of benefits that include stronger, more sustainable economic growth, a more cohesive society with a more equitable distribution of the region's prosperity, cleaner air and water, less congestion, more attractive communities, and a rich legacy for future generations.

Many of these benefits cannot be quantified, either because they represent qualitative improvements in the lives of the region's citizens or because we lack the tools to measure them effectively. For example, we have only gross measures of the contributions of health and education in a productive society and no clear understanding of the role that informal businesses, volunteers, and family workers have in our economy. The true costs of production, investments, and public services are even more difficult to ascertain because we do not incorporate the costs of depleted natural or public resources in our economic accounting systems, nor do we determine the full costs of highways, real estate development, and public facilities and services in making public investment choices.[1]

Even for traditional measures of economic growth, benefits estimates are constrained by a lack of data at the regional level. Within these constraints, however, a plausible scenario can be depicted for the difference between current trends and the result of a proactive strategy to reinvest in the region's human, physical, and natural resources. For decades, the region has become an increasingly smaller portion of the nation's economy, a trend that has accelerated since the late 1980s. If our share of national growth declines at the same rate that it has averaged since 1970, then we would decline from approximately 9% of U.S. gross domestic product, the primary measure of the nation's output of goods and services, to near 7% by the year 2020. On the other hand, holding our share of the nation's growth constant over the next 25 years would translate into an additional $200 billion per year in the region's economy, in constant dollars, by the year 2020.[2]

In the short term, it is unrealistic to expect the region to grow at the same rate as the nation. The region's deficits in quality of life, cost, and efficiency will take several years of investment to overcome. However, in the long term, growth in the world economy is likely to accelerate while growth in the national economy will slow. With stronger financial and institutional connections to the international economy than the rest of the nation, the

223

| Scenario | 1995 | 2000 | 2005 | 2010 | 2015 | 2020 |
|---|---|---|---|---|---|---|
| 1. Continued Decline in National Share | $640 | $690 | $730 | $760 | $780 | $800 |
| 2. Stabilized Share of National Growth | $640 | $700 | $760 | $830 | $900 | $1,010 |
| *Difference* | *$0* | *$10* | *$30* | *$70* | *$120* | *$210* |

*Notes:*

    Scenario 1 assumes that the region's share of the gross domestic product declines at the same rate that it did in the 1975 to 1995 period.

    Scenario 2 assumes that investments in education, infrastructure, and the environment, as well as government reforms, generate sufficient growth to stabilize the region's share of national growth.

**Figure 97**: *Two Scenarios for Regional Growth (estimated gross regional product in billions of 1994 dollars).*

region has an opportunity to approach, or even surpass, national growth—if it invests in the attributes that will maintain the region as a vibrant world center. And, unlike many other regions, this region already has most of its essential infrastructure systems in place. Here, investments are generally required to repair, modernize, and connect existing systems, rather than the more expensive proposition of expanding or creating new systems.

The investments, policies, and governance reforms recommended in the plan's five campaigns will not guarantee that the region can achieve a change of this magnitude. Such variables as the pace of technological change, national and global politics, and changes in consumer tastes can have a profound impact on both worldwide economic growth and the region's relative advantages in capturing a share of national and global expansion. However, attaining a stable share of the nation's economy is a reasonable long-term expectation given the region's advantages in the global economy and the significant improvements in quality of life and economic efficiency that would result from the plan's recommendations.

If equaling the national growth rate is possible, is it also desirable? There is nothing intrinsically valuable in growing faster, slower, or at the same rate as the nation. Indeed, a strong argument can be made that slower growth is more sustainable and reduces environmental damage, particularly in such a mature, densely developed region. However, it is important to keep in mind that national growth will probably slow considerably in the decades to come.

Even if the region does exceed the national growth rate, its rate of growth will still be slower than that experienced during the "boom" years of the late 1970s and 1980s. Another point is that downward pressure on wages for low-income workers is likely to increase regardless of aggregate growth levels. Faster growth will provide more resources to address this pressure on wages. Combined with redirecting employment to centers and improving the skills and labor market access for low-skill workers, growth in the region's economic wealth provides an opportunity to reduce disparities in income, both by expanding job growth and by increasing revenue available to address workforce needs.

The opportunities to increase growth in the next decade are not as great as for the years following, but they are still significant. Short-term benefits of the plan include: construction-related economic stimulus from infrastructure investments; immediate efficiency improvements such as the Tri-State *Rx* and greater consistency and speed in land use regulatory processes; and quality of life improvements ranging from new parks and recreational opportunities to reduced congestion on highways and bridges. Not the least of these improvements would be a renewed sense of optimism for the region and a turnaround of its current image as a place where quality of life is deteriorating. A reasonable prospect for the next decade is that the region could slow its decline in share of national growth to half the rate predicted by an extension of past trends, resulting in a $30 billion increase in gross regional product by 2005.

## Estimates of Cost and Revenue Potential

Achieving this growth potential and the other benefits of the plan will require an investment of financial resources, political will, and civic energy. Of the five campaigns outlined in this plan, four—*Greensward*, *Centers*, *Mobility*, and *Workforce*—call for additional public investment in systems to restore the region's competitiveness, social equity and quality of life. The final campaign, *Governance*, illustrates ways that new funds could be raised and public services reorganized. The investments carry significant price tags that must be put in the context of current spending, potential revenue sources and estimated return. With the movement in Washington toward devolution of government responsibilities—a reality, at least in the short run—the region needs to develop its own investment strategy and the means to finance it with declining guidance and support from the federal government. Currently, public sector expenditures in the region from state and local government, excluding infrastructure spending, total approximately $80 billion.[3] In addition, RPA estimates from available agency data that the region spends an additional $12 billion annually on infrastructure investments. Transportation expenditures—which are weighted heavily in favor of highway maintenance and construction—dominate the region's capital budget.

RPA estimates that the region will need to spend $75 billion in capital expenditures above current levels over the next 25 years to implement the recommendations of the *Greensward*, *Centers*, and *Mobility* campaigns. Some of the larger region-shaping investments, such as Regional Express Rail (*Rx*), regional reserves and revitalized downtowns can be completed within a 15-year time period, increasing capital investments by approximately $4 billion per year during that period.

The total cost of the human capital investments identified in the *Workforce* campaign have not been estimated, but fully addressing the needs of public education, early childhood development, and adult education and training could require resource commitments approaching those of the other three campaigns combined. With the region's school-age population expected to surge by 700,000 over the next 15 years, additional enrollment alone will re-

| Jurisdiction | Infrastructure Expenditure (in billions) |
|---|---|
| New York City | $4.2 |
| MTA | $1.9 |
| NJ TRANSIT | $0.6 |
| Port Authority | $0.8 |
| New York State—Transportation | $1.9 |
| New York State—Other | $0.8 |
| Connecticut State | $0.6 |
| New Jersey State | $1.0 |
| Tri-State Localities | $0.5 |
| **Total** | **$12.3** |

*Figure 98: 1995 State and Local Infrastructure Investments.*

Source: Compilation based on available agency capital expenditure reports, prepared for RPA by Albert A. Appleton.

quire a significant increase in both capital and operating expenditures in public schools. The capital requirements to bring schools to a state of good repair and meet expansion needs could be as high as $25 billion for New York City alone.[4] Actual improvements in instruction—reductions in class size; expanded programs in science, the arts, and foreign language instruction; and implementation of school-to-work initiatives—could require region-wide expenditures of similar magnitude even with aggressive efficiency measures. Investments in early childhood development, daycare, and adult literacy are also essential components of workforce development that carry significant price tags.

Specific investments for the campaigns in Figure 99 include:

- Establishing the 11 reserves, greenways, and urban open spaces envisioned in the *Greensward* campaign will cost an estimated $11 billion, with the largest expenditures for wetland restoration, improved access, and waterfront redevelopment for Long Island Sound and the New York–New Jersey Harbor Estuary.

- The *Centers* campaign calls for $17 billion to attract jobs and development to the region's downtowns and to make significant progress in building affordable housing. At $10 billion the housing recommendations represent the largest expenditure in this category.

- Building a world-class express rail system and improving both highway and freight movement, as outlined in the *Mobility* campaign, will cost an estimated $47 billion. Regional Express Rail, the largest single capital budget item in the plan, has a price tag of $21 billion.

The plan's capital investment recommendations do not include funding for essential maintenance needed to keep transportation and environmental systems in a state of good repair, for required new or upgraded wastewater collection, and for treatment plants. These costs, along with currently planned projects and plan recommendations, should be included in a regional capital investment plan that sets priorities based on a comprehensive cost–benefit analysis.

RPA proposes that these investments be funded through a combination of strategies that increase government efficiency or charge users for services, rather than through increases in general taxes. RPA's strategy is for the region to make better use of public funds by streamlining and restructuring government, in much the same way that every other sector of the economy has restructured over

| Proposal | Estimated Cost (in billions) |
|---|---|
| **The Greensward Campaign** | |
| Regional Reserves | $6 |
| Greenways | $1 |
| Urban Parks, Natural Resources, and Waterfront Redevelopment | $4 |
| *Total Greensward* | $11 |
| **The Centers Campaign** | |
| Housing | $10 |
| Downtown Revitalization | $4 |
| Arts and Historic Preservation | $2 |
| Brownfields | $1 |
| *Total Centers* | $17 |
| **The Mobility Campaign** | |
| Regional Express Rail (Rx) | $21 |
| Transit Upgrade | $15 |
| Highways | $4 |
| Freight and Airports | $7 |
| *Total Mobility* | $47 |
| **Total Capital Costs** | **$75** |

*Figure 99: RPA's Recommended Infrastructure Investments.*

the last decade, to take advantage of new approaches to organization, communications, and data management. In so doing, government can purchase the same services and meet the same objectives with less money. All three states and New York City have already initiated restructuring efforts of the type envisioned here. New or restructured revenues for investments should be raised through fee systems that charge those who either create the need or would benefit most from the new investments.

## Increasing Public Efficiency

Just as sustainable business principles call for private enterprise to invest more efficiently by focusing on pollution prevention rather than environmental cleanup, government should use public funds with much greater cost-effectiveness. Four approaches are proposed that could fund a substantial portion of the plan's recommendations: smart infrastructure, right-sizing government (both described in *Governance*), redirecting inefficient economic development incentives, and reducing the costs of sprawl.

### Smart Infrastructure

Existing examples of smart infrastructure in New York City and other places have demonstrated the potential to save half or more of the cost of some projects compared with conventional approaches. Three examples described previously include:

- The restoration of Jamaica Bay by using an ecosystem restoration strategy is expected to be $1.1 billion less expensive than the originally proposed $2.3 billion treatment facility.

- The region's ongoing shift toward an integrated solid waste management system, including waste prevention, will save public agencies an estimated $475 million per year in waste management costs by 2015 over disposal-based strategies.

- Expenditures of about $1.5 billion for a comprehensive New York City watershed protection program should avoid the estimated $6 billion otherwise required to build the world's largest water filtration system, while achieving at least the same water quality standards.

Less dramatic savings may be available from transportation and other types of infrastructure than from the environmental examples cited above. Studies also indicate substantial savings potential in procurement reform, the elimination of duplicative oversight, and privatization of some systems and facilities. If the region were to save just 10% overall through smart infrastructure reforms and strategies, it would translate into a $1.2 billion saving annually, or $30 billion over 25 years.[5] The trend toward privatization, in particular, is only now beginning in a series of controversial and experimental programs that go beyond private service contracting to the actual investment of private capital—and subsequent private ownership of facilities—for public services. These efforts need to be examined and, where promising, nurtured and developed. However, this must not mean an abrogation of public oversight but rather a new role for public agencies in setting appropriate standards for construction and operation of privatized infrastructure.

### Right-Sizing Governance

Right-sizing governance also presents the opportunity for dramatic savings in public spending, particularly in this region. State and local government expenditures, excluding public authorities, have more than doubled in real terms since 1967.[6] Much of this increase represents expansion in medical, social welfare, and environmental protection costs, in addition to higher service levels in much of the region. Other regions have experienced tremendous growth in government expenditures over this period, and many are also now implementing aggressive efficiency and privatization measures. Excluding capital outlays, but including the operating expenditures of public authorities, current expenditures total approximately $80 billion. If institutional reforms, governmental consolidation, and better inter-regional cooperation could produce a 5% reduction in these expenditures, then an additional $100 billion in savings would be produced over 25 years.

Currently, the political leadership of the region recognizes the need to improve government efficiency but is coupling efficiencies primarily with reductions in taxes. While tax reductions may make the region marginally more competitive in the

short run, some of these savings should be invested wisely in human capital that both increase long-term economic growth and address the widening divide between well-educated and low-skill workers. Particularly since low-skill workers and minorities are likely to bear the brunt of reduced government employment, the need to provide these workers with the means to obtain other employment becomes more compelling.

### The Cost of Sprawl

Successful implementation of the plan's *Greensward*, *Centers*, and *Mobility* campaigns would result in a third category of investment savings and increased efficiency: a reduction in the costs of sprawl development patterns. Various studies have demonstrated through case study analysis that planned forms of urban development cost local governments less in services, particularly in roads and utilities. For example, with compact development patterns, fewer miles of roads and utilities have to be built and school districts can more efficiently operate at full capacity. Savings of around 25% in road construction and maintenance, 15% in utilities, and smaller savings in public education offer potentially large savings overall in service costs.[7] A comprehensive study of the New Jersey State Plan has indicated potential savings of up to $400 million annually to municipalities and school districts statewide if new development proceeded in accordance with State Plan guidelines.[8] Region-wide, these savings could be twice the estimate for New Jersey alone. Assuming that it will take a decade before significant savings from reduced sprawl could begin to accrue, the cost of government could be reduced by as much as $1 billion per year by the end of the first decade of the next century.

### Eliminating Border Warfare

A fourth approach that would more efficiently use government resources would be to end "border warfare" economic development strategies in which different sections of the region compete against each other to lure businesses with tax breaks. Tax waivers and economic development incentives represent a substantial source of forgone revenue for investment. New York City alone exempts commercial and industrial taxpayers from some $800 million each year in real property, business, and excise taxes to induce business to remain in or relocate to the city.[9]

Some of these waivers are included in specific incentive packages designed to lure or retain particular companies, such as deals in 1995 to attract Swiss Bank to Stamford or to keep CS First Boston in New York City. These transactions add nothing to the region's economy and deplete revenues that could be used for general tax reductions, service improvements, or capital investments. The bulk of these expenditures, however, are "as of right" programs (available to any firm moving to a designated area), such as New York City's $96 million Industrial and Commercial Incentive Program for companies locating outside Manhattan's central business district; industry-wide programs; or exemptions for property owned by public authorities, such as Battery Park City or the World Trade Center. Even for as-of-right programs, intra-regional competition for jobs and tax base is often a strong motivating force, as municipalities respond to relocations in particular industries or areas.

As levers for economic development, it is highly questionable that targeted incentives are more effective than general tax reductions or equivalent investments in infrastructure or education. While they reduce business costs for selected recipients, they do nothing to improve overall productivity or efficiency, or to improve the region's attractiveness as a place to live and work. They also tend to ratchet up destructive border warfare.

Complete elimination of tax waivers and targeted incentive programs is not feasible in the short run, or completely desirable. Many transactions are legally binding for years to come, and some as-of-right programs may be important tools if they are part of a comprehensive strategy to redirect employment to centers. As a general policy direction, however, the thrust should be to reduce reliance on incentives in favor of investments in workforce, transportation, and the environment. Assuming that economic development incentives currently total well over $1 billion region-wide, a reasonable goal would be to gradually redirect them to investments in centers and communities. Assuming an immediate moratorium on new incentive agreements and a gradual reduction of $50 million per year, the size of incentive programs could be cut in half over a ten-year period.

## New Revenues from User Fees and Dedicated Taxes

Even with the savings outlined above, this plan calls for investments that will require new sources of public funding. But rather than looking simply for more money to go to public expenditures, RPA recommends a transformation in the manner by which new public funds are procured and allocated. Rather than increases in general taxation rates, greater emphasis should be given to methods of finance that create visible links between fees collected and services provided. Relating revenues directly to services provides the public with greater assurance that their taxes and fees fund specific service improvements, and it lets government rely more on market forces to achieve public purposes. For example, pricing tolls differently during peak and off-peak periods can reduce congestion and lets users decide whether time or price is a higher priority. Dedicated taxes, such as a cigarette tax to fund health care or a gasoline tax to fund transportation improvements, do not have as direct a link between a user and a specific service, but they affect consumption rates of activities that have external costs to society—such as medical costs and highway maintenance.

To produce new revenues for public investment, the plan proposes user fees or dedicated taxes for transportation and other systems. Research has demonstrated both that certain user fees can efficiently achieve public goals, such as reduced congestion, and make political sense, as RPA's 1995 Quality of Life Poll demonstrated. The significant finding of the poll was that, in an era of cost cutting and government cutbacks, people would be willing to pay for increased services as long as the new fees are directly and visibly tied to the production of improved public service.[10]

To finance a Tri-State Infrastructure Bank, RPA proposes various user fees and dedicated taxes on automobile travel. A 20 cent per gallon regional gasoline tax would produce approximately $1.2 billion a year, and a 1.5 cent vehicle-per-mile (VMT) charge, to be collected when vehicles are registered, would create a $1.5 billion revenue stream.[11] By combining these two—for example, a 10 cent per gallon gas tax and a one cent per mile VMT charge—around $1.6 billion would be raised annually for the Tri-State Infrastructure Bank. This strategy would introduce long-overdue market forces to the region's transit-funding policies. In addition to raising capital for infrastructure improvements, congestion on the region's highway system would be reduced, particularly as new or improved transit alternatives come on line.

Over time, the goal should be to replace as much of this dedicated tax revenue as possible with user fees. New technology, such as automated toll and fare collection, represents significant potential to charge users according to how much they use the transportation system with both distance and congestion-based pricing. Once the technology is in place, revenue from differential tolls and fares could allow dedicated taxes to be reduced. Until such systems are in use, however, it is difficult to determine how much revenue would actually be generated.

While these vehicle taxes and fees may seem excessive to some, they represent a fraction of the current direct subsidy provided to automobile and truck users by taxpayers. In New York State alone, these subsidies were estimated at $1.9 billion in 1990. They also represent an even smaller fraction of vehicle taxes paid in competing European and Asian countries.[12]

Similarly, new fee systems and dedicated taxes should be implemented to finance acquisition and protection of the region's natural resources and open spaces. As experience in the New Jersey Pinelands has demonstrated, land values increase significantly in areas where open space and ecological systems are protected. A portion of this increased value should be used to pay for conservation measures. Specific options, outlined in *Greensward*, include a dedicated real estate tax tied to development activity of large landowners or short-term transactions and a property tax surcharge that would capture a portion of the rise in property values associated with adjacent conservation lands. In addition, a surcharge on water bills for areas that draw water from the Regional Reserves could be used to finance land conservation, water quality infrastructure, and pollution prevention programs in

the Appalachian Highlands and other water-producing areas. These incremental fees, tied to those who directly benefit from improved environmental quality, could raise in excess of $300 million a year for environmental investments.

## Revenue from Expanded Growth

A final source of revenue is the potential for increased tax revenues if the region is able to increase its rate of economic growth. If the implementation of the plan is successful in enabling the region to stabilize its share of national growth, then tax revenues would increase substantially.

As described above, stabilization of the region's share of national economic activity would result in an additional $200 billion per year in gross regional product (GRP) by 2020. Currently, state and local tax revenues approach 13% of GRP. Revenues equivalent to 10% of GRP increases would yield an additional $20 billion per year in tax revenues by 2020, if this rate of growth is achieved. Over the next 25 years, $180 billion in revenue could be raised without an increase in tax rates, with most of the increase coming in the later years.

## A Twenty-Five Year Investment Strategy

The potential revenue sources described above are a combination of potential savings from government efficiencies, fees, and dedicated taxes that could be adopted by state and city governments, reallocations of existing revenues in the case of economic development incentives, and revenue potential from faster economic growth. All will require considerable effort and ingenuity to implement but are achievable if the political will exists.

To provide public assurance that efficiency efforts and new revenue streams result in improved services and a stronger economy, the plan recommends that specific funding mechanisms and protocols be instituted, including:

1. A Tri-State Infrastructure Bank to administer a coordinated long-range capital budget for transportation and environmental improvements.

2. Along with state assumption of education financing, a requirement that productivity savings in the education system be reinvested in schools. In recent years, cost-saving efficiencies implemented in the schools have been used to balance municipal budgets, reduce taxes, or fund other purposes. At a minimum, the increasingly heard refrain in all levels of government that children are the highest priority should result in the reinvestment of these savings, if not savings achieved from right-sizing government in other areas.

3. Identification of dedicated revenue streams for specific workforce-related objectives, combined with the implementation of strong management reforms to insure that objectives are achieved. In this regard, implementation of the investment plan advocated by the Commission on School Facilities and Maintenance Reform can be a first step, as well as serve as a model for other jurisdictions and issues.

The Infrastructure Bank would receive funds from environmental- and transportation-related fees and taxes. A portion of this revenue stream should be devoted to training and employment services to provide low-income communities with access to the increased job opportunities, particularly in construction jobs directly tied to the infrastructure investments. These expenditures could also help reduce the total construction costs by easing labor shortages during peak construction periods.

Capital costs funded by the Infrastructure Bank could be paid directly out of government receipts ("pay-as-you-go") or through government bonds with debt service paid from the above mix of revenues. The "pay-as-you-go" approach has the advantage of reducing government debt ratios and relying more on committed rather than expected revenues. It has the disadvantage of increasing upfront costs and reducing the early stimulative effect of the capital program. The scenario below assumes that the entire program is funded through the more traditional approach of government bonding. However, a "pay-as-you-go" approach for at least part of the expenditures might be appropriate for a program of this size, even though it might slow the initial pace of implementation.

Figure 100 describes one scenario for funding the $75 billion in recommended capital expenditures over 25 years; it assumes that all dedicated revenues are used to support debt service for bonded projects. If smart infrastructure is able to achieve a 10% efficiency in the plan's infrastructure recommendations, then the cost of the capital plan would be reduced by $7.5 billion. Debt service for the remainder would total approximately $100 billion during the 25-year plan period.

Capital expenditures are somewhat less during the first five "start-up" years than the following ten years, but they then decline again on the assumption that $Rx$ and other large systems are completed by 2010. If user fees and taxes are fully implemented from the first year of the program, then

| | 1996 to 2000 | 2001 to 2005 | 2006 to 2010 | 2011 to 2015 | 2016 to 2020 | Total |
|---|---|---|---|---|---|---|
| Capital Costs | 15.0 | 22.5 | 22.5 | 7.5 | 7.5 | **75.0** |
| 10% Efficiency Savings [13] | 1.5 | 2.3 | 2.3 | 0.8 | 0.8 | **7.5** |
| **Debt Service on Remaining Costs** [14] | **3.5** | **12.8** | **23** | **29** | **32.4** | **100.7** |
| Auto-use Fees and Dedicated Taxes [15] | 8.0 | 8.0 | 8.0 | 8.0 | 8.0 | **40.0** |
| Conservation Fees [16] | 1.5 | 1.5 | 1.5 | 1.5 | 1.5 | **7.5** |
| Employment and Training Fund [17] | -0.8 | -0.8 | -0.8 | -0.8 | -0.8 | **-4.0** |
| Interest on Fees and Taxes [18] | 0.7 | 1.6 | 0.9 | 0 | 0 | **3.2** |
| Redirected Incentives [19] | 0.8 | 2.2 | 2.5 | 2.5 | 2.5 | **10.4** |
| **Total User Fees and Dedicated Taxes** | **10.2** | **12.5** | **12.1** | **11.2** | **11.2** | **57.1** |
| Fees Less Debt Service | 6.7 | -0.4 | -10.9 | -17.8 | -21.2 | **-43.6** |
| **$ Needed from Increased Growth** [20] | **0** | **0** | **4.6** | **17.8** | **21.2** | **43.6** |

*Figure 100*: *Estimated Costs and Potential Revenues for Third Plan Capital Expenditures (in billions of 1994 dollars).*

dedicated revenue streams from these fees can fully pay for debt service in the first part of the program. As debt levels rise in later years, accelerated growth should be more than sufficient to cover increased costs.

The auto-use fees and taxes would yield $1.6 billion per year, or $40 billion total, enough to finance the debt service on the *Mobility* investments until approximately 2008. The $300 million in annual conservation fees, $7.5 billion total, would finance *Greensward* investments until approximately 2005. Likewise, redirected economic development incentives would fund more productive investments in *Centers* until around 2000.

Combined, fees and taxes cover more than half of the debt service payments. The remaining $44 billion needed from additional revenues is less than one-quarter of what the region might achieve if it can only maintain its current share of national growth. For the years beyond 2020, debt service will stabilize at approximately $7 billion per year, but revenues should continue to rise as the productivity and quality of life improvements of the plan generate additional economic growth. Growth could be well below full potential and still be more than sufficient to fund increasing debt service.

Clearly, implementing the efficiency savings and user fees recommended here represents an imposing challenge for a region with more than its share of fiscal difficulties. However, the means are available if the civic and political will exists. In many ways, today's challenge is no less than the one faced by the region at the time of RPA's first regional plan. In spite of an infrastructure system with needs even greater than those we face today, and in spite of a depression even more severe than our recent downturn, the region was able to build the foundations for two generations of growth. Building on past successes to create more equitable and sustainable growth will require a similar level of commitment.

## Notes

1. On a national and global level, several ongoing efforts have been underway for up to a decade to incorporate into public accounts the values of such factors as cleaning or dirtying air and water and using up nonrenewable resources. The United Nations Statistical Office, the Bureau of Economic Analysis of the U.S. De-

partment of Commerce, and such private organizations as the World Wildlife Fund, Redefining Progress, and the business-oriented Global Environmental Management Institute are among the contributors to an expanded view of the components and measurement of growth.

2. The only definitive calculation of the region's gross regional product (GRP) was computed by Regina B. Armstrong (*Regional Accounts: Structure and Performance of the New York Region's Economy in the Seventies*, Regional Plan Association, 1980). Per that study, GRP was 10.8% of gross national product in 1975. DRI/McGraw-Hill has estimated the region's share of total national industry output since 1970. This is a different measure from gross product but tends to change at a similar rate. If the region's share of GRP declined at the same rate as industry output between 1975 and 1995, it would account for 8.9%, or $640 billion, in 1995.

3. Unpublished monograph prepared by Lynndee Kemmet and Jerry Benjamin of the Rockefeller Institute of Government, SUNY at Albany, September 1995.

4. See assessment of the Board of Education's 1993 Master Plan in *Report of the Commission on School Facilities and Maintenance Reform*, June 1995, pp. 4–10.

5. "Infrastructure, Environmental Investment and the Tri-State Region: A Monograph Prepared for the Regional Plan Association Third Regional Plan." Albert F. Appleton, Senior Fellow, RPA. June 30, 1995, pp.16–17.

6. Data for 1967 from Census of Governments' "Compendium of Government Finances." The 1993 data for New York is from New York State Comptroller's Special Report on Municipal Affairs, 1993. The 1993 data for Connecticut comes from "Fiscal Indicators for Connecticut Municipalities, Fiscal Years Ended 1992–93." The 1993 data for New Jersey is 1991 data from New Jersey State Department of Education and the "54th Annual Report of the Division of Local Government Services, 1991," with the 1991 dollars adjusted to 1993 figures.

7. See New Jersey Office of State Planning, *Impact Assessment of the New Jersey Interim State Development and Redevelopment Plan. Report II: Research Findings*, Trenton, NJ, 1992; and Burchell and Listoskin, *Land, Infrastructure, Housing Costs and Fiscal Impacts Associated with Growth: The Literature on the Impacts of Sprawl versus Managed Growth*, 1995.

8. "Impact Assessment of the New Jersey Interim State Development and Redevelopment Plan: Executive Summary," prepared by Rutgers University Center for Urban Policy Research for the New Jersey Office of State Planning, February 1992.

9. New York City Department of Finance, Annual Report on Tax Expenditures, Fiscal Year 1994, pp. 8 and 63.

Some $511 million in property tax waivers and the vast majority of the $267 million in business and excise tax waivers go to commercial and industrial taxpayers to promote economic development. Data for the rest of the region is not available, but likely would amount to an additional several hundred million dollars.

10. Regional Plan Association and Quinnipiac College Polling Institute, *Comparative Quality of Life Poll*, 1995. The poll found that 66% of the region's residents would be willing to pay money to ensure clean air and water, 56% of the region's residents would be willing to pay for preserved open space and managed parks, and 24% were willing to spend money to eliminate traffic congestion.

11. John D. Dean and Jeffrey M. Zupan, "Financing Transportation in the New York Region," Regional Plan Association, Working Paper #10, March 1992.

12. Charles Komanoff and Brian Ketcham, *Win-Win Transportation: A No Losers Approach to Financing and Transport in New York City and the Region*, an unpublished paper delivered for the American Association for the Advancement of Science, 1993.

13. Assumes the region's capital costs can be reduced by a minimum of 10% through efficiencies described earlier as "Smart Infrastructure."

14. Assumes 1/10 ratio of annual debt service to capital expenditures.

15. Includes $600 million per year from 10 cent per gallon gas tax and $1 billion per year from 1 cent vehicle-per-mile tax.

16. $300 million per year as described in the *Greensward* campaign.

17. Set-aside of 10% for construction-related employment and training services targeted to low-skill and minority workers.

18. Assumes 5% annual interest on fees held in trust during early years when revenues run a surplus over expenditures.

19. $200 million in redirected economic incentives in 1996, rising to an annual level of $500 by 2002.

20. Revenue to be generated by increased economic growth induced by plan investments.

# Chapter 12

# Coordinating Implementation of the Plan

TO ACHIEVE RESULTS on the wide range of issues addressed in the plan, RPA proposes coordination of political and civic leadership on several levels, ranging from governors and chief executive officers to municipalities and grassroots organizations. In this manner, the implementation of the plan will be both a *top down* and a *bottom up* process, utilizing RPA's history of advocacy in the first and second regional plans.

Actions by the federal government will also determine how well the region can implement these recommendations. Federal tax and expenditure policies, as well as the delineation of federal and state responsibilities, will affect the condition of urban regions throughout the country, including this region's ability to invest in people and infrastructure.

## A Tri-State Business Council

A major recommendation emerging from the Competitive Region Initiative was that the region must do a better job of promoting itself to the rest of the world. Most current promotion efforts deal only with one state or subregion, with the result that a

European or Japanese executive seeking a U.S. headquarters or manufacturing site could visit several corporate and government trade fair exhibits and leave with the impression that Newark, Long Island, New York City, and Connecticut have little or no proximity or relationship to each other. With the reduction in 1995 of the Port Authority promotional activities, it is more important than ever that new ways be found for the region to avoid this duplication and speak to the world with one voice.

A related concern is that area-wide chambers of commerce and business partnerships find new ways to cooperate in their lobbying and advocacy activities, particularly with regard to federal and state investments and policies affecting the whole region.

In the long run, it may make sense for a new regional chamber of commerce to assume these responsibilities, although rivalries between existing groups could make it difficult for a regional chamber to gain financial and political support. An interim—and possibly alternative—step would involve getting the existing groups—including SACIA, the Westchester County Association, The Hudson Valley Coordinating Committee, the New York City Partnership, greater Newark's Regional Business Alliance, the Long Island Association, and

233

other groups—together for regularly scheduled meetings around agendas of common concern. This group, which could be called the Tri-State Business Council, could begin as an ad hoc group but might evolve into a more formal coordinating body. RPA will work to convene the council and provide initial staff support. Activities could include:

- Joint efforts to promote the whole metropolitan region through trade fair exhibits, advertising, and other national and international promotional efforts.

- Coordination of lobbying for federal investments and legislation (e.g., the reauthorization of the Federal Transportation Act, banking reform, and the Clean Water Act).

- Promotion of interstate cooperation on transportation, environmental, and tax issues, such as *Rx*, the cleanup of Long Island Sound, or proposed commuter taxes.

## A Tri-State Compact

To secure these outcomes RPA will promote adoption of a Tri-State Compact, in which the governors, municipal officials, and business and civic leaders would pledge to take key actions.

The governors of New Jersey, New York, and Connecticut should pledge to support the following actions:

- Begin reducing the use of financial incentives to promote intra-regional business relocations.

- Continue tax, budget, and regulatory reform needed to make these systems competitive with those of other U.S. regions.

- Make the priority infrastructure and education investments called for in the plan, including *Rx*, workforce initiatives, and environmental improvements.

- Create a Tri-State Infrastructure Bank to finance these investments, financed by user fees paid by the beneficiaries of the investments.

- Reform existing regional authorities such as the Port Authority and the MTA so that they can build and operate world-class infrastructure.

- Adopt effective state growth management plans that improve local land use decision-making and that make state infrastructure programs consistent with plan recommendations, promoting development opportunities in centers.

- Protect the greensward and other natural systems to safeguard the region's quality of life and its green infrastructure of public water supplies, clean air, and productive farms and estuaries.

- Investigate ways to create more equitable local tax and school finance systems.

Mayors and other chief elected officials of the region's counties, cities, towns, and villages should pledge to:

- Adopt plans and regulations that promote "region building," not "region busting" patterns of growth by encouraging transit-oriented and downtown development and discouraging commercial strips and isolated office parks.

- In greensward areas, participate in regional efforts to protect and manage important natural, agricultural, and recreational landscapes.

- Work with neighboring communities where appropriate to share services and facilities and reduce costs.

Business leaders should pledge to:

- Participate in or lead third sector coalitions organized to promote action on priority initiatives identified in the plan.

- Participate in or lead school-to-work initiatives and education reform efforts.

- Work with community-based organizations to expand economic opportunity.

- Attempt to make locational or expansion decisions that are transit-accessible or center-supporting.

- Adopt accounting practices and production processes that minimize pollution and reflect the realities of sustainable economics.

Civic leaders should pledge to:

- Participate in or lead third sector coalitions organized to promote key outcomes identified in the plan.

- Provide leadership in addressing the region's pressing social, environmental, and other concerns.

## Tri-State Governors' Summit

In much the same way that the annual G7 Summit brings together the heads of state of the seven largest industrial democracies to discuss common economic concerns, RPA proposes that the governors of New Jersey, New York, and Connecticut hold an annual meeting, which could be called the G3 Summit.

The initial summit should be held in 1996 to sign the Regional Compact, and in subsequent years to monitor progress toward achieving the region's goals, to set targets for upcoming action, to coordinate region-shaping infrastructure investments and policies, and to sustain public support for plan implementation. The G3 Summit should include both public and private sessions to build confidence among the governors and other political leaders, as well as to encourage the media, civic groups, and others to participate in key issues facing the region.

RPA could help organize and staff these meetings, aid in setting agendas, coordinate media coverage, and prepare an annual report card on implementation of the Tri-State Compact and the plan, to be released at each year's summit.

## Tri-State Congressional Caucus

At least annually, the members of the Tri-State Congressional delegation should meet to coordinate legislative strategies and discuss national legislation, budget concerns, and related issues affecting the Tri-State region. Collectively this delegation would have as much clout in Congress as any state delegation, and three times the voting power in the Senate. Special attention should be paid to federal funding of transportation, the environment, and the arts; regulation of finance, communications, and other key industries; and immigration policy and other priority concerns outlined in the plan.

## Partnerships with Federal Agencies

In addition to implementing broad national policies, federal agencies can assist the region's rejuvenation through technical assistance, funding of demonstration projects, and program development. Senior officials of key federal agencies, including HUD, Labor, Education, Commerce, Interior, and Transportation, should meet with the Tri-State Congressional Caucus, the three governors, and regional civic and business organizations to coordinate federal policy with the implementation of regional initiatives. In many cases, federal support can provide the critical spark to launch important new initiatives, such as school-to-work programs,

transit infrastructure, or housing revitalization. As the nation's largest metropolitan region and most important global center, federal programs here will affect the health of the nation as a whole.

For example, the Interstate Reimbursement Program was created by Senator Moynihan as a provision of the Intermodal Surface Transportation Efficiency Act (ISTEA) of 1991. This program pays in today's dollars funds expected by states that built interstate roads in the early 1950s in advance of federal funding for interstate highways. Under this program, over a 15-year period New York State should receive about $5 billion, New Jersey about $1.9 billion, and Connecticut about $1.7 billion, although the relevant provision of ISTEA must be renewed in successor legislation after fiscal year 1997. These funds do not represent a windfall; they only ensure that these states are not shortchanged. Half of these funds can be used for any transportation purpose eligible under ISTEA. It would be appropriate for the three states to use the funds to put in place the first installments of the *Rx* proposal.

## Commissioners' Summits

At least twice annually, state commissioners of transportation, environmental protection, economic development, and arts and tourism should meet to coordinate actions and investments, with a special focus on region-shaping activities. In addition, officials responsible for state planning—New Jersey's Director of the Office of State Planning, Connecticut's Secretary of Policy and Management, and an official to be designated by the Governor or New York—should meet to coordinate steps by each state to adopt, strengthen, and implement effective state growth management systems.

## Regional Indicators

Since its founding in the 1920s, RPA has been an active voice as a monitor of progress on regional issues. With the release of the Third Regional Plan, RPA will focus attention on tracking the plan's recommendations through measurable indicators as a report card of progress toward regional goals.

Indicators that show where a system is headed, and at what speed, have long been useful in science, economics, public policy, health, and many other fields as a feedback mechanism. The current wide-spread development and use of indicators is attempting to bring larger systems into focus.[1] For RPA this means a picture of how the whole region is doing as a society. Indicators are often used to integrate trends and concepts that have not been linked before and to build a base of information from which more precise statistical analyses can be developed. Indicators that reflect the status of larger regional systems would show a basic aspect of the long-term economic, social, or environmental health of this area. They need to be measurable within a specific geographic area and lend themselves to a practical form of data collection and monitoring. Most importantly, indicators must be understood and accepted by members of the community as a valid measure of the trend or condition they describe.

Current indicators of the region's progress often give contradictory or misleading results. How can we attach a plus or minus sign to quality of life in the region if—as is now the case—the overall average income is rising, even as increasing numbers of children are living below the poverty line? Is mobility improving if the number of cars per capita is multiplying, even as road congestion becomes worse? Is the economy healthy if the gross regional product is growing, even as fewer people are working?

RPA will seek to develop a list of indicators that takes into account regional and interrelated issues and encourage their widespread use (see accompanying box). These indicators will also better reflect the increasing awareness of economic and environmental sustainability. Choosing and using the right indicators can help us make appropriate choices in public policy, growth management, and even individual life-styles. Air and water quality, road con-

---

### Indicators of the Third Plan

The following indicators will be used to track the Third Regional Plan. Data on some of these indicators are shown in other sections of the plan. Some indicators will be tracked annually, while others will be tracked on a longer term basis. Data will be presented so as to show whether the condition described is getting better or worse. RPA will issue an annual progress report on the implementation of the Third Regional Plan, using these indicators and others.

Economy
- Per capita income
- Number of jobs in the region
- Percentage of population employed
- Real average wage.
- Gross regional product growth

Equity
- Average household income: highest 20% versus lowest 20%
- Below poverty line, by race

Environment
- Acres of open space and developed areas
- Air quality

- Material recycled as a percentage of waste stream
- Solid waste collected per person

Transportation
- Delay time for trucks at bridges and tunnels
- Passenger comfort level
- Passenger miles traveled by public transportation

Centers and Mobility
- Percentage of population in compact communities
- Trips to centers
- Jobs in downtowns

Housing
- Median house price to median income ratio

Arts and Culture
- Arts as an occupation
- Attendance at museums and theaters
- Financial support of arts by public and private institutions
- Graduates of arts teaching institutions

Public Safety
- Serious crimes

gestion, transportation efficiency, acres of open space, employment figures, and communications networks are interconnected. Indicators allow us to track how effectively these systems are working together and on our behalf.

In addition to the use of quantifiable statistical data, more general qualitative indicators of progress toward implementation of some of the plan's recommendations will be prepared. For example, efforts in each of the three states at land use planning or growth management will be followed and evaluated. Initiatives to reform tax disparities between cities and suburbs, to provide greater equity in school financing, and to share services between municipalities will also be tracked. Accountability, cost-effectiveness, and service delivery are other evaluation criteria for the region's political institutions.

RPA is cooperating with groups in the region, such as the New Jersey Office of State Planning, the New Jersey Department of Transportation, and others, to share both data collection and data and to develop indicators in compatible forms so as to strengthen both public understanding and the base for community and regional action.

## Note

1. The 1992 Earth Summit in Rio galvanized international, national, and community efforts to develop and link indicators. The worldwide United Nations Commission on Sustainable Development, the U.S. President's Council on Sustainable Development, and many U.S. states and cities, including Oregon, Seattle, Jacksonville, and Chattanooga, are adopting indicators that aim both to measure and to stimulate progress toward a sustainable quality of life.

# Conclusion: Recapturing the Promise

REGIONAL PLAN ASSOCIATION has prepared an ambitious plan that targets new investments necessary for sustained growth and continued prosperity in an uncertain future. The plan calls for radical changes in the status quo and bold initiative on the part of citizens. Some of the recommendations carry significant price tags, but the Tri-State Metropolitan Region cannot afford not to make these investments. Projections and analysis demonstrate that we are reaching the end of credible short-term solutions and must begin to look at the fundamental causes of our mounting problems. At their root, these issues are all regional and will require comprehensive approaches for meaningful improvements.

Each campaign needs the active help and cooperation of government, business, and civic leadership. To the degree that our elected officials opt not to provide the necessary leadership, we must form new civic coalitions demanding change. New coalitions are already being formed that bring together competing interests and forge new ways to address old problems—coalitions between environmentalists and developers, between government and business, between local interests and regional imperatives. By looking at the long-term, and considering the interlocking goals of economy, equity, and environment, we can build on our successes and enter the next millennium strategically positioned for another century of growth and prosperity. But we must act now. The region's competitiveness and sustainability in a changing world hangs in the balance.

# Appendix:
# Envisioning Two Futures

ONE WAY TO ENVISION the importance of these choices and illustrate the effects of alternative policies is to create a pair of hypothetical scenarios for the region's future, one that assumes continuation of current trends and policies of a *"de facto"* plan and a second that assumes the adoption of the policies, plans, and investments proposed in the Third Regional Plan.

## The *"De Facto"* Plan

In this scenario, the region develops according to the *"de facto"* regional plan—the aggregate of current public and private policies, investment plans, and locational decisions.

The year is 2020 and the region has changed in many ways over the past quarter century. Its outer boundaries are hard to define, since the growing exurban areas 100 and more miles from Manhattan have merged with similar exurbs growing out from Philadelphia, Albany, Hartford, and Boston.

New York City's share of the region's employment base has dropped to about 20% of the total as employers and entrepreneurs have fled to the exurbs and other parts of the country. Newark, Stam-

ford, Bridgeport, and White Plains have also lost their share of employment, as cities have continued to lose business—many to the growing number of exurban office parks—and home workers have moved to isolated suburbs.

What was once the financial district in Lower Manhattan has become an upscale residential area, where historic 20th century high-rise office buildings have been converted to residences as financial institutions have left for Midtown, the suburbs, and other regions. Downtown streets that once hummed with activity on workdays are now as eerily quiet as they had once been on weekends when this area had been a critical center in the world economy, only a quarter century ago.

Many of these residences have a view of the picturesque ruin of the Manhattan Bridge, which was closed after a section of the main roadway collapsed in 2008, the result of more than a decade of reduced investment in maintenance and capital improvements. The bridge was not rebuilt because the volume of downtown commuters had dropped and because the city's capital budget had been preempted by the expense of new water treatment facilities, needed to keep the supply from the upstate watersheds potable, and new prisons to house the growing numbers of criminals. Meanwhile, studies and regulatory reviews have been underway for more than a decade to determine how the Manhattan Bridge might best be restored and possibly returned to service.

In New Jersey the cities have lost jobs and nearly all of their middle-class residents, and the pressure to develop formerly rural areas has increased. The last commercial farm north of Trenton was protected in 2007 as an outdoor museum to preserve this important part of the Garden State's heritage. It became one of the most popular tourist attractions in what has become the nation's most suburbanized state.

Areas of New York and Connecticut have had similar experiences as a result of increased suburbanization since the 1990s. Residents of central and eastern Long Island have to travel several hours to get to real countryside. Many families have purchased virtual reality programs simulating mountain trails and fly-fishing experiences.

Most areas of New York City's outer boroughs and other large cities have become increasingly isolated and poor ethnic enclaves where the dominant concerns are high tax and unemployment rates, racial strife, and street crime. The departure of middle- and upper-income whites and African-Americans that began in the 1980s accelerated after the turn of the century, adding to the region's economic decline. Mayor Kim, New York City's first Korean-American Mayor, has promised to break down ethnic barriers, in part, by promoting her concept for a new urban cultural center in the former United Nations headquarters in Manhattan. The UN left for Geneva in 2005 in frustration over the city's deteriorating conditions and poor airport access. Unfortunately, New York City and other cities throughout the region have been able to do little to provide access for poor residents to the education and employment opportunities of the distant exurbs.

The fastest growing employment centers in the region are the new office parks and distribution centers adjoining the Interstate 84–287 inner beltway in portions of Connecticut, the Hudson Valley, and northern New Jersey.

Most business transactions are handled electronically, with all but the most complicated negotiations handled through video "meetings." Consequently, these exurban areas make ideal business locations, despite the gridlocked highways jammed with commuters and trucks carrying freight in a region that manufactures little of its own material needs and that lacks the rail infrastructure to effectively tie into the expanding national rail freight system. A major problem for employers and their professional employees in these areas is getting to the nearest supersonic jetports in Pittsburgh and Virginia. First, they have to get to one of the region's three airports on decaying and overcrowded highways, then transfer at these other airports. The lack of supersonic international jet service in this region has encouraged expansion of other cities that have this service, leaving the region with a declining share of the nation's decentralized financial and business system.

In any event, most executives have few reasons to go into New York City or the region's other cities. The vast majority of jobs are in the outer ring of the region. Some adventurous exurbanites do make occasional visits to Manhattan for its cultural offerings and the offbeat culinary and retail activities of the city's growing Asian, African, and Russian émigré populations. But they do not get there by transit.

The region's mass transit system has been suffering from disinvestment and threatening collapse since the late 1990s, as market share and political support have fallen. Even the oil price shocks of 1999 and 2006 failed to increase ridership for any sustained period, leaving the region increasingly dependent on unreliable foreign petroleum supplies.

Reverse commuting from the cities to the suburbs represents a significant share of remaining ridership. Mostly immigrant and minority workers, needed in the labor-short exurbs, ride to suburban stations where shuttle buses take them on congested highways to office parks 50 or more miles from New York, Newark, and Bridgeport. Most new jobs are located ten or more miles from the nearest station in a transit system that has not grown with the region for nearly a century.

Jobs and suburban residents have been pushed farther and farther out by growing congestion and crime in the cities and inner suburbs, where widespread housing abandonment began right after the turn of the century, as new federal laws reduced legal immigration levels. Despite extreme congestion, high taxes, expensive housing, and the lack of a sense of community, the exurbs located 50 to 100 miles from the region's former center have become the communities of choice for the middle- and upper-middle-income residents who remain in the region.

Growing numbers of elderly residents have been forced to choose between increasingly unsafe cities and inconvenient exurbs, neither or which meet their needs for social services and transportation access.

In the exurbs, much of what had recently been picturesque countryside and rural villages has, of course, been converted into three- to five-acre housing lots, shopping strips, and office parks, undercutting the amenity that brought residents there in the first place. Water and air quality have also suffered as traffic has increased and housing has developed in places where municipal wastewater collection and treatment facilities have been unavailable.

Still, the exurbs are convenient to the remaining open spaces of the Adirondacks, Poconos, and Berkshires—at least until these places succumb to the same development pressures that have permanently altered the region's landscape.

## Regional Plan Association's Alternative

In this scenario, the region has adopted many of the policy and investment recommendations of the Third Regional Plan.

The year is 2020 and the region has changed in many ways—mostly for the better. Glimpses of the better life of most of the region's residents can be seen by looking at several typical places that have benefited from the bold leadership and prudent investments that emerged in the 1990s.

By 8:20 A.M. the crowds of morning rush hour commuters grow on the platforms of Bridgeport, Brewster North, Huntington, Morristown and other *Rx* (high-speed Regional Express Transit) stations, where sleek hybrid-electric shuttle vans arrive like clockwork from nearby neighborhoods and suburbs just before the full *Rx* trains depart for the region's offices, media centers, world government centers, research parks, and specialty manufacturing plants. At the Bridgeport *Rx* Station, many of the younger commuters have just dropped the kids at school and daycare centers after leisurely breakfasts.

Many of their spouses are working at home, linked to their virtual offices and clients by the region's advanced telecommunications system. As a result, small cities and town centers across the region have gained new close-to-home employment opportunities, and, for people who choose to drive, reduced highway congestion has made commutes easier and more energy-efficient.

How life has changed since the 1990s, when the region's economic future had been so uncertain! One manifestation of the changes was the increase in choices for living, working, and moving about the region, including a significant reduction in commuting times and housing prices. Since the Tri-State *Rx* Service opened in 1998, the commuting time from Bridgeport to Manhattan and other regional employment centers has been significantly shortened, turning what had been a time-consuming daily ordeal into a fast, pleasant trip.

*Rx* trains arrive every few minutes on the outbound platform, bringing workers and visitors to the new custom manufacturing centers and vibrant tourist destinations lining Bridgeport's reclaimed harborfront. Many of these firms moved to Bridgeport and other centers to take advantage of the expanded labor market areas made possible by *Rx* service, although significant numbers of workers walk or take vans from the city's revitalized working class neighborhoods. The city's reformed schools and community colleges provide every young person and adult with the basic technical skills and literacy needed to participate in the region's expanding technology- and information-based industries.

The prosperous looking crowd on the inbound *Rx* platform consists equally of men and women of what seems like every racial and ethnic group represented in the region. Some of them work on Long Island, others in Newark and White Plains. Only a small share of the credit for the region's growing prosperity belonged to the *Rx* system, however. Dramatic expansion of the information and media industry and other industries exporting services and high-value manufactured products to world markets helped burnish the region's image as the world's leading financial and service center. Many of these companies have relocated or expanded to benefit from the region's exceptionally well-educated and creative workforce and world-class transportation and telecommunications systems. In 2002 the CEO of one major company that moved its headquarters to Virginia in 1988 was unceremoniously fired for his lack of foresight.

Other important ingredients in the region's rejuvenation were the successful campaigns, led by New York City's Mayor Kim, the city's first Korean-American chief executive, to make neighborhoods and the Manhattan business district safer and more inviting and to restructure the city's primary and secondary school systems. These schools graduate large numbers of well-trained professional and support staff who collectively are fluent in nearly every language, one of the region's unique assets among world centers. Mayors of other cities in the region have emulated Mayor Kim's strategies, and state governments have redirected necessary funds to the cities to support these successful initiatives.

Soon after boarding the hub-bound *Rx* train, some passengers look up briefly as the train travels through the revived neighborhoods and parks in the Bronx, and they see the racing sculls on the Harlem River and its luxuriant green backdrop. From the Hell Gate Bridge, passengers get a view of Harlem, the site of the "Second Harlem Renaissance" in the late 1990s as the neighborhood became the global media center for African-American and African-Diaspora culture.

The rampant unemployment, crime, and drug addiction of this and other urban neighborhoods in the early 1990s has become a distant memory as growing job and business opportunities, improved education, and strategic investments in housing and retail services led to community rebirth early in the new century.

Many *Rx* commuters leave the train at the elegantly rebuilt Pennsylvania Station on 8th Avenue, which older residents remember had once been a post office. At the time of its rededication in 1999, the glistening restored station was pictured on the cover of *The Economist* magazine, which called it a symbol for the city and region's rebirth. Those who stayed on the train, and others who get on at Penn Station, head to destinations in Newark, New Brunswick, and Trenton. Commuters on other *Rx* lines make transfers at the restored Grand Central Terminal to the Downtown *Rx*, providing them with an eight-minute trip to the revived Wall Street financial and new media district.

From both terminals commuters take the Cross-town Light-Rail line to the rapidly expanding United Nations City complex on the Queens Waterfront, which has added to the region's cachet as the center of international government. Here are located the United Nations Parliament, an elected advisory body to United Nations agencies that serves as the world's conscience, and main offices of agencies formerly located in Paris, Geneva, Tokyo, and other centers. Decisions to locate the parliament and the United Nation's common seat in New York were made after the United States Congress threatened to quit the United Nations in 1997. The Congress and President elected in 2004, on a platform to re-engage the country in world affairs, helped bring these UN activities to New York City through political arm-twisting and loan guarantees, along with federal funds for the new *Rx* airport links to provide easy connections between UN City and the rest of the region.

Another major new international presence in the region is the headquarters of the Inter-American Economic Community—the Western Hemisphere's answer to the European Community—which located on Avenue of the Americas in 2002 after a group of prominent philanthropists purchased a Rockefeller Center building at auction from bankruptcy court and donated it to the IAEC.

One of the major attractions in this area, and in the adjoining Times Square district, which re-emerged as America's most elegant and vital entertainment center, are the hundreds of restaurants purveying cuisine from all over the world, catering to the region's multinational business and government clientele. These restaurants benefit from one of the region's major assets—the availability of fresh produce, dairy products, and fine wines produced in the agricultural reserves of eastern Long Island, central New Jersey, the Hudson Valley, and the Catskills, and fresh fish and shellfish from the newly cleaned waters of Long Island Sound and the New York Bight.

The proximity of the city to the prosperous rural working landscapes, where residents struck a balance with nature, enhanced the region's success as a major international tourist destination. Also nearby are the recreational areas of the Highlands Reserve, stretching from the Delaware River to the Litchfield Hills, which provide a permanent green edge for the region's urban areas. And in the Hudson Valley and the Catskills the scenic farms and forests adjoin vibrant towns and villages containing small offices and factories linked to the world by the region's advanced telecommunications system. One of the prime destinations in the region is the "Source Schoharie," where the reservoir's waters are bottled and carbonated for distribution to upscale consumers in Europe and East Asia—a global symbol of the region's environmental quality and success.

The oil shocks of 1997 and 2006—resulting from worldwide petroleum shortages induced by rapidly expanding economies in East Asia and the Second Gulf War of 1997—dramatically raised gasoline prices. This provided the region, endowed with an extensive public transit system, with an enormous competitive advantage over Los Angeles, Atlanta, and other regions that were almost totally dependent on automobile use.

Looking back from 2020, historians wonder how the region's prospects changed so dramatically since the "doom and gloom" days of the mid-1990s. Some suggest that the transformation had begun in 1996, when the region's leaders and concerned citizens rallied around a new vision for the region and took the initial steps toward creating a better future.

# Acknowledgments

THE ONCE-IN-A-GENERATION PROCESS of building a regional plan was only made possible by the guidance, advice, and support of hundreds of individuals from across the Tri-State region and beyond.

More than two dozen other Board Members reviewed and commented on drafts and gave freely of their time in a special Board committee that shaped the plan in 1994 and 1995. Four members of the Board, Christopher Daggett, Co-Chair, New Jersey; William Parrett, Treasurer; Serafin Mariel; and Dr. Roscoe Brown, deserve special recognition for reviewing several drafts of the plan and working closely with the staff on the plan's policy recommendations. In addition, Dr. John Lahey of Quinnipiac College provided extraordinary support for the 1995 Quality of Life Poll, Ruth Sims advised the staff on a broad range of issues, and Barbara Fife contributed significantly to sections on the arts. Three members of RPA's state committees also deserve special credit: Michael Cacace, Esq., chaired the Connecticut Land Use Coalition; Ingrid Reed of Rockefeller University helped with several areas of the plan; and Msgr. William Linder of Newark's New Communities Corporation guided staff in developing the equity and workforce sections. Diana Jepsen, assistant for community affairs at GE Capital, provided important input throughout the process.

The fundamental shape of the plan was provided by The Council for The Region Tomorrow, a group of more than 100 business, civic, religious, and community leaders, chaired by Richard Ravitch that met several times from 1990 to 1992. Later in the process, the Committee on the Third Regional Plan (chaired initially by Robert F. Wagner, Jr., and then by Robert Kiley) brought together a smaller group of academic, business, and civic leaders to hammer out the policy and investment recommendations included in the plan.

The Competitive Region Initiative (CRI) provided much of the plan's economic rationale. This process was chaired initially by Richard Leone of the 20th Century Fund and then by Richard Kahan of the Urban Assembly. Mark Rockefeller was CRI's first director and led in organizing the research and working groups. CRI brought together more than 220 business leaders in working groups representing eight of the region's leading industries. From the deliberations of these groups emerged the plan's focus on quality of life concerns and the importance of investments in workforce and infrastructure to the region's competitiveness.

Through all three processes—the Council for The Region Tomorrow, the Committee on the Third Regional Plan, and the Competitive Region Initiative—the plan received the guidance of many of the region's most dedicated and able leaders, representing a cross section of its communities and business and civic leadership. Their input was supplemented, critiqued, and vetted by that of thousands of concerned citizens who participated in RPA's annual Regional Assemblies and Regional Forums.

But RPA has also benefited from the input of a loose network of advisors, including some of the leading thinkers and doers on regional issues from the Tri-State Metropolitan Region, the rest of North America, as well as Europe and Japan.

While it would be impossible to list all of these people here, several individuals deserve special recognition. Within the region, Robert Geddes provided invaluable assistance in several areas of the plan, including conceptualizing the new physical structure of the region and developing the Crosstown concept with input from the Architects Committee, which he chaired. Richard Kahan of the Urban Institute chaired the Competitive Region Initiative and led efforts to shape the plan's workforce and governance sections. Richard Kaplan of the J.M. Kaplan Fund helped in many ways, including guiding RPA's thinking on regional design, natural resource protection, and downtown revitalization, and sustained support for the whole plan.

Harry Dodson developed the regional simulations and helped RPA envision better development patterns for cities, suburbs, and countryside. Jonathan Barnett guided the regional design and transit-friendly communities programs. Michael Kwartler of the New School developed RPA's thinking on reclaiming suburban sprawl. Joel Russell and Philip Herr developed model plans and regulations for rural communities. Diane Brake helped shape the plan's suburban design concepts. Janet Lussenhop , a former RPA vice president, initiated the Brownfield project.

Norman Glickman and other staff at Rutgers University's Center for Urban Policy Research analyzed the regional economy and the relationship between the economy of New York City and other areas of the region. Dr. Glickman also helped initiate and chaired the American side of the US–Japan

Metropolitan Planning Exchange (Metroplex). Luther Tai, Stuart Nachmias of Con Edison, and Patrick Mulhearn of NYNEX helped shape the CRI process and its economic development recommendations for the plan. Mitchel Moss and Hugh O'Neill both provided valuable insights for the plan, first identifying the growing importance of a knowledge-based economy in this region.

Boris Pushkarev, RPA's former vice president for research and planning, assisted in developing the transportation and land value study and in researching and engineering *Rx*. Robert Olmsted also assisted in developing the *Rx* program, and Herb Levinson advised RPA on a broad range of other transportation issues. *Rx* maps were produced by Marc Italia-RE/Locate. New York University's Emanuel Tobier helped conduct RPA's research on immigration, with assistance from several academic and community advisors. Professor Jameson Doig shaped RPA's thinking on the restructuring of regional authorities. Jerry Benjamin and Richard Nathan of the Rockefeller Institute shaped RPA's thinking on the structure of state and local governments. Hooper Brooks, former vice president of RPA, helped conceptualize the Greensward proposal and developed RPA's greenways network plan. Douglas Schwartz at the Quinnipiac College Poll conducted the 1995 Quality of Life Poll.

Ed Skloot of the Surdna Foundation, Colin Campbell and Ben Shute of the Rockefeller Brothers Fund, Tony Wood of the Ittleson Foundation, Bob Crane of the Joyce Mertz-Gilmore Foundation, Joan Davidson of the J.M. Kaplan Fund, and Ron Aqua of the US–Japan Foundation provided sounding boards for ideas throughout the process and backed our work with important financial support. Bob Sellar, Randy Bourscheidt, Nancy Meier, George Wachtel, and Ted Berger all participated in RPA's arts initiative and contributed valuable insights. John Schall and Michael Simpson, both with the Tellus Institute in Boston; Kendall Christianssen, now with Resource, Inc.; and Benjamin Miller have all helped develop our Discarded Materials Management Program.

Beyond the region, Ethan Seltzer from the Institute for Portland Metropolitan Studies in Portland, Oregon, and Henry Richmond from the National Growth Management Leadership Project (also in Portland) provided broad guidance on several issues, including ways to reform state and regional planning systems and intra-regional equity concerns. Gardner Church from Toronto's York University helped shape the governance section of the plan and suggested the "Three E" graphic diagrams. Former Toronto Mayor David Crombie, one of the continent's great regionalists, urged the focus on the region's *raison d'être*. John DeGrove of Florida Atlantic University provided critical advice on state and regional planning concerns at several points. Nancy Connery from Woolwich, Maine, helped develop the Infrastructure Bank concept. State Representative Myron Orfield from Minneapolis shaped RPA's thinking about the potential to create urban–suburban coalitions around tax, infrastructure, and equity issues.

Armando Carbonell from the Cape Cod Commission advised on the creation of regional land use regulatory commissions, including the Long Island Central Pine Barrens Commission. Peter Calthorpe from San Francisco helped initiate the regional design program and provided helpful comments at key points. Rob Atkinson of the Office of Technology Assessment in Washington, D.C., Andrea Saveri from the Institute for the Future in Menlo Park, California, and Peter Huber of the Manhattan Institute helped RPA's staff understand the impacts that new telecommunications technologies could have on urban form and economic activities. Roger Starr of the Manhattan Institute provided constructive criticism on a number of issues. Steve Waldhorn, Jim Gollub, and Richard Gross of DRI/McGraw-Hill's San Francisco office helped develop and staff the CRI process.

Larry Orman of San Francisco's Greenbelt Alliance, Gerry Adelman of Chicago's Open Land Project, Joanne Denworth and Patrick Starr of the Pennsylvania Environmental Council, and Robert Neville of the USDA Forest Service helped shape the Greensward project through their participation in the National Metropolitan Greenspace Initiative.

A number of environmental leaders within the region helped develop the Greensward concept and reviewed drafts of this section of the plan, including Timothy Dillingham, New Jersey Sierra Club; Joann Dolan, New York–New Jersey Trail Conference; Paul Dolan, ABC News; Charlotte Fahn and Linda Davidoff, Parks Council; Thomas Gilmore,

Bill Neil, and Rich Kane, New Jersey Audubon; Glen Hoagland, Mohonk Preserve; Nancy Jones, Delaware River Greenway; Steward Pickett and Alejandro Flores, Institute of Ecosystem Studies; Richard Pouyat, Bob Neville, and Wayne Zipperer, USDA Forest Service; David Sampson, Hudson River Greenway Communities Council; Andy Stone, Trust for Public Land; Karl Wagener, Connecticut Council on Environmental Quality; Bob Wagner, American Farmland Trust Lynn Werner, Housatonic Valley Association; Richard White-Smith, New York Parks and Conservation Association; Andy Willner, American Littoral Society; and Nancy Wolf, Environmental Action Coalition.

To better understand how other world centers dealt with similar issues, RPA initiated, in collaboration with the Center for Urban Policy Research at Rutgers University, the US–Japan Metropolitan Planning Exchange ("Metroplex"). This process allowed teams of planners and government and civic leaders from New York and Tokyo to work together on case study projects in both countries. These projects inspired *Rx*, transit-friendly communities and other concepts. This ongoing collaboration was funded by the US–Japan Foundation and the Japan Foundation Center for Global Partnership. More than 20 Japanese planners participated in the Metroplex exchange project. Special contributions were made by Prof. Hidehiko Tanimura of Tsukuba University (Japanese Chair of the Metroplex), Akihiko Tani of Nagoya's Soken, Ltd. (coordinator of the project), and Andy and Won Min Higuchi, now at Harvard University.

Richard Lloyd of the Countryside Commission, in Cheltenham, England, helped shape the concept for the Greensward and also helped to explain it to groups in the region. Paul Milmore of England's East Sussex Council advised RPA and Long Island and Catskill residents and officials on green tourism and countryside management. And Eric Britton of EcoPlan International in Paris helped RPA grapple with the "new work" issues facing this and other metropolitan regions.

Within the region, dozens of business, environmental, and community leaders contributed to the plan in many ways. Special thanks are due to Kevin McDonald of the Group for the South Fork; Bob Wiebolt of the New York State Homebuilders;

Roger Akeley of the Dutchess County Planning Department; Patrick Mulhearn of NYNEX; Kent Barwick of the Municipal Art Society; Bob Bendick, formerly of the New York State Department of Environmental Conservation; Michael LoGrande of the Suffolk County Water Authority; Richard Amper of the Long Island Pine Barrens Society; Paul Marinaccio of Deloitte & Touche; Saskia Sassen and Elliott Sclar of Columbia University; Marilyn Taylor of Skidmore, Owings & Merrill; Howard Permut of Metro-North Railroad; Ernest Tollerson of *Newsday;* and Lee Wasserman of Environmental Advocates. Shirley Bishop of the New Jersey Council on Affordable Housing, David Listokin of Rutgers University, and Kathryn Wylde of the New York City Housing Partnership all reviewed the housing section of the plan. G. M. Williams, Jr., provided advice on transportation. David Johnson at the University of Tennessee reviewed early drafts of the plan.

Finally, it must be noted that this plan would not have been initiated without the leadership of former RPA presidents John Keith and Richard Anderson, and former chairmen William Woodside and William Knowles.

*Robert D. Yaro*
*Executive Director, RPA*

## RPA Board of Directors

*(Members of the Executive Committee are indicated with an asterisk.)*

CHAIRMAN
Gary C. Wendt*, Chairman & CEO, GE Capital

VICE CHAIRMAN AND CO-CHAIRMAN, NEW JERSEY
Christopher J. Daggett*, Managing Director, William E. Simon & Sons

VICE CHAIRMAN AND CO-CHAIRMAN, NEW JERSEY
Aristides W. Georgantas*, Chairman & CEO, Chemical Bank, NJ

VICE CHAIRMAN AND CO-CHAIRMAN, CONNECTICUT
John L. Lahey*, President, Quinnipiac College

VICE CHAIRMAN AND CO-CHAIRMAN, CONNECTICUT
Bruce L. Warwick*, Executive Vice President, The Galbreath Company

PRESIDENT
H. Claude Shostal*, President, Regional Plan Association

TREASURER
William G. Parrett*, Group Managing Partner, Deloitte & Touche

COUNSEL
Peter W. Herman*, Partner, Milbank, Tweed, Hadley & McCloy

DIRECTORS
Stephen R. Beckwith, Chief Administrative Officer, Scudder, Stevens & Clark, Inc.

Donald L. Boudreau, Vice Chairman, Chase Manhattan Bank

Hamilton V. Bowser, President, Evanbow Construction Company

J. Frank Brown, Managing Partner, Price Waterhouse LLP

Roscoe C. Brown, Jr., Professor & Director, Center for Urban Education Policy, Graduate School, City University of New York

David E.A. Carson, Chairman, President & CEO, People's Bank

Alice Chandler*, President, The College at New Paltz, State University of New York

David C. Chang, President, Polytechnic University

Jill M. Considine*, President, New York Clearing House Association

Aldrage B. Cooper, Jr., Vice President, Community Relations—Corporate Staff, Johnson & Johnson

Michael J. Critelli*, Vice Chairman, Pitney Bowes, Inc.

Alfred E. DelliBovi, President, Federal Home Loan Bank of New York

Brendan J. Dugan, Executive Vice President, European American Bank

Jerry Fitzgerald English, Partner, Cooper, Rose & English

Sandra Feldman, President, United Federation of Teachers

Barbara J. Fife, School of Public Affairs, Baruch College

Frank F. Flores, President, Marsden Reproductions, Inc.

Emil H. Frankel, Counsel, Day, Berry & Howard

Wendell W. Gunn, Vice President, Strategic Research Group, Metropolitan Life Insurance Company

Richard S. Hayden, Partner, Swanke, Hayden, Connell Architects

Marian S. Heiskell, Director, *The New York Times*

Eugene R. McGrath

Diane G. Millstein

Herbert E. Morse

William M. Raveis

Frederic V. Salerno

James J. Schiro

James S. Schoff, Jr.

Gary F. Sherlock

Winthrop H. Smith, Jr.

Robert C. Timpson

William H. Turner

Annmarie H. Walsh

William J. Wilkinson

Robert C. Winters

Frank N. Zullo

### *Committee on the Third Regional Plan*

Robert R. Kiley, New York City Partnership (Chair)

Diana Balmori, Balmori Associates

Gerald Benjamin, Rockefeller Institute

Henry A. Coleman, Center for Government Studies, Rutgers University

Gordon Davis, Lord, Day & Lord, Barrett Smith

Jameson Doig, Woodrown Wilson School, Princeton University

Donald H. Elliott, Mudge, Rose, Guthrie, Alexander & Ferdon

Robert Geddes, Robert Geddes Architects

Charles Hamilton, Battle Fowler

Tony Hiss, New York University

Richard A. Kahan, The Urban Assembly

Richard Kaplan, J. M. Kaplan Fund

Edward M. Kresky, New York State Council on the Arts

Donald Kummerfeld, Magazine Publishers of America

Nathan Lenventhal, Lincoln Center for the Performing Arts

Michael LoGrande, Suffolk County Water Authority

Alton G. Marshall, Alton G. Marshall Associates

Richard P. Nathan, Rockefeller Institute of Government

Dick Netzer, Wagner School of Public Administration, New York University

Rodney W. Nichols, New York Academy of Sciences

Preston D. Pinkett, Chemical Bank New Jersey

Alan J. Plattus, Architectural School, Yale University

Ingrid W. Reed, Rockefeller University

Roger Starr, *City Journal*

Marilyn J. Taylor, Skidmore, Owings & Merrill

Ernest Tollerson, *The New York Times*

Richard Wade, CUNY Graduate School

Kathryn Wylde, NYC Housing Partnership

### *Major Consultants*

Harry Dodson, Dodson Associates, Ashfield, MA

Jonathan Barnett, Washington, DC

DRI/McGraw-Hill, San Francisco, CA

Kendall Christianssen, Brooklyn, NY

Benjamin Miller, New York City

John Schall and Michael Simpson, Tellus Institute, Boston, MA

Phil Herr, Herr Associates, Newton, MA

Joel Russell, Salt Point, NY

Steward Pickett, Institute for Ecosystem Studies, Millbrook, NY

Norman Glickman, Rutgers University, Center for Urban Policy Research, Piscataway, NJ

Michael Kwartler, New School Environmental Simulation Laboratory, New York City

Meir Gross and E. Bruce MacDougall, University of Massachusetts, Department of Landscape Architecture & Regional Planning, Amherst, MA

Herbert Levinson, New Haven, CT

Robert Olmsted, New York City

Nancy Campbell, New York City

Michael Bernick, University of California, Berkeley

Tuevo Airola, Department of Environmental Resources, Rutgers University, New Brunswick, NJ

George Colbert, New York City

Tom Miner, Conway, MA

Donna Plunkett, Westhampton, NY

### *Competitive Region Initiative Leadership Group*

Richard Kahan, The Urban Assembly (Chair)

Richard C. Leone, The Twentieth Century Fund (former Chair)

Jeremiah A. Barondess, M.D., New York Academy of Sciences

Robert Beckman, Intergen Co.

Barbara J. Fife, Baruch College

Albert J. Giunchi, Hartz Mountain

Henry F. Henderson, Jr., H. F. Henderson Industries

Bruce Herman, Garment Industries Development Corporation

Edward Higgins, Loral, Inc.

Edward Martino, IBM Corporation

William Parrett, Deloitte & Touche

Preston D. Pinkett III, Chemical Bank New Jersey

Jonathan Plutzik, CS First Boston

Joseph A. Ripp, Time, Inc.

Robert Sellar, IBM Corporation

Elaine Stone, Fashion Institute of Technology

Gery Williams, Conrail

### *Manhattan Crosstown Architects Committee*

Robert Geddes, Robert Geddes Architect (Chair)

Wayne Berg, Pasanella & Klein Stolzman & Berg Architects

J. Max Bond, Jr., Davis Brody & Associates

Colin Cathcart, Kiss & Cathcart Architects

Keller Easterling, Columbia University

Jordan Gruzen, Gruzen Samton

Frances Halsband, Kliment & Halsband

John Keenen, Keenen Riley Architects

Robert M. Kliment, Kliment & Halsband

Michael Kwartler, New School for Social Research Environmental Simulation Center

Terence Riley, Director, Architecture & Design, Museum of Modern Art

Jane Thompson, Thompson & Wood

### *Regional Plan Association Research Staff*

Albert Appleton, Senior Fellow/Environment

Regina Armstrong, Senior Fellow/Economics

Winifred Armstrong, Consulting Economist

Nicole Crane, Executive Assistant

John Dean, Senior Planner

John Feingold, Director, New York

Raymond Gastil, Director, Regional Design Program

Christopher Jones, Director, Economic Programs

Elizabeth McLaughlin, Director, Connecticut

Linda Morgan, Director, New Jersey

John James Oddy, Director, Arts Program

Robert Pirani, Director, Environmental Projects

Jeffrey Raven, Director, Downtown Brooklyn Project

William Shore, Senior Fellow/Urban Affairs

Graham Trelstad, Director, Connecticut Land Use Coalition

Thomas Wright, Manager of Research Information

Robert Yaro, Executive Director

Jeffrey Zupan, Senior Fellow/Transportation

### *Administrative Staff*

H. Claude Shostal, President

Reginald French, Vice President for Finance

Aram Khachadurian, Director of Development

Lillie Balinova, Director of Communications

Lilly Chin, Executive Assistant to the President

Tanya DeVonish, Administrative Assistant

Dorina Herscowicz, Office Manager

Linda R. Hoza, Administrative Assistant

SanDonna Bryant, Administrative Assistant

### *Contributors*

Major funding for the Third Regional Plan was provided by the following:

### *Businesses, Foundations, and Government Agencies*
$100,000 AND ABOVE

Brooklyn Union Gas

Champion International Corporation

The Chase Manhattan Bank, N.A.

Chemical Banking Corp.

Consolidated Edison Company of New York, Inc.

Jessie B. Cox Charitable Trust

Deloitte & Touche

The First Boston Corporation

Fund for the Campaign to Reform Transportation Systems in the New York City Region

General Electric Company

Joyce Mertz-Gilmore Foundation

Goldman, Sachs & Co.

GTE Corporation

IBM Corporation

The Japan Foundation—Center for Global Partnership

Johnson & Johnson

The J.M. Kaplan Fund, Inc.

KPMG Peat Marwick

The Andrew W. Mellon Foundation

Merck & Co., Inc.

Merrill Lynch & Co., Inc.

Metropolitan Life Insurance Company

Metropolitan Transportation Authority

National Westminster Bancorp Inc.

New York City Department of Environmental Protection

New York Life Foundation

New York State Department of Transportation

The New York Times Company, Inc.

Newsday, Inc.

NYNEX

Office of the Bronx Borough President

Pfizer, Incorporated

Pitney Bowes

The Prudential Insurance Company of America

The Port Authority of New York & New Jersey

Public Service Electric & Gas Company

Charles H. Revson Foundation

Rockefeller Brothers Fund

Alfred P. Sloan Foundation

State of New Jersey

Surdna Foundation, Inc.

United States-Japan Foundation

UST, Inc.

Warner-Lambert Company

Xerox Corporation

**$50,000 TO $99,999**

Allied-Signal Inc.

Amerada Hess Corporation

American Conservation Association, Inc.

American Express Company

American International Group, Inc.

The Vincent Astor Foundation

AT&T

Bell Atlantic–New Jersey

The Blackstone Group

Bristol-Myers Squibb Company

Cablevision Systems Corporation

The CIT Group, Inc.

Geraldine R. Dodge Foundation

Donaldson, Lufkin & Jenrette, Inc.

Forbes Magazine

Fortunoff

The Fund for New Jersey

Gannett Suburban Newspapers

McGraw-Hill, Inc.

Morgan Stanley Group Inc.

People's Bank

Philip Morris Companies, Inc.

The Rockefeller Group, Inc.

Salomon Brothers Inc.

The Schumann Fund for New Jersey

Sidley & Austin

Southern New England Telephone Company

Suffolk County Water Authority

The Sulzberger Foundation, Incorporated

TIAA-CREF

USDA Forest Service

UDC/R.E.D.'s Partnership

Victoria Foundation

Andy Warhol Foundation for the Visual Arts, Inc.

Weil, Gotshal & Manges

**$10,000 TO $49,999**

Amelior Foundation

American Brands Inc.

American Home Products Corporation

American Public Transit Association

American Re-Insurance Company

American Stock Exchange, Inc.

Apple Bank for Savings

Arnold & Porter

Arthur Andersen & Co., SC

Automatic Data Processing, Incorporated

The Bank of New York

BankAmerica Foundation

Bankers Trust Company

Bear Stearns Companies, Inc.

Beneficial Management Corporation

Bloomingdale's

Boston Properties

Capital Cities/ABC, Inc.

Central Hudson Gas & Electric Corporation

Law Offices of Leon H. Charney

Chemical Bank New Jersey

The Chubb Corporation

Citicorp

The Edna McConnell Clark Foundation

Cleary, Gottlieb, Steen & Hamilton

Colgate-Palmolive Company

Consolidated Rail Corporation

Continental Corp.

CPC International, Inc.

Charles E. Culpeper Foundation

The Nathan Cummings Foundation Inc.

Cushman & Wakefield, Inc.

Dewey Ballantine

Downtown Brooklyn Development Association

The Dun & Bradstreet Corporation

Edward S. Gordon Company, Inc.

Empire Blue Cross Blue Shield

The Equitable Companies Incorporated

European American Bancorp

Exxon Corporation

Finlay Enterprises, Inc.

Fleet Bank

Ford Motor Company

Forest City Ratner Companies

Fund for the City of New York

The Furthermore Program of the J.M. Kaplan Fund

The Galbreath Company

Gannett Foundation

GE Capital

The General Contractors Association of New York, Inc.

General Re Corporation

Great Atlantic and Pacific Tea Company, Inc.

The Guardian

Hackensack Water Company

The Hearst Corporation

Helmsley-Spear Inc.

Hoffmann-La Roche, Inc.

K. Hovnanian Enterprises, Inc.

Independence Savings Bank

James D. Wolfensohn Incorporated

Joelson Foundation

Johnson & Higgins

H.J. Kalikow Properties, Inc.

Kekst and Company

The Larsen Fund

Lazard Freres & Company

Lehman Brothers

Loral Corporation

The Macklowe Organization

R. H. Macy & Company, Incorporated

Manufacturers Hanover Trust Company

Metro Newark Chamber of Commerce

Milbank, Tweed, Hadley & McCloy

Mutual Benefit Life Insurance Company

Nabisco Brands, Inc.

National Endowment for the Arts

National Park Service

New Jersey Economic Development Authority

New York Community Trust

The New York Daily News

New York National Bank

Newmark & Co. Real Estate, Inc.

Olin Corporation

Open Space Institute

Park Tower Realty Corporation

Parsons Brinckerhoff, Inc.

The Perkin-Elmer Corporation

Pinchot Institute

Price Waterhouse

The Reader's Digest Association Inc.

The Record

Reliance Group Holdings, Inc.

F. D. Rich Company

Anne S. Richardson Fund

Rose Associates, Inc.

Rudin Management Company, Inc.

Russell Sage Foundation

Saks Fifth Avenue

Schering-Plough Corporation

Scudder, Stevens & Clark, Inc.

Sills, Cummis, Zuckerman, et al.

Marilyn M. Simpson Charitable Trust

Smith Barney Inc.

State of Connecticut—Department of Environmental Protection

Swanke Hayden Connell Architects

Syms Corp.

Texaco Incorporated

Transport Workers Union of Greater New York, Local 100

Tri-State Transportation Campaign

The Trump Organization

Turner Construction Company

U.S. Department of Agriculture–Forest Service

UJB Financial Corp.

Union Carbide Corporation

Union Trust Company–A First Fidelity Bank

United Federation of Teachers Local 2

United States Surgical Corporation

Vinmont Foundation, Inc.

Wachtell, Lipton, Rosen & Katz

The Mary Warfield Fund

Warnaco Inc.

Westvaco Corporation

White & Case

Wien, Malkin & Bettex

Winston & Strawn

$5,000 TO $9,999

A.J. Contracting Co., Inc.

Alliance for Downtown New York Inc.

American Cyanamid Company

Aquarion Company

Bowater Incorporated

Bozell Worldwide, Inc.

Castle Harlan Inc.

Cooper, Rose & English

Coopers & Lybrand

Corporate Conservation Partnership

County of Putnam

Cubic Automatic Revenue Collection Group

Davis Polk & Wardwell

Debevoise & Plimpton

The Depository Trust Company

The Dreyfus Corporation

Durst Organization, Inc.

Dynamics Corporation of America

Elberon Development Co.

Elizabethtown Gas Company

Elizabethtown Water Company

Emigrant Savings Bank

Fairfield County Community Foundation

Farrel Corporation

Grenadier Realty Corp.

Grow Tunneling Corporation

Haines Lundberg Waehler

Hellmuth, Obata & Kassabaum, P.C.

The Hertz Corporation

International Paper Company

J. General Real Estate

JWP Forest Electric Corp.

Kidder, Peabody Group Inc.

The Leavens Foundation

Lowenstein, Sandler, Kohl, Fisher & Boylan

McKinsey & Company, Inc.

McManimon & Scotland

Midlantic National Bank

Mitsui Fudosan (New York), Inc.

National Reinsurance Corporation

National State Bank

New Jersey Transit Corporation

New York Elevator Company, Inc.

New York–New Jersey Trail Conference

Newsweek

Northeast Utilities Service Company

Office of the Manhattan Borough President

The Omega Group

Partners Cleaning Corp.

PHH Homequity Corp.

Podell, Rothman, Schechter & Banfield

Quantum Chemical Corporation

Richard Ravitch Foundation

Rutgers University

The Segal Company

Selective Insurance

Simpson Thacher & Bartlett

Skidmore, Owings & Merrill

Sterling Forest Corporation

Structure Tone, Inc.

Summit Bank

TAMS Consultants, Inc.

Time Warner Inc.

Tishman Speyer Properties, Inc.

United Ways of Tri-State, Inc.

Vollmer Associates

Waldenbooks

Walter & Samuels, Inc.

Winoker Realty Company

Woolworth Corporation

Young & Rubicam Inc.

## *Individuals*

### INDIVIDUALS WHO GAVE $5,000 OR MORE

Isabelle Feher

Elizabeth B. Gilmore

Albert W. Merck

Francis W. Murray III

David Rockefeller

Robert W. Wilson

### INDIVIDUALS WHO GAVE $1,000 TO $4,999

Frances Beinecke

George Bugliarello, Jr.

Morris D. Crawford, Jr.

Alan M. Fortunoff

Pearl H. Hack

Peter W. Herman, Esq.

William T. Knowles

Leonard Lieberman

Marianne Pollak

Jonathan F. P. Rose

James S. Schoff

Thomas J. Stanton, Jr.

Howard C. St. John

William S. Woodside

# Index

## Figure Credits

Figure 31: Harry Dodson
Figure 32: Fairfield Conservation Commission
Figure 39: New York City Department of Environmental Protection
Figure 41: © Frederick Gilbert
Figure 44 (*clockwise from top left*): National Park Service; D & R Canal Commission; National Park Service; Housatonic Valley Association
Figure 46 (*top*): Henry C. Eno, Courtesy Museum of the City of New York
Figure 46 (*bottom*): Central Park Conservancy
Figure 48: John Turner
Figure 52: Glen Hoagland
Figure 53: Harry Dodson
Figure 54: National Park Service
Figure 56: Fairfield Conservation Commission
Figure 57: Harry Dodson
Figure 60: Green Guerrillas
Figure 61: Newark Land Conservancy
Figure 62: © Wallace Roberts & Todd, 1994
Figure 75: © Frederick Gilbert
Figure 79: Regional Plan Association/Fairfield 2000
Figure 81: New Jersey Performing Arts Center
Figure 82: © Stephanie Berger, Courtesy Lincoln Center for the Performing Arts
Figure 88: Conrail
Figure 93: Cara Lise Metz, Courtesy Garment Industry Development Corporation

## Plate Credits

Plate 1A: © George M. Aronson
Plate 1C: © Regional Plan Association/Dodson Associates, 1991
Plate 2A: © Regional Plan Association/Dodson Associates, 1991
Plate 2B: © Regional Plan Association/Dodson Associates, 1991
Plate 2C: © Regional Plan Association/Dodson Associates, 1991
Plate 2E: Max Bond, Davis Brody & Associates
Plate 2F: Robert Geddes, Robert Geddes Architect
Plate 2G: John Keenen and Terence Riley, Keenen/ Riley Architects
Plate 2H: Wayne Berg, Pasanella + Klein Stolzman + Berg Architects
Plate 2I: Colin Cathcart, Kiss + Cathcart Architects
Plate 2J: Jane Thompson, Thompson & Wood
Plate 2K: Robert Kliment and Frances Halsband, R. M. Kliment & Frances Halsband Architect